BASIC

English
Grammar

FOURTH EDITION

TEACHER'S GUIDE

BASIC

English
Grammar

FOURTH EDITION

TEACHER'S GUIDE

Martha Hall
Betty S. Azar

Basic English Grammar, Fourth Edition
Teacher's Guide

Pearson Education, 10 Bank Street, White Plains, NY 10606

Staff credits: The people who made up the *Basic English
Grammar, Fourth Edition Teacher's Guide* team,
representing editorial, production, design, and manufacturing,
are Dave Dickey, Daniel Dwyer, Nancy Flaggman, Amy
McCormick, Joan Poole, and Marian Wassner.
    Text composition: S4Carlisle Publishing Services
    Text font: Helvetica

ISBN 10: 0-13-336096-2
ISBN 13: 978-0-13-336096-7

Printed in the United States of America

11

Contents

Preface

This *Teacher's Guide* is intended as a practical aid to teachers. You can turn to it for notes on the content of a unit and how to approach the exercises, for suggestions for classroom activities, and for answers to the exercises in the text.

General teaching information can be found in the *Introduction*. It includes:

- the rationale and general aims of *Basic English Grammar*.

- classroom techniques for presenting charts and using exercises.

- suggestions for using the *Workbook* in connection with the *Student Book*.

- supplementary resource texts.

- comments on differences between American English and British English.

- a key to the pronunciation symbols used in this *Guide*.

The rest of the *Guide* contains notes and instructions for teaching every chapter. Each chapter contains three main parts: the Chapter Summary, the background notes on charts and exercises (found in the shaded boxes), and the bulleted step-by-step instructions for the charts and most of the exercises.

- The Chapter Summary explains the objective and approach of the chapter. It also explains any terminology critical to the chapter.

- The background notes in the gray boxes contain additional explanations of the grammar point, common problem areas, and points to emphasize. These notes are intended to help the instructor plan the lessons before class.

- The bulleted step-by-step instructions contain detailed plans for conducting the lessons in class.

The back of the *Guide* contains the answer key for the *Student Book* and an index.

Acknowledgments

The author would like to acknowledge Mr. Charles Jordan, one of her most inspiring friends. She is equally grateful to her colleagues at The New England School of English, Anna Shine, Kate Orellana, Rose François-Gill, and Lori Rosner, and to Pearson editor Marian Wassner and freelance editor Margo Grant.

Introduction

General Aims of *Basic English Grammar*

Basic English Grammar (BEG) is a beginning-level ESL/EFL developmental skills text. The corpus-informed grammar content of *BEG* reflects discourse patterns, including the differences between spoken and written English.

In the experience of many classroom teachers, adult language learners like to spend at least some time on grammar, with a teacher to help them. The process of looking at and practicing grammar becomes a springboard for expanding the learners' abilities in speaking, writing, listening, and reading.

Most students find it helpful to have special time set aside in their English curriculum to focus on grammar. Students generally appreciate the opportunity to work with a text and a teacher to make sense out of the many forms and usages. This understanding provides the basis for progressing in a relaxed, accepting classroom. Successful English classrooms and instructors foster risk taking as students experiment, both in speaking and writing, with ways to communicate their ideas in a new language.

Teaching grammar does not mean lecturing on grammatical patterns and terminology. It does not mean bestowing knowledge and being an arbiter of correctness. Teaching grammar is the art of helping students make sense, little by little, of a sometimes-puzzling construct and engaging them in various activities that enhance skill areas and promote easy, confident communication.

The text depends upon a partnership with a teacher; it is the teacher who animates and directs the students' language-learning experiences. In practical terms, the aim of the text is to support you, the teacher, by providing a wealth and variety of materials for you to adapt to your individual teaching situation. Using grammar as a base to promote overall English skill, teacher and text can engage students in interesting discourse, challenge their minds, and intrigue them with the power of language as well as the need for accuracy to create successful communication.

Suggestions for the Classroom

THE GRAMMAR CHARTS

Each chart contains a concise visual presentation of the structures to be learned. Presentation techniques often depend upon the content of the chart, the level of the class, and students' learning styles. Not all students react to the charts in the same way. Some students need the security of thoroughly understanding a chart before trying to use the structure. Others like to experiment more freely with using new structures; they refer to the charts only incidentally, if at all.

Given these different learning strategies, you should vary your presentation techniques and not expect students to "learn" or memorize the charts. The charts are simply a starting point (and a point of reference) for class activities. Some charts may require particular methods of presentation, but generally any of the following techniques are viable.

Technique A: Present the examples in the chart, perhaps highlighting them on the board. Add your own examples, relating them to your students' experiences as much as possible. For example, when presenting simple present tense, talk about what students do every day: come to school, study English, and so on. Elicit other examples of the target structure from your students. Then proceed to the exercises.

Technique B: Elicit target structures from students before they look at the chart in the *Student Book*. Ask leading questions that are designed to elicit answers that will include the target structure. (For example, with present progressive, ask, "What are you doing right now?") You may want to write students' answers on the board and relate them to selected examples in the chart. Then proceed to the exercises.

Technique C: Instead of beginning with a chart, begin with the first exercise after the chart. As you work through it with your students, present the information in the chart or refer to examples in the chart.

Technique D: Assign a chart for homework; students bring questions to class. (You may even want to include an accompanying exercise.) With advanced students, you might not need to deal with every chart and exercise thoroughly in class. With intermediate students, it is generally advisable to clarify charts and do most or all of the exercises in each section.

With all of the above, the explanations on the right side of the charts are most effective when recast by the teacher, not read word for word. Focus on the examples. By and large, students learn from examples and lots of practice, but they also find clear explanations helpful. In the charts, the explanations focus attention on what students should be noticing in the examples and the exercises.

Additional Suggestions for Using the Charts

The Here-and-Now Classroom Context

For every chart, try to relate the target structure to an immediate classroom or real-life context. Make up or elicit examples that use the students' names, activities, and interests. For example, when introducing possessive adjectives (Chart 2-5), use yourself and your students to present all the sentences in the chart. Then have students refer to the chart. The here-and-now classroom context is, of course, one of the grammar teacher's best aids.

Demonstration Techniques

Demonstration can be very helpful to explain the meaning of a structure. You and your students can act out situations that demonstrate the target structure. For example, the present progressive can easily be demonstrated (e.g., "I *am writing* on the board right now"). Of course, not all grammar lends itself to this technique.

Using the Board

In discussing the target structure of a chart, use the classroom board whenever possible. Not all students have adequate listening skills for "teacher talk," and not all students can visualize and understand the various relationships within, between, and among structures. Draw boxes, circles, and arrows to illustrate connections between the elements of a structure. A visual presentation helps many students. As much as possible, write students' production on the board.

Oral Exercises with Chart Presentations

Oral exercises follow a chart in order to give students increasingly less controlled practice of the target structure. If you prefer to introduce a particular structure to your students orally, you can always use an oral exercise prior to the presentation of a chart and its written exercises, no matter what the given order in the text.

The Role of Terminology

Students need to understand the terminology, but don't require or expect detailed definitions of terms, either in class discussion or on tests. Terminology is just a tool, a useful label for the moment, so that you and your students can talk to each other about English grammar.

Balancing Teacher and Student Talk

The goal of all language learning is to understand and communicate. The teacher's main task is to direct and facilitate that process. The learner is an active participant, not merely a passive receiver of rules to be memorized. Therefore, many of the exercises in the text are designed to promote interaction between learners as a bridge to real communication.

The teacher has a crucial leadership role, with teacher talk a valuable and necessary part of a grammar classroom. Sometimes you will need to spend time clarifying the information in a chart, leading an exercise, answering questions about exercise items, or explaining an assignment. These periods of teacher talk should, however, be balanced by longer periods of productive learning activity when the students are doing most of the talking. It is important for the teacher to know when to step back and let students lead. Interactive group and pairwork play an important role in the language classroom.

EXERCISE TYPES

Warm-up Exercises (See Exercise 2, p. 1 and Exercise 20, p. 38.)

The purpose of these exercises is to let students discover what they already know and don't know about the target structure in order to get them interested in a chart. Essentially, the Warm-up exercises exemplify the technique of involving the students in the target as a springboard for presenting the grammar in a chart.

Any exercise can be used as a Warm-up. You do not need to follow the order of material in the text. Adapt the material to your own needs and techniques.

First Exercise after a Chart (See Exercise 26, p. 13 and Exercise 16, p. 67.)

In most cases, this exercise includes an example of each item shown in the chart. Students can do the exercise together as a class, and the teacher can refer to chart examples where necessary. More advanced classes can complete it as homework. The teacher can use this exercise as a guide to see how well students understand the basics of the target structure(s).

Written Exercises: General Techniques

The written exercises range from those that are tightly controlled to those that encourage free responses and require creative, independent language use. The fourth edition of *Basic English Grammar* provides expanded "micropractice" exercises to provide incremental practice with a single grammar structure (see Chart 5–7, Exercises 25–28, pp. 139–141). Here are some general techniques for the written exercises.

Technique A: A student can be asked to read an item aloud. You can say whether the student's answer is correct, or you can open up discussion by asking the rest of the class if the answer is correct. For example:

TEACHER: Juan, would you please read item 3?
STUDENT: Ali *speaks* Arabic.
TEACHER (to the class): Do the rest of you agree with Juan's answer?

The slow-moving pace of this method is beneficial for discussion not only of grammar items, but also of vocabulary and content. Students have time to digest information and ask questions. You have the opportunity to judge how well they understand the grammar. This technique is time-consuming, but it allows students to develop a variety of skills and respond to spontaneously posed questions about vocabulary, content, and context as well as the grammar itself.

Technique B: Give students time to complete the exercise, in class, as seatwork. They should be instructed to write their answers in the book while you circulate and provide assistance. When most students have completed the exercise, invite students to begin reading their completions aloud. Correction can be provided immediately, and corrections can be readily illustrated on the board.

Technique C: Read the first part of the item, and then pause for students to call out the answer in unison. For example:

ITEM entry: "Ali (*speak*)_____ Arabic."
TEACHER (with the students looking at their texts): Ali . . .
STUDENTS (in unison): speaks (with possibly a few incorrect responses scattered about)
TEACHER: . . . speaks Arabic. *Speaks.* Do you have any questions?

This technique saves a lot of time in class, but is also slow paced enough to allow for questions and discussion of grammar, vocabulary, and content. It is essential that students have prepared the exercise by writing in their books, so it must be assigned ahead of time either in class or as homework.

Technique D:	Students complete the exercise for homework, and you go over the answers with them. Students can take turns giving the answers, or you can supply them. Depending on the importance and length of the sentence, you may want to include the entire sentence or just the answer. Answers can be given one at a time while you take questions, or you can give the answers to the whole exercise before opening it up for questions. When a student supplies the answers, the other students can ask him or her questions if they disagree.
Technique E:	Divide the class into groups (or pairs) and have each group prepare one set of answers that they all agree is correct prior to class discussion. The leader of each group can present its answers.
	Another option is to have the groups (or pairs) hand in their sets of answers for correction and possibly a grade.
	It's also possible to turn these exercises into games wherein the group with the best set of answers gets some sort of reward (perhaps applause from the rest of the class).
	One option for correction of group work is to circle or mark the errors on one paper the group turns in, make photocopies of that paper for each member of the group, and then hand back the papers for students to rewrite individually. At that point, you can assign a grade if desired.

Of course, you can always mix these techniques—with students reading some aloud, with you prompting unison responses for some, with you simply giving the answers for others, or with students collaborating on the answers. Much depends on the level of the class, their familiarity and skill with the grammar at hand, their oral-aural skills in general, and the flexibility or limitations of class time.

Technique F:	When an exercise item has a dialogue between two speakers, A and B (e.g., Exercise 45, p. 83), ask one student to be A and another B and have them read the entry aloud. Then, occasionally, say to A and B, "Without looking at your text, what did you just say to each other?" (If necessary, let them glance briefly at their texts before they repeat what they've just said in the exercise item.) Students may be pleasantly surprised by their own fluency.
Technique G:	Some exercises ask students to change the form but not the substance, or to combine two sentences or ideas. Generally, these exercises are intended for class discussion of the form and meaning of a structure.
	The initial stages of such exercises are a good opportunity to use the board to draw circles and arrows to illustrate the characteristics and relationships of a structure. Students can read their answers aloud to initiate class discussion, and you can write on the board as problems arise. Or, students can write their sentences on the board themselves. Another option is to have them work in small groups to agree upon their answers prior to class discussion.

Open-ended Exercises

The term *open-ended* refers to those exercises in which students use their own words to complete the sentences, either orally or in writing.

Technique A:	Exercises where students must supply their own words to complete a sentence (e.g., Exercise 15, p. 455) should usually be assigned for out-of-class preparation. Then, in class, one, two, or several students can read their sentences aloud; the class can discuss the correctness and appropriateness of the completions. You can suggest possible ways of rephrasing to make the students' sentences more idiomatic. Students who don't read their sentences aloud can revise their own completions, based on what is being discussed in class. At the end of the exercise discussion, you can tell students to hand in their sentences for you to look at or simply ask if anybody has questions about the exercise and not have them submit anything to you.
Technique B:	If you wish to use a completion exercise in class without having previously assigned it, you can turn the exercise into a brainstorming session in which students try out several completions to see if they work. As another possibility, you may wish to divide the class into small groups and have each group come up with completions that they all agree are correct and appropriate. Then use only those completions for class discussion or as written work to be handed in.

Technique C:	Some completion exercises are done on another piece of paper because not enough space has been left in the *Student Book* (e.g., Exercise 50, p. 157). It is often beneficial to use the following progression: (1) Assign the exercise for out-of-class preparation; (2) discuss it in class the next day, having students make corrections on their own papers, based on what they are learning from discussing other students' completions; and (3) ask students to submit their papers to you, either as a requirement or on a volunteer basis.

Writing Practice (See Exercise 61, p. 94; Exercise 44, p. 124.)

Some writing exercises are designed to produce short, informal paragraphs. Generally, the topics concern aspects of the students' lives to encourage free communication as they practice their writing skills. While a course in English rhetoric is beyond the scope of this text, many of the basic elements are included and may be developed and emphasized according to your needs.

These new writing tasks help students naturally produce target grammar structures. They are accompanied by models and checklists that teach students the basic conventions of clear and grammatical expository writing. The checklist can be used to guide students' own writing and to allow for peer editing.

By providing examples of good compositions written by you (or previous classes, perhaps) or composed by the class as a whole (e.g., you write on the board what students tell you to write, and then you and your students revise it together), you give your students clear models to follow.

In general, writing exercises should be done outside of class. All of us need time to consider and revise when we write. And if we get a little help here and there, that's not unusual. The topics in the exercises are structured so that plagiarism should not be a problem. Use in-class writing if you want to appraise the students' unaided, spontaneous writing skills. Tell your students that these writing exercises are simply for practice and that—even though they should always try to do their best— mistakes that occur should be viewed simply as tools for learning.

Encourage students to use a basic dictionary whenever they write. Discuss the use of margins, indentation of paragraphs, and other aspects of the format of a well-written paper.

Error-Analysis Exercises

For the most part, the sentences in this type of exercise have been adapted from actual student writing and contain typical errors. Error-analysis exercises focus on the target structures of a chapter but may also contain miscellaneous errors that are common in student writing at this level (e.g., final -*s* on plural nouns or capitalization of proper nouns). The purpose of including them is to sharpen the students' self-monitoring skills.

Error-analysis exercises are challenging, fun, and a good way to summarize the grammar in a unit. If you wish, tell students they are either newspaper editors or English teachers and that their task is to locate all the mistakes and then write corrections. Point out that even native speakers— including you yourself—have to scrutinize, correct, and revise their own writing. This is a natural part of the writing process.

These exercises can be done as written homework but, of course, they can be handled in other ways: as seatwork, group work, or pairwork.

Let's Talk Exercises

The fourth edition of *Basic English Grammar* has many more exercises explicitly set up for interactive work than the last edition had. Students work in pairs, in groups, or as a class. Interactive exercises may take more class time than they would if teacher-led, but it is time well spent, for there are many advantages to student-student practice.

When students are working in groups or pairs, their opportunities to use what they are learning are greatly increased. In interactive work, the time students have for using English is many times greater than in a teacher-centered activity. Obviously, students working in groups or pairs are often much more active and involved than in teacher-led exercises.

Group work and pairwork also expand students' opportunities to practice many communication skills at the same time that they are practicing target structures. In peer interaction in the classroom, students have to agree, disagree, continue a conversation, make suggestions, promote cooperation, make requests, and be sensitive to each other's needs and personalities—the kinds of exchanges that are characteristic of any group communication, whether in the classroom or elsewhere.

Students will often help and explain things to each other during pairwork, in which case both students benefit greatly. Ideally, students in interactive activities are "partners in exploration." Together they go into new areas and discover things about English usage, supporting each other as they proceed.

Group work and pairwork help to produce a comfortable learning environment. In teacher-centered activities, students may sometimes feel shy and inhibited or may experience stress. They may feel that they have to respond quickly and accurately and that *what* they say is not as important as *how* they say it. When you set up groups or pairs that are noncompetitive and cooperative, students usually tend to help, encourage, and even joke with one another. This encourages them to experiment with the language and to speak more often.

- Pairwork Exercises: Tell the student whose book is open that s/he is the teacher and needs to listen carefully to the other student's responses. Vary the ways in which students are paired up, ranging from having them choose their own partners to counting off or drawing names or numbers from a hat. Walk around the room and answer questions as needed.

- Small Group Exercises: The role of group leader can be rotated for long exercises, or one student can lead the entire exercise if it is short. The group can answer individually or chorally, depending on the type of exercise. Vary the ways in which you divide the class into groups and choose leaders. If possible, groups of three to five students work best.

- Class Activity (Teacher-Led) Exercises:

  a. You, the teacher, conduct the oral exercise. (You can also lead an oral exercise when the directions call for something else; exercise directions calling for pairwork or group work, for example, are suggestions, not ironclad instructions.)
  b. You don't have to read the items aloud as though reading a script word for word. Modify or add items spontaneously as they occur to you. Change the items in any way you can to make them more relevant to your students. (For example, if you know that some students plan to watch the World Cup soccer match on TV soon, include a sentence about that.) Omit irrelevant items.
  c. Sometimes an item will start a spontaneous discussion of, for example, local restaurants or current movies or certain experiences your students have had. These spur-of-the-moment dialogues are very beneficial to your class. Fostering such interactions is one of the chief advantages of a teacher leading an oral exercise.

Listening Exercises

Two audio CDs can be found at the back of the *BEG Student Book*. You will find an audio tracking list on p. 514 to help you locate a particular exercise on the CDs. The scripts for all the exercises are also in the back of the *BEG Student Book*, beginning on p. 489.

A variety of listening exercises introduce students to relaxed, reduced speech and the differences between written and spoken English (see Exercise 18, p. 168 and Exercise 42, p. 249). They reinforce the grammar being taught—some focusing on form, some on meaning, most on both.

Depending on your students' listening proficiencies, some of the exercises may prove to be easy and some more challenging. You will need to gauge how many times to replay a particular item. In general, unless the exercise consists of single sentences, you will want to play the dialogue or passage in its entirety to give your students the context. Then you can replay the audio to have your students complete the task.

It is very important that grammar students be exposed to listening practice early on. Native speech can be daunting to new learners; students often say that they cannot distinguish individual words within a stream of language. If students can't hear a structure, there is little chance it will be reinforced through interactions with other speakers. The sooner your students practice grammar from a listening perspective, the more confidence they will develop and the better equipped they will be to interact in English.

Pronunciation Exercises

A few exercises focus on pronunciation of grammatical features, such as the endings on nouns or verbs and contracted or reduced forms. Some phonetic symbols are used in these exercises to point out sounds that should not be pronounced identically; for example, /s/, /əz/, and /z/ represent the three predictable pronunciations of the grammatical suffix that is spelled -s or -es (see Exercise 17, Listening, p. 68). It is not necessary for students to learn a complete phonetic alphabet; they should merely associate each symbol in an exercise with a sound that is different from all others. The purpose is to help students become more aware of these final sounds in the English they hear to encourage proficiency in their own speaking and writing.

In the exercises on spoken contractions, the primary emphasis should be on students' hearing and becoming familiar with spoken forms rather than their accurate pronunciation of these forms.

The goal of these exercises is for students to listen to the oral production and become familiar with the reduced forms. Beginners' attempts at reduced or contracted forms may sound strange or even unrecognizable to other beginners. Keep students' focus on being able to recognize these forms when listening to native speakers.

Language learners know that their pronunciation is accented, and some of them are embarrassed or shy about speaking. In a pronunciation exercise, students may be more comfortable if you ask groups or the whole class to say a sentence in unison. After that, individuals may volunteer to speak the same sentence. Students' production does not have to be perfect, just understandable.

Expansions and Games

Expansions and games are important parts of the grammar classroom. The study of grammar is (and should be) fun and engaging. Some exercises in the text are designated as Games. In this *Teacher's Guide*, other exercises have Expansions that follow the step-by-step instruction. Both of these activity types are meant to promote independent, active use of target structures.

If a game is suggested, the atmosphere should be relaxed and not overly competitive. The goal is clearly related to the chapter's content, and the reward is the students' satisfaction in using English to achieve that goal.

MONITORING ERRORS IN ORAL WORK

Students should be encouraged to monitor themselves and each other to some extent in interactive work. Not every mistake must be corrected, particularly when students are just beginning to learn the language. Mistakes are a natural part of language learning. However, students generally ask for more correction rather than less. Adult students in particular do not want an incomprehensible level of English to be tolerated by their teachers. Learners want to speak more grammatically and fluently, and with you openly and immediately correcting global errors, students can learn to correct themselves. In an attempt to spare students' feelings, teachers undercorrect or correct so subtly that students don't recognize which part of the sentence is wrong. In fact, when a teacher merely repeats what the student has said but says it correctly, the student may not realize that the teacher is correcting him at all. Therefore, supportive and explicit correction is best.

Students shouldn't worry that they will learn one another's mistakes. Being exposed to imperfect English in an interactive classroom is not going to impede their progress in the slightest. In today's world, with so many people using English as a second language, students will likely be exposed to all levels of English proficiency in people they meet—from airline reservation clerks to new neighbors from a different country to a coworker whose native language is not English. Encountering imperfect English is not going to diminish their own English language abilities, either now in the classroom or later in different English-speaking situations.

Make yourself available to answer questions about correct answers during group work and pairwork. Use time at the end of an exercise to call attention to mistakes that you heard as you monitored the groups. Another way of correcting errors is to have students use the answer key in the back of the book to look up their own answers when they need to. If your copy of *BEG*, fourth edition, doesn't include the answer key, you can make student copies of the answers from the separate *Answer Key* booklet.

OPTIONAL VOCABULARY

Students benefit from your drawing attention to optional vocabulary for many reasons. English is a vocabulary-rich language, and students actively want to expand both their passive and active vocabularies in English. By asking students to discuss words, even words you can safely assume they recognize, you are asking students to use language to describe language and to speak in a completely spontaneous way (they don't know which words you will ask them about). Also, asking students to define words that they may actually know or may be familiar with allows students a change of pace from focusing on grammar, which may be particularly challenging at any given time. This gives students a chance to show off what they do know and take a quick minibreak from what they may occasionally feel is a "heavy" focus on grammar.

One way to review vocabulary, particularly vocabulary that you assume students are familiar with, is to ask them to give you the closest synonym for a word. For example, if you ask students about the word *optimistic*, as a class you can discuss whether *positive*, *hopeful*, or *happy* is the closest synonym. This is, of course, somewhat subjective, but it is a discussion that will likely engage students. Similarly, for a more advanced group, you can ask them for the closest antonym of a given word, and thus for *optimistic* students could judge among *sad*, *negative*, and *pessimistic,* for example. However you choose to review optional vocabulary, most students will greatly appreciate and profit from your doing so.

HOMEWORK

The *Student Book* assumes that students will have the opportunity to prepare some of the written exercises by writing in their books prior to class discussion. Students should be assigned this homework as a matter of course.

Whether you have students write their answers on paper for collection or let them write the answers in their books is up to you. This generally depends on such variables as class size, class level, available class time, your available paper-correcting time, and your preferences in teaching techniques. Most of the exercises in the text can be handled through class discussion without the students' needing to hand in written homework. Most of the written homework that is suggested in the text and in the chapter notes in this *Teacher's Guide* consists of activities that will produce original, independent writing.

Some exercises are managed in class, as "seatwork," whereby you ask students to do an unassigned exercise in class immediately before discussing it. Seatwork may be done individually, in pairs, or in groups.

THE WORKBOOK AS INDEPENDENT STUDY

Particularly eager students can use the *Workbook* to supplement their learning. It contains self-study exercises for independent study, with a perforated answer key located at the end of the book. Encourage your students to remove this answer key and put it in a folder. It's much easier for students to correct their own answers if they make their own booklet.

If you prefer students not to have the answers to the exercises, ask them to hand in the answer key at the beginning of the term (to be returned at the end of the term). Some teachers may prefer to use the *Workbook* for in-class teaching rather than independent study.

The *Workbook* mirrors the *Student Book*. Exercises are called "exercises" in the *Student Book* and "practices" in the *Workbook* to minimize confusion when you make assignments. Each practice in the *Workbook* has a content title and refers students to appropriate charts in the *Student Book* and in the *Workbook* itself.

Workbook practices can be assigned by you or, depending on the level of maturity or sense of purpose of the class, simply left for students to use as they wish. They may be assigned to the entire class or only to those students who need further practice with a particular structure. They may be used as reinforcement after you have covered a chart and an exercise in class or as introductory material prior to discussing a chart.

In addition, students can use the *Workbook* to acquaint themselves with the grammar from any units not covered in class.

Additional Resources
TEST BANK

The *Test Bank for Basic English Grammar* is a comprehensive bank of quizzes and tests that are keyed to charts and chapters in the student book. Each chapter contains a variety of short quizzes which can be used as quick informal comprehension checks or as formal quizzes to be handed in and graded. Each chapter also contains two comprehensive tests. Both the quizzes and the tests can be reproduced as is, or items can be excerpted for tests that you prepare yourself.

FUN WITH GRAMMAR

Fun with Grammar: Communicative Activities for the Azar Grammar Series is a teacher resource text by Suzanne W. Woodward with communicative activities correlated to the Azar-Hagen Grammar Series. It is available as a text or as a download on AzarGrammar.com.

AZARGRAMMAR.COM

Another resource is AzarGrammar.com. This website is designed as a tool for teachers. It includes a variety of additional activities keyed to each chapter of the student book including additional exercise worksheets, vocabulary worksheets, and song-based activities tied to specific grammar points. This website is also a place to ask questions you might have about grammar (sometimes our students ask real stumpers), as well as also being a place to communicate with the authors about the text and to offer teaching/exercise suggestions.

Notes on American English versus British English

Students are often curious about differences between American English and British English. They should know that the differences are minor. Any students who have studied British English (BrE) should have no trouble adapting to American English (AmE), and vice versa.

Teachers need to be careful not to inadvertently mark differences between AmE and BrE as errors; rather, they should simply point out to students that a difference in usage exists.

DIFFERENCES IN GRAMMAR

Differences in article and preposition usage in certain common expressions follow. These differences are not noted in the text; they are given here for the teacher's information.

AmE	BrE
be in the hospital	*be in Ø hospital*
be at the university (be in college)	*be at Ø university*
go to a university (go to college)	*go to Ø university*
go to Ø class/be in Ø class	*go to a class/be in a class*
in the future	*in Ø future (OR in the future)*
did it the next day	*did it Ø next day (OR the next day)*
haven't done something for/in weeks	*haven't done something for weeks*
ten minutes past/after six o'clock	*ten minutes past six o'clock*
five minutes to/of/till seven o'clock	*five minutes to seven o'clock*

DIFFERENCES IN SPELLING

Variant spellings can be noted but should not be marked as incorrect in student writing. Spelling differences in some common words follow.

AmE	BrE
jewelry, traveler, woolen	*jewellry, traveller, woollen*
skillful, fulfill, installment	*skilful, fulfil, instalment*
color, honor, labor, odor	*colour, honour, labour, odour*
-ize (realize, apologize)	*-ise/ize (realise/realize, apologise/apologize)*
analyze	*analyse*
defense, offense, license	*defence, offence, licence (n.)*
theater, center, liter	*theatre, centre, litre*
check	*cheque (bank note)*
curb	*kerb*
forever	*for ever/forever*
focused	*focused/focussed*
fueled	*fuelled/fueled*
jail	*gaol*
practice (n. and v.)	*practise (v.); practice (n. only)*
program	*programme*
specialty	*speciality*
story	*storey (of a building)*
tire	*tyre*

DIFFERENCES IN VOCABULARY

Differences in vocabulary usage between AmE and BrE usually do not significantly interfere with communication, but some misunderstandings may develop. For example, a BrE speaker is referring to underwear when using the word "pants," whereas an AmE speaker is referring to slacks or trousers. Students should know that when American and British speakers read each other's literature, they encounter very few differences in vocabulary usage. Similarly, in the United States, Southerners and New Englanders use different vocabulary but not so much as to interfere with communication. Some differences between AmE and BrE follow.

AmE	BrE
attorney, lawyer	*barrister, solicitor*
bathrobe	*dressing gown*
can (of beans)	*tin (of beans)*
cookie, cracker	*biscuit*

corn	maize
diaper	nappy
driver's license	driving licence
drug store	chemist's
elevator	lift
erasers	rubber
flashlight	torch
gas, gasoline	petrol
hood of a car	bonnet of a car
living room	sitting room, drawing room
math	maths (e.g., a maths teacher)
raise in salary	rise in salary
restroom	public toilet, WC (water closet)
schedule	timetable
sidewalk	pavement, footpath
sink	basin
soccer	football
stove	cooker
truck	lorry, van
trunk (of a car)	boot (of a car)
be on vacation	be on holiday

Key to Pronunciation Symbols

THE PHONETIC ALPHABET (SYMBOLS FOR AMERICAN ENGLISH)

Consonants

Phonetic symbols for most consonants use the same letters as in conventional English spelling: /b, d, f, g, h, k, l, m, n, o, p, r, s, t, v, w, y, z/.*
Spelling consonants that are *not* used phonetically in English: *c, q, x.*

A few additional symbols are needed for other consonant sounds.

/ θ / (Greek theta) = voiceless *th* as in **thin**, **thank**
/ δ / (Greek delta) = voiced *th* as in **then**, **those**
/ ŋ / = *ng* as in **sing**, **think** (but not in *danger*)
/ š / = *sh* as in **shirt**, **mission**, **nation**
/ ž / = *s* or *z* in a few words like *pleasure*, *azure*
/ č / = *ch* or *tch* as in **watch**, **church**
/ ǰ / = *j* or *dge* as in **jump**, *le***dge**

Vowels

The five vowels in the spelling alphabet are inadequate to represent the twelve to fifteen vowel sounds in American speech. Therefore, new symbols and new sound associations for familiar letters must be adopted.

Front	**Central**	**Back** (lips rounded)
/I/ or /Iy/ as in **beat**		/u/, /u:/, or /uw/ as in **boot**
/I/ as in **bit**		/ʋ/ as in **book**
/e/ or /ey/ as in **bait**		/o/ or /ow/ as in **boat**
		/ɔ/ as in **bought**
/ɛ / as in **bet**	/ə/ as in **but**	
/æ/ as in **bat**	/a/ as in **bother**	

Glides: /ai/ or /ay/ as in **bite**
/ɔi/ or /ɔy/ as in **boy**
/au/ or /aw/ as in a**bout**

British English has a somewhat different set of vowel sounds and symbols. You might want to consult a standard pronunciation text or a BrE dictionary for that system.

*Slanted lines indicate phonetic symbols.

Chapter 1
Using Be

CHAPTER SUMMARY

OBJECTIVE: In this chapter, students learn to describe themselves and their classmates by using pronouns in combination with the verb *be*. Students become comfortable making basic statements about the world, using the names of countries, the names of languages, and basic geographical vocabulary, and using nouns that describe categories of everyday things. This chapter presents singular and plural nouns, pronouns, affirmative and negative statements, and contractions. It also introduces basic vocabulary for people, family roles and jobs, and animals and combines these common nouns in *be*-statements, simple descriptive adjectives, and common prepositions.

APPROACH: This book presents basic English in its most recognizable style and register. For this reason, contractions, which are among the first important colloquialisms students are exposed to, are presented immediately after affirmative statements with *be*. The first exercise provides an opportunity for beginners to introduce themselves to classmates and exchange basic information. The charts and exercises then focus on the structure of *be*-statements with nouns, adjectives, and pronouns. Chart 1-1 conjugates the verb *be* with singular subject pronouns and highlights third person gender differences; Chart 1-2 highlights plural forms. Later charts model contractions and negative forms. The text emphasizes the accurate use of the verb *be* with common vocabulary. Chart 1-8 introduces the verb *be* in conjunction with prepositions of place, which allows beginners to describe the physical placement of objects. Finally, Chart 1-9 summarizes basic sentence patterns with *be* and provides written and aural practice with these patterns.

Beginning students have varyingly limited degrees of language to utilize when trying to comprehend classroom instructions and grammar explanations. It is critical that instructors make exercise instructions clear in every way possible — by writing on the board, of course, but also by being prepared to demonstrate and act out various instructions and speech acts until students can understand them. Teaching beginners requires strong communicative skills on the part of teachers, who should monitor their own reliance on the book to ensure that students truly understand the tasks.

TERMINOLOGY: The text uses the term *tenses* to describe verb forms that express time relationships, because most students are comfortable with the term. The idea of tense as related to time has meaning in many other languages. The text presents and explains structures with a minimum of technical terminology and a maximum of repetition to ensure ready acquisition. This strategy ensures that students will gain good control of basic grammar structures and enough working terminology to further their study of the language.

❑ EXERCISE 1. Let's talk: class activity.
Page 1
Time: 10 minutes

- Model the first cloze statements by writing them on the board with the blanks *uncompleted*.
- Tell the class that you are going to introduce yourself. Then complete the blanks with *your* information.
- Write the words and examples for each column on the board:

first name (names):	*Juan, Koji, Chun Hua, Madonna, Igor, Ahmed*
country (countries):	*Colombia, Japan, Korea, England, Russia, Saudi Arabia*
city (cities):	*Bogotá, Tokyo, Seoul, London, Moscow, Riyadh*
language (languages):	*Spanish, Japanese, Korean, English, Russian, Arabic*

- Beginning students may have little passive language to call on when listening to instructions. Provide support by modeling the exercise with a few students first.
- Erase the information that applies to you, and write a student's name above the model on the board.
- Complete the model with information from two or three students before asking students to complete their own information in their books.
- Once students have completed their own information in Exercise 1, ask them to stand up and move around the room, getting information from others.
- Circulate around the room, assisting first any students who did not immediately respond to your instructions / explanations. Students who do not immediately grasp an exercise will more readily understand what is asked of them if you model the exercise directly with them. True beginners will especially benefit from this approach.

Optional Vocabulary

Depending on the level of the students in your class, you will need to decide how much additional vocabulary to teach for active use or simply "use" without detailed explanation. This teacher's guide will provide lists of optional vocabulary; however, you should be wary of overloading students with vocabulary. When deciding what vocabulary and associated words to teach with targeted material, you should take into account the combination of true beginners and near beginners in your class.

hi	talk
hello	from
speak	come from

❑ EXERCISE 2. Warm-up. Page 1
Time: 5 minutes

- Write the words *happy* and *sad* on the board.
- Ask students if they know what the words mean and incorporate any responses actively into the discussion.
- Add students' contributions to the board work.
- Make simple drawings on the board to show the meaning.

    happy = draw a smiley / smiling face
    sad = draw a frowning face

- Write *he = man* and *she = woman* on the board.
- Ask one student to read item 1 aloud.
- As a class, circle the appropriate picture.
- Repeat the process for item 2.
- Ask students to complete item 3 individually.
- Tell students how you are and write this on the board, using a simple adjective.

    I am <u>happy</u>.

Expansion: Invite students to use other adjectives they may know. Exercise 5 does just this, but you may find some students are bursting to show off what they know. A few minutes of spontaneous sharing will not take away from the impact of Exercise 5 and, in fact, may make students more confident when approaching it.

bored	hungry
cold	nervous
excited	thirsty
hot	tired

If students can readily produce *I am* + *adjective,* put student-generated sentences on the board, using students' names.

Juan is hungry.
Hiroko is nervous.
Ahmed is tired.

CHART 1-1. Singular Pronouns + *Be.* Page 2
Time: 10–15 minutes

Though students won't have full control of the verb *be* in its simple present form, most or many will have seen it before and some may be able to repeat it as a rote-learned task.

At this level, students will probably not be able to give full explanations in English. It is still important that you ask questions and incorporate whatever explanations they can produce—even something as basic as a raised index finger, to indicate *1*—into your board work. Doing so prompts students to respond immediately to your use of English and activates their passive knowledge of English. Using whatever language they can produce will help beginning students realize that they are communicating meaningfully, however stilted and limited it may seem.

Get good at writing on the board without turning your back to the students! This allows you to maintain eye contact while continuing to elicit and encourage student interaction with both you and the material. Teaching beginners requires not only becoming a superb actor but also developing the ability to multitask and maintain a connection with students even more consistently than you would need to in more advanced classes, where you can use more English to explain English.

- Write the chart heading "Singular Pronouns + *Be*" on the board.
- Ask students if they know what *singular* means and write the word on the board.
- Ask students if they know what *plural* means and write the word on the board.
- Incorporate any and all feedback as inclusively as you can to define the words.

    singular = 1
    plural = 2, 3, 4, 5 . . . 10 . . . 50 . . . 500 . . . 1000, and so on.

- Ask student(s) to read the sentences (a)–(h) on the left side of Chart 1-1 aloud while you write them on the board.
- Write and say *singular pronoun* while demonstrating the person referred to:

I	*Point to yourself.*
you	*Point directly to one student and one student only.*
he	*Point to a male in the class.*
she	*Point to a female in the class.*
it	*Point to an object in the class.*

- In the sentences you have written on the board, highlight the three singular forms of *be* by underlining them and drawing an arrow back to the singular pronoun that requires their use.

    I <u>am</u> late.

Expansion: Point to each student in the class and have the class say whether the person is a *he* or a *she*. Start by pointing at yourself. Keep track of *he* versus *she* on the board.

he = 7 students
she = 9 students + 1 teacher

Optional Vocabulary

refer to	bus
person	pronoun(s)
forms	feminine
late	masculine
early	

❏ EXERCISE 3. Looking at grammar. Page 2
Time: 5–7 minutes

- Ask a student to read the completed example aloud.
- Explain that students have to choose which pronoun they need for each noun.
- Write *he*, *she*, or *it* on the board.
- Allow three to four minutes to complete and then have students read correct answers aloud.
- Stress that because the titles *Dr.* and *Professor* are not gender specific, two answers are possible.

❏ EXERCISE 4. Looking at grammar. Page 2
Time: 5–7 minutes

- Write *am*, *is*, and *are* on the board.
- Without completing the blanks, give each student a sentence to read and complete.
- Ask students for explanations of *hot* and *cold*. Write on the board any helpful words that may come up (e.g., *weather*, *summer*, *winter*, *food*, *soup*, *ice cream*, etc.).

❏ EXERCISE 5. Let's talk. Page 3
Time: 10 minutes

Part I
- Introduce the task by writing on the board a few adjectives that are true for you right now, in combination with a simple *be* sentence. For example:

  Now I am happy and tired.

- Have students independently check adjectives that are true for them right now.
- Go around the room and assist students who do not recognize the adjectives given or who don't think enough are true for them. Assist them in coming up with more adjectives as needed.

Part II
- Pair students.

> It can take more time for beginners to pick their own partners or even understand that you expect them to work in pairs. Thus, it can be more effective for you to pair students so that maximum time is spent on the speaking task and momentum is not lost.

- Ask pairs to tell their partners what is true for them right now.
- Write some of the sentences you hear students telling each other, on the board and in quotes.

  Hiroko: *"I am nervous."*
  Ahmed: *"I am tired."*

Part III
- Ask each pair to tell the class two things about their partner.
- Write a few third person sentences on the board below the *I* statements from Part II.

- Show the difference between an *I* statement and one about a third person by crossing out the *I* and *am* in an *I* statement and replacing the pronoun and verb form. For example:

  "~~I am~~ tired."
  <u>She is</u> *tired.*

❏ EXERCISE 6. Warm-up. Page 3
Time: 5 minutes

- Read the question *How many people?* and write it on the board.
- Have students read each sentence and choose the correct response.
- Use your hands, gestures, and tone of voice to indicate whom each plural pronoun refers to. Monitor the different ways in which you act out target structures, to ensure that your actions illustrate without patronizing students.
- For item 1, clearly include the entire class or more than one student by using your hand to indicate that *we* is always plural and always first person (i.e., the people doing the speaking).
- For item 2, show that *you* can refer to one person or several people by speaking *directly to* either one student or more than one student.
- For item 3, show that *they* is always plural and always third person by speaking *about* more than one person and using appropriate gestures.

CHART 1-2. Plural Pronouns + *Be.* Page 4
Time: 10–15 minutes

> Be prepared to tap into each student's learning style by presenting new material in several ways—for example, by writing on the board as well as modeling directly with students. Students will be ready for the presentation of plural pronouns in this chart both because they have probably been exposed to them before and because the singular forms have recently been presented. However, speak slowly and clearly and illustrate meaning by gesturing toward students and objects in the class. Be sure students understand that *be* has only one plural form.

- Write the chart title on the board, "Plural Pronouns + *Be.*"
- Ask a student to remind the class what *plural* means and write it on the board:

  plural = 2, 3, 4, 5 . . . 50, and so on.

- Demonstrate and write *we*, *you* (plural), and *they* on the board.
- Add *are* after all three plural pronouns.

  We are
  You are
  They are

- Have three students read chart examples (a)–(c) aloud while you complete them on the board with *here.*
- Ask three more students to take turns reading (d)–(f), and write the examples on the board.

- Point out that plural pronouns and verbs are *easy*: each plural pronoun is followed by *are*.
- Tell students that for *be* and other verbs, the plural forms stay the same in every tense.

Optional Vocabulary
here
there
persons / people

❑ **EXERCISE 7.** Looking at grammar. Page 4
Time: 5 minutes

- Read the example.
- Ask why *they* is circled.
- Lead students to the conclusion that *we* always includes *I*. Demonstrate *we* (*you, he, she, they* + *I*) if necessary.
- Complete the exercise by having students take turns reading each item and selecting the correct plural pronoun.
- Remind students that unlike third person singular (*he* / *she* / *it*), the plural form has no gender difference. *They* is used for all combinations of third person plural.

❑ **EXERCISE 8.** Looking at grammar. Page 4
Time: 7–10 minutes

- Instruct students to complete the sentences independently.
- Read each completed sentence aloud.
- Ask students the meanings of adjectives not yet discussed and write them on the board.

Expansion: After working through the meaning of *homesick* as a class, ask students what makes them homesick when they are away from home. Lead the discussion by suggesting things that make a person homesick. For example:

language
family
food
weather

Optional Vocabulary
ready   homesick
late   funny
sick

❑ **EXERCISE 9.** Looking at grammar. Page 5
Time: 10–15 minutes

- Because this is the first exercise in the text requiring students to make original sentences from cue words, explain the task carefully.
- Model the example by writing the cue words and example sentence on the board.
- Tell students to make sentences using the words for each item. Go around the classroom to ensure that students understand the task and are able to work through it.

- Have students read the newly completed sentences aloud to you while you write the correct versions on the board.
- For those sentences students had trouble with, write very overt corrections on the board, crossing out the incorrect verb with a flourish and writing the new verb. For example, if a student produces the sentence "You and I am homesick," cross out "am" and write "are" just above or below it.

        are
You and I ~~am~~ homesick.

It is critical to students' acquisition of new and unfamiliar grammar that you correct them overtly and definitively. Do so in a level-appropriate and supportive way, but do so readily and clearly. Many times newer teachers or teachers of beginning students are so concerned about inhibiting students' production that they undercorrect speaking (and overcorrect writing). Often, when a teacher hears a mistake in the targeted structure, she will tell the student the correct form. However, the student may not recognize that a correction is being given. The student may even hear the correction as a repetition of what he or she said originally, or he may confuse the correction for a confirmation. It is far more useful to students, particularly beginners, to be very direct and overt in making corrections, and even to write errors on the board.

It is also important to choose carefully when and what to correct to avoid discouraging students. Most learners find clear corrections extremely helpful, particularly when they are beginning their study of English. Lengthy discussions of why something is incorrect may not always be helpful, because beginners simply don't have enough language to follow such a detailed discussion. Therefore, keep explanations brief and clear and, above all, leave no doubt in the student's mind what the correct form is.

Because beginning students can't easily comprehend the "filler" language that teachers use when making supportive corrections, don't give lengthy explanations in which you use many (possibly new) words to show your support of students' efforts. Get students used to receiving straightforward feedback. For example: "Good try, Luis, but wrong. *Is*, not *are*, goes with the pronoun *he*."

Correct overtly, definitively, and dynamically. Write corrections on the board, and modulate your voice to emphasize what is right or wrong grammatically.

❑ **EXERCISE 10.** Warm-up. Page 5
Time: 5 minutes

- Ask students to name a few cities and countries they know.
- Write these on the board.
- Ask students if they know what an island is.
- Draw an island in the middle of water on the board.
- Have students complete the Warm-up independently and review as a class.

CHART 1-3. Singular Nouns + *Be*. Page 6
Time: 10–15 minutes

This chart presents singular indefinite articles. Students must be able to identify which words are preceded by *an* and which words by *a*. They thus need to recognize words that begin with vowels. It matters less whether they remember the terminology (*vowels* and *consonants*) or can name which letters are which. Recognition and production are more important than terminology at this stage.

- Write the chart title on the board, "Singular Nouns + *Be*."
- Ask a student to remind the class what *singular* means and write the definition on the board. For example:

  singular = 1

- Write the word *noun* on the board and elicit the working definition below and / or present it by writing it on the board.

  noun = person, place, or thing

- Explain that *a* and *an* both mean "one" and that these words are called *articles*.
- Write on the board:

  a / an = 1
  a / an = articles

- Tell students that *a* is the more common article and it goes before most words.
- Write on the board:

  a city
  a country
  a school
  a student

- Explain that *an* is the form of the article used before words that begin with *vowels*.
- Ask students if they know what a *vowel* is. Write the following on the board:

  an goes before words starting with vowels
  vowels = a, e, i, o, u
  an animal
  an egg
  an island
  an office
  an umbrella

- Ask a student to read sentence (a) in the chart while you write it on the board.
- Review the notes accompanying sentence (a) with students and write key words on the board.
- Ask another student to read sentence (b) while you write it on the board.
- Review the notes accompanying sentence (b) with students and write key words on the board.

❑ EXERCISE 11. Looking at grammar.
Page 6
Time: 5–10 minutes

- Give students a few minutes to select the correct articles independently.
- Review as a class.

Optional Vocabulary

consonant(s)	street
vowel(s)	avenue
town	ocean
island	continent
place	

❑ EXERCISE 12. Vocabulary and grammar.
Page 7
Time: 10–15 minutes

Part I
- Write the word *geography* on the board and create a quick word map.
- Ask students if they know any vocabulary words about *geography* and write any related words they come up with on the word map.
- Possibilities include:

map	*rivers*
world	*mountains*
land	*cities*
countries	*towns*
oceans	*areas*
seas	*continents*
places	*languages*
islands	

- Write each of the four headings in the exercise on the board.
- Tell students to put the words in the box above the chart into the appropriate categories in the chart.
- Give students five to seven minutes to complete the chart independently.

Part II
- Have students get into smaller groups.
- Ask students to make sentences similar to the examples given.

Expansion: Keep students in groups and circulate, providing help as needed. For groups and students who find the task less challenging, ask them to add to the appropriate column as many countries, languages, cities, and islands they can think of.

Next, give individual students one word from the original list in the box. Ask one student to make a sentence and write it under the correct column heading on the board.

Finally, invite those students who managed the task most quickly and easily to make additional sentences with geographical words and write their sentence in the correct columns on the board.

Students in beginning classes may have a relatively wide range of abilities, so you should be ready to accommodate the different speeds at which they complete tasks. For controlled exercises presented and reviewed in class, have the most competent students tackle the more difficult questions and invite students who struggle the most to read the completed exercise items and give synonyms for basic vocabulary. Because students don't know which vocabulary words you will ask about, all will benefit from discussing the words and formulating responses to your questions. In addition, have extra seatwork tasks for those students who tend to finish independent work more quickly than others. The Expansion on page 5 is an example of such an additional task, and it includes instructions for incorporating it into the exercise given.

❏ EXERCISE 13. Warm-up. Page 7
Time: 5 minutes

- Ask students to complete the Warm-up with *book* or *books*.
- Ask students to explain how the two words differ and what the extra *-s* on *books* means.
- Ask students to compare the verbs in red. When is *is* used? When is *are* used?

Optional Vocabulary
textbooks
dictionaries
reference books

CHART 1-4. Plural Nouns + *Be*. Page 8
Time: 10–15 minutes

In this chart, you will present plural nouns with *be*. Because the text doesn't introduce the use of *some* at this stage, the use of a plural noun will always indicate the most general sense of the noun.

Spend ample time explaining that a singular noun + a singular noun = a plural noun, as this is the most challenging aspect of this chart.

- Write the chart title on the board, "Plural Nouns + *Be*."
- Ask a student to remind the class what *plural* means and write it on the board. For example:

  plural = 2, 3, 4, 5 . . . 50, and so on.

- Ask students to remind you of the definition of a noun.

  a noun = a person, place, or thing

- Explain that plural nouns end in *-s* and because *a / an* mean one, they are not used before plural nouns.
- Tell students that when we use a plural noun, we are talking about the noun in all cases, in the most general sense.
- Ask students to take turns reading (a)–(e) while you put the additional examples and explanatory notes on the board.
- Explain sentence (c) carefully and tell students that nouns ending in *-y* change their spelling to *-ies* in the plural.

- Write additional examples to illustrate sentences (d) and (e). For example:

  Tokyo and Moscow <u>are cities</u>.
  Textbooks and dictionaries <u>are books</u>.

❏ EXERCISE 14. Looking at grammar.
Page 8
Time: 5 minutes

- Have students read the nouns on the left and select the appropriate number on the right.
- Remind students that when a noun has a final *-s*, it usually means the noun is plural.

❏ EXERCISE 15. Looking at grammar.
Page 8
Time: 4–7 minutes

- Give students a few minutes to complete each blank with the plural form on their own.
- Have students read each correct plural aloud and check that they know the meanings of the words.

❏ EXERCISE 16. Looking at grammar.
Page 9
Time: 7–10 minutes

- Ask a student to read the example sentences.
- Have students complete each sentence on their own.
- Review as a class.

❏ EXERCISE 17. Looking at grammar.
Page 9
Time: 10–12 minutes

- Ask a student to read the example sentence.
- Explain to students that they will need to make three items in each sentence plural:

  1. *the first noun*
  2. *the verb* be
  3. *the second noun*

- Give students time to complete the exercise on their own. Circulate, helping any students who need support.
- Review and correct as a class. Assist students with the correct pronunciation of *vegetables* (sometimes difficult with so many syllables) and *months* (the *-ths* ending may be difficult to pronounce).

Optional Vocabulary

As the text progresses and students gain competence, the Optional Vocabulary lists will appear more sporadically, after several exercises. Discussing vocabulary gives beginning students a chance to use their newly acquired English in spontaneous ways. It also gives you the opportunity to encourage students to use the target structures (singular noun + *be* and plural noun + *be*) correctly as they describe the words you ask them about.

When you introduce new vocabulary, ask students about related words. Beginning students often have seen many more words than they can readily produce, and guiding them to think about words in topical categories may help them recall words they know passively. As you go through the list below, ask students to add to the names of animals, sports, vegetables, months, and seasons. Write all vocabulary on the board and encourage students to write notes.

animal	pea
dog	machine
cat	airplane
cow	month
horse	June
sports	July
tennis	season
soccer	winter
vegetable	summer

Expansion: Do the following quick oral exercise for additional practice with *be* + noun. (Charts 1-3 and 1-4) Ask students to close their books. Tell students they will complete the sentences with a form of *be* + *a student / students*. Indicate the student or students as you name them.

Example:
TEACHER: (name of a student in the class) Yoko
STUDENT: Yoko is a student.

1. *(name of a student)*
2. *(name of a student) and (name of a student)*
3. *I*
4. *(name of a student) and I*
5. *We*
6. *(name of a student)*
7. *(name of a student) and (name of a student)*
8. *They*
9. *You*
10. *(name of a student) and (name of a student) and (name of a student)*

❏ EXERCISE 18. Game. Page 10
Time: 10–12 minutes

- Instruct all students to close their books.
- Put students into teams of two or three.
- Have each team pick one member to write their sentences.
- Tell students you will read ten nouns, and for each noun that you read, they will make a sentence using that noun and another noun in the same category.
- Model the example given in the book.
- Read each item included in the game.
- If students are readily engaged, give five to ten more items.
- Have teams write their answers on the board and correct as a class.
- Announce the winning team.

❏ EXERCISE 19. Let's talk: pairwork.
Page 10
Time: 10–12 minutes

Remind students that pairwork practice helps them gain confidence with the structures.

Students often work well in pairs when background music is played at a low volume. The music helps students feel less self-conscious and can also be stopped and started to indicate when to begin speaking and when to stop.

Circulate with paper and pen and write down any common mistakes of production, pronunciation, or factuality that you hear. Bring common errors to the attention of the class and correct overtly and visually by explaining and illustrating on the board.

- Put students into pairs.
- Explain that each partner will ask the other to name a thing, an animal, a place, a food, and so on.
- After the first partner reads the category, the other partner must give an example and use a complete sentence in response.
- Model the example in the book with one of the stronger students.
- Tell students that as they work through the exercise, you will help each pair.
- Review the exercise as a class and invite students from each pair to share alternative answers.

❏ EXERCISE 20. Warm-up: listening.
Page 11
Time: 5 minutes

Whenever using CDs, be fully prepared. Know which track number you will be using and make sure the player is turned on. Understanding a new language exclusively by listening is challenging. Students cannot see the mouths of those speaking, and the contexts are unknown. Students may become nervous or easily distracted when they are asked to listen to a CD, so give them very clear instructions about the task before you begin playing it.

- Play the CD.
- Write the contractions on the board.
- Invite students to tell you the long form for each contraction and write it on the board.

CHART 1-5. Contractions with *Be*. Page 11
Time: 10 minutes

Most students have already been exposed to contractions and will recognize them. Tell students they will hear contractions more often than they will see them in print and that contractions are extremely common in speaking.

- Write the chart title on the board.
- Ask the class if anyone can explain what a contraction is.
- Write the first example on the left side of the chart on the board.

    I + am ⇒ I'm.

- Explain that the apostrophe (') takes the place of the verb *be*.
- Explain that in English, the sound is *I'm* . . . as though the two words are "pushed together," with no verb and no space in between.
- Have students read examples (a)–(g) to you while you write them on the board.
- Pronounce each contraction in (b)–(g) carefully and have students repeat the contracted form after you.

❏ EXERCISE 21. Looking at grammar.
Page 11
Time: 5–10 minutes

- Have students write the contraction for each long form.
- Correct both by writing the contractions on the board as students say them and by pronouncing them carefully.
- Overtly correct students' pronunciation of the contracted verbs.

❏ EXERCISE 22. Looking at grammar.
Page 11
Time: 5–10 minutes

- Have students write the long form for each contraction individually, as seatwork.
- Review by having students read each item aloud.

❏ EXERCISE 23. Looking at grammar.
Page 12
Time: 5–10 minutes

- Have a student read the example sentence.
- Point out that *Sara* was replaced with the correct subject pronoun in contracted form.

    Sara is = She's

- To show the changes made, cross out *Sara* and the *i* in *is*.
- Without allowing prior preparation, have students complete each sentence aloud, correcting as you review.
- Have students write the pronouns and correct.

❏ EXERCISE 24. Listening. Page 12
Time: 10 minutes

Part I
- Explain to students that they will write the contractions they hear but that these contractions are missing from the printed exercise.
- Play the track from the CD.
- Play the CD a second time if needed before correcting.

Part II
- Play the track again, pausing to correct with students.

Optional Vocabulary

substitute	early
contraction	cafeteria
push together	funny
apostrophe	too
nice / happy to meet you	seat
absent	same
late	nice

❏ EXERCISE 25. Warm-up: pairwork.
Page 12
Time: 5–10 minutes

- Have students look at the list of nouns.
- Invite students to define any words they can.
- Ask students to make true sentences using *not* plus the words in the box.
- Ask students to make true affirmative sentences (sentences without *not*) if they can.

CHART 1-6. Negative with *Be*. Page 13
Time: 10 minutes

> Most students will have heard *not* and understand that it negates the action of the verb.

- Write the chart title on the board.
- Ask students to define the word *negative*.
- Write some negative example sentences that apply to you and the class you are in and show students the negative with a contraction. For example:

    I am <u>not</u> a doctor. (I am a teacher.) ⇒ I'<u>m not</u> a doctor.
    We are <u>not</u> in England.
    (We are in the USA.) ⇒ We'<u>re not</u> in England.
                        AND
                        We <u>aren't</u> in England.
    Satoko is <u>not</u> Spanish.
    (She is Japanese.) ⇒ She'<u>s not</u> Spanish.
                AND
                She <u>isn't</u> Spanish.

- Invite students to give you more examples and write these on the board. For example:

    A city is <u>not</u> an animal. ⇒ A city'<u>s not</u> an animal.
                        AND
                        A city <u>isn't</u> an animal.

- Ask students to take turns reading sentences (a)–(h) from the chart aloud. Then ask other students to read the contracted forms aloud.
- Spend adequate time on the stress and pronunciation of each contraction and have students repeat after you as you model each one.
- Review the notes to the right of the chart with students.
- Emphasize that *I + am* has only one contracted form:

    I + am <u>not</u> tired. ⇒ I'<u>m not</u> tired.

❑ EXERCISE 26. Looking at grammar.
Page 13
Time: 7–10 minutes

- Begin the exercise by asking a student to read the full form and then the contracted form in item 1 aloud.
- Go around the room, asking first one student to complete the full negative form and then two others to provide both contracted forms.
- Provide immediate pronunciation and stress correction of the two forms.

❑ EXERCISE 27. Looking at grammar.
Page 14
Time: 7–10 minutes

- Begin the exercise by reading the two examples aloud.
- For seatwork, have students complete the exercise and create full sentences from the cues.
- Review as a class by having students read their completed sentences aloud.

❑ EXERCISE 28. Vocabulary and listening.
Page 14
Time: 10–12 minutes

Most beginners know at least a smattering of family terms. Family vocabulary is considered essential, and practicing it gives students a chance to talk about their families. Allow this vocabulary work to take as much time as it naturally needs. Students may bring up additional family words (*niece, nephew, cousin, grandfather, grandmother, grandparents, in-laws,* etc.). Welcome discussion of passive vocabulary in relation to this topic.

Part I
- Ask students what a family tree is.
- Have students look at the Peterson family tree and, using the nouns to the left of the chart, identify the members by their family roles.
- Invite students to contribute other family words they may know: *niece, nephew, cousin, grandfather, grandmother, grandparents, in-laws,* etc.
- Expand on the Peterson family tree or create a family tree of your own, and write all related vocabulary on the board.
- Ask students to write the correct article in front of each noun listed.
- Have students take turns reading the items, correct their article choices, and discuss the meaning of each noun further.

Part II
- Tell students you will play the CD track for the exercise.
- Explain that they will determine whether the verb in each statement is affirmative or negative and circle the form they hear.

- Before you begin, instruct students to listen carefully for the final *-t* sound as it can be hard to hear in negative contractions.
- Review the correct answers with students.

❑ EXERCISE 29. Looking at grammar.
Page 15
Time: 10–15 minutes

This exercise is ideal for vocabulary expansion. Write words that students produce on the board, as often as possible, showing that their production is meaningful. Writing student-generated vocabulary gets students into the habit of writing words, which aids both memory and appropriate categorization.

- Before having students look at the names of jobs in the book, ask them to look at the pictures.
- Ask students to identify the jobs they see and name any other objects they see in the pictures. (Naming these objects may help other students recall the names of the jobs themselves.)
- Write the vocabulary that students produce on the board.

Part I
- Give students time to complete this exercise as seatwork.
- Review as a class, encouraging any further discussion of the jobs named.

Part II
- Have students complete this part as seatwork.
- Correct as a class.

❑ EXERCISE 30. Warm-up. Page 16
Time: 5 minutes

- Begin by writing a few basic *be* + adjective sentences about yourself on the board. For example:

I am	short.
I am	hungry.
I am not	tired.

- Complete the Warm-up with students.
- Ask students how they know Bill is old and Sam is young. What age clues can they see in the picture?
- Invite any other *be* + adjective combinations and write these on the board.
- Ask the class if anyone can explain what an adjective is.
- If no one can, go to the three sample sentences you wrote and circle the adjectives.
- Doing so may lead students to give you other examples of adjectives, rather than a definition. Write the words students produce on the board for further discussion.

CHART 1-7. *Be* + Adjective. Page 16
Time: 10–15 minutes

> This chart presents sentences in which the subject of the verb *be* is described by an adjective. Explain that adjectives tell us more about the subject (and nouns in general). Stress that adjectives do not change in terms of person or number. Point out that *round* and *intelligent* used in example sentences (a)–(d) do not change in form at all.

• Write the chart title on the board.
• Ask students to take turns reading example sentences (a)–(d) on the left aloud while you write these on the board.
• Underline the subjects of each sentence as well as the adjective.
• Explain to students that though the subject changes in person and number, the adjective form always remains the same, whether it describes a singular or plural noun.
• Remind students that the noun subject can be replaced by a pronoun, and invite other students to read (e)–(g) aloud, while you write these sentences on the board.
• Review the notes on the right side of the chart with students.

❏ EXERCISE 31. Grammar and vocabulary.
Page 16
Time: 10–12 minutes

• Write the word *opposite* on the board and ask students to give you examples of opposites.
• Write any examples students give on the board. For example:

   sick ≠ healthy

• Ask one student to read the completed example to the class.
• Without allowing prior preparation, have students complete the rest of the exercise. Give other students different sentences to complete aloud.
• As students complete the sentences, they may use other vocabulary words and adjectives.
• Write any additional vocabulary on the board along with examples of opposites that students use.

❏ EXERCISE 32. Grammar and vocabulary.
Page 17
Time: 10–15 minutes

• Instruct students to complete the exercise independently as seatwork.
• Remind students that they will need to supply the correct form of the verb *be*.
• Correct the exercise by having students read their individual completions aloud.
• Discuss all possible completions and ask students to explain and justify their choices of adjectives.

Optional Vocabulary

intelligent	round
hungry	square
thirsty	flat
happy	triangular
sad	dangerous
dirty	safe
tidy	sweet
clean	sour
ugly	elephant
beautiful	rain forest
rich	joke
poor	coin
cheap	bill
expensive	

❏ EXERCISE 33. Let's talk: game. Page 18
Time: 10–15 minutes

• Explain to the class that you are going to play a game but first you will model how it goes.
• Write on the board *Things that are big . . .*
• Ask student to come up with names of things that are big and write these on the board. For example:

   an elephant
   a continent
   a country
   a planet

• Put students into groups of three or four and ask one student to be the writer.
• Using the nine adjectives in the exercise, have each group write as many items for each adjective as they can.
• Compare lists.

Expansion: Explain to your class that you would now like them to try the negative version of the game. With this version, they have to write lists of things that are *not* each of the nine adjectives above. Compare the lists as above.

❏ EXERCISE 34. Let's talk: pairwork.
Page 18
Time: 10–15 minutes

• Put students into pairs or keep students in their previous groups from the last activity.
• Explain that they will create sentences using *be* + adjective and *be* + *not* + adjective to describe the pictures they see.

Expansion: Ask students to come up with their own adjectives for the pictures and to make affirmative and negative sentences to describe each picture in their own words. Write students' contributions on the board and review all as a class.

❏ EXERCISE 35. Grammar and vocabulary.
Page 19
Time: 10–15 minutes

- Ask students to complete the exercise as seatwork.
- Circulate around the room as students are working and assist with any vocabulary questions that come up.
- While reviewing, ask students for additional names of colors, fruits, vegetables, or other foods.
- Ask students which of the foods included in the exercise they like, and so on.
- Put all additional vocabulary on the board.

❏ EXERCISE 36. Let's talk: game. Page 20
Time: 10–15 minutes

Part I
- Give students time to check all the words they know. Given their collective passive vocabulary, there should be strong familiarity with all or most of the words.
- Write words that few students know on the board and, with the help of students, explain these words.

Part II
- Ask students to move their desks into a circle.
- Explain that using the list of words in Part I, they will make sentences about themselves.
- Model the Student A–Student B–Student C pattern with one or two students.
- Tell students the goal is to recall what all the other students have said about themselves, using *be* and *not* as required.
- As the teacher, you will be in the last position and will need to restate what all students have said.

❏ EXERCISE 37. Let's talk: pairwork.
Page 20
Time: 10–15 minutes

- Ask students to think about the city or town they are now studying in.
- Explain that the list of adjectives in the book can be used to describe cities, towns, and other places.
- Have students first check all the adjectives that describe the city or town they are currently studying in.
- Circulate around the room, helping students as needed while they go through the list and decide which adjectives describe their current location.
- After students have chosen the adjectives they think apply to their cities or towns, put them into pairs to compare notes.
- Have each pair dictate a sentence to you and discuss whether both partners agree on the content of the sentence.

Expansion: While students are still in pairs, ask them to use the same list of adjectives to describe either their favorite city or town or their favorite place in the world. Have them write five sentences on a piece of paper and then circulate and find a new partner. Using these sentences, new partners have to guess each other's favorite places. Ask students to read their sentences to the class to see if the class can guess the place as a group.

Optional Vocabulary

well	married
easy	single
difficult	lazy
banana	hardworking
orange	famous
apple	shy
pea	dangerous
strawberry	safe
fruit	inexpensive
vegetable	

❏ EXERCISE 38. Warm-up. Page 21
Time: 5 minutes

- Ask students to read items 1–3.
- Ask students what information items 1–3 give us and lead them to the answer, *where*.
- Explain that *be* + a place lets us say *where* things are.

CHART 1-8. *Be* + a Place. Page 21
Time: 10 minutes

Beginners will already know at least some prepositions of place and will recognize them in the chart. Prepositions have many uses in English, and some students will also be familiar with their use in time phrases. Because prepositions are also used in phrasal verbs and idioms, and the varied ways they are used challenge even advanced students, stress only their use to show location for now.

- Write the chart title on the board.
- In order to help students understand what *place* means, write the following list of words on the board and ask them to tell you which are places.

  school   summer   grocery store   airport   face   tree

- Ask students to tell you some of the places they are in or at during the day and write these on the board. Accept all nouns that can be considered a place (for example, *class* can be a place and also a group of people or a course in a subject). For example:

the bathroom	*class*
the shower	*school*
my room	*the bus*
a café	*the subway*
work	

- Even at this early stage, show students that some of these places are always used with an article or personal pronoun.
- Ask students to tell you any prepositions they already know that can be used with these places. If they are not able to give you any, introduce *at, in,* and *on*.
- Explain that *at, in,* and *on* show general location and are used very frequently in English.

- Explain that the meaning of *at* is similar to *in* but *at* indicates a less specific physical place than *in* or *on*. *At* stresses the activity done in this place rather than exact physical location inside the place. For example, *at the gym*, *at the dentist*, *at the movies*.
- Put a number of examples with *at* on the board. *At* is more difficult to illustrate physically than *in* or *on*, and students can best master it through repeated examples.

  at school
  at work
  at the movies
  at the supermarket
  at the airport
  at the hospital
  at home
  at a restaurant

- Draw examples of *on* and *in*, using the illustrations in the chart as a guide. For example, draw an illustration of a book on a table.
- Explain to students that you are *on* a flat surface (floor, street, etc.) but that you are *in* anything that is three-dimensional and can physically hold you inside of it (e.g., a room).
- Explain that people frequently use *in* and *on* with some of the same places. This happens because one person may be thinking of the floor or surface of the place (*I was on the bus*) and someone else may be thinking of the capacity of the place—the fact that his or her whole body was inside (*I was in the bus*).
- Tell students not to worry about that difference for now but rather simply to get used to using prepositions + places to describe locations.
- Have students take turns reading the example sentences from the chart while you reiterate the particular points included on the right side of the chart.
- When looking at the illustrations of the boxes, explain that certain prepositions give very exact locations and are even more specific than *at*, *in*, and *on*.

❑ EXERCISE 39. Looking at grammar.
Page 22
Time: 10 minutes

- Give students time to complete the exercise independently as seatwork.
- Review the exercise by having different students read each item aloud.
- Invite students to give other prepositions that they know and that accurately describe each picture. For example, for item 4, students could also say, "The cat is near the desk."

❑ EXERCISE 40. Let's talk: pairwork.
Page 23
Time: 10–15 minutes

- Put students into pairs.
- Explain that they will practice using prepositions of place with *be*.

- Because students have not yet studied the imperative, briefly introduce (or reintroduce) its form and use. Explain that you give orders by using the basic verb without a subject. In every case, the subject *you* is understood. Because the subject is always *you*, it does not need to be stated each time.
- Ask a student to be Partner B and model the first exchange.
- Give students time to instruct each other and perform the actions accordingly.
- Circulate throughout the room, assisting students as you go.

Expansion: To give students more practice with prepositions, have them give and follow directions by drawing objects in relation to one another. This exercise allows students to tap into their own visual and creative styles of learning and apply additional learning styles to the acquisition of structures. Put students into pairs and distribute paper. Begin by asking one student to go to the board and give the student an instruction.

Example: Draw a box under a table.

Once the student has drawn this recognizably, thank the student and ask him or her to be seated. Explain that students will now continue this exercise by giving instructions and drawing in pairs.

Pairwork:

Work with a partner. Give and follow directions.

Partner A: Give directions. Your book is open. You can look at your book before you speak. When you speak, look at your partner.

Partner B: Draw the pictures Partner A describes. Your book is closed.

Example: Draw a ball on a box.

Partner A (book open): "Draw a ball on a box."

Partner B (book closed): (Draw the picture Partner A described.)

1. Draw a ball on a box.
2. Draw a ball above a box.
3. Draw a ball next to a box.
4. Draw a ball under a box.
5. Draw a ball in a box.
6. Draw a banana between two apples.
7. Draw a house. Draw a bird above the house. Draw a car next to the house. Draw a cat between the car and the house.
8. Draw a flower. Draw a tree next to the flower. Draw a bird above the tree. Draw a turtle under the flower.

Switch roles.

Partner A: Close your book.

Partner B: Open your book. Your turn to talk now.

9. Draw a circle next to a triangle.
10. Draw a circle in a triangle.
11. Draw a circle above a triangle.
12. Draw a triangle between two circles.
13. Draw a circle under a triangle.
14. Draw an apple on a banana. Draw an apple above a banana.

15. Draw a tree. Draw bananas in the tree. Draw a person next to the tree. Draw a dog between the person and the tree.

16. Draw a cloud. Draw a bird under the cloud. Draw a bird above the cloud. Draw a bird in the cloud.

❏ EXERCISE 41. Listening. Page 23
Time: 10 minutes

- Ensure that the CD player is ready and you have the correct CD track number.
- Tell students you will be playing a CD recording and that they must complete the missing information with the words they hear in the recording.
- Explain that among other words, students will need to write the verb *be* in its contracted form.
- Monitor how successfully students are able to complete the cloze exercise after just one listening.
- If needed, play the track a second time.
- Review by having students read their completions aloud.
- Correct the spelling and pronunciation of the completions. Use the board as much as possible.

❏ EXERCISE 42. Reading and writing.
Page 23
Time: 10 minutes

- Give students an opportunity to read the paragraph through once, at their own pace, as seatwork.
- Have students then take turns reading aloud each sentence in the paragraph. Ask students to define the adjectives. For example, ask students if they know another word for *good* or another way to say *at home*—(in his house).
- Ask for volunteers to complete items 1–5 on the board. Do not require complete sentences, only completions.
- Because the cues are somewhat open-ended, invite as many completions as are accurate and have students write the different options on the board.

CHART 1-9. Summary: Basic Sentence Patterns with *Be*. Page 24
Time: 15–20 minutes

> Stress that this chart is a review and that students will benefit from seeing all the patterns they have learned thus far in one place.

- Write the chart title on the board.
- Have students read patterns (a)–(d) aloud. Take time after each sentence is read to ask questions that will lead to the notes on the right side of the chart.
- For example, after sentence (a), ask students what the noun or pronoun at the beginning of the sentence is called.
- Review the notes on the right side as interactively as possible and write additional examples on the board.

❏ EXERCISE 43. Looking at grammar.
Page 24
Time: 10 minutes

- Explain to students that this exercise requires them to think about the noncontracted form of *be*.
- Explain that they also need to consider the part of speech that follows the verb.
- Give students ample time to complete the exercise on their own and then review and correct as a group.

Optional Vocabulary
basement
library
downtown
explanations
clear
upstairs
downstairs

❏ EXERCISE 44. Listening. Page 25
Time: 10 minutes

- Have the CD ready and tell students that in this listening exercise they will hear contracted versions of the sentences they see.
- First have students listen to the sentences. Then have them try pronouncing the contracted versions with your help.
- Correct immediately and overtly so that students learn the standard pronunciation of contractions definitively.

❏ EXERCISE 45. Looking at grammar.
Page 25
Time: 10 minutes

- Have students complete this exercise without prior preparation, as seatwork.
- Have students take turns reading and completing. The approach used here will help them quickly recognize the right forms, both by reading and by trying out the different options to hear what sounds right.
- Correct immediately and clearly.

❏ EXERCISE 46. Reading and writing.
Page 26
Time: 15–20 minutes

Part I
- Have students take turns reading aloud the sentences that make up the paragraph.
- Correct pronunciation and ask vocabulary questions that naturally present themselves for the words included under the heading *Do you know these words?* For example, *What does* bright *mean?* Name something that is bright.

Part II
- Give this writing assignment as homework after reviewing the conventions of a simple paragraph.
- Review paragraph format, referring back and forth to the Venus paragraph in Part I.

- Teach the elements targeted in Part III in class by composing a simple paragraph on the board as a class.
- Start a sample paragraph on the board about a topic everyone knows well, such as the city in which students are currently studying or learning English.
- Have students contribute ideas and expand these into full sentences.

Part III
- As you expand each sentence, check for all elements included in Part III:

   capital letter at the beginning of each sentence
   period at the end of each sentence
   indenting the first line of the paragraph
   a subject and a verb in each sentence
   correct spelling

- After students have completed Part II as homework, have students exchange paragraphs and use the five items in Part III to edit their partner's work.
- Give students a chance to correct mistakes and then collect a final draft after peer editing.

Expansion: The following simple review activities can be used at any point either following a cumulative review or while presenting the various charts and points.

Suggested review activities:

1. Describe yourself.

Ask students to write twenty sentences about themselves. Tell them to use the verb *be* + adjective, nouns, prepositions, and noun phrases of place. These sentences can then become a poem about the student. Alternatively, students can exchange papers and read some of the sentences about one another aloud, prompting the rest of the class to guess who is being described.

2. Picture writing prompts.

Use pictures that show many items that students are able to name, describe with adjectives, or describe in terms of location. Norman Rockwell reproductions or actual photos can prove good writing prompts.

3. Peer-editing sentences.

Have students complete the following sentences by using *is* or *are*. Ask students to exchange papers and correct each other's sentences.

1. _____ an animal.
2. _____ here.
3. _____ languages.
4. _____ not cheap.
5. _____ friendly.
6. _____ not expensive.
7. _____ an insect.
8. _____ countries.

Chapter 2
Using Be and Have

CHAPTER SUMMARY

OBJECTIVE: In this chapter, students learn yes / no questions and short answers with *be* as well as *where*-questions and answers with *be*. This practice gives them increased confidence in using *be* and prepares them to use *have*. Students learn the most common uses of *have*: to show possession of belongings, to describe having common ailments and conditions, and to explain the composition of one's family. Following the presentation of *have*, students learn possessive pronouns and the use of *this / that* and *these / those*, enabling them to indicate both their own and other people's possessions. Finally, they learn to ask questions with *What* and *Who*.

APPROACH: The chapter repeats and expands students' knowledge of the verb *be* and provides practice of spoken questions and answers in short yes / no forms. This practice enables students to use their English beyond the confines of the classroom as they learn how to ask practical questions. The presentation of the verb *have* highlights the third person singular form as distinct from all other forms of *have* and provides ample practice asking questions and answering them. Acquiring *have* allows students to talk about themselves, their bodies, their health, and their possessions more confidently and easily. The book provides repeated, short controlled practices as well as increasingly longer exercises that require more open-ended production.

TERMINOLOGY: In keeping with the goal of getting students to recognize and use the targeted structures, the book keeps the use of terminology to a minimum. *Yes / No questions* and *short answers* are standard and descriptive terms; thus, their inclusion allows students to identify the target structures as such. In the case of *this / that* and *these / those,* the term *demonstrative pronoun* is not used or mentioned as a type of pronoun, because it is far less important than students' immediate understanding of their meanings and readiness to use them. Teachers should take their cues about using terminology from the book itself. The names of the major parts of speech are useful for students to know as well as subject-verb-object word order. However, too much terminology will confuse students and could interfere with their ready acquisition of targeted structures.

❏ **EXERCISE 1.** Warm-up. Page 28
Time: 5 minutes

- Ask students to read the questions in the Warm-up to the class as a whole.
- Ask students if they can think of other questions with *be* to prompt them to generate yes / no questions and answers. For example:

  Are you thirsty?   *Is your teacher tall or short?*
  Are you tired?   *Is English easy?*
  Is the classroom   *Is English hard?*
  * warm or cold?*

- Write student-generated questions and short answers on the board.

CHART 2-1. Yes / No Questions with *Be*.
Page 28
Time: 10–15 minutes

> Whenever possible, use students' lives and names when introducing new structures. Be sure to use all students' names and lives at varying times (to ensure no perception of favoritism). Make such examples very student specific, so as to involve everyone maximally in the content on the board, which differs from the generic content in the book. Always make sure such examples are positive and nonthreatening in content.

- Write the chart title on the board.
- Write a simple *be*-statement below the title, using content that can easily be derived from the actual context of your class and its unique makeup of students. For example:

  Yukiko is early.

- Highlight the subject and verb by adding labels above the subject and verb in the sentence on the board.

      S + V
  Yukiko is early.

- Explain that in English, yes / no questions are formed by inverting, or changing the order of, the subject and the verb.
- Using arrows, show the change in position of the subject and verb when you ask a question.

      V   +   S
  Is   Yukiko   early?

- Explain that in addition to inverting the subject and verb, a question ends with a question mark.
- Stress that a yes / no question has only two possible answers: *yes* or *no*.
- Ask students to read sentences (a)–(c) in the chart aloud. Reiterate the notes on the right side of the chart, writing them on the board and referring to them as much as is useful.

❏ EXERCISE 2. Looking at grammar.
Page 28
Time: 5–7 minutes

> With newly introduced structures, do the exercises first as a class, providing ample guidance. You will need to lead some of your students to the appropriate responses. By directing these first controlled exercises, you will help your students gain confidence for later exercises. In addition, completions where the first few words are missing are often harder for students than completions where a few words at the end of a sentence are missing. As there is no example to model with Exercise 2, be prepared to complete the first item for students.

- Ask the strongest students in the class to complete the first two or three items in the exercise.
- Correct indicative word order to interrogative word order immediately and definitively, and use the board for further clarification.

❏ EXERCISE 3. Looking at grammar.
Page 29
Time: 5–10 minutes

> Now that students have practiced the target structure in the previous exercise, they are ready to try supplying the missing questions independently as seatwork. Students often find it difficult to supply missing words (or in this case entire questions) at the beginning of an item, so be prepared to help individuals as they work through the exercise.

- Write item 1 on the board and model with a student.
- Tell your students to find the subject and verb in the response, and then to invert these to create the appropriate question.
- Give students time to complete as seatwork and review completions as a class.

❏ EXERCISE 4. Listening. Page 29
Time: 7–10 minutes

> Stress to students that one way to identify questions is to listen for the rising intonation at the end of the sentence. They should both listen for rising intonation and recreate it when they speak. But even in a listening exercise, they should then model what they have heard.

- Explain to students that they will hear sentences spoken by Speaker A and questions spoken by Speaker B.
- Tell them to listen and then complete Speaker B's questions for each item.
- Explain to students that they will write the correct form of *be* for each question.
- Review aloud as a class, correcting intonation.

Optional Vocabulary

> Though some words in this Optional Vocabulary serve as review of vocabulary in the previous chapter, asking students to explain some of the words below allows them to produce English using simple descriptors and the verb *be*. Frequent vocabulary checks allow students to use their newly acquired English in fresh ways and thus help build student confidence, self-correction, and autonomy.

late	absent
early	planets
new	exercise
vegetables	slck

❏ EXERCISE 5. Warm-up. Page 30
Time: 5 minutes

- Ask students to read through the Warm-up and discuss which contractions they prefer for the negative statements.
- Tell students that most native speakers use both interchangeably.

CHART 2-2. Short Answers to Yes / No Questions. Page 30
Time: 10–15 minutes

> Explain to students that native speakers give short answers to yes / no questions very frequently. In fact, to give a long response to a yes / no question would seem odd to most native speakers.

- Write the chart title on the board.
- Using an example similar to sentence (a) in the chart (and based on actual students' lives), create a question that will resonate with the whole class. For example:

    Is Juan from Mexico?

- Explain to students that when they respond in the affirmative, there is only one possible short answer and it is never contracted.
- Stress that the verb *be* is never contracted in short answers that begin with *yes*. In response to the question *Is Juan from Mexico?* it is not possible to say, *Yes, he's.*
- Draw a line through this mistake and repeat that responses with *yes* cannot be contracted.

    ~~Yes, he's.~~

- Tell students that *Yes, he is* is the correct and only short answer.
- Explain that students may choose to contract or not contract if the short answer begins with *no* and that there are two negative contractions with *be*.
- Explain that one negative contraction uses the pronoun contracted with *be*. Write *pronoun + be* as option 1 on the board.
- Explain that another negative contraction uses the verb *be* contracted with the word *not*. Write *be + not* as option 2 on the board.
- Repeat the example above, but change the country of origin to force a negative response. For example:

  Is Juan from Holland?

- Write the two possible answers on the board, inviting students to give you each word.

  No, he's not.
  No, he isn't.

- Finally, ask students to change both responses back into their noncontracted forms and write these forms on the board.

  No, he is not.
  No, he is not.

❑ EXERCISE 6. Looking at grammar.
Page 30
Time: 10–15 minutes

> This exercise requires students to create whole questions and sentences rather than simply complete cloze exercises. Because this level of production can be challenging for students this early on, be ready to support them by writing the example items on the board.

- Explain that students will be creating both the questions and the short answers based on the sentence in parentheses.
- Give students time to complete the exercise as seatwork.
- Circulate and help those students who need extra support.
- Review by having students take turns reading both their questions and their responses aloud.
- Correct target grammar, pronunciation, and intonation and put challenging items on board for further clarification.

Expansion: Listening (questions with *be*). (Teacher makes questions.)
1. Is Boston a city?
2. Are tigers cats?
3. Are oceans salty?
4. Is Great Britain a city?
5. Is the president of the United States a man?
6. Is New Zealand a continent?
7. Are fast-food restaurants cheap?
8. Is English easy?
9. Is Indonesia a country?

Listen to the questions. Circle (or write) *yes* or *no*.
Example: Is Africa a continent? (yes) *no*

1. yes no	4. yes no	7. yes no
2. yes no	5. yes no	8. yes no
3. yes no	6. yes no	9. yes no

Let's talk: find someone who . . . (questions with *be*)

Print the chart below and give it to students. Tell them to walk around the room and ask their classmates questions. Ask them to find someone who can answer *yes* to each question and write down his or her name. Use *Are you . . . ?*

Example:
SPEAKER A: *Are you hungry?*
SPEAKER B: *No, I'm not.*
SPEAKER A: *(Ask another student.) Are you hungry?*
SPEAKER C: *Yes, I am. (Write down his or her name.)*
(Now ask another student a different question.)

	First name		First name
1. hungry		8. tired	
2. sleepy		9. nervous	
3. thirsty		10. friendly	
4. married		11. lazy	
5. a parent		12. cold	
6. single		13. comfortable	
7. happy		14. from (*name of country*)	

❑ EXERCISE 7. Let's talk: pairwork. Page 31
Time: 10 minutes

- Put students into pairs.
- Model the examples with a student by reading Partner A's role.
- Tell students to read the cues first and then form their questions. Tell them to look at their partner when they ask their yes / no questions.
- Remind partners that they can choose between two ways of contracting negatives.

Expansion: While students are working through Exercise 7, write additional examples on the board. When one pair has completed the exercise in the book, direct them to the extra examples on the board. For example:

rain: wet / dry	the desert: dry / wet
chairs in class: comfortable / uncomfortable	ice cream: sweet / bitter
your cell phone: with you / at home	chess: easy / difficult
rock music: loud / soft	sharks: cute / dangerous

❑ EXERCISE 8. Looking at grammar.
Page 31
Time: 10 minutes

- Give students time to complete the exercise on their own as seatwork.

- Review completions as a class, correcting accuracy and pronunciation.
- Discuss and compare the content of each item.

❑ EXERCISE 9. Warm-up. Page 32
Time: 5 minutes

- Remind students that in the last chapter, they used *be* with prepositions to describe exact location.
- Explain that by using *where*, they can ask questions about exact location.
- Complete the Warm-up with students.

CHART 2-3. Questions with *Be*: Using *Where*.
Page 32
Time: 10–15 minutes

Explain to students that questions with *Where* ask for specific information, not for yes / no confirmation or negation. Some beginners may already know other information question words (*what, who, when, how*), and you should encourage students to demonstrate their passive knowledge during this discussion.

- Write the chart title on the board.
- Ask students to take turns reading questions and answers (a)–(d) aloud.
- Write sentences (a)–(d) on the board, underlining the verb *be*. In sentences (c) and (d), underline *where* for additional emphasis.
- Emphasize the long answer as opposed to the short answer and be sure students understand what the short answer is short for. Students should easily be able to produce both but should know that short answers are more common.
- Using the classroom as a physical context, ask and write *where*-questions on the board. For example:

    Where is the board?
    Where is the door?
    Where is Eun Jung?

- Underline the verb *be* and draw an arrow back to the word *where*, showing that the verb comes after the word *where*.
- Elicit answers from students and write the responses beneath the original questions. For example:

    Where is the board?
    It's in the front of the room.
    Where is the door?
    It's in the back of the room.
    Where is Eun Jung?
    She is next to Pablo.

Expansion: Send two to three students out of the room for five minutes. During their absence, hide or remove from the classroom an item that is usually in plain sight of all class members. For example, put the board eraser in a book bag or briefcase, move the wastebasket behind a desk, or even hide a student. When the students who have left the room return, they

have to identify what has been removed or hidden and formulate a grammatically correct question, which the rest of the class can answer. For example:

    Question: Where is the eraser?
    Answer: It's behind the DVD player.

❑ EXERCISE 10. Looking at grammar.
Page 33
Time: 5 minutes

- Clarify the directions by saying that there are two questions but only one matches the one response given.
- Remind students that if they see *Yes* or *No* as the first word of the response, the question must begin with a form of *be*. If the answer consists of a statement indicating place, the question must begin with *Where*.
- Because students may find the format of this exercise challenging, do it as a group, helping them identify key words.

❑ EXERCISE 11. Looking at grammar.
Page 33
Time: 5–10 minutes

- Give students time to complete this exercise independently first as seatwork.
- Review as a class by having students take turns reading completed items aloud.
- Correct grammar and pronunciation immediately and definitively.

❑ EXERCISE 12. Let's talk: pairwork. Page 34
Time: 5–10 minutes

- Put students into pairs.
- Model with one student by taking the role of Partner A.
- Remind students to look at the book for the cues but at their partner when speaking.
- Circulate, assisting pairs as needed.

Optional Vocabulary

single / married	boxes
intelligent / dumb	closet
sweet / sour	kitchen counter
glasses	

❑ EXERCISE 13. Warm-up. Page 34
Time: 5–10 minutes

Most beginners are familiar with *have*. You may therefore wish to have students complete the Warm-up independently. To support students unfamiliar with this verb, write an open-ended question using *have* on the board and direct their attention to it as necessary. For example: *What other things do you have with you in class today?*

- Ask students to complete the Warm-up and then read each item aloud, discussing who has what.
- Correct *have / has* errors right away and very directly from this point on.

CHART 2-4. Using *Have* and *Has.* Page 34
Time:10–15 minutes

> Depending on the native languages of students in your classroom, you may want to mention that *have* is not used to describe a person's age or whether a person feels hungry or thirsty. If you have Romance language speakers, be ready to correct such direct translations.

- Write the chart title on the board.
- Using an observable classroom object in the example, conjugate *have* on the board. For example:

I have a red grammar book.	*We have red grammar books.*
You have a red grammar book.	*You have red grammar books.*
Ahmad <u>has</u> a red grammar book.	*Ahmad and Kyung Min have red grammar books.*

- Stress that the only form that differs from *have* is the third person singular, *has*. Underline this form in the written conjugation.
- Have students take turns reading through the chart aloud and again, giving special emphasis to the third person singular form *has*.

□ **EXERCISE 14.** Looking at grammar.
Page 35
Time: 5–10 minutes

- Without allowing prior preparation, have students take turns completing the sentences in the exercise.
- Discuss types of vehicles known to students. Ask questions that will allow students to show their passive knowledge of vehicles and to tell you what kinds of vehicles they have.
- Write related questions on the board to help students use prior knowledge. For example:

   Who has a van?
   Who has a motorcycle?
   Who has a bike?
   Who has a truck?
   Who has a bus?

□ **EXERCISE 15.** Looking at grammar.
Page 35
Time: 5–10 minutes

- Give students a chance to work through the exercise on their own, as seatwork.
- Remind students that third person singular is followed by *has*.
- Circulate and help students as needed.
- Review by having students read their completions aloud, with the correct circled response.
- Discuss optional vocabulary.

Optional Vocabulary
daughter
interesting

journalist
laptop computer
screen
website designer
battery / batteries

Expansion: In Exercise 15, one item states that being a journalist is an interesting job. Ask your students what other jobs are interesting. Use yes / no questions and short answers to allow students to practice recently learned structures and write on the board to prompt discussion. For example:

   Does a teacher have an interesting job?
   Does a doctor have an interesting job?
   Does a police officer have an interesting job?
   Does an army member have an interesting job?
   Does a cleaner have an interesting job?
   Does an athlete have an interesting job?
   Does a computer programmer have an interesting job?
   Does a website designer have an interesting job?
   Do you have an interesting job?

□ **EXERCISE 16.** Vocabulary and grammar.
Page 36
Time: 10–15 minutes

> While you do need to be respectful of students' privacy, most students enjoy knowing the names for common ailments and feel empowered when they can discuss their own health.

- Before beginning the exercise, explain that students will learn new vocabulary for body parts and common health problems.
- Tell students that some common health problems are considered temporary and are therefore used with an article. Write some examples on the board. For example:

   a headache
   a stomachache

- Explain that other health problems are considered ongoing conditions or diseases and are therefore not used with an article. Write examples on the board. For example:

   high blood pressure
   diabetes

- Allow students to complete this exercise as seatwork.
- Review as a class, having students take turns reading the correct matches aloud.
- This topic will likely prompt students to ask about additional common ailments and symptoms. Encourage this and write new vocabulary on the board as words and phrases arise. For example:

a fever	*joint pain*
allergies	*a rash*
asthma	*a sunburn*
migraine	*a sore*
muscle pain	

Expansion: Bring in some additional pictures or photos that show various ailments. Show each picture and have a volunteer describe the health problem using *have* or *has*. Write the descriptions on the board as each student speaks.

❑ EXERCISE 17. Let's talk: pairwork. Page 37
Time: 10–15 minutes

> Remind students that they will benefit most from pairwork if they first read the cues in the book and then look at each other to speak. Doing so will prepare them to speak in real exchanges with native speakers.

- Model the Partner A–Partner B exchange by taking Partner A's role and having a strong student take Partner B's role.
- As students practice, walk around the room taking note of mistakes in grammatical accuracy, pronunciation, and intonation.
- Review by discussing each item and reviewing overheard mistakes on the board.

Expansion: The scene is in a doctor's office. Put students into groups of three (the doctor, the parent, the son or daughter). The parent describes the son's or daughter's health problem to the doctor. One student in the group writes down the conversation. Then the group presents the conversation to the class.

❑ EXERCISE 18. Looking at grammar.
Page 37
Time: 10 minutes

- Explain to students that they will rewrite each sentence in the paragraph so that Dr. Lee becomes the person talked about (grammatically, the third person) rather than the person doing the talking (grammatically, the first person).
- Remind them that subject pronouns and verbs will need to be changed to switch from first person to third person.
- When students have rewritten all sentences in the paragraph, review as a class.
- Have students read the transformed sentences aloud.
- Discuss the following related vocabulary:

  patients
  clinic
  experience
  hospital
  downtown

❑ EXERCISE 19. Looking at grammar.
Page 37
Time: 10–15 minutes

Part I
- Give students time to complete each sentence with either *is* or *has*, according to the context of the sentence.

- Remind students that an adjective can be preceded only by the verb *be* and never *have*.
- Review as a class by asking students to read completions aloud.

Part II
- Tell students that in this part they will use either *are* or *has*.
- Explain that they should look at the picture and be prepared to discuss what parts of the picture give them exact information.
- Review as a class, inviting students to read their completions aloud.

Optional Vocabulary
smart phone	noisy
quiet	messy
pet bird	parties on the weekends
serious	low / high grades

❑ EXERCISE 20. Warm-up. Page 38
Time: 5–10 minutes

> Most beginners have some knowledge of possessive adjectives, though they may confuse *his* and *her*, for example, or confuse these adjective forms with object pronouns. Help students show what they do know by encouraging them and writing their contributions on the board.

- Give students time to match the possessive adjective to the person.
- Review as a class.
- Expand by naming class members and asking what the appropriate pronoun word is to show that something belongs to each person—for example, *Maria, Slav, Hiroko, Hiroko and me,* and so on.
- Write these names and pronouns on the board. Use an equal sign to show the correct possessive adjective to use with each one. For example:

Maria = her	*Slav and Maria = their*
Slav = his	*Aya and you = your*
Hiroko = her	*you = your*
Hiroko and me = our	*I = my*

CHART 2-5. Using *My, Your, Her, His, Our, Their.* Page 39
Time: 10–15 minutes

> Stress the usefulness of these possessive adjectives in distinguishing one owner of an item (for example, the red Azar grammar book) from another owner of the same item.

- Write the chart title on the board.
- Show the class your grammar book and say, *My grammar book is red.*
- Write the above sentence on the board.
- Ask a student to give you his or her grammar book.

- Say and write the following sentence on the board:

  Ali's grammar book is also red.

- Explain that *Ali* can be replaced with the possessive adjective *his.*

- Rewrite the above sentence by crossing out *Ali* and replacing it with *his.* For example:

  His ~~Ali's~~ grammar book is also red.

- Ask students to take turns reading example sentences (a)–(g) aloud.

- Write the material on the right side of the chart (the comparison between the subject form of pronouns and the possessive adjective form) on the board while you say each form aloud.

- Review additional notes on the right side of the chart with students, encouraging them to show you what they already know.

❏ EXERCISE 21. Looking at grammar.
Page 39
Time: 5–10 minutes

- Tell students you will ask them to complete the sentences aloud without prior preparation.

- Have students take turns completing the items given.

- To involve more students, give students alternative sentences to transform. For example, as an alternative for item 1:

  Susana and Slav are next. It's <u>their</u> turn.

❏ EXERCISE 22. Vocabulary and grammar.
Page 40
Time: 10–15 minutes

- Begin by discussing what an ID card is and what types of ID students have and / or carry.

- Ask students what types of information are included on different types of IDs, such as passports, student IDs, driver's licenses, and so on.

- If students feel comfortable doing so, ask them to show their own IDs to their peers and ask about whether different types of information (for example, street address, date of birth, height, etc.) are included on various types of ID. This can be interesting if you have a class made up of students from a wide variety of countries.

- Give students four to five minutes to complete each part of the exercise.

- Circulate to ensure that students are referring to the correct ID for each set of information.

- When students have completed the entire exercise on their own as seatwork, review as a class.

- Encourage students to discuss the ID content by using the target grammar and to be prepared to discuss the various items (zip code, area code, etc.) they refer to.

- Correct readily and overtly to prepare students for using these necessary parts of speech independently.

Expansion: Make copies of a blank ID card with the zip code, area code, and birth date required. You can create a simple one on a computer. Have students work with a partner. First, they fill out their own form.

Then they exchange IDs and report the information on their partner's ID to the class.

  This is Maria. Her last name is _____. Her first name is _____.

❏ EXERCISE 23. Vocabulary: pairwork.
Page 42
Time: 10–15 minutes

- Put students into pairs.

- Explain that together with their partner, they will first check vocabulary words they know independently and then discuss the words their partner knows but they don't.

- Tell students to refer to page 43 to see clothing items illustrated.

- Ask pairs to try to expand upon the lists they see in the exercise with more specific terms for colors they may know, as well as additional clothing and jewelry items or other accessories.

- Discuss these items as a group and encourage questions.

In general, beginning students want to know terms for practical items like the ones in these lists and they can use this vocabulary readily, helping build both their confidence and their active vocabulary.

Expansion: Ask pairs to write the items of clothing, jewelry, and accessories their partners are wearing today. Ask pairs to be specific and use actual color names, and so on.

❏ EXERCISE 24. Looking at grammar.
Page 42
Time:10–15 minutes

- Without allowing prior preparation, ask students to take turns completing each sentence.

- Correct students readily and ask them to describe optional vocabulary during the review.

❏ EXERCISE 25. Listening. Page 43
Time: 10 minutes

- Have all equipment ready to go and be prepared with the CD track you will play.

- Ask students to look at the illustration of Anna before you play the CD, so they can anticipate what they are listening for.

- Play the audio through once and review with students.

- Depending on students' comfort level for listening to a CD, you may need to play the CD a second time to allow them to review what they have written.

- Repeat appropriate pronunciation and correct any incorrect completions.

❏ EXERCISE 26. Looking at grammar.
Page 43
Time: 10–15 minutes

- Give this exercise to students as seatwork.
- Remind students that before deciding which possessive adjective to use, they will need to identify the subject of each sentence and, if the subject includes more than one person, the subject pronoun that can replace it.
- Tell students that after identifying the subject pronoun, they will need to choose the corresponding possessive adjective.
- Circulate to help any students having difficulty choosing the correct forms or comprehending the associated vocabulary.

Optional Vocabulary
turn
next
first / middle / last name
initial
birth date / birthday
address
zip code
area code

❏ EXERCISE 27. Reading and grammar.
Page 44
Time: 10–15 minutes

Part I
- Before assigning the reading to students, have them look at the vocabulary listed to the right and discuss these words.
- Put the words on the board and invite students to participate in defining them. Write student-generated words and descriptions on the board.
- Have students read sentences from the paragraph aloud. Ask both vocabulary questions and paraphrasing questions based on the text.
- Ask students to complete the yes / no items on their own and then review as a class.

Part II
- Ask students to complete the sentences with the possessive adjectives *his*, *her*, or *their* and remind them that in one sentence more than one completion is possible.
- Review as a class.

Part III
- Ask students to complete the story as seatwork.
- Have students take turns reading the completions aloud. Correct pronunciation and grammatical accuracy immediately.
- Discuss more optional vocabulary, as useful.

Expansion: Invite students to discuss the title, "One Big Happy Family." If you have adult students, even those who have limited language, this topic lends itself to a somewhat sophisticated discussion. Beginning students enjoy the chance to use their newly acquired language to discuss a topic that is real to them.

Specific Expansion Questions: The following questions will serve as a preview for questions with *Who* and *What*, which will be taught later in the chapter. Most beginners will have encountered these forms and be able to handle them receptively.
  Is the title true for most families?
  What is good about a big family? What is challenging?

Ask questions about students' own families:
  Is your family big or small?
  Who are the people in your family? What are their names?
  Are they busy?

Optional Vocabulary

nice	several
cousins	different
friendly	countries
brother / sister	busy
college	airline pilot
doctor	overnight
disabled	stay-at-home
adopted	helpful
single	

❏ EXERCISE 28. Warm-up. Page 45
Time: 5 minutes

- Model *this* / *that* differences by touching *this* items (those close to you and belonging to you), and pointing at *that* items (those far from you).
- Have two students complete the Warm-up aloud.

CHART 2-6. Using *This* and *That*. Page 45
Time: 10–15 minutes

In order for students to understand *this* versus *that,* you will need to emphasize that *this* refers to something close, or something that a person owns or has claim to. *That* refers to an object that is not close, and generally not one the person owns.

- Write the chart title on the board.
- Show the class your grammar book and say, *This is my grammar book.*
- Point to yourself when using *this* and write the example on the board, underlining *this*.
- Ask a student to show you his or her grammar book and say, *That is (Pietro's) grammar book.*
- Write this sentence on the board and underline *that*.
- Have students take turns reading example sentences (a)–(f).
- Review the contraction of *that* and *is* (*that's*) and model correct pronunciation. Tell students they will hear this frequently.
- Explain that it is harder to make a contraction with *this* and *is* (*this's*) because it is hard to make the two s's sound distinct. Tell students they will not see the contracted form in writing.

❏ EXERCISE 29. Looking at grammar.
Page 46
Time: 5–10 minutes

- Have students do this exercise on sight, without prior preparation.
- Have students read the completed sentences aloud.

❏ EXERCISE 30. Let's talk: pairwork.
Page 47
Time: 10 minutes

Part I
- Put students into pairs.
- Encourage students to look at each other when speaking.
- Review the vocabulary items included in the exercise.

Part II
- Ensure that students feel comfortable using their own items from school bags, backpacks, purses, and so on, in order to practice their use of *this / that*.

Expansion: Bring additional items (school, office, personal) into class to allow students plenty of practice using the target grammar with additional and sometimes unknown items.

Optional Vocabulary
backpack
credit card
checkbook
business card
computer bag

❏ EXERCISE 31. Warm-up. Page 48
Time: 5 minutes

- Explain that *these* and *those* are simply the plural forms of *this* and *that*.
- Have two students complete the Warm-up aloud.

CHART 2-7. Using *These* and *Those*. Page 48
Time: 10–15 minutes

- Ask students who may participate more reluctantly to read sentences (a) and (b) from the chart aloud.
- Review the notes to the right.
- Explain to students that the contractions for *these + are* and *those + are* are commonly heard in English but less frequently seen in writing.

❏ EXERCISE 32. Looking at grammar.
Page 48
Time: 10 minutes

- Have students do this exercise on sight, without prior preparation.
- Have students read the completed sentences aloud.

❏ EXERCISE 33. Vocabulary and grammar.
Page 49
Time: 10 minutes

- Point out the heading of the exercise, "In our dorm room."
- Explain that *our* indicates that the dorm room is shared and, therefore, that some of the objects will be plural.
- First review the vocabulary presented in the exercise: *pillow, sheets, blankets, mattresses, TV*. Then review optional vocabulary, inviting students to name additional items they see in the illustration for Exercise 33.

Optional Vocabulary

window	books
bed	pencils
desks	notepads
chairs	waterproof
computers	erasers
bookshelf	

❏ EXERCISE 34. Looking at grammar.
Page 49
Time: 5–10 minutes

- Give students time to complete the items as seatwork, using *this / that / these / those* as appropriate.
- Review the completions with students and discuss the Optional Vocabulary included above.

❏ EXERCISE 35. Let's talk: pairwork.
Page 50
Time: 5–10 minutes

- Model Partner A with a student, who will take the role of Partner B.
- Remind students of the cases in which *this / these* are used.
- Circulate as students practice with each other.
- Review vocabulary items used in the exercise.

❏ EXERCISE 36. Listening. Page 52
Time: 10 minutes

- Ensure that the CD player is ready to go and be prepared with the CD track you will play.
- Read the example sentences and remind students that all sentences describe items found in the kitchen.
- Review students' completions and write corrected answers on the board.
- Replay the CD track if necessary.

❏ EXERCISE 37. Warm-up. Page 52
Time: 5 minutes

- Explain that *What* is used to get information about an object and *Who* is used to ask for a person's name.
- Have two students complete the Warm-up aloud.

CHART 2-8. Asking Questions with *What* and *Who* + *Be*. Page 52
Time: 10–15 minutes

> Many beginners have some practice using *Who* and *What* to get information. Invite them to participate in the descriptions and explanations found in the chart. You can draw on their knowledge by asking questions such as *Who is your teacher? What is your class?* and so on.

- Write the chart title on the board.
- Ask students to take turns reading (a)–(f) aloud.
- Review with students the notes on the right.
- Explain the contracted forms and write these on the board.

❑ EXERCISE 38. Looking at grammar.
Page 53
Time: 10 minutes

- Model item 1 by taking the role of speaker A and having a student read the response of speaker B.
- Without their preparing the remainder of the exercise as seatwork, ask students to read it through and complete the exercise on sight.
- Have students take turns reading the completions aloud, correcting their answers immediately.

❑ EXERCISE 39. Vocabulary and speaking: pairwork. Page 54
Time: 10–15 minutes

> Because this exercise requires discussing general body parts, you may want to pair students of the same gender, depending on the cultural makeup of your class. (For example, it would not be appropriate for a female student from Saudi Arabia to discuss ankles with a male student of any nationality.) Also, be prepared for students to ask about additional body parts and organs.

Part I
- Put students into pairs.
- Using the body words in the box and each partner's prior knowledge of these words, encourage students to write in all the body parts for which there are boxes.

Part II
- Have students remain in the same pairs and use the examples given to ask and answer questions about all the body parts.
- Circulate around the room and help those students who need additional assistance.

❑ EXERCISE 40. Let's talk: class activity.
Page 54
Time: 10–15 minutes

> This is a teacher-led activity and you will interact with all of your students as you work through the exercise. Be ready to choose items that work best with the students you call on.

- Write the words *this*, *that*, *these*, and *those* on the board.
- Tell students to close their books and be ready to respond in complete sentences using *this*, *that*, *these*, and *those*.
- Model the examples in the book with some of the strongest students.
- Complete the exercise, calling on other students in the class. Repeat different body parts with different students to give everyone ample practice.
- Correct pronunciation as well as accuracy.

❑ EXERCISE 41. Check your knowledge.
Page 55
Time: 10 minutes

- Give students time to complete as seatwork.
- Have students take turns identifying and correcting each mistake, as review.

❑ EXERCISE 42. Looking at grammar.
Page 55
Time: 10 minutes

> This review will help students self-correct and identify which completion among the three possible choices sounds correct. Go through this exercise at a quick clip when possible to train students' ears so that they can better self-correct.

- Without allowing prior preparation, have students take turns reading the sentences aloud and choosing the correct completion as "automatically" as possible.
- When questions arise, discuss with the class what other changes would have to be made in the item to allow an incorrect completion to work.
- Particularly because you may move through this exercise quickly, write on the board as much as possible to support students who are challenged by the material.

❑ EXERCISE 43. Looking at grammar.
Page 56
Time: 10 minutes

- Give students time to prepare this exercise on their own as seatwork.
- Correct and review by having students read aloud.

Optional Vocabulary

keys	favorite
dessert plates	only child
sponges	bats
dishcloths	banana
frying pan	math book
saltshaker, pepper shaker	apartment
empty	art history
camera	

❑ **EXERCISE 44.** Looking at grammar.
Page 57
Time: 10 minutes

> Tell students to complete the conversations within the exercise with any words that work and remind them that multiple completions can be correct.

- Give students time to complete the conversations.
- Circulate and help those students who need it.
- Ask students to read their completions aloud, discuss the content, and write alternative versions on the board.

❑ **EXERCISE 45.** Grammar and writing.
Page 57
Time: 10–20 minutes

Part I
- Have students complete the cloze exercise independently.
- Ask students to read their completions aloud to each other in small groups while you visit each group, checking on content.
- Point out the conventions of writing in paragraphs and giving descriptions—that is, the type of information usually given when people are described. Read corrected versions aloud or write a completed and correct version on the board.

Part II
- Assign students the four paragraphs outlined in Part II.
- Have student read the information for each paragraph carefully and write notes that can be expanded into sentences.
- Give students ample time to plan and write (perhaps as homework) their paragraphs.

Part III
- Discuss again the mechanical conventions of writing, including capitalization, punctuation, and indentation.
- Remind students to use *be* and *have* correctly, in person (first, second, or third) and number (singular or plural), and to be ready to edit their own work or others' work.
- Remind students to check that each sentence is complete and that it has a subject and a verb.
- Have students edit their own work or share as peer editing.
- Put common errors on the board and review as a class.

Chapter 3
Using the Simple Present

CHAPTER SUMMARY

OBJECTIVE: In this chapter, students learn to use the simple present tense to describe usual activities and habits. Because students have already gained familiarity with third person singular forms (with *be* and *have*), they are prepared to pay special attention to third person singular verb forms. The presentation of frequency adverbs allows students to master simple present verbs in a meaningful way, by describing their daily lives. They gain further linguistic autonomy and prepare to use infinitives by learning how to use *like to*, *want to*, and *need to*. Students round out their knowledge of the simple present by learning how to make negative statements, how to use the auxiliary *do / does* in questions, and how to give short answers. Finally, they learn how to ask and answer information questions using simple present verbs.

APPROACH: The chapter builds on students' knowledge of *be* and *have* and their familiarity with conjugations. Exercises move from more controlled (cloze completions) to more productive. Vocabulary is interwoven throughout the presentation of the simple present. The introduction and use of frequency adverbs promotes autonomous use of verbs. Finally, the chapter presents the use of negative forms and questions. By comparing the use of these previously learned forms (as taught with *be* and *have*) with regular verbs, students can identify patterns and thus gain confidence.

TERMINOLOGY: The introduction of the term *frequency adverbs* helps students to compare these common adverbs to adverbs of manner, which they will learn later. The verb terminology used in this chapter helps students compare and contrast what they have learned about verbs with new information about the simple present.

❏ EXERCISE 1. Warm-up. Page 59
Time: 5 minutes

> Some beginners will be familiar with the conjugation of regular verbs. In addition, all beginning students who have completed the first two chapters of this book will anticipate that, as with *is* and *has*, third person singular ends with a final *-s*.

- Ask students to take turns reading the paragraph aloud, sentence by sentence.
- Ask students to explain the vocabulary used in the paragraph, and write any related words and phrases

generated by students on the board, in categories. For example:

> *take videos: film students' experiments, make a movie, use a camera*
>
> *post videos: place / put videos (on Facebook / Twitter), upload*
>
> *share videos: show videos to others, friends watch my videos*

- Have students work as a class to complete items 1–6 and underline the final *-s* used consistently with third person singular.

CHART 3-1. Form and Basic Meaning of the Simple Present Tense. Page 59
Time: 10–15 minutes

> Because the simple present is review for many beginners, involve students and reactivate all that they have learned thus far by asking for their help in putting example sentences on the board. Remind students of all they learned in previous chapters, and, whenever possible, ask pointed questions to engage them further and activate their knowledge as they do board work. For example (from below):
>
> *Every morning and night, Ana brushes _____ teeth.*
>
> *What possessive adjective goes before teeth? His? Her?*

- Write the chart title on the board.
- Ask students when they use simple present tense and anticipate phrases to add to the board. For example:

> *something that usually happens*
>
> *habits*
>
> *everyday activities*

- If students don't give you these expected responses, begin by stating that you use the simple present tense to show things you do regularly.
- Ask students, *What is something you do every day or every night?*
- Write students' responses on the board. For example:

> *eat*   *work*
>
> *sleep*   *go to class*
>
> *study*   *send email*

- Using student-generated information, write simple sentences on the board and underline the verb forms.
- If your class is not very responsive, begin with *I* statements and the phrase *Every day* or *Every night*. For example,

    Every day, I *teach* English grammar.

    Every day, I *send* emails to my friends.

    Every night, I *sleep*.

- Explain that there are some activities most people do every day. For example:

    Every day, people *eat*.

    Every day, people *work*.

- Ask students to read the conjugation for *talk* aloud as you write the complete conjugation on the board.
- You may wish to ask students if they can guess why the verb *talk* is used for all pronouns except *It*. If they cannot guess the reason, point out that *talk* is usually a human action and *it* is not a human subject; *it* describes impersonal actions.
- Have students take turns reading example sentences (a)–(d) aloud.
- Review the notes on the right with students and discuss the illustrated sentences beneath them.
- Remind students that the simple present expresses a habit and then ask students to discuss additional habits they may have.
- Write these on the board, using third person singular and the names of the students who contributed the ideas.
- Ask students for help in writing the sentences. For example:

    Every night, Marcus *makes* dinner and *eats* it with his mother.

    Every weekend, Jin Ok *exercises* at the gym.

    Every morning and every night, Ana *brushes* her teeth.

❏ EXERCISE 2. Looking at grammar.
Page 60
Time: 5–10 minutes

> Lead controlled exercises immediately following presentation of new grammar as class-wide completions, calling on the stronger students to provide answers to the more challenging items.

- Without allowing prior preparation, have students complete the eleven items on sight with either *speak* or *speaks*.
- Ask students to explain why they need a final *-s* and get them in the habit of identifying the subject as third person singular.

Optional Vocabulary
online
experiments
several
fluently

❏ EXERCISE 3. Let's talk: pairwork. Page 60
Time: 10–15 minutes

> Give students plenty of time to complete this pairwork. They need the speaking practice, and the topic should naturally activate a lot of passive vocabulary.

- Put students into pairs.

Part I
- Ask students to read through the list of daily activities and check off those that they do.
- Tell students to discuss unfamiliar phrases with their partner. Let them know that you will also be going around the room to assist with vocabulary.
- Ask students to write independently the order of their own habits on the lines provided.

Part II
- Once students have ordered and prioritized their lists of activities, ask them to tell their partner their habits.
- Ask students to look at their books as little as possible while comparing schedules with their partner.
- Write down mistakes, mispronunciations, or any other questions that need clarification as a group and review these as board work.

Expansion: Ask pairs how their routines change on the weekend. Write specific examples on the board to promote further discussion. Encourage students to do most of the talking; your role is to correct, clarify, and present, as needed. For example:

    On the weekend, I *don't turn off* my alarm.

    On the weekend, I *get up* later.

- Finally, ask each partner to tell the class one habit they learned about their peer's schedule, whether daily or weekend.
- Use this comparison of habits to further discussion of vocabulary when possible.

❏ EXERCISE 4. Listening. Page 61
Time: 10 minutes

- Have the CD player ready and know which track you will play.
- Tell students they will hear complete sentences and will need to listen for the final *-s*, as it occurs in sentences with third person singular subjects.
- Play the track through once and correct as a class, having students say the correct verb form aloud.
- If students require further clarification, replay the items from the CD so they can hear the verb form themselves.

❏ EXERCISE 5. Looking at grammar.
Page 61
Time: 10 minutes

- Give students time to complete the twelve items as seatwork.
- For review, have students read their completions aloud and discuss as a class.

- Write any items that posed particular challenges on the board, as needed.
- Ask students about nontarget grammar and vocabulary to get them and keep them speaking spontaneously as much as possible while reviewing.

Optional Vocabulary

shave	bring
brush	library
wash	

❑ EXERCISE 6. Warm-up. Page 62
Time: 5–10 minutes

- Write the percentages on the board and ask a student to write *always* or *usually* or *sometimes* or *never* beside each percentage.
- Ask students to take turns reading the Warm-up sentences.
- Ask students to tell you something they *always*, *usually*, *sometimes*, and / or *never* do.

CHART 3-2. Frequency Adverbs. Page 62
Time: 10–15 minutes

> Because most students will probably know percentages well, write these on the board first.

- Write the chart title on the board.
- Ask students what *frequency / frequent* means and write both these key words and any related words on the board.
- From the Warm-up above, write *always*, *usually*, *sometimes*, and *never* on the board.
- Ask students to take turns reading sentences (a)–(g) from the chart aloud.
- Write the sentences on the board and underline the frequency adverb in each one.
- Explain that these frequency adverbs come between the subject and the verb, and explain that this is not the usual placement of adverbs.
- Introduce other frequency phrases to students.
- Ask students to explain how many times a day *once* is and write this on the board.
- Have students take turns reading examples (h)–(l) aloud.
- Explain that *a day*, *a week*, and *a month* are the same as *per day*, *per week*, and *per month*.
- Introduce *every day / week / month / year*, and have students read sentence (l) aloud.
- Have students close their books. Ask quick questions to elicit spontaneous use of frequency adverbs from the chart before moving on to controlled exercises.
- Write students' answers on the board. For example:

  Marcia, do you always eat breakfast at the same time every day? Yes?

  Marcia eats breakfast at 7:30 every day.

  Wen, do you exercise every day? No?

  He exercises twice a week.

❑ EXERCISE 7. Looking at grammar.
Page 63
Time: 5–10 minutes

- Have students look at the chart.
- Lead students through this exercise on sight, having them pick the correct frequency adverb based on the number of cups of tea per name.

❑ EXERCISE 8. Looking at grammar.
Page 63
Time: 10–15 minutes

- Ask students to explain what a subject and a verb are, and write the example on the board.
- Look at the completed example with students and ask which word is the subject and which is the verb. Have a student read the sentence with *always*.
- Tell students to write *S* above the subject and *V* above the verb in each sentence.
- Tell them to insert the frequency adverb between the subject and verb and then rewrite each sentence.
- Give students time to complete the exercise as seatwork.
- Review aloud as a class, correcting both pronunciation and accuracy.

❑ EXERCISE 9. Let's talk: class activity.
Page 64
Time: 10–15 minutes

- Ask students to close their books.
- Lead the discussion by asking both the questions in the book and ones that you come up with and direct these questions to specific students.
- Write students' responses on the board in complete sentences.

❑ EXERCISE 10. Looking at grammar.
Page 64
Time: 10 minutes

> Explain and practice the phrase *that means* before starting the exercise.

- Read through the completed example with students, referring back to the chart.
- Give students time to complete the items.
- Review and correct as a class.

Optional Vocabulary

something happens	cafeteria
carrots	that means

❑ EXERCISE 11. Warm-up. Page 65
Time: 5 minutes

- Have students take turns reading the sentences aloud and have the class answer *yes* or *no* as a group, and in reference to the city in which the class takes place.
- Write the sentences on the board.

- Ask student(s) to go to the board and underline the frequency adverbs.
- Ask students to explain how the position of the frequency adverbs in items 3 and 4 differs from their position in 1 and 2.

CHART 3-3. Position of Frequency Adverbs.
Page 65
Time: 10–15 minutes

This chart presents an exception to what students just learned in the previous chart, that frequency adverbs are placed between the subject and the verb. Irregular verbs and other exceptions to grammar "rules" can be particularly frustrating to beginners. Remind students that many of the exceptions in English grammar are related to irregular verbs. Therefore, when they are using irregular verbs, they can anticipate additional irregularities in the grammar. Discussing the fact that this chart shows an exception can help students feel better prepared.

- Write the chart title on the board.
- Remind students that there are different rules for the placement of frequency adverbs with *be* than for the placement of frequency adverbs with other verbs in the simple present. However, the actual verb forms remain the same.
- Conjugate and write the forms of *be* on the board.
- Write a frequency adverb next to each subject-and-verb combination and then write the adjective *late*, as in the book, or another adjective (*cold*, *hot*, etc.).
- Have students read the conjugation of *be* aloud, sentence by sentence.
- Next have students read the sentences with *comes* aloud. Then ask them to compare the placement of the frequency adverb in the sentences with *be* with the placement of the frequency adverb in the sentences immediately below. What is different between the two groups of sentences?
- Before moving on, write on the board:

    Frequency adverbs come before all simple present verbs except *be*.

❑ EXERCISE 12. Looking at grammar.
Page 65
Time: 10 minutes

- Read the first two example sentences aloud, and write them on the board.
- Underline the frequency adverbs, and highlight the different placement in each item.
- Lead this exercise as a group, assigning the first items to stronger students to complete and read aloud.
- Continue through the exercise, giving different students items to complete and read aloud, and writing on the board as necessary.
- Correct immediately and overtly.

❑ EXERCISE 13. Let's talk: class activity.
Page 66
Time: 10–15 minutes

Part I
- Give students time to complete the chart as thoroughly as possible by describing their own habits and checking off the appropriate frequency adverb for each one.

Part II
- Assign partners.
- Ask students to exchange books.
- Give students several minutes to review their partner's chart and write a few complete sentences based on their partner's habits.
- Ask students to read two or three sentences about their partner's habits aloud.

Expansion: Have partners write their sentences on the board and ask the rest of the class to read aloud, correct for accuracy, and compare similar habits among class members.

❑ EXERCISE 14. Writing. Page 66
Time: 15–20 minutes

Lead writing exercises for beginners as class-wide activities in coauthoring a piece on the board. By collaborating on one piece on the board, you can model basic writing skills while also engaging all students in their newly acquired grammar mastery. This also promotes spontaneous contribution and speaking on the part of students. Because students write at very different speeds, doing one version together as a class on the board before assigning writing as homework works best for beginners.

Expansion: Have students collaborate on one paragraph, which you write on the board, from sentences students contribute. Ask students to describe what usually happens in your class and at different time(s). You can personalize the paragraph by referring to students' particular behavior as long as this is done in a warm and supportive way. For example:

Class always starts at 9:00 A.M. Otavio sometimes arrives late and often brings coffee. Our teacher usually corrects our homework with us. We usually learn new grammar, but we never watch movies.

Optional Vocabulary
hometown
skip
have time
spend time
surf (the Internet)

❏ EXERCISE 15. Warm-up: listening.
Page 66
Time: 5–10 minutes

> Some beginners may be familiar with syllables, but in any case, clapping out syllables, which may seem juvenile at first, is often very helpful to beginners. As with all directions in this teacher's guide, complete instructions are written for exposing students to new concepts and structures. However, if your students don't need this step, proceed without overexplaining.

- Write the word *syllable* on the board.
- Elicit any student explanations of the word and write associated vocabulary on the board. For example:

  syllable = sound, beat, clap

- Explain and write the following simple definition of *syllable* on the board:

  A syllable is a part of a word or a whole word that has just one distinct vowel sound.

- Clap (or count by slapping a desk) the syllables in the names of some of the students in the class.
- Write the names of a few students and have students supply you with the number of related syllables. For example:

  Mar-ta = 2 syllables
  Hyun-chae = 2 syllables
  Rolf = 1 syllable
  Abdullah = 3 syllables

- Now have students take turns reading items 1–6 and circling the correct number of syllables for each word.

CHART 3-4. Spelling and Pronunciation of Final *-es*. Page 67
Time: 10–15 minutes

> The reason for this spelling presentation becomes clear if you try to have your students add a final *-s* to the end of a single-syllable word ending in *-sh*, *-ch*, *-ss*, or *-x*. It is physically impossible to do, and having students try to do it can show them why this rule exists.

- Write the chart title on the board.
- Write the verbs in (a)–(d) on the board.
- Ask students how they make the third person singular simple present of each verb and elicit that they should add a final *-s*.
- Have students try to do only that and pronounce the resulting words (*pushs*, etc.).
- Demonstrate the ease of adding an *-es* as opposed to just *-s*.
- Model and reiterate the spelling and pronunciation in the chart.

❏ EXERCISE 16. Looking at grammar.
Page 67
Time: 10 minutes

- Read through the completed example (item 1) with students.
- Give students just a few minutes to look at the exercise so that they understand the task and then call on students to complete items on the spot.
- Correct immediately and overtly.
- Write out on the board the correct completion for each item as a student completes it and give others an opportunity to repeat the correct version aloud.

Optional Vocabulary

> When teaching, practicing, and reviewing vocabulary, demonstrate physically as much as is possible and effective. Words like *stretch* and *yawn* lend themselves to gesture and physical demonstration.

fix	wash
watch	stretch
kiss	yawn
wear	

❏ EXERCISE 17. Listening. Page 68
Time: 5–10 minutes

- Have the CD player and track number ready.
- Read the direction line aloud and make sure students understand the task.
- Play the track through once.
- Review as a class, correcting and clarifying as needed.
- Play the sentences and review a second time if needed.

❏ EXERCISE 18. Looking at grammar.
Page 68
Time: 10–12 minutes

- Briefly review the direction line and completed example with students.
- Give students ample time to complete the exercise as seatwork.
- Ask students to read their completed responses aloud.
- Correct and review challenging items on the board.

Optional Vocabulary

leave	sit down to eat
turn on	pick up
schedule	

❏ EXERCISE 19. Warm-up. Page 68
Time: 5–7 minutes

- Ask students to give you examples of consonants and vowels and write them on the board.
- Review the two *y*-ending verbs with students.

CHART 3-5. Adding Final -s / -es to Words That End in -y. Page 69
Time: 10–15 minutes

- Write the chart title on the board.
- Explain that in verbs ending in a consonant + -y (where the vowel sound is /y/),the -y changes to -ies.
- Explain that if a vowel comes before the -y, -s is added immediately after the -y.
- Ask a student to read the sample items in example (a) aloud while you write them on the board. Then write two complete sentences using a verb with the -ies spelling. For example:

    I cry sometimes.   *The baby <u>cries</u> sometimes.*

- Ask another student to read the items in example (b) aloud while you write them on the board. Then write two complete sentences using a verb with the -ys spelling. For example:

    You enjoy movies.   *Josephine <u>enjoys</u> movies.*

❏ EXERCISE 20. Looking at grammar.
Page 69
Time: 10 minutes

- Read the direction line and completed example.
- Have students complete each item on sight and then read each one aloud in turn.
- Correct and review immediately.

❏ EXERCISE 21. Looking at grammar.
Page 69
Time: 10 minutes

- Read the direction line and completed example.
- Give students time to complete the items as seatwork.
- Correct and review by asking students to read items aloud.

Optional Vocabulary

enjoy	passengers
worry	debit card
employ	

❏ EXERCISE 22. Warm-up. Page 70
Time: 5–7 minutes

Many beginners will know the third person singular forms of the three irregular verbs in the chart. The chart students create in this exercise gives them a chance to explain what they already know about regular third person singular forms; it also activates their passive knowledge of irregular verb forms.

- Ask students to complete the third person singular forms of *have*. Write these forms on the board while students write them in the chart.
- Ask students if they know the third person endings for *go* and *have*, and with their help, write these forms on the board while students write them in the chart.
- Review the completed chart.

CHART 3-6. Irregular Singular Verbs: *Has, Does, Goes.* Page 70
Time: 10–15 minutes

- Write the chart title on the board.
- Ask students to read example sentences (a)–(f) aloud.
- Write example sentences (b), (d), and (f) on the board and underline *has*, *does*, and *goes*.
- Have students practice the /z/ sound these forms end in.

❏ EXERCISE 23. Looking at grammar.
Page 70
Time: 8–10 minutes

- Ask a student, perhaps a student who may have difficulty with on-sight production, to read the two example sentences.
- Lead this exercise as a class, having students complete the cloze questions on sight.
- Correct for accuracy and pronunciation as you complete the exercise.

❏ EXERCISE 24. Listening. Page 71
Time: 10–15 minutes

- Have the CD player and track number prepared.
- Play only the first two example items and review with students to ensure they understood the first completions.
- Explain to students that they will complete each blank with the correct third person singular verb, as heard on the CD track.
- Once students have completed the missing items, have individual students read their completions aloud in turn, reading each whole sentence.
- Correct immediately, writing correct completions on the board as needed.
- Replay the track as needed.

❏ EXERCISE 25. Looking at grammar.
Page 72
Time: 10–15 minutes

- Read the direction line with students and review the completed example in item 1.
- Give students ample time to complete the exercise independently as seatwork.
- Review as a class and make corrections both orally and on the board as needed.
- Ask students to paraphrase content and vocabulary to provide additional speaking opportunities while correcting.

❏ EXERCISE 26. Let's talk: game. Page 72
Time: 10–15 minutes

Part I
- Tell students you will give them a verb from which to make a complete sentence.
- You may wish to prepare the verbs and verb phrases on index cards beforehand.

- Give students one to three minutes to create and remember a sentence for their respective verbs.
- Tell students to circulate around the room and tell their sentence to as many classmates as possible.

Part II
- Put students into teams of five to eight.
- Ask students in each team to elect one member to write all the sentences their team has heard.
- After five to ten more minutes, have students read their sentences aloud and have the originators of those sentences correct them for accuracy and content.
- The team with the most correct sentences wins.

❑ **EXERCISE 27.** Let's talk: pairwork.
Page 73
Time: 10–15 minutes

Part I
- Put students into pairs.
- Have each pair use the chart to create sentences about the content of the chart.
- Walk around the room taking notes and assisting students.
- Review common errors and challenges as a class, using the board.

Part II
- Ask students to write ten complete sentences for homework.
- Collect the homework for correction at the following class meeting.

Expansion: Ask a few students to tell the class how often they do the five things listed in the chart. Have those students write their sentences on the board. Have the class correct the sentences.

❑ **EXERCISE 28.** Looking at grammar.
Page 73
Time: 10–15 minutes

- Give students time to add -s or -es to each verb in the paragraph.
- When students have completed this task, have them take turns reading the correct sentences aloud.
- Ask students about content and correct pronunciation as well as target grammar.

❑ **EXERCISE 29.** Speaking and writing:
pairwork. Page 73
Time: 10–15 minutes

- Put students into pairs and explain that they will share information and practice sentences in the third person, with final -s or -es.
- Instruct students in each pair to refer to the list they made for Exercise 3, if possible, or simply generate five to ten sentences about things they do every morning.

- Direct pairs to take turns telling each other their sentences.
- Have each listening partner takes notes.
- Have each partner write a paragraph, either in class or for homework, describing the actions of his or her partner.
- Ask pairs to exchange paragraphs and pay special attention in the use of final -s and -es.

Optional Vocabulary

part-time job	strange
do dishes	bite fingernails
snack	pay attention
exercises	get up
volleyball	put on
unusual	catch a bus
take a break	communicate
come up	roommate

❑ **EXERCISE 30.** Warm-up. Page 73
Time: 5 minutes

- Have three students read the sentences aloud.
- Ask various class members to respond with *yes* or *no* and discuss content.

CHART 3-7. *Like To, Want To, Need To.*
Page 74
Time: 10–15 minutes

Many beginners will understand these verbs without necessarily understanding their use in an infinitive verb phrase. However, some students may understand the infinitive verb phrases. Discuss verbs with students and encourage them to compare the differences in meaning among these three verb phrases and their similarity in terms of form.

- Write the chart title on the board.
- Ask students what an infinitive is and write any student feedback on the board.
- Have a student read example sentence (a) to the class while you write it on the board.
- Discuss the meaning of *like to* with the class and elicit sentences from students explaining what they *like to* + verb (*do*).
- Repeat the steps above for example sentences (b) and (c) with the class.
- Illustrate the differences among the verbs as needed, especially explaining the difference between *want to* and *need to*.

❑ **EXERCISE 31.** Looking at grammar.
Page 74
Time: 5–10 minutes

- Lead this exercise as a class activity after reviewing the completed example in item 1.
- Ask students in turn to create sentences from the cues on sight and read the new sentences aloud.

- Correct the target structures and pronunciation of each item so that students can hear the *to* part of the verb.

❑ EXERCISE 32. Reading and grammar.
Page 74
Time: 10–15 minutes

Part I
- Have students take turns reading parts of the story aloud.
- Ask students to explain vocabulary and paraphrase sentences to give them spontaneous speaking practice.

Part II
- Lead the students in completing the cloze exercise with the correct words.
- Have students give corrected answers and discuss content.

Expansion: Ask students questions about cooking and cleaning to get them using some of the vocabulary spontaneously and in reference to their own lives. Get students speaking as much as possible and put student-generated sentences on the board.

Sample questions to expand the conversation:
Do you like to cook?
Do you like to invite friends for meals?
Do you need to cook? Who cooks in your home?
Do you need to use recipes?
Do you like to clean up?
Do you have favorite recipes?
What is your favorite food?
Is it easy to make?
Do you like to try new recipes?

❑ EXERCISE 33. Let's talk: pairwork.
Page 75
Time: 10–15 minutes

- Put students into teams of three or four.
- Have students take turns reading the statements about mosquitoes and choosing *yes* or *no*.
- When the teams have completed the exercise, have team members read the statements aloud while you provide the correct responses. The team with the most correct answers wins.

Optional Vocabulary
sweets	pots
quietly	stove
wonderful	delicious
recipes	clean up
arrive	invite

❑ EXERCISE 34. Warm-up. Page 75
Time: 5 minutes

- Have students read the sentences and, for each item, choose whether a or b is true for them.

- Discuss other tastes and preferences that students / people have in terms of food.
- Ask students if they know people who don't eat any meat products. What are they called? (*Vegetarians*).

Expansion: Have students get together with a partner and write five sentences about what food they think their partner *likes* and *doesn't like*. Have students read their sentences aloud while their partner says *true* or *false*.

You may want to include yourself. Have the class make up sentences about what you like or don't like. You respond with *true* or *false*.

CHART 3-8. Simple Present Tense: Negative.
Page 76
Time: 10–15 minutes

Many beginners will already know how to form the negative of the simple present tense. If they don't know how to produce this form, they will almost certainly recognize it. Therefore, when writing the conjugation of the verb in the chart on the board, encourage students to provide the words needed in the correct order. This is also an ideal opportunity to get students talking about their own likes and dislikes.

- Write the chart title on the board.
- Explain that in order to make a simple present verb negative, the helping verbs *do* and *does* are needed.
- Ask students to tell you some foods, drinks, or conditions they don't like.
- Write their responses as complete sentences on the board, and underline the complete verb. For example:

  Maya does not like fish.
  I do not like soda.
  Jun Long does not like any sweets.
  Ahmad does not like snow.

- Use one of these student-generated sentences to conjugate the verb *like*. Underline the complete verb and circle the third person singular helping verb.
- Have students tell you the words to write as you complete this conjugation.

  I do not like snow.
  You do not like snow.
  He / She / It does not like snow.
  We do not like snow.
  You do not like snow.
  They do not like snow.

- Explain that the final *-s* on the third person singular is found on the helping verb *does*.
- Review the notes on contractions with students and make sure they know when to anticipate them.

❑ EXERCISE 35. Looking at grammar.
Page 76
Time: 10 minutes

- Review item 1 with students.
- Have students complete the items in the exercise on sight by calling on individual students to read each correct item aloud.

❑ EXERCISE 36. Looking at grammar.
Page 77
Time: 10 minutes

- Read the direction line and completed example items 1 and 2 with students.
- Remind students that the third person singular is the only negative form that requires the helping verb *does*. The other forms take the helping verb *do*.
- Have students complete the items in the exercise on sight by calling on individual students to read the completed items aloud.
- Correct items immediately and make sure that students enunciate *doesn't / don't* sufficiently so that others can distinguish between the two.

❑ EXERCISE 37. Let's talk: pairwork.
Page 77
Time: 10–12 minutes

- Put students into pairs.
- Read the direction line and tell students to take turns, with one partner making a positive sentence and one making a negative one.
- Go around the classroom and help students working in pairs.

❑ EXERCISE 38. Let's talk: game. Page 79
Time: 10–15 minutes

- Have students pull their chairs into a circle.
- Start by giving students one verb to use from the box below the example.
- Instruct the first student to make a sentence that is true for him or her, using the verb in the negative.
- Tell the next student to repeat the first student's sentence and then add another sentence.
- Continue around the circle and add your own sentence last.
- Correct students' pronunciation and use of the target grammar as you use the other verbs for the game.

❑ EXERCISE 39. Looking at grammar.
Page 79
Time: 10 minutes

- Read the direction line aloud and review the completed example sentence in item 1.
- Explain to students that they need to both select the appropriate verb from the box above the exercise and put the verb in the appropriate negative form, using the correct helping verb.

- Give students time to complete the exercise on their own as seatwork.
- Move around the room and help those students who need additional support.
- Correct and review as a class by having students read their completions aloud.
- Write any particularly challenging items on the board.

❑ EXERCISE 40. Looking at grammar.
Page 80
Time: 10 minutes

- Explain that completing the two charts in this exercise will help students see the difference between the negative forms of the verb *be* and the negative forms of an action verb, which requires the helping verb *do / does*.
- Give students a few minutes to complete the charts.
- Have students read the correct completions aloud; for direct comparison of any forms, write them on the board.

❑ EXERCISE 41. Looking at grammar.
Page 80
Time: 10 minutes

- Read the direction line and discuss the completed example with students.
- Remind students that if the verb *be* is used, it will be followed directly by an adjective, noun, or prepositional phrase.
- Give students time to complete the exercise.
- Review as a class. Emphasize which words and parts of speech indicate whether the verb *be* or another verb is used.

❑ EXERCISE 42. Let's talk: class activity.
Page 80
Time: 10–15 minutes

Part I
- Put students into pairs.
- Explain the direction line and examples to students and have them make true sentences using the negative simple present.
- Circulate and assist pairs making sentences. Write down any common errors for later correction.

Part II
- Tell students to remain with their partner.
- Have students write true sentences from the cues in Part II.
- Correct and review all possible sentences from both Part I and Part II as a class.
- Write any common errors you overheard on the board, and write the correction for each error on the board.

Optional Vocabulary

play soccer	shaves
understand	cigarettes
rain / snow	smoke
much	careful
strangers	barefoot
umbrella	citizens
showers / baths	tails
beard	serve
mustache	driver's license
puts on	whiskers

❏ EXERCISE 43. Warm-up. Page 81
Time: 5–7 minutes

- Ask a student to read the questions in the speech bubble aloud.
- Ask students to say what the situation is, why the woman is asking these questions, and where the two women are.
- Ask students specifically which verbs need helping verbs to form questions.

CHART 3-9. Simple Present Tense: Yes / No Questions. Page 82
Time: 10–15 minutes

Many beginners know how to make simple yes / no questions for simple present tense verbs. Again, this is an ideal chance to have students supply you with the correct verb forms as you write on the board. In this way you will maximally involve students in this class presentation of the target grammar.

- Write the chart title on the board.
- Ask students a simple question, other than the one in the chart, in order to engage the class in actively presenting yes / no questions. For example:

    Do you exercise?

- Write the question on the board.
- Explain that as with negative forms of simple present regular verbs, the helping verb *do / does* must be used with yes / no questions.
- Write the pronouns on the board to prompt formation of questions:

    I

    You

    He / She / It

    We

    You

    They

- Ask a student to use *do* to make the question you have written on the board into one that uses the pronoun *I*. From there, have students give you the correct question forms by looking at the chart and by activating their passive English.
- Write the entire conjugation on the board.

- Underline the helping verbs.

I	<u>Do</u> *I exercise?*
You	<u>Do</u> *you exercise?*
He / She / It	<u>Does</u> *he / she / it exercise?*
We	<u>Do</u> *we exercise?*
You	<u>Do</u> *you exercise?*
They	<u>Do</u> *they exercise?*

- Have students read the questions (h)–(m) aloud.
- Ask students to read questions (n) and (o) aloud.
- Remind students of the short-answer forms and correct use of the helping verbs.
- Read sentences (p) and (q) aloud and explain that *do* is also used as a main verb, meaning "to complete an action or execute a task."

❏ EXERCISE 44. Looking at grammar. Page 82
Time: 10 minutes

- Give students a few minutes to read through the items and decide what the original question in each item should be.
- Have one student read the correct question (created from cues in each item) and ask a second student to respond with the correct short answer (a or b).
- Correct right away and put any challenging items on the board.

❏ EXERCISE 45. Speaking and grammar: pairwork. Page 83
Time: 10–15 minutes

Part I
- Put students into pairs.
- Read the direction line and completed examples at the beginning of the exercise.
- If necessary, write the examples on the board so that students understand the task thoroughly.
- Explain that the first student (Partner A) asks a question about another class member based on the cues given.
- The second student (Partner B) responds with a short answer, using the cues given.
- Explain that for Part I, students should first do the entire exercise orally and not write the questions and answers until they are finished working with their partner.

Part II
- Ask students to work in pairs to write the correct questions and answers in their books.
- Review as a class and write the more challenging items on the board.

❏ EXERCISE 46. Vocabulary and speaking. Page 84
Time: 10 minutes

Part I
- Ask students to go through the items individually and check the activities they do at least once a week, as indicated in the direction line.

Part II

- Have students move around the room and ask other students questions about their daily / weekly habits.
- Instruct students to keep asking questions (and changing the time frames, etc.) until they get *yes* responses.
- Review both parts of the exercise in a class discussion.
- Ask students to share the *yes* responses they got from other students with the class.

Expansion: Ask students to write five sentences about themselves, telling what they do at least once a week. (Ten minutes.) Then have students exchange papers with a student they have not exchanged with before. That student reports the five sentences to the class, using the student's name or *he* or *she*.

❑ **EXERCISE 47.** Looking at grammar.
Page 84
Time: 10–15 minutes

Part I
- Ask students to complete the statement forms of both *live* and *be* as directed.

Part II
- Have students complete the negative forms of both verbs as directed.
- Tell students they can use the full form or the contracted form, as they choose.

Part III
- Have students complete the sentences for both verbs, using question forms.
- Finally, have students compare all three lists perhaps by writing the completed forms on the board.

❑ **EXERCISE 48.** Let's talk: game. Page 85
Time: 10 minutes

- Put students into teams of three or four.
- Instruct teams to form the correct question and answer it correctly. Tell them they may not use their smart phones!
- When the teams have completed the questions, have team members read the questions and answers aloud while you provide the correct responses.

Optional Vocabulary

wear jeans	go around (orbit)
take a nap	planets
make a snack	easy / hard to see
do the laundry	windy

❑ **EXERCISE 49.** Warm-up. Page 86
Time: 5 minutes

- Ask students what a "lost-and-found" is and encourage discussion of the term.
- Have students read each question on the left aloud as a class and decide which answer corresponds.

CHART 3-10. Simple Present Tense: Asking Information Questions with *Where* and *What*.
Page 86
Time: 10–15 minutes

Because information questions are so important at the earliest stages of learning a new language, it is very likely that this chart will be review for many of your students. Remind them that information questions and yes / no questions are formed in different ways.

- Start by asking students yes / no questions as in the chart and write them on the board.
- To engage students, ask questions based on what you know about the actual people in your class. For example:

  Do your parents live in this city, Monica?
  Does your sister want a new bike, Akiko?

- Ask the class to tell you how to change these yes / no questions into information questions.
- Ask what kind of words introduce information questions, and elicit any information words students know, such as *what, where, who, when,* and *how.* Tell students this chart focuses only on *where* and *what.*
- Elicit help from students to write information versions of the above yes / no questions on the board. For example:

  Do your parents live in this city, Monica? Where?
  <u>Where do</u> *your parents live?*
  Does your sister want a new bike, Akiko? What?
  <u>What does</u> *your sister want?*

- Have students read example sentences (a) and (b) and then (c) and (d) from the chart aloud, while you write them on the board.
- Ask other students to read the short answers and write them on the board.
- Review the notes in the right column with students and underline the inverted word order in the questions in the left column that use the helping verb *do / does.*
- Ask other students to read example sentences (e) and (f) and (g) and (h) aloud while you write them on the board.
- Ask still other students to read the short answers aloud and write them on the board.
- Review all the notes from the chart and, if needed, generate additional examples with the help of students.

❑ **EXERCISE 50.** Looking at grammar.
Page 86
Time: 10 minutes

- Have students read the direction line.
- Make sure they understand the task by highlighting the completed example items 1 and 2 with them, guiding them to start with the statement in parentheses that follows each item.
- Ask students to create the appropriate questions by looking at Speaker B's answer and rephrasing the information in parentheses to form an information question.

- Without having students prepare as seatwork, walk around the room, giving the first items to stronger students.
- Correct immediately and write more challenging items on the board.

❏ EXERCISE 51. Let's talk: pairwork.
Page 87
Time: 10 minutes

- Put students into pairs.
- Ask each student to look at the book in order to prepare information questions based on the cues given for Partner A and Partner B.
- Tell students there may be more than one information question that can be made from the information included in this exercise.
- Move around the room and help students speak more fluidly by providing them with vocabulary and / or help getting started.

❏ EXERCISE 52. Reading. Page 87
Time: 10 minutes

- Ask students to describe the word *opposite*.
- Ask them if they have a roommate or have lived with a roommate before. Tell them to talk about some of the challenges, as best they can.
- Write any student-generated information you can on the board and involve students as much as possible by asking questions. For example:

  Is your roommate messy or clean?

  Does your roommate go to bed early or late?

  Do you like your roommate?

  Do you want to have a roommate?

- Ask students to take turns reading the paragraph aloud and answer the related questions as a group.

  Expansion: As a class, write a paragraph about how a dog and a cat act very differently. Show an action picture of a cat and one of a dog. (Perhaps the dog is jumping all over its owner as the person arrives home, and the cat is looking very independent.) Encourage students to volunteer sentences that you then write on the board.

❏ EXERCISE 53. Let's talk: class activity.
Page 88
Time: 10 minutes

- Explain to students that you have more information about the lives of each character named in the chart on page 88.
- Tell students that in order for them to complete the chart, they have to ask you information questions about the lives of these characters.
- Tell students that in order for you to give them more information, they must use the correct format in their questions.
- When students ask you *correct* questions, give them the information they requested.

- Write incorrect questions on the board and correct them with the help of the entire class.
- When everyone has the correct information, have students compare the lives of the people in the exercise. Discuss who has the best life and why.

Optional Vocabulary
front row
school supplies
go on vacation
neat
smell
make his bed
hang up his clothes
put things away

❏ EXERCISE 54. Warm-up. Page 88
Time: 5 minutes

Any time you can get students to produce language using newly acquired structures, it should be encouraged. Thus, even with very short Warm-ups, get students to compare the contexts described in the book with their real lives.

- Ask students to look at the two pictures to answer the questions.
- Engage students in the topic by asking them what time their alarm goes off and what time they wake up. Have questions ready to go to provide opportunities for conversation. For example:

  Do you use an alarm clock to wake up?

  What time do you get up Monday to Friday?

  Is this time different on Saturday and Sunday?

  Is it ever hard for you to sleep?

  How many hours of sleep do you need?

- Write student-generated information on the board.

CHART 3-11. Simple Present Tense: Asking Information Questions with *When* and *What Time*. Page 89
Time: 10–15 minutes

As with the last chart, it is likely students will be familiar with these information words. Correct students right away so that they use the question forms accurately.

- Write the chart title on the board.
- Ask students yes / no questions that have to do with time first and write them on the board. For example:

  Do you wake up early on weekends?

  Does your father work late?

- As with the previous chart, ask students what question words and phrases can be used to ask questions about time.

- Write the question words that will elicit answers explaining *when* and *what time*. For example:

    Do you wake up early? When?
    When do you wake up?

    Does your father get home late? What time?
    What time does your father get home?

- Ask students to answer the questions. Put student-generated information on the board.
- Ask students to read each section of the chart aloud while you write the actual questions on the board.
- Ask students to help you write the word order for information questions. For example:

    Tell me the word order for information questions.
    Question word + does / do + subject + main verb.

- Write one of the sentences from the chart on the board. Then point to each word or phrase and identify it. For example:

    When do you go to class?

- Review the note on the placement of frequency adverbs in the last cell of the right column of the chart.

❏ EXERCISE 55. Looking at grammar.
Page 89
Time: 10 minutes

- Without having students prepare the exercise as seatwork, have students look at the exercise as you read the direction line to them.
- Make sure students know they have to form correct information questions that ask *when* or *what time*.
- Give the first item to one of the stronger students.
- Move from student to student, and have each one complete the question aloud.
- Have other students provide the short answer.
- Correct by writing on the board whenever necessary.

❏ EXERCISE 56. Let's talk: interview.
Page 90
Time: 10–15 minutes

- Instruct students to move around the room with their books, asking peers *when / what time* questions with the correct format.
- Circulate around the room yourself to help any students who are struggling and to provide immediate correction and assistance with word order and / or vocabulary.
- Have students compare answers as a class by writing on the board grammatically correct sentences that describe the habits of the classmates they talked to.
- Remind those students writing sentences to use the third person singular correctly in their responses. Have those students not writing provide feedback on the grammar.

❏ EXERCISE 57. Looking at grammar.
Page 91
Time: 10 minutes

- Read the direction line to students and highlight the completed examples in items 1 and 2.
- Give students time to complete the remainder of the exercise as seatwork.
- Review as a class by having students read both questions and answers aloud.
- Correct target grammar and all associated words.
- Correct pronunciation.

❏ EXERCISE 58. Looking at grammar.
Page 91
Time: 10 minutes

- Give students time to complete each of the three conversations independently as seatwork.
- Walk around the room, helping as needed and making notes on anything that should be raised with the group.
- Correct as a class by having students read the completions. Provide immediate and clear correction.
- Then have pairs read the completed conversations aloud.

❏ EXERCISE 59. Check your knowledge.
Page 93
Time: 10 minutes

- Explain the direction line and highlight the corrected word in item 1.
- Without having students prepare as seatwork, ask them to read each sentence as it is aloud and then correct it on the spot.
- Correct for accuracy and pronunciation.

❏ EXERCISE 60. Looking at grammar.
Page 93
Time: 10 minutes

- Have students think of questions that will elicit the answers given.
- Give students time to complete the exercise as seatwork.
- Review as a class and allow any natural conversation that begins to unfold.
- Correct grammar and put challenging items on the board, as needed.

❏ EXERCISE 61. Speaking and writing:
pairwork. Page 94
Time: 15–20 minutes

> Because students often complete writing at different
> speeds, have them do the preparation for writing in
> class and with their partner. Assign independent
> writing as homework, and remind students that this
> exercise allows them to practice everything they have
> learned in Chapter 3.

Part I
- Put students into pairs.
- Read the direction line as well as the example section.
- Have students take turns asking each other about what they do and do not have. Tell them to ask questions not only about material objects. They can also ask about other things such as friends, health, etc. For example:

  Do you have some good friends?

  Do you have a backache? A headache?

- Ask students to take notes on their partner's responses.

Part II
- Tell students they will now discuss what they like and what they do not like, and read the direction line aloud.
- Have students exchange information and take notes on what they learn from their partner.

Expansion: Ask students questions about what they *like to do*. This structure is used in the sample paragraph, so it would be good to practice.

Do you like to eat pizza?

Do you like to go to movies?

Do you like to listen to rock music?

Do you like to come to school?

Part III
- Tell students to read the sample paragraph very carefully.
- Ask them to describe their partner in writing as homework.

Part IV
- Tell students to exchange papers.
- Explain to students that they should complete the editing check with their partner.
- When both partners are satisfied that their paragraphs have been appropriately edited, ask them to turn in their completed work.

Optional Vocabulary
opens / closes
office hours
pocket
set of keys
good luck
carry
physical description

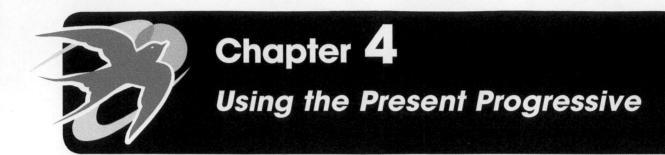

Chapter 4
Using the Present Progressive

CHAPTER 4 SUMMARY

OBJECTIVE: In this chapter, students learn to use the present progressive to describe actions that are currently in progress. Students gain practice using the negative and interrogative forms of the present progressive. The simple present tense and its use in describing habits and scheduled events is then contrasted with the present progressive and its use in describing actions in progress. The chapter presents non-action verbs that do not normally occur in the present progressive and the difference between *think about* + present progressive and *think that* + simple present as an example of how certain non-action verbs are used.

APPROACH: The chapter introduces the present progressive by focusing on its form: *be* + *-ing*. Students are given opportunities to practice in response to visual and written cues, and spelling changes required for present progressive are reviewed. Students are asked about their daily habits as a means of focusing on usage differences between the simple present and present progressive.

TERMINOLOGY: The term *present progressive*, rather than *present continuous*, is used for the *be* + *-ing* form of verbs. The term *non-action verb*, rather than *stative verb*, is used to talk about verbs that express physical or emotional need, mental awareness, and sensory experience. The term *non-action* is more descriptive than *stative* and reminds students of the function of these verbs.

❏ **EXERCISE 1.** Warm-up. Page 96
Time: 5 minutes

Some beginners may already be familiar with the present progressive. Explain that present progressive verb forms are used to describe temporary situations at the moment of speaking.

• Ask students to look at the two pictures and complete items 1 and 2.
• Ask students to talk about any other conditions and / or actions they see in the illustrations. Write these on the board. For example:

David is not sad.	*Nancy is tired.*
David is not unhappy.	*Nancy is unhappy.*
David is singing.	*Nancy is rubbing her eye.*
David is smiling.	*Nancy is not smiling.*

CHART 4-1. *Be* + *-ing*: the Present Progressive. Page 96
Time: 10–15 minutes

Though the present progressive may be review for some beginners, they may not recognize the term. Explain that the term *present continuous* is used in some texts and that it describes an action that is in progress at the moment of speaking.

• Write the chart title on the board.
• Ask students what they are doing right now and write this question on the board.
• Underline the important elements of the question— that is, the elements of the present progressive:

  What <u>are</u> you do<u>ing</u> right now?

• Write all answers that students give on the board, and explain as you reformulate them into the correct present progressive form, if incorrect when given. For example:

  Maya: I listen to my teacher.
  You: For present progressive, we need the verb be + -ing form, as in the question. So, Maya <u>is</u> listen<u>ing</u> to her teacher.
  Han: I am reading my book.
  You: Very good. We can say, Han <u>is</u> read<u>ing</u> his book.

• Ask students to read example sentences (a)–(c) aloud, in turn.
• Write these sentences on the board and underline the *be* and *-ing* forms.
• Read or review the notes in the chart and stress that we use this tense to describe something that is happening right now, and we can observe.
• Because forms of the verb *be* will occur as helping verbs in most tenses, reiterate that these forms are called helping verbs and that they will appear as helping verbs in both past and future tenses.

❏ **EXERCISE 2.** Looking at grammar.
Page 97
Time: 5–10 minutes

• Have students respond to these items on sight, without prior preparation.
• Ask students to take turns reading their completions,

using the correct form of the verb *be* for the subject pronoun used.

- Stress that only the helping verb changes and not the *-ing* form and provide immediate and overt correction of target grammar and pronunciation.
- Remind students that the actions and events in these items are happening right now. Tell them that observations of actions in progress must be described by the present progressive.

❏ EXERCISE 3. Looking at grammar.
Page 97
Time: 5–10 minutes

- Give students a few minutes to prepare these answers as seatwork.
- Correct by having students take turns reading their completions aloud.

❏ EXERCISE 4. Let's talk: class activity.
Page 97
Time: 10–15 minutes

- Instruct students to close their books.
- Tell them that you will act out verbs and that they will tell you what you are doing.
- Write the following prompt on the board to support students as they respond spontaneously to your actions:

    Teacher: What <u>am</u> I do<u>ing</u>?
    Class: You <u>are</u> xxxx<u>ing</u>.

- Act out items 1–6 and write students' correct responses on the board.

Expansion: Put students into pairs. Ask the first student to begin by miming or acting out a verb of his or her choice while his or her partner says what the verb is, using the correct present progressive form. The first student then instructs his or her partner by saying, *You are combing your hair* until the partner acts out that instruction. Then tell the second student to give an instruction. This back-and-forth gives both students a chance to direct the action and practice the target grammar in an engaged fashion. Circulate, assisting students who need help getting going, and taking notes on any mistakes made during this exercise. Review the errors before moving on.

❏ EXERCISE 5. Let's talk: pairwork. Page 98
Time: 10 minutes

- Put students into pairs.
- Review the direction line.
- Walk around the room helping those pairs who need it and taking notes on any repeated errors that should be the focus of later review.
- Assign one item to each pair.
- Correct the exercise by having one member of each pair go to the board and write a complete sentence for the item.
- The rest of the class will determine whether the sentence is correct.

❏ EXERCISE 6. Let's talk: class activity.
Page 99
Time: 10–15 minutes

- Instruct students to close their books.
- Explain to students that you will be giving them instructions that they will then carry out and describe using the present progressive.
- To demonstrate this expectation, go to the board.
- Begin writing *I am writing on the board* on the board.
- Say, *I am writing on the board* while you are still doing so.
- Next turn to one student in the class and give him or her an instruction, either from the examples modeled in the book or of your own invention. For example:

    You: Please stand on one foot.
    Student: (stands on one foot)
    You: What are you doing?
    Student: I am standing on one foot.

- Continue with the models and directions given in the book.

Expansion: The activity above can be expanded into the children's game Simon Says, which you can play with the entire class. However, before going ahead, you should first assess whether your students may find it too juvenile.

Tell students they will play a game called Simon Says, but in this case it is called (Your Name) Says. Have students stand up as you explain the rules. Tell them they should do whatever you tell them to do when you start by saying, for example, *Martha Says*. However, if your instructions do not start with those words, students should not follow the instructions. As an example, tell the class *Martha says, look out the window*. Then ask them what they are doing. As a group, they need to respond by using the first person plural (*we*) and the present progressive: *We are looking out the window*. After five to eight Martha Says–style instructions, give an instruction without this initial statement. Tell any student who follows the instruction that does not start with *Martha Says* to sit down. The winner is the only student who does not follow the non–*Martha Says* instructions.

This game has the following goals: (1) to expand students' abilities to respond to context cues and directions in English, (2) to provide an opportunity for students to describe what they are doing by using the present progressive, (3) to permit students to expand their understandings of random vocabulary, and (4) to allow students to feel more autonomous as they acquire more vocabulary.

Before you begin the game, perform or have students perform the actions in the suggested instructions.

Suggested instructions:
hop on one foot
close your eyes
turn around repeatedly
hum your favorite song
count silently to fifty, in English
sit in someone else's desk or chair

clear your throat
wink
march in place
dance around your desk
blink
wave to an imaginary friend

❑ **EXERCISE 7.** Listening. Page 99
Time: 10–15 minutes

- Make sure that the CD player is ready and you have the correct CD track number.
- Read the direction lines to the class.
- Have students take turns reading the brief paragraph describing Tony. Ask students what guesses they can make about Tony's behavior.
- Review any unfamiliar vocabulary from the paragraph before starting the CD track.
- Play the CD track.
- Pause the CD if necessary to give students time to finalize their answers.
- After students have completed all ten items, correct as a group and write any particularly challenging items on the board.

Optional Vocabulary

helping verbs	fix (a computer)
snowing	kick (a ball)
counting	clap
waving	lazy
ceiling	

❑ **EXERCISE 8.** Warm-up. Page 100
Time: 5 minutes

- Review the direction line with your students.
- Review the following: consonants, vowels.
- Have students respond to items 1–4 and ask them to explain what the verbs mean.

CHART 4-2. Spelling of -ing. Page 100
Time: 10–15 minutes

> Though beginners are likely to be somewhat familiar with the present progressive, it is unlikely that they are very familiar with the spelling rules, which are important to know for writing. Tell students that their energies are best spent memorizing spelling rules and exceptions rather than trying to understand how each rule came about.

- Write the chart title on the board.
- Tell students that it is best to learn spelling rules in a rote fashion.
- Have a student read Rule 1 aloud while you write the accompanying example, the conditions for each rule, and the spelling change on the board. For example:

Rule 1
smi<u>le</u>   →   smi<u>ling</u>
consonant + -e   →   drop the -e and add -ing

- Repeat this presentation of the remaining rules, presenting each one slowly and clearly so that students can become familiar with the pattern for each rule.
- After you have completed the chart, review the exceptions and tell students that they will now practice the rules.

❑ **EXERCISE 9.** Looking at spelling.
Page 100
Time: 5–10 minutes

- For this exercise have individual students go to the board to write the -ing form of the items given.
- You can likely fit five students at a time at the board.
- Have students who do not go to the board check if the items written on the board are correct.

❑ **EXERCISE 10.** Looking at spelling.
Page 101
Time: 5–10 minutes

- Read the direction line.
- Explain that students will write the actions you do, in the present progressive form, as you are doing the actions.
- Remind students to follow the spelling rules as they change each verb to the -ing form.
- Correct students' work immediately and overtly.

❑ **EXERCISE 11.** Looking at grammar.
Page 101
Time: 10 minutes

- Give students time to complete these items first as seatwork.
- Correct by reviewing as a class.
- Make sure to ask students how to spell the -ing form and provide immediate and precise correction.

Optional Vocabulary

double	staff
plan	manager
bake	battery
lobby	

❑ **EXERCISE 12.** Warm-up. Page 101
Time: 5 minutes

- Ask students to look at the illustration and choose the affirmative or negative form of the verb for each item.
- Correct and review. Correct pronunciation as well.

CHART 4-3. Present Progressive: Negatives.
Page 102
Time: 10–15 minutes

> In presenting this chart, emphasize the placement of *not* and the formation of contractions. Remind

students that the word *not* comes after the helping verb and that contractions are made with the helping verb, not with the *-ing* participle. Some beginners will probably be familiar with the negative forms of the present progressive.

- Write the chart title on the board.
- Ask your students what they are *not* doing at the moment, and write this question on the board. For example:

  What are you not doing right now?

- Encourage students to be as imaginative in their responses as possible and provide them with a creative example of your own. For example:

  What are you not doing right now?
  I am not skiing right now.

- Write as many student-generated examples as you can on the board and try to use a variety of persons and numbers.

  We are not dancing in the streets of Paris.
  Mika is not flying in an airplane.
  Carlos and Ahmad are not rock climbing.
  You are not sleeping . . . or are you?

- Have students read example sentences (a)–(c) aloud. Write these examples on the board along with the formulaic conjugation shown on the right of the chart.

❏ EXERCISE 13. Looking at grammar.
Page 102
Time: 10 minutes

- Model the example given in the book with one or two of the stronger students.
- Give students time to complete the sentences in each situation as seatwork.
- Remind students that one student should write a negative sentence and one should write an affirmative sentence.
- Have students take turns reading their completions aloud and provide immediate correction of the target grammar and its pronunciation.

❏ EXERCISE 14. Looking at grammar.
Page 104
Time: 10 minutes

Part I
- Write the sentences about Jamal on the board and establish his occupation, his work situation, and his personal qualities as a way of preparing students to describe the activities he is doing at the moment.
- Have students check the sentences that make sense and discuss any unfamiliar vocabulary.

Part II
- Give students time to create their own sentences based on Part I.
- Have students write their completed sentences on the board and read them aloud.

- Call on students who haven't written their sentences on the board to correct the board work. Tell them to focus on the spelling of the *-ing* words as well as the placement of the negatives (contractions with *not*).

❏ EXERCISE 15. Let's talk. Page 105
Time: 10–15 minutes

- Put students into groups of three or four.
- Read the direction line to students and explain that they must use their imaginations to describe what various people are doing right now, as, of course, they cannot know.
- Circulate around the room and assist students as they generate sentences describing what various people are doing.
- Have students read their sentences aloud and correct for accuracy, spelling, and pronunciation.

Expansion: For each group, prepare index cards stating the name of a person not included in the list in Exercise 15. The groups have to generate sentences describing what that person is doing right now. Each group then reads its unique sentences aloud, and the other groups must guess about whom the sentences have been written.

Suggested people (use actual names if you sense your students share enough of a cultural frame of reference to do so; if not, use descriptions and titles):

  the head of Apple or Microsoft (or Bill Gates)
  a famous pop star (Katy Perry, Madonna, Usher, or Psy)
  the head of the United Nations
  the president of the United States (or the leader of another country)
  an Olympic athlete (Michael Phelps or Kim Yuna)
  a wealthy businessperson (Donald Trump)
  the pope
  the Dalai Lama
  an Oscar-winning actress (Lupita Nyong'o)
  an Oscar-winning actor (Matthew McConaughey)
  a new mother / father
  a new infant
  the originator of Facebook (Mark Zuckerberg)

Optional Vocabulary
drive by
daydream
change the oil
a bill
repair an engine
neighbor
garden

❏ EXERCISE 16. Warm-up. Page 105
Time: 5 minutes

- Have students take turns reading an item aloud and giving the correct answer.
- Ask students what they notice about the possible answers given.

CHART 4-4. Present Progressive: Questions.
Page 105
Time: 10–15 minutes

> Remind students of what they learned about this topic in earlier chapters. Be prepared to stress the placement of the helping verb in yes / no questions.

- Write the chart title on the board.
- Ask students yes / no questions in the present progressive and write both the questions and the answers on the board.
- If students answer incorrectly, correct them right away and explain that short answers contain only *yes* or *no*, the subject and the helping verb, and a negative word, if needed. For example:

  Marta, are you studying Italian right now?
  No, I'm not.
  Ali, are you learning English right now?
  Yes, I am.

- Have students take turns reading the example sentences (a) and (b) to you aloud. Write these on the board.
- Underline the important elements of the short answers. Also ask students to supply the long (complete) answer that each short answer represents.
- Tell students that, as they learned before, information questions (those that begin with *wh*-question words) require responses that include additional, specific information, not just an affirmation or negation.
- Have students read example sentences (c)–(e). Write the questions on the board and ask students what the expected answers are.
- Stress that with information questions, the *wh*-question word is placed before the helping verb.

❑ EXERCISE 17. Looking at grammar.
Page 106
Time: 10 minutes

- Make sure that students understand the task at hand: They must make questions from the sentences that are in parentheses.
- Give students time to complete these items as seatwork.
- Review and correct by having students read their completions aloud.

❑ EXERCISE 18. Vocabulary and speaking:
pairwork. Page 106
Time: 10–15 minutes

- Put students into pairs.

Part I
- Tell students to discuss the phrases in Part I with their partner and put a check mark next to the phrases they know.

- Circulate around the room and help students by eliciting their explanations of the phrases they know and carefully leading them toward understanding the phrases they don't know (or don't think they know).

Part II
- Read the direction line carefully, making sure that students understand what is required.
- Stress that Partner A must ask questions about the activities that are represented in the pictures on page 107, thus giving Partner B a chance to respond with *No*, and then use the appropriate vocabulary to describe the actions in the pictures on page 501 in the present progressive.
- Review Parts I and II by asking pairs to read aloud the exchanges they prepared and correcting as needed.

Expansion: Make this a lively speaking opportunity in your class. Ask students questions for which the answer will be *No*. Tell them to answer and then make a correct statement as in this exercise. For example:

  Are we speaking French?
  Are you driving to school?
  Is your classmate eating an ice-cream cone?
  Is your dinner cooking now?

Continue with students asking the questions.

❑ EXERCISE 19. Looking at grammar.
Page 108
Time: 10 minutes

- Read the direction line and explain that students must read the sentence in parentheses carefully in order to have the correct information to make a question.
- Review the completed example sentence.
- Have students respond to each item on sight and ask associated questions for each item, without prior preparation.
- Correct immediately and overtly and put any particularly challenging exercises on the board for further discussion.

❑ EXERCISE 20. Looking at grammar.
Page 108
Time: 10 minutes

- Review the two completed example items and restate the direction line.
- Remind students that they need to do two things: make questions and also provide the short answers.
- Give students time to complete the exercise as seatwork.
- Have students take turns reading their questions and short answers aloud and correct as needed.

Optional Vocabulary
lie
dance
do, make, take (phrases from page 106)
take a break
do an exercise
why? . . . because

□ EXERCISE 21. Warm-up. Page 109
Time: 5–10 minutes

- Have students think about their daily habits and remind them of what they have already learned regarding simple present tense and daily habits.
- Ask students to add to the daily activities and create questions in addition to those in items 1–3 in this Warm-up.
- Write any additional questions students generate on the board. For example:

  Do you use your computer every day?

  Do you exercise every day?

  Do you send e-mails every day?

  Do you watch TV every day?

- Next, have students use the simple present questions they generated above to create questions in the present progressive, like those in items 4–6 of the Warm-up exercise. Write these questions on the board. For example:

Do you use your computer every day?	*Are you using your computer now?*
Do you exercise every day?	*Are you exercising now?*
Do you send e-mails every day?	*Are you sending e-mails now?*
Do you watch TV every day?	*Are you watching TV now?*

- Review the items on the board along with those in the Warm-up. From this work, have students articulate their own rules for how these two tenses are used.

CHART 4-5. Simple Present Tense vs. the Present Progressive. Page 110
Time: 10–15 minutes

> The Warm-up has prepared students to articulate the differences between the simple present and the present progressive. As much as possible, use the information students have provided to present the information in the chart.

- Write the chart title on the board.
- Write two columns on the board. For example:

  Simple Present   *Present Progressive*

- Write the rules for the use of both tenses in students' own words (as given during the Warm-up) on the board, under the appropriate heading.
- Ask a student to read the notes about the simple present (in the first box on the left) aloud. This should expand upon the usage rules generated by students, which you will have already put on the board. Add to the student-generated rules in the *Simple Present* column.
- Ask another student to read the notes about the present progressive (in the first box on the right) aloud and write additions to student-generated rules in the *Present Progressive* column.

- Ask students to read the simple present conjugation of *talk* aloud as you write the Statement, Negative, and Question simple present conjugations of *talk* on the board.
- Then ask students to read the present progressive conjugation of *talk* aloud as you write the complete Statement, Negative, and Question present progressive conjugations of *talk* on the board.
- Involve as many students as you can in presenting the conjugations above.
- Ask students to ask additional questions about daily activities.
- Write any questions students generate on the board. For example:

  Do you drink coffee for breakfast every day?

  Do you walk to school every day?

  Do you send a text message every day?

  Do you eat lunch at noon every day?

- Next, have students use the simple present questions they have just generated to create questions in the present progressive. Write these questions on the board. For example:

Do you drink coffee for breakfast every day?	*Are you drinking coffee now?*
Do you walk to school every day?	*Are you walking to school now?*
Do you send a text message every day?	*Are you sending a text message now?*
Do you eat lunch at school every day?	*Are you eating lunch at school now?*

- Ask students to answer the sets of questions on the board and have students articulate the rules for how these two tenses are used.

□ EXERCISE 22. Looking at grammar.
Page 110
Time: 5–10 minutes

- Review the completed example item with students.
- Have students read the items in the exercise on sight, without prior preparation.
- Have students select, on sight, the correct completion and be prepared to explain and justify their completions.

□ EXERCISE 23. Looking at grammar.
Page 111
Time: 10 minutes

- Read the direction line with students and review the completed examples in item 1.
- Give students time to complete the exercise as seatwork.
- Circulate around the room and assist students as needed.
- Correct for accuracy and pronunciation and ask students to define and discuss any vocabulary that will provide an opportunity to speak in class. For example: *hometown, cook, vegetarian.*

❏ EXERCISE 24. Listening. Page 111
Time: 10 minutes

- Make sure the CD player is ready and you have the correct track number.
- Read the direction line and review the completed example in the book with students.
- Tell students to listen to the sentences and then decide whether each sentence describes an action that is happening right now or an action that happens every day.
- Play the track through once and have students select the correct completion for each sentence they hear.
- Correct and review by playing the track again and stopping after each item to allow students to correct and discuss. Alternatively, read the script aloud, taking as much time as needed between each item.

❏ EXERCISE 25. Let's talk: pairwork.
Page 112
Time: 10–15 minutes

- Put students into pairs.
- Read the direction line to students.
- Explain that students will first ask a question using the present progressive and then ask a question using the simple present. Then model the example with one student.
- Emphasize that when giving a short answer, students need to use the helping verb *is* for a question in the present progressive and *does* for a question in the simple present.

Expansion: Give an index card containing one of the phrases in the box to each student. Ask students to write a question using their phrase. Have volunteers choose someone, ask their question, and then ask a follow-up question:

    Do you drink tea in the morning?

    No, I don't.

    What do you drink?

    I drink coffee.

❏ EXERCISE 26. Looking at grammar.
Page 113
Time: 10 minutes

- Explain the directions carefully. Make sure students understand that each question may be completed with more than one of the words listed in the box.
- Tell students that for each item they will need to make a question with all the words from the box that can be combined with the initial question words.
- Have students review the completed example carefully so they understand the task fully. For example, call on different students to read, separately, each possible question in item 1.
- Give students time to complete this exercise independently as seatwork.
- Review as a class by having different students read different possible questions.
- Have students tell you which of the words in the boxes *cannot* be combined with the initial question words.

❏ EXERCISE 27. Looking at grammar.
Page 113
Time: 10 minutes

- Explain that students need to choose the correct helping verb for each question.
- Guide students to state the two questions they must answer for each item: *Which tense is being used (to determine whether the helping verb do or be is needed)?* and *Which person and number is needed (to determine the correct form of the helping verb)?*
- Have students complete the exercise on sight by having various students take turns reading the completion aloud.

❏ EXERCISE 28. Listening. Page 114
Time: 10 minutes

- Make sure the CD player is ready and you have the correct track number.
- Review the completed example with students.
- Read the direction line with students. Make sure they understand that they must complete each blank with all the words they hear on the CD that do not appear on the page.
- Tell students they will need to listen very carefully as they read each sentence, because sometimes the printed sentence includes the subject and sometimes it does not. Sometimes both the subject and verb are missing, and sometimes only the verb is missing.
- Play the track through once as students listen. Then play each exchange again, pausing for students to write the missing words for each sentence they hear.
- Review by reading the script, pausing at each blank to allow students to read their completions aloud. Correct for accuracy and pronunciation.

❏ EXERCISE 29. Looking at grammar.
Page 114
Time: 10 minutes

- Read the direction line to students.
- Have two students read the completed Student A–Student B dialogue in item 1.
- Give students time to complete the remaining five items on their own.
- Review by having students read their completions aloud in turn.
- Provide immediate and complete correction.

❏ EXERCISE 30. Reading and grammar.
Page 115
Time: 15–25 minutes

Part I
- Have students read the paragraph silently.
- Have students take turns reading the sentences in the paragraph aloud.
- Review the new vocabulary items listed in the yellow flag as well as familiar vocabulary in the paragraph. Ask students to paraphrase parts of the text in their own words.

Part II

- Give students time to read through and complete the questions.
- Tell students to try to refrain from referring back to the paragraph above unless they really need to.
- Have students take turns providing the helping verbs required, asking the newly completed questions, and answering the questions based on the paragraph.
- Encourage discussion of the parts of the paragraph that contain the answers to the questions students have read aloud.

Part III

- Have students check the important qualities for a server in item 1. Ask students whether they are getting their ideas only from the text or also from their own experiences (either eating in a restaurant or working in one or both).
- Review any words in item 1 that may require clarification (for example, *formal*) by asking students to try to define or explain them.
- Lead discussions about the questions in items 2–4 and encourage as many diverse and complementary points of view as possible.
- Write ideas, responses, and associated vocabulary (especially vocabulary generated by students) on the board and encourage students to take notes. Focus on facilitating a lively and engaging discussion by asking additional unscripted questions that will stimulate conversation.

Optional Vocabulary

rain	conductor
shine	hallway
hometown	online
help	hang
rice and beans	closet
meat	minimum wage
vegetables	server
vegetarian	tips
check phone for messages	formal
text	talkative
ticket	workday
wallet	workweek

❏ EXERCISE 31. Warm-up. Page 116
Time: 5 minutes

- Have students take turns reading the sentences in the Warm-up.
- Following the direction line, ask students what they notice about the verbs in red.
- Ask students if they can guess why *see* and *hear* are not in the progressive form.
- Ask students to describe what happens when they *see*, *hear*, *think*, and so on, and lead them to discuss how these verbs do not express visible action.

CHART 4-6. Non-Action Verbs Not Used in the Present Progressive. Page 116
Time: 10–15 minutes

Building on the Warm-up, continue your discussion of other verbs that are considered non-action. These verbs describe conditions or sensory experiences rather than actions. Because many beginners already have some familiarity with these verbs, encourage students to contribute to the discussion of this topic. As noted earlier in the chapter, this text refers to these verbs as non-action verbs, but other grammar books call the same category of verbs stative. Because some students may know the term *stative*, it may be useful to mention this term.

- Write the chart title on the board.
- Have two different students read example sentences (a) and (b), in turn. Write these sentences on the board.
- Review the notes on the right with students and discuss the fact that these non-action verbs describe certain types of experiences—such as physical needs, emotions, mental states, and sensory experiences—rather than actions.
- Ask students to list other non-action verbs, without looking further at the chart.
- For each additional non-action verb that students provide, generate a sentence using a present progressive verb. Then ask students to build upon your sentence with a sentence containing a non-action verb. For example:

hate	*I am changing the TV channel.*	*I hate violence.*
like	*I am now watching a comedy.*	*I like it.*

❏ EXERCISE 32. Looking at grammar.
Page 116
Time: 10 minutes

- Read the direction line to students.
- Explain to students that they will be using the present progressive or simple present, according to the context.
- Tell students to be prepared to explain each use of a non-action verb.
- Have students complete the items in the exercise as seatwork.
- Review as a class by having students read the completed items aloud.
- Correct target grammar and pronunciation while also checking on nontarget vocabulary.
- Have students explain each use of a non-action verb.

❏ EXERCISE 33. Let's talk: interview.
Page 117
Time: 10–15 minutes

- Have students stand up with their books and move around the classroom to conduct their interviews.
- Encourage students to get detailed information from the classmates they interview.

- After most students have completed their interviews, have them return to their seats.
- Ask students to say aloud the complete question they asked for each item in the interview. Write these questions on the board, leaving space below each question to write answers.
- Ask students to share the information they learned by writing complete sentences on the board, below the appropriate question.
- Have the class compare and contrast the information students discovered in their interviews by calling on different students to read their responses for each question.

❏ EXERCISE 34. Warm-up. Page 118
Time: 5 minutes

- Give students time to complete the items.
- Ask students if they can explain the difference between *look at* and *watch*.
- Ask students if they can explain the difference between *hear* and *listen to*.
- Write on the board and discuss any ideas students give about the differences between these verbs.

CHART 4-7. *See, Look At, Watch, Hear,* and *Listen To.* Page 118
Time: 10–15 minutes

> The basic differences among these verbs have to do with the level of active attention on the part of the subject. Some beginners may be able to articulate these differences. Making an effort to explain these differences will help students activate their passive language and gain confidence.

- Write the chart title on the board.
- Write the following verbs on the board:

  See   *Look At*   *Watch*

- Also on the board, make a list of items that a person normally *sees*, *looks at*, or *watches*. For example:

a movie	*Exercise 35*
a baseball game	*a boat*
my watch	*snowflakes*

- Have students decide which items they normally *see*, *look at*, or *watch*, and write each item below the appropriate verb on the board.
- You will use this information to demonstrate whether each verb is an action or non-action verb.

See	*Look At*	*Watch*
a boat	*my watch*	*a movie*
snowflakes	*Exercise 35*	*a baseball game*

- Using the list above, discuss the differences between the three verbs and explain the notes in the right column of the chart.
- Have students read example sentences (a)–(c) aloud. Write them on the board.

- Explain that *see* is used when you have your eyes open and notice what is in front of you. It describes a sensory experience and not an action you actively take.
- Explain that *look at* means to actively direct the sense of sight in a particular direction.
- Explain that *watch* means to actively direct the sense of sight to something that is in motion rather than still.
- Write *Hear* and *Listen To* on the board along with a list of items that we normally hear or listen to. For example:

  music on my MP3 player

  a train in the distance

  birds

  a voice mail message

- Ask students to decide which items a person normally *listens to* and which ones a person *hears*.

Hear	*Listen To*
a train in the distance	*music on my MP3 player*
birds	*a voice mail message*
	birds

- Explain that we hear birds, and we also listen to the birds singing.
- Ask one student to read the example sentences in (d) and one to read the example sentences in (e) aloud.
- Write these sentences on the board.
- Review the notes to the right with students.
- Emphasize that *hear* is used for a sensory experience that happens if you are not deaf and have healthy ears. It describes an activity that is passive, that happens whether you want it to or not. Therefore, *hear* is a non-action verb.
- Explain that *listen to* is used when the subject directs the sense of hearing to something specific. The subject is actively engaged in the activity. Therefore, *listen to* is an action verb.

❏ EXERCISE 35. Let's talk: class activity.
Page 118
Time: 10 minutes

- Ask students to close their books.
- Remind students that *see* and *hear* are physical senses that happen involuntarily.
- Tell students that you will ask questions. They should answer each question using the verb you use in that question.
- Ask different students items 1–9. Ask the same item more than once to give as many students as possible the chance to participate.
- Write student responses on the board to illustrate both content and the target grammar.

❏ EXERCISE 36. Looking at grammar.
Page 119
Time: 15 minutes

- Give students time to read through and complete the sentences as seatwork.
- Walk around the room helping students who need additional support. As this is a lengthy exercise, keep students on track and focused if needed.

- Stop students after they have completed Situation 1 and review it by having students take turns reading their completions aloud.
- Correct immediately and make sure you explain why certain verbs need the simple present and others require the present progressive.
- Have students continue and complete the remainder of the exercise.
- Correct and review Situation 2 as you did Situation 1. Write challenging items on the board for further illustration.

Expansion: Game. Bring in a big picture or a photo that shows a lot of activities going on. It could be a picture of a playground, a zoo, or a beach. Put students into groups of three or four with one student writing down sentences that the group creates about the activities going on. Go around to each group and check the sentences. The group with the most correct sentences wins.

Optional Vocabulary

podcast	gum
weather	bench
taste	accountant
smell	joggers
believe	squirrels
sniff-sniff	ground
teenagers	nut
elderly	ducks
corner	park
chew	picnic

❏ **EXERCISE 37.** Warm-up. Page 120
Time: 5 minutes

Warm-up exercises like this one get students talking because they are interested in the topic. It is critical to students' whole language acquisition as well as their mastery of accurate grammar that they gain the ability to speak comfortably about a wide range of topics. Therefore, get students speaking as often as possible by using topics of personal interest that they are likely to have something to say about. Students' need to speak kindles their interest in learning the grammatical structures they need to express themselves. If you can present grammar when students have just "exercised" their speaking, they are more primed to attend with enthusiasm.

- Ask different students to read items 1–3 aloud.
- Discuss the items and put student-generated vocabulary on the board.
- Ask students to explain the difference between item 1 and item 2 in terms of the tense used in each sentence.
- If possible, encourage students to say why they think it is difficult to be a parent and help them expand their vocabulary in doing so.

- Write any words that may come up on the board while facilitating a dynamic minidiscussion. For example:

parenting	*joy*
responsibility	*expense*
love	*education*
fear	*freedom*

CHART 4-8. *Think About* and *Think That.*
Page 121
Time: 10–15 minutes

The target grammar, *think about* and *think that*, allows students to express their opinions and feelings. For the first time, they can talk about something other than what is actually happening right here and now. This is an important leap for beginners. The grammatical structure that follows *think that* is a noun clause. Although students have not yet encountered sentences with more than one clause, teaching them to express their thoughts is extremely valuable to their growth as English language learners and users. The book presents this more sophisticated grammar formulaically, as a simple pattern students can follow. The instructor should anticipate questions and concerns accordingly. However, the focus should be on the ability students gain to speak more meaningfully at an earlier stage of their language acquisition rather than on the somewhat-advanced nature of the pattern itself. Although students are not yet ready to manipulate the elements involved, they can readily express themselves by using the *think that + statement* formula.

- Write the chart title on the board.
- Ask students a variety of *think about* and *think that* questions and write these on the board. For example:

    Do you often think about your family?

    Do you often think about your future?

    Do you think that English is an important language?

    Do you think that English is an easy language?

    Do you think that education is more important than experience?

    Do you think that the world has too many people?

    Do you think that laughter is the best medicine?

- Elicit answers and show students, step-by-step, how to put their answers in the correct form. For example:

    Ricardo: I think my future every moment.

    You: Okay, Ricardo. You are missing the preposition about but let's get your sentence on the board.

    Ricardo thinks about his future every moment.

    Xian: Yes, English is an important language.

    You: Okay, Xian, you think that English is important. Let's write that on the board:

    Xian thinks that English is an important language.

- Using this interactive approach, try to get as many student thoughts into correct sentences on the board as possible.

- As you correct and write students' ideas on the board, be very explicit about what you are correcting and make sure that students recognize each correction you are making by asking them leading questions.
- Now turn to the chart and ask students to take turns reading example sentences (a) and (b) aloud.
- Write these sentences on the board and review the notes in the right column of the chart.
- Ask other students to take turns reading example sentences (c)–(e) aloud.
- Stress that *think that* + statement expresses an opinion and that as we all like talking about our opinions, this is very important grammar to learn.
- Read the notes in the right column of the chart and emphasize that the present progressive is used with *think about* and not with *think that*.
- Ask other students to read example sentences (f) and (g).
- Explain that when giving an opinion, *that* is often omitted. Demonstrate this by reading sentences (f) and (g) again, omitting *that*.
- Finally, read the note in the right column of the chart aloud.

❏ EXERCISE 38. Grammar and speaking.
Page 121
Time: 10 minutes

- Have students create sentences with the adjectives given, without prior preparation.
- Review the completed example item with them.
- Ask a strong student to complete item 2 and write on the board as he or she is speaking, using the proper sentence format.
- Review and correct the sentence so that what is on the board is completely accurate.
- Invite other students to make sentences using the other adjectives provided. Discuss these opinions.
- Repeat the process above with the final two items so that items 2–4 are written correctly on the board.
- If students don't seem confident about the grammar, ask them to find the subject and verb and also the opinion in each sentence, and mark these on the board.
- Try to get students to discuss item 2 and item 4 actively. Encourage their disagreement while you correct their grammar and pronunciation.

❏ EXERCISE 39. Writing and speaking.
Page 121
Time: 10–15 minutes

- Give students time to complete the sentences by using their own words.
- Encourage them to express real opinions, albeit ones they are willing to discuss with the class.
- Once students have completed all the sentences, have them read their completions aloud.
- Write the completions that contain grammatical errors on the board. Correct these as a class as visually and clearly as possible.

- Discuss the opinions expressed in the completed sentences. Encourage students to express related opinions using the target grammar.

❏ EXERCISE 40. Let's talk: game. Page 122
Time: 10 minutes

- Explain to students that this game resembles 20 Questions, a well-known guessing game.
- Put students into small groups and make sure they understand the way the game works. One student first names the general category of the animal or food item he or she is thinking about, and then others in the group ask and get answers to yes / no questions until they guess what the student is thinking about.
- Move around the room and assist students to participate as actively as possible.
- Be ready to supply vocabulary as needed.

❏ EXERCISE 41. Reading. Page 122
Time: 10–15 minutes

- Give students time to read through the passage once.
- Instruct them to circle *T* or *F* for true or false and to be ready to justify their answers by referring to the paragraph.
- Have students take turns reading aloud. Ask questions about nontarget words.

❏ EXERCISE 42. Looking at grammar.
Page 123
Time: 10 minutes

- Conduct as a whole-class exercise whereby students respond to each item on sight.
- Read the direction line aloud and review the completed example with the class.
- Have students take turns reading and completing items on sight.
- If a student doesn't get an item correct, invite others to respond and explain why his or her answer is correct.

❏ EXERCISE 43. Check your knowledge.
Page 123
Time: 10 minutes

- Review the corrected example item with students and explain that they will have to identify the errors and write the corrections.
- Give students time to complete this exercise as seatwork.
- Correct as a class, and have students explain why they made each correction.
- Put particularly challenging items on the board for the entire class to work on.

❑ EXERCISE 44. Reading and writing.

Page 124

Time: 10–15 minutes

Part I

- Give students time to read through the paragraph independently.
- Have students take turns reading the sentences in the paragraph aloud.

Part II

- Explain that students' task is to imagine themselves awake and unable to sleep.
- Explain that students should write what they are thinking about. Encourage students to use a combination of both simple present and present progressive verbs in their paragraphs.

- Assign the paragraph for homework or have students do it in class and exchange with a partner to complete Part III.

Part III

- Tell students to exchange paragraphs.
- Have six students take turns reading aloud the six items listed. Remind them that these items are required in their paragraphs.
- Write the items on the board.
- Have students check each item in the list to indicate that it is included in their paragraph.
- Return to the original paragraph, "A Sleepless Night," and have students point out the location of each required item.

Chapter 5

Talking About the Present

CHAPTER SUMMARY

OBJECTIVE: In this chapter, students learn to use accurate grammar to discuss their present situations. The text presents the present tense in combination with prepositional phrases of time and location to describe when and where scheduled events take place. Phrases and questions with *it* and *there* are taught in order to give students the ability to describe their surroundings concretely and ask for further specific information. By learning additional prepositions and prepositional phrases, students are able to describe the present more accurately. Finally, students learn to talk about their needs and wants grammatically, and they also learn to present these needs and wants more politely and formally by using *would like*.

APPROACH: The chapter begins with using *it* to talk about time and moves on to prepositions of time. It then presents *it* and *what* to talk about the weather, followed by statements and questions with *there* + *be* and prepositions of place. Finally, in teaching first how to express present needs and wants, and then how to express these needs and wants politely with *would like*, the chapter fosters more autonomy and productive speech, which in turn solidifies mastery.

TERMINOLOGY: The text continues to use a minimum of grammatical terminology and to refer to phrases using the grammar form so that students immediately grasp their purpose. Most grammar points are described as *using ___ to talk about ___*, which further emphasizes that the point of grammatically accuracy is meaningful expression.

❏ **EXERCISE 1.** Warm-up. Page 125
Time: 5–10 minutes

> Some beginners may already be familiar with *it* + time phrases. Capitalize on their knowledge by asking them to use what they know.

- Ask students to tell you what time it is, what day it is, and what month it is right now.
- Ask the questions above orally and then, with the assistance of students, write accurate and complete responses on the board. For example:

  Ask: What time is it? *Write the students' response: It is 11:45 A.M.*

  Ask: What day is it? *Write the students' response: It is Friday.*

  Ask: What month is it? *Write the students' response: It is March.*

- Ask students to look at the three pictures in the Warm-up and respond to items 1–3.
- Review students' responses as a class and write any additional vocabulary that arises on the board.

CHART 5-1. Using *It* to Talk About Time.
Page 125
Time: 10–15 minutes

> The chart presents *it* + *is* with various time-and-date phrases. Although beginners will be familiar with many of these phrases, explain which ones are most common. For example, in speech, *September 15th* is more common than *the 15th of September*. Students will benefit from knowing which phrases they are most likely to hear and / or read.

- Write the chart title on the board.
- Ask different students to read the example questions and answers, (a)–(e), aloud.
- Write the questions and answers on the board.
- Ask students additional questions about times, dates, and months, and write their responses on the board. For example:

  Ask: What is your birthday? *Write: It is October 1.*

  Ask: What is your favorite day of the week? *Write: It is Friday.*

  Ask: What is your favorite month of the year? *Write: It is June.*

❏ **EXERCISE 2.** Looking at grammar.
Page 126
Time: 8–10 minutes

- Read the direction line and ask a student to read the completed example item aloud.
- Give students time to read the answers in each item and supply the correct question.
- Correct together, asking students to take turns reading the questions and answers aloud.

❏ **EXERCISE 3.** Warm-up. Page 127
Time: 5 minutes

- Ask students to think about their weekly schedules.
- Have them read through and complete items 1–3.

- Ask students to read the items aloud as completed sentences.
- Invite students to share and compare other scheduled events that they may have in their lives by asking additional questions.
- Write your questions and student-generated information on the board. Underline the expressions of time. For example:

  Ask: Do you exercise every week? When?
  Write: Marco exercises <u>on Monday and Wednesday</u>.
  Ask: Do you do laundry every week? When?
  Write: Pei-Lin and Noriko do laundry <u>on Sunday</u>.
  Ask: What time do you go to bed every night?
  Write: Gabriela, Fernanda, and Ahmad go to bed <u>at 11:00 P.M.</u>

CHART 5-2. Prepositions of Time. Page 127
Time: 10–15 minutes

> The chart presents prepositions of time, many of which beginners may already know. Prepositions often pose challenges for beginning and advanced students alike as there are so many prepositions used in English and their use is idiomatic rather than literal. In addition, though many patterns can be observed, there are many exceptions within these patterns.
>
> One way to approach prepositions of time is to indicate the types of time periods governed by each preposition: *At* is used for the most specific time, an actual time on the clock. *On* is used for a day of the week or a specific date. *In* is used for periods of time, such as weeks, months, and years.

- Write the chart title on the board.
- Write *at* on the board and ask students to read example sentences (a)–(c) aloud.
- Discuss the notes on the right of the chart and write a few examples and notes on the board. For example, ask students what time their English class starts *at* and what time it finishes *at* and write their answers on the board. Underline the time phrases with *at*. For example:

  What time does English class start at?
  Class starts <u>at 9:00 A.M.</u>
  Class finishes <u>at 11:00 A.M.</u>

- Write *in* on the board. Ask students to read example sentences (d)–(h) aloud.
- Explain that *in* is used for periods of time such as *the morning*, *the evening*, and *the afternoon*.
- Explain that *in* is also used for specific months, years, and centuries.
- Ask students questions to elicit the use of *in*. Write their answers on the board. Underline the time phrases with *in*. For example:

  When do you prefer to study? <u>In the morning or in the evening</u>?
  Lam prefers to study <u>in the evening</u>.
  What month is Christmas in? It is <u>in December</u>.

- Refer to the notes in the right column of the chart. Write the notes and sentences illustrating their use on the board. For example:

  in + a specific month: Febria's birthday is <u>in May</u>.
  in + specific periods of time: Mahmoud visits his mosque <u>in the afternoon</u>.

- Write *on* on the board.
- Ask students to read example sentences (i)–(k) aloud.
- Explain that *on* is used with specific days of the week and dates.
- Ask students questions that will elicit the use of *on* and write the questions and sentences on the board. For example:

  When is your birthday?
  My birthday is <u>on October 31</u>.

- Write *from . . . to* on the board.
- Explain that *from . . . to* is used to show the duration of an activity.
- Have a student read example sentence (l) aloud and write the accompanying note on the board.
- Ask students questions that elicit the appropriate use of *from . . . to*.
- Write questions, examples, and reminders on the board. For example:

  When do you do your homework?
  from + a specific time to + a specific time: I do my homework <u>from 7:30 to 9:00 P.M.</u>

❑ EXERCISE 4. Looking at grammar.
Page 127
Time: 10–12 minutes

- Give students time to read through and complete the items as seatwork.
- Have students take turns reading their completed items aloud.
- Correct overtly and immediately, referring to notes on the board from Chart 5-2 (on page 127).

❑ EXERCISE 5. Let's talk: pairwork. Page 128
Time: 10–15 minutes

- Put students into pairs.
- Read the direction line and review the completed model item.
- As students are working through the items, circulate and assist them.
- Encourage students by asking the questions of both partners at once.
- When students have completed the exercise, review by asking them to read their partner's responses aloud.

Expansion: Do a quick poll about students' study habits by comparing how many students prefer to study in the morning, in the afternoon, and in the evening. Write the results of the poll on the board, using students' names. For example:

  Pierre, Hiro, and Sadaf study <u>in the morning</u>.
  Carolina, Chun Ja, Francis, and Ahmad study <u>in the afternoon</u>.

Junko, Pedro, Maria C., Maria B., and Jing Wen study <u>in the evening</u>.
Marta studies <u>at night</u>.

❏ **EXERCISE 6.** Listening and grammar.
Page 129
Time: 10–15 minutes

Part I
• Have the CD player ready and know which track you will play.
• Read the direction line and tell students they will hear four descriptions. They must match each description to one of the pictures.
• Play the appropriate track while students identify each description.

Part II
• Instruct students to complete the items by using the information they learned in the listening.
• Have students read the completed items aloud.
• Correct students for content and accuracy. Correct students' pronunciation as you go.

Optional Vocabulary
the day *versus* the date
express
be born
was born

❏ **EXERCISE 7.** Warm-up. Page 129
Time: 5 minutes

• Write the word *weather* on the board.
• Ask students to tell you any words they know having to do with weather. Make a word web and write student-generated vocabulary on the board.
• Explain that some weather vocabulary has to do with temperature, some with the air quality or movement, and some with precipitation (rain and snow). For example:

<u>temperature</u>	<u>air</u>	<u>precipitation</u>
mild	sunny	rainy
warm	clear	snowy
hot	cloudy	
chilly	foggy	
cool	windy	
cold	calm	

• Have students read the questions in the Warm-up aloud.
• Compare responses among students and discuss the differences in weather in students' hometowns.
• Ask students to talk about their favorite weather.

CHART 5-3. Using *It* and *What* to Talk About the Weather. Page 130
Time: 10–15 minutes

• Write the chart title on the board.
• Write *It + is + weather adjective* on the board. Explain that English speakers use this formula to describe the weather.

• Ask a student to read example sentences (a)–(c) aloud.
• Ask students to describe the current weather by using specific adjectives.
• Ask other students to read example questions (d)–(f) aloud while you write the three questions on the board.
• Use these questions to ask about weather in parts of the world known to have extreme conditions.
• Write these questions and students' responses on the board. For example:

What's the weather like in the Sahara?
It's very windy and very hot.
How's the weather at the North Pole?
It's extremely cold.
What's the temperature in Jakarta, in summer?
It's above 100 degrees Fahrenheit!

❏ **EXERCISE 8.** Let's talk: pairwork. Page 130
Time: 10–15 minutes

This activity can be a very interesting cross-cultural exercise if your students are from very different parts of the world. Before beginning, ask students what temperatures, for them, are cold, hot, and / or just right. Explain that peoples' perceptions of the weather are determined by the weather they are used to, along with their own personal preferences.

• Put students into pairs and read the direction line aloud.
• Write the question *How's the weather today?* on the board.
• Walk around the room, helping pairs as they compare their opinions on the weather.
• Review as a group.

Expansion: To illustrate the fact that people's perceptions of weather are determined by the weather they are used to as well as their personal preferences, draw a simple x-y graph on the board. Label one end *cold* and the other *hot*. Have students write temperature-related weather adjectives on the board and say what weather temperature they like best.

cold_____|_____hot

❏ **EXERCISE 9.** Let's talk: small groups.
Page 130
Time: 5–10 minutes

• Put students into small groups.
• Ask them if they are familiar with the Fahrenheit temperature scale.
• Ask if they know places, other than the United States, that use the Fahrenheit scale. (It is used in the Bahamas, the Cayman Islands, Palau, and Belize.)
• Give the groups time to complete the items with Celsius temperatures from the box and also to describe the temperature in words.
• Discuss and compare as a class, and remind students that words such as *warm* and *cool* are not scientific: What one person thinks is *cool,* another person might find *mild*.

❑ EXERCISE 10. Let's talk: small groups.
Page 131
Time: 10–15 minutes

> When pair or small-group exercises follow one another, be ready to move students from one group to another. Sometimes, simply moving one person out of each group and into a new group can keep pair and small-group work dynamic. In any case, observe pair, group, and seatwork exercises carefully to see how you can optimize student attention and class momentum.

- Put students into new small groups if such a change could benefit class momentum.
- Explain to students that being able to convert temperature quickly from Celsius to Fahrenheit will allow them to function more independently in a setting where Fahrenheit is used.
- Discuss *exact* versus *approximate*.
- Have a student read the completed example aloud.
- Ask groups to complete the remaining six items.
- Review the items as a group.

❑ EXERCISE 11. Let's talk: interview.
Page 132
Time: 10–15 minutes

- Read the direction line to students.
- Write the Student A questions on the board while having students read the modeled exchange aloud.
- Encourage students to get up and move around during this exercise.
- Review the interviews as a class, asking students to share information they learned about the persons they interviewed.
- Write shared information on the board, as much as possible.
- Correct for accuracy and pronunciation.

Optional Vocabulary
hometown	windy
cloudy	stormy
partly cloudy	location
humid	population
chilly	average temperature
freezing	

❑ EXERCISE 12. Warm-up. Page 133
Time: 5–8 minutes

> It is likely that some beginners will already be familiar with *there is / there are*.

- Ask students to look around the room.
- Ask students to take turns reading and completing items 1–3 on sight.

- Once students have supplied the correct form of *there is / there are*, ask them to make other observations about the classroom and surroundings.
- Write student-generated observations on the board. For example:

  There is a wastebasket in the room.
  There are maps on the wall.

CHART 5-4. *There + Be.* Page 133
Time: 10–15 minutes

- Write the chart title on the board.
- Explain that *there + be* is used to describe what is in a certain place.
- Preteach the word *exists* and give students examples of concrete things that physically exist in the classroom. For example:

  a teacher: There is a teacher in the room.
  chairs: There are chairs in the room.
  tables: There are tables in the room.

- Ask students to read example sentences (a) and (b) aloud.
- Write the accompanying notes on the board.
- Ask students to read example sentences (c) and (d) aloud.
- Write the accompanying notes about contracted forms on the board.

❑ EXERCISE 13. Looking at grammar.
Page 133
Time: 10 minutes

- Read the direction line for students and review the two completed example items with the class.
- Have students complete the remaining items independently as seatwork.
- Correct the exercise by having students take turns reading items aloud.
- Ask students about additional vocabulary embedded within the exercise.

❑ EXERCISE 14. Let's talk: pairwork.
Page 134
Time: 10 minutes

- Put students into pairs.
- Read the direction line aloud and stress that students should look at their partner, not at their books, while completing the exercise.
- Walk around the room, joining pairs and assisting them.
- Remind students to look at each other and remind them that the basic task is to switch from singular *There is* to plural *There are*.

❏ EXERCISE 15. Let's talk: small groups.
Page 134
Time: 10–15 minutes

- Put existing pairs together into small groups.
- Ask everyone to put some of their own personal items on the table.
- Explain the direction line to students and write *There is . . . There are . . .* on the board if it is no longer there.
- Walk around the room, assisting and encouraging students and correcting them in close proximity.

Expansion: Alternatively, bring paper or opaque plastic bags containing odd items to give to each small group. Each bag can contain several of the same items, such as paper clips or rubber bands, along with an odd item or two that you have around your house (a ladle, a bow, a candle, a deck of cards, batteries, soap, etc.). Contents of a typical junk drawer are great for such exercises. To give students additional time practicing *There is / There are*, have students put their items back into their bag and close it up. You can then redistribute the bags to different groups, giving students a new set of items to name. This is also a fun way both to teach daily vocabulary and to invite students to share what they may already know about the names of random items found in a house.

❏ EXERCISE 16. Listening. Page 134
Time: 5–10

- Have the CD player ready and know which track you will play.
- Read the direction line to students and review the completed example with them, emphasizing that they will hear both singular and plural contractions of *there + be.*
- Tell students to listen for a /z/ sound in the ending of *there's*. Listening for this final consonant sound will help them distinguish *there's* from *there're*.
- Remind students to listen also for other words and indicators of singular or plural, such as singular articles and the plural endings of nouns.
- Play the CD.
- Correct the exercise as a class, writing any challenging items on the board for further review.

Optional Vocabulary
comfortable
view
activities
difficult

❏ EXERCISE 17. Warm-up. Page 135
Time: 5–10 minutes

Students will already be familiar with yes / no questions as well as *there + be.*

- Ask students to read the two questions in the Warm-up aloud and respond to them.

CHART 5-5. *There + Be*: Yes / No Questions.
Page 135
Time: 10–15 minutes

Remind students that they are already familiar with this basic form. They have answered questions with short answers and the verb *be*. Now they will learn how to ask these questions.

- Write the chart title on the board.
- Ask a student to read sample question (a) aloud while you write the elements of the structure of yes / no questions on the board. For example:

Question	*Answer*
Be + there + subject?	*Yes, there is / are.*
	No, there isn't / aren't.

- Ask another student to read sample question (b) aloud while you write both the question and the possible short answers on the board.
- Emphasize that students need to read the question carefully to determine if the subject is singular or plural.

❏ EXERCISE 18. Let's talk: pairwork.
Page 135
Time: 10 minutes

Because students have not yet been exposed to quantity / container vocabulary, ask them to focus on the singular article *a* when identifying whether the phrase is singular or plural.

- Put students into pairs.
- Read the direction line to students and have them ask and answer questions about what is in the refrigerator, using the respective items (1–6) for Partner A and Partner B.
- Walk around the room, engaging with different pairs and helping students interact with each other.
- Lead the review of the exercise by asking questions for all twelve items of different members of the class.

❏ EXERCISE 19. Let's talk: small groups.
Page 136
Time: 10 minutes

- Put students into groups.
- Read the direction line to the students.
- Write the name of the city where the class is being held on the board.
- Model the example questions and responses with students and then tell students to begin with one student asking the question.
- Move around the room and assist students.
- Review grammatical accuracy and content as a class by asking the class as a whole if *there is / there are* the items in 1–12 in this city.

❏ EXERCISE 20. Let's talk: class activity.
Page 136
Time: 10 minutes

> Turn to the grid on page 502 which has all the information needed for this exercise and solves "the puzzle" of which hotel students should choose.

- Ask students to take turns reading sentences about the Romero family.
- Explain that students must ask you questions, using the correct structure, to discover whether a particular hotel has a particular feature the family wants.
- As students ask questions about each hotel, answer with the appropriate form: *Yes, there is / are* or *No, there isn't / aren't.*
- The questions will lead students to the name of the correct hotel.

Optional Vocabulary

a bottle of	a public transportation
a bowl of	system
a bag of	hiking trails
a subway system	horses to ride
	ocean-view rooms

❏ EXERCISE 21. Warm-up. Page 137
Time: 5 minutes

> Teach students how to *estimate*, or give approximate numbers, in response to the Warm-up items. Point out that estimating is very useful when discussing numbers that are constantly changing or beyond an ordinary person's experience. Because students learned *approximate* before, encourage them to use this word. Teach *on average, about, almost,* and any other words (*population, guess, roughly, over, under*) that may help them with this task.

- Ask students the first question, *How many students are there at this school?*
- Write the question on the board and discuss with students how they could arrive at an estimate.
- Ask for students' ideas about estimating this number and encourage scientific reasoning, asking them how many classrooms there are and how many students are in each class, on average.
- Write students' responses on the board, along with any additional reasoning they provided.

> *There are 20 classes and there are, on average, 10 students in each class. So, there are about 200 students in this school.*

- Have students read items 2 and 3 aloud and give you their best estimates of the populations of both their country and the world.
- Write student-generated answers on the board, using the target grammar.

> *There are about 190 million people in Brazil.*
> *There are almost 1.5 billion people in China.*
> *There are over 7 billion people in the world.*

CHART 5-6. *There + Be*: Asking Questions with *How Many*. Page 137
Time: 10–15 minutes

- Write the chart title on the board.
- Ask a student to read question (a) aloud, along with its short answer, while you write the question's components on the board. For example:

  How many + subject + are + there?

- Explain that the short answer to a question with *how many* must have a number, an amount, or a quantity word.
- Have another student read question (b) aloud, along with its short answer.
- Stress that *how many* must be followed by a plural noun.

❏ EXERCISE 22. Let's talk: class activity.
Page 137
Time: 10 minutes

- Start this exercise by asking your students the sample question.
- Have various students ask the questions. Students can answer spontaneously or, alternatively, you can direct their questions.
- Correct immediately and clearly, referring back to the board work from the previous chart as needed.

Expansion: Instruct students to look around the room and observe as much as they can. Tell them to look carefully at what objects their classmates have with them, what they are wearing, and what objects are in the room. Then tell students to close their eyes and keep them closed. Ask students *how many* questions using the items from Exercise 22.

Add additional questions. For example:

> *How many pairs of sneakers are there in this classroom?*
> *How many students with glasses are there in this classroom?*
> *How many students with dark / red / short / long hair are there in this classroom?*
> *How many students with red shirts are in this classroom?*
> *How many maps / posters are on the walls of this classroom?*

❏ EXERCISE 23. Let's talk: pairwork.
Page 137
Time: 10–15 minutes

> As students gain comprehension and confidence using English, they will be ready to start pairwork with minimal instruction.

- Put students into pairs.
- Model the example with a student. Then instruct students to ask and answer questions with the items for Partner A and Partner B in the book.
- Walk around the class and monitor student progress, taking notes on mistakes or other matters to address with the whole class.

- Review as a group by asking the whole class to respond to the partner items. Discuss any discrepancies that arise and encourage students to name the states in the United States, the provinces in Canada, and the countries in North America.

□ **EXERCISE 24.** Warm-up. Page 138
Time: 10 minutes

- Give students a chance to read items 1–3 aloud.
- Discuss any related vocabulary and correct pronunciation.

Expansion: To expand this Warm-up, prepare index cards describing famous people by location (expressed by using prepositions of place). Put students into groups of three or four and distribute index cards that can be used to elicit the names of famous people. There may be more than one correct response for each set of clues. For example:

I live in Rome.
I live at St. Peter's Basilica, the Apostolic Palace.
I live on Vatican Hill.

I live in Washington DC.
I live on Pennsylvania Avenue.
I live at the White House.

I work in a firehouse.
I ride on a fire truck.
I arrive at the scene of a house fire.

I work on the ground floor of the building.
I work at a restaurant.
I work in the kitchen.

I sing on the stage.
I work at an opera house.
I wait in the wings.

I work on the maternity floor.
I work at Mass General Hospital.
I work in Boston.

CHART 5-7. Prepositions of Place. Page 138
Time: 10–15 minutes

> One way to approach prepositions is to use schematic diagrams to show what each preposition expresses. Make three diagrams: a specific point on an x-y axis, a specific point on a two-dimensional flat surface, and a point in a three-dimensional space big enough to hold a person. When *at*, *on*, and *in* are used as prepositions of place, *at* indicates a specific point or position, *on* shows location on a two-dimensional flat surface, and *in* shows location in a space that can enclose a person.

- Write the chart title on the board.
- Building on the general physical explanation given above, mention some specific examples of the types of locations governed by *on*, *in*, and *at*. For example:

  on: used for two-dimensional flat surfaces (roads, etc.)
  in: used for a location big enough to contain the subject (in a city, in a country)
  at: used for specific places (at a street address, at the corner of x and y)

- Have a student read example sentence (a) aloud while you write the corresponding notes in the right column of the chart on the board. Stress that *on* is for a flat surface, and draw a simple diagram to illustrate this. For example:

  _____X_____

- Ask other students to read example sentences (b)–(e) aloud while you write the corresponding notes on the board. Explain that *in* is for a bigger, three-dimensional space, one that can enclose the subject. Draw a simple diagram to illustrate this. For example:

  | X |

- Bring in a box and ask a couple of students to put a small object in it. Then ask, *Where is the pen? Where is your pencil?*
- Have other students read sentences (f)–(h) aloud. Explain that in addition to signifying very specific location, *at* shows engagement in certain *activities*. Illustrate the specificity of location and explain the importance of the activity done at this location. For example:

  John works at the Green Market.
  I study at my friend's house.
  Linda is sitting at her desk.

- Read the notes in the right column of the chart and write them on the board. Explain that people who are *at work* and *at school* are not just physically inside those buildings. Rather, they are doing work and school activities.
- Have students read example sentences (i)–(l) aloud. Write the corresponding notes on the board, and explain each of the situations expressed by the prepositional phrases.

□ **EXERCISE 25.** Looking at grammar.
Page 139
Time: 10 minutes

- Read the direction line to students.
- Give them time to complete the exercise as seatwork.
- Have students read the completed sentences aloud.
- Call on more than one student to read answers to questions 8–11.
- Correct prepositional phrases and target grammar immediately.

□ **EXERCISE 26.** Game. Page 140
Time: 10–15 minutes

- Put students into small groups or teams.
- Read the direction line aloud.
- Because the direction line may not be clear to beginning students, explain that students need to do two things: First choose the correct preposition and then match the proper names from the box with the locations in items 1–3.
- Because the directions do not include a completed example, write one of your own on the board and complete it with students. For example:

  Building:
  I am _____ Pennsylvania Avenue.
  I am _____ Washington, DC.
  (The White House)

- Give students time to complete all items with their team.
- Review by having students read corrected items aloud and keep score visibly on the board.
- Remind students that in order to receive one point, they must get both the preposition and the name of the person, building, or company correct.

❏ EXERCISE 27. Looking at grammar.
Page 140
Time: 10 minutes

- Ask students to complete this exercise on sight, with no independent preparation.
- Have different students read each completed item aloud.
- Correct and discuss as needed.

❏ EXERCISE 28. Looking at grammar.
Page 141
Time: 10 minutes

- Give students time to complete as seatwork.
- Circulate, assisting any students who may need it.
- Review by having students take turns reading each item. Correct immediately for both accuracy and pronunciation.
- Review optional vocabulary for this section.

Optional Vocabulary
resting
prisoner
prison / jail
free
hall
surgery
fire extinguisher
headache

❏ EXERCISE 29. Warm-up. Page 141
Time: 5 minutes

Some beginners will know more than the most basic prepositions. Before having students attempt the items in the Warm-up, model some of the prepositions of place presented in Chart 5-8 by using yourself as the object of the preposition.

- Look at the class and tell the students who is in front of you, and write this on the board. For example:

  Mina is in front of me.

- As the board (or another classroom feature) is likely to be right behind you, say this and write the corresponding sentence on the board. For example:

  The board is in back of me.

- Instruct students to answer the questions.
- Have different students tell you their answers in complete sentences.

CHART 5-8. More Prepositions of Place:
A List. Page 142
Time: 10–15 minutes

Many beginners are familiar with many of the prepositions in this chart. Before presenting the explanations in the chart, have students demonstrate their knowledge by physically positioning themselves according to the meaning of each preposition, as indicated in the instructions below. This will help activate students' knowledge of these prepositions and will engage them more fully in the material.

- Write the chart title on the board.
- Before having students read through the example sentences, tell them you want them to demonstrate the meanings of all the prepositions they already know.
- Using yourself as a point of reference, ask a specific student to stand beside you and write _beside_ me on the board as you do so.
- Move through the prepositions listed in the box by asking different students to stand in various places around the room, demonstrating the meanings of the prepositions. For example:

  Say: Shinko, please stand <u>at</u> the door.
  Write: <u>at</u> the door

- Write each preposition on the board as you work through the list.
- When you have completed the list, have students read the sample sentences (a)–(p) aloud.
- If any prepositional phrase is still not clear, write the corresponding sentence on the board and draw or physically demonstrate the preposition and its relationship to the object until you are sure students understand.

❏ EXERCISE 30. Looking at grammar.
Page 143
Time: 10 minutes

- Give students time to work through this exercise as seatwork.
- Correct and review by having students read completed sentences aloud.
- Accept all answers that could be correct (for example, *under* and *below*).

❏ EXERCISE 31. Let's talk: pairwork.
Page 144
Time: 10 minutes

- Put students into pairs.
- Read and explain the direction line.
- Call on one student to model the role of Partner A while you take the role of Partner B.
- Have students work through the first nine items before changing roles.
- Circulate around the room, assisting students as you go.

- Review by having the class respond to some of the questions as a group and writing their responses on the board.

❑ EXERCISE 32. Listening. Page 145
Time: 10 minutes

- Have the CD player ready and know which track you will play.
- Read direction line to students and stress that for all fifteen items, they will need to listen for the prepositional phrase in order to respond with T or F.
- Play the CD track.
- Correct by either replaying the track or reading the script aloud, calling on individual students to provide the *true* or *false* responses.
- For false statements, make sure students understand which part of the statement was false.

❑ EXERCISE 33. Let's talk: pairwork.
Page 145
Time: 10 minutes

- Put students into pairs.
- Explain that they will practice using prepositions of place with *be*.
- Because students have not yet studied the imperative, briefly reintroduce its form and use. Explain that you give orders by using the basic verb without a subject. In every case, the subject *you* is understood. Because the subject is always *you*, it does not need to be stated each time.
- Ask a student to be Partner B and model the first exchange.
- Give students time to instruct each other and perform the actions accordingly.
- Circulate throughout the room, assisting students as you go.

❑ EXERCISE 34. Vocabulary and grammar.
Page 146
Time: 10–15 minutes

Gauge how well your students are responding to pairwork. As they will have had a couple of pairwork exercises in a row, it may be more effective for you to lead this exercise as a class-wide activity.

Give those students who struggle more or seem reluctant to respond in a class-led activity an opportunity to speak by calling on them by name while also asking open-ended questions to the class.

Part I
- Have students look at the vocabulary and invite them to explain words to the class.
- Direct students to look at the illustration as you ask the first question, inviting more than one response.
- To draw in reluctant students and / or those whose level is lower than average, ask those students to read the questions aloud.

- Have students correct one another spontaneously, and put any challenging items on the board.

Part II
- Ask students to complete the cloze exercise as seatwork.
- Correct as a class by asking students to take turns reading their completions aloud.

❑ EXERCISE 35. Vocabulary and grammar.
Page 147
Time: 10–15 minutes

Part I
- Have students look at the vocabulary and invite them to explain words to the class.
- Direct students to look at the illustration as you ask the first question, inviting more than one response.
- To draw in reluctant students and / or those whose level is lower than average, ask specific students to read questions aloud.
- Have students correct one another spontaneously, and put any challenging items on the board.

Part II
- Ask students to complete the cloze exercise as seatwork.
- Correct as a class by asking students to take turns reading their completions aloud.

❑ EXERCISE 36. Vocabulary and grammar.
Page 148
Time: 10–15 minutes

Part I
- Have students look at the vocabulary and invite them to explain words to the class.
- Direct students to look at the illustration as you ask the first question, inviting more than one response.
- To draw in reluctant students and / or those whose level is lower than average, ask specific students to read questions aloud.
- Have students correct one another spontaneously, and put any challenging items on the board.

Part II
- Ask students to complete the cloze exercise as seatwork.
- Correct as a class by asking students to take turns reading their completions aloud.

Optional Vocabulary

boots	server
bridge	cut
butterflies	circulation desk
fishing pole	shelf / shelves
picnic bench	cash a check
picnic table	bank teller
burn	line of people
candle	counter
saucer	beard

❑ EXERCISE 37. Warm-up. Page 149
Time: 5–10 minutes

- Ask students what phrases and words they know to make their English more polite.
- Beginners will certainly know *please* and *thank you* and may also be familiar with using modals to make polite questions, so encourage students to tell you all the expressions they know.
- Write the phrases they produce on the board. For example:

    Please
    Thank you.
    You're welcome.
    Could I_____?
    Pleased to meet you.

- Have one student read aloud the statement from the woman in the illustration. Have another student read aloud the statement from the man in the illustration.
- If students are able to do so, invite discussion of the ways they express politeness in their language. Compare their responses with the ways people express politeness in English.

CHART 5-9. *Would Like.* Page 149
Time: 10–15 minutes

Explain that when a request is made, *I would like* is much more polite than *I want*. Be ready to discuss the effect that *I want* statements tend to have on others.

There is a lot of information in this chart, and students will probably not grasp all of it equally well. Stress the use of *would like* as a polite way to state a want or need. The remainder of the chart presents structural variants of this phrase. Try to keep students' focus on the main presentation of *would like* and, most important, the usefulness of this phrase.

Students have not yet had an introduction to the infinitive in the text. To minimize the focus on grammatical terminology, explain that the infinitive is the *to* form. Many beginners will understand this. Stress that the infinitive allows verbs to combine with other verbs to create very specific meanings.

- Write the chart title on the board.
- Have students read example sentences (a) and (b) aloud while you write both on the board.
- Repeat each sentence in an appropriate tone of voice so that students can hear how differently each sentence is received by native speakers and readily identify the softness in *would like*.
- Ask different students to take turns reading the sentences in example (c) aloud.
- Emphasize that neither *would* nor *like* is conjugated, and thus there is no final *-s* on either.
- Write both the long forms in (c) and the contracted forms in (d) on the board. Read aloud so students can hear the correct pronunciation of the contracted version.
- Explain the corresponding chart notes for contractions of *would* in (d).

- Have a student read example sentence (e) while you write it on the board.
- Explain that *would like* can be followed by the *to* form of the verb to show what people *would like to do*.
- Put example question (f) on the board and write its elements above each corresponding word.
- Emphasize that in a question, *would* comes before the subject.
- Ask a student to read short answer (g) aloud. Write it on the board and remind students of the way that *Yes, I would* is similar to *Yes, I am*.

❑ EXERCISE 38. Grammar. Page 150
Time: 10 minutes

- Read the direction line and review the completed examples with students.
- On sight, have students read item 3 aloud and then transform it, using *would like*.
- Provide immediate correction.
- Complete the exercise in this fashion—reading, transforming, and correcting each item.
- Have students read the sentences aloud, contracting *would* and *like*.
- Have students practice repeating the contracted form.

❑ EXERCISE 39. Let's talk: class activity.
Page 150
Time: 15 minutes

- Tell students that they will answer questions about their current state of mind and mood and what they would like to do right now.
- Write *I would like to ____* and *I'd like to ____* on the board.
- Instruct students to close their books and direct different questions to different students.
- Expand on the items in the book by including your own and tailoring them to specific students in your class.
- If the class activity is building momentum, use one of the Expansion questions below to maximize student production.

Expansion: Ask students additional questions to promote the use of *would like*. Explain the term *bucket list* and write it on the board. Encourage students to share their bucket lists using *would like*. Put student-generated sentences on the board.

If you could have a party and invite famous people, dead or alive, who would you like to invite?

If you had unlimited time and money, what would you like to do?

If you could relive any day in your life, what day would you like to relive?

Optional Vocabulary
polite
infinitive
bucket list
party
invite
relive

❑ EXERCISE 40. Warm-up. Page 151
Time: 5–10 minutes

- Have students describe some of their likes, in terms of food, drink, ways to relax.
- Write student-generated responses on the board. For example:

  I like movies.
  I like to watch movies.
  I like Italian food.
  I like to eat Italian food.

- Ask students what they *would like* right now.
- Write their responses on the board. For example:

  I would like a snack. I am hungry.
  I would like to take a nap. I am tired.

- Have students read the two Warm-up sentences aloud and discuss the difference.
- Focus on the fact that *like* indicates a general preference, something that is *always* true.
- Stress that *would like* indicates something a person wants to do or have *now*.

CHART 5-10. *Would Like* vs. *Like*. Page 151
Time: 10–15 minutes

- Write the name of the chart on the board.
- Ask a student to read example sentence (a) aloud.
- Write the sentence on the board and discuss the accompanying notes.
- Ask a different student to read example sentence (b) aloud.
- Write the sentence on the board and review the accompanying notes.

❑ EXERCISE 41. Listening. Page 151
Time: 5–10 minutes

- Have the CD player ready and know which track you will play.
- Write *like* and *'d like* on the board.
- Say these sentences and ask a volunteer to circle *like* or *'d like* for each one:

  1. *They like coffee.*
  2. *They'd like a cup of coffee.*
  3. *We like basketball.*
  4. *We'd like to play basketball tonight.*

- Review the example item with students before playing the track and instruct them to listen specifically for the difference between *like* and *'d like* (the contraction for *would like*).
- Either replay or read the items aloud in order for students to correct and review the exercise.

❑ EXERCISE 42. Let's talk: class activity.
Page 152
Time: 10–15 minutes

- First give students an opportunity to think about and write completions to the items.

- Leading the discussion, ask various students to share their completions and expand on their likes and dislikes and so on.
- Put student-generated sentences on the board and, as much as possible, get students to speak in full sentences and explain their completions.

❑ EXERCISE 43. Let's talk: pairwork.
Page 152
Time: 10 minutes

- Put students into pairs.
- Read and explain the direction line to students.
- Model the completed Partner A and Partner B dialogues with a few students and put example questions and short answers on the board.
- Have students determine who is Partner A and who is Partner B and work through each item.
- Circulate around the room, assisting students and ensuring that they understand their partner and can respond in complete sentences.
- Take notes on common mistakes and present these on the board while reviewing and discussing the items.

❑ EXERCISE 44. Vocabulary and grammar.
Page 153
Time: 15–20 minutes

Many students may never have written a check in their own language, let alone in English. Use this exercise as an opportunity to ask students how they usually pay for things in their countries, whether they use credit and debit cards more frequently than cash and what kinds of uses a written check has.

Part I
- Have students read through the vocabulary in the box.
- Ask students to explain the vocabulary in their own words as best they can and ask specific questions to help them. For example:

  When do you use your full name? What documents is it on?

- Lead the exercise or put students into pairs, but give students an opportunity both to read each question in Part I aloud and to answer it.

Part II
- Give students a few minutes to complete each item.
- Correct by having students read their completed items aloud.

❑ EXERCISE 45. Vocabulary and grammar.
Page 154
Time: 15–20 minutes

Most students have some experience with cooking. Engage them in the topic by asking questions about whether they like to cook, what they like to cook, and so on.

Part I
- Have students read through the vocabulary in the box.
- Ask students to explain the vocabulary in their own words as best they can and ask specific questions to help them. For example:

  When you go to the grocery store, do you always bring a grocery list?

- Lead the exercise or put students into pairs, but give students an opportunity both to read each question in Part I aloud and to answer it.

Part II
- Give students a few minutes to complete each item.
- Correct by having students read their completed items aloud.

❏ EXERCISE 46. Vocabulary and grammar.
Page 155
Time: 15–20 minutes

Engage students by asking what they like to watch on TV and how often they do so. Ask questions that allow students to use newly acquired vocabulary and structures and that provide an opportunity for them to talk about their own lives.

Expansion: Ask a variety of questions to engage students.

What do you like to do in the evening?

Do you like to watch TV?

Do you like to watch TV alone or with friends and family?

How often do you watch TV during the week?

What are your favorite shows?

Do you know the term reality TV?

Part I
- Have students read through the vocabulary in the box.
- Ask students to explain the vocabulary in their own words as best they can and ask specific questions to help them.
- Lead the exercise or put students into pairs, but give students an opportunity both to read each question in Part I aloud and to answer it.

Part II
- Give students a few minutes to complete each item.
- Correct by having students read their completed items aloud.

❏ EXERCISE 47. Let's talk: game. Page 156
Time: 15 minutes

- Put students into groups of three or four and tell them they will be functioning as a team.
- Explain the direction line.
- Explain that each team needs to make as many sentences as possible and that every sentence they write must have at least one preposition. Further, tell them that all the sentences must be grammatically correct.

- Have students choose a writer to record their team's sentences on one piece of paper.
- Give students ten minutes to write their sentences.
- Collect each team's sentences and read them aloud, having all students correct for grammatical accuracy.
- Write sentences on the board as needed.

❏ EXERCISE 48. Looking at grammar.
Page 156
Time: 10–12 minutes

- Give students time to complete this review as seatwork.
- Have students take turns reading the corrected items aloud. Discuss any challenging items and write them on the board.

❏ EXERCISE 49. Check your knowledge.
Page 157
Time: 10–15 minutes

- Read the direction line and review the completed example.
- Give students time to correct the items on their own, as seatwork.
- Ask students to take turns reading the corrected sentences aloud.
- Discuss those items that contain more than one correction.

❏ EXERCISE 50. Looking at grammar.
Page 157
Time: 10–15 minutes

- Ask students to read these items aloud, completing them on sight.
- Compare content among different class members by inviting several completions to each item.
- Should any discussions arise naturally, encourage students to engage with one another and simply correct for accuracy and pronunciation.

❏ EXERCISE 51. Reading and writing.
Page 158
Time: 15–20 minutes

Expansion: To engage students in the topic, ask them questions about dreaming in general and their own dreams in particular. For example:

What do you dream about?

Do you have good dreams and bad dreams? Do you ever have nightmares?

Do you usually remember your dreams?

Do you know what a recurring dream is? Have you ever had the same dream more than once?

Do you dream in color?

Part I
- Ask students to read through the passage, "A Happy Dream," underlining the verbs.

- Have students take turns reading the sentences in the passage aloud and ask about any words or phrases you choose. Doing so will provide students with an opportunity to speak English in a spontaneous fashion.

Part II
- Read through the direction line with students.
- Encourage students to think about dreams they have actually had or can imagine.
- Tell students to use the questions to write about their own dreams.

Part III
- Have students exchange paragraphs with a partner and use the editing check to check and correct each other's work. Alternatively, tell students to use the editing check to correct their own work.

Expansion: Have students as a class collaborate on writing a paragraph on the board by asking them to contribute to a common theme—a collective dream that they have for their own lives. Use the editing check to edit the collaborative work.

Invite students to collaborate on a paragraph about an ideal English class. They should write as "we" while working as a whole class, creating their sentences right on the board. They should discuss and write about what they envision as the perfect class.

Chapter 6
Nouns and Pronouns

CHAPTER SUMMARY

OBJECTIVE: In this chapter, students learn about the different functions of nouns in sentences—as subjects of verbs, objects of verbs, and objects of prepositions. The chapter also focuses on how nouns are modified by adjectives and teaches the pronouns (subject, object, possessive) that nouns refer to and are replaced by. The chapter teaches plural forms for regular nouns and nouns that have irregular plural forms. Mastering nouns and pronouns allows students to move from simply naming items to using nouns in more sophisticated ways. Students become adept at speaking about their own and others' actions in a way that naturally includes the people, places, and things in their lives.

APPROACH: The chapter begins by introducing the important distinction between subject nouns and object nouns, and accordingly, the distinction between transitive and intransitive verbs. It also teaches the distinction between the noun as object of a verb and the noun as object of a preposition. Students then learn that subject and object pronouns can be used in place of subject and object nouns. The chapter goes on to present the function and position of adjectives in a sentence and then possessive adjectives and possessive pronouns. Finally, *whose* is introduced, as its use allows students to speak more autonomously about nouns, enabling them to ask what noun belongs to what person.

TERMINOLOGY: The text teaches grammar terminology when doing so is helpful for students. For example, since *transitive* and *intransitive* remain the most meaningful words to describe verbs that can or cannot be followed by an object, this terminology is taught in the first chart. *Subject* and *object* are equally functional terms, and their use serves students' understanding. However, when grammar terminology does not support students' understanding, it is avoided. Accordingly, when *whose* is introduced , the term *interrogative possessive pronoun* is not used, because this lengthy phrase would not promote greater understanding on the part of beginning students.

❏ EXERCISE 1. Warm-up. Page 159
Time: 10–15 minutes

> Beginners are likely to know many names of objects and somewhat fewer names of categories of objects. In order to engage students maximally, think of additional categories of which they can name members. As much as possible, help them show the many words they do know.

- Put students into small groups of three or four.
- Ask students if they can explain what a noun is.
- Write the students' (or your) explanation on the board, and give an example of a person, place, or thing. For example:

  A noun is a person (a grammar teacher), a place (a classroom), or a thing (a grammar book).

- With students sitting in groups, have them write as many nouns for each category as possible and give those groups who work fastest additional categories. For example:

  Name kinds of meat (beef, chicken, pork, etc.).
  Name kinds of vegetables (carrots, beets, potatoes, etc.).

- Walk around the room, monitor progress, and encourage students and groups who appear stuck.
- Review as a class by having group members give their nouns for each category and writing these on the board.

CHART 6-1. Nouns: Subjects and Objects.
Page 159
Time: 10–15 minutes

> There are several important concepts here, and by using simple language and clear examples, you will help your students grasp them. Be prepared to reiterate the idea of the *doer* of an action and the *receiver* of an action. Beginners may be able to explain what a subject does but will probably have more difficulty articulating and perhaps even understanding what an object is.

- Write the chart title on the board.
- Ask students if they can explain what a subject is.
- Put students' ideas on the board and include related ideas.
- Explain that some traits of subjects are often, but not always, true. For example:

	does the action
A subject:	is a person or a thing
	comes in front of the verb
	controls the verbs

  Jeanne broke the window.
  The cat is watching the birds.

- Have a student read example sentence (a) from the chart and discuss the explanatory notes with the class.
- Ask another student to read example sentence (b) from the chart and discuss the notes with your students.
- Write on the board:

	"receives" the action
An object:	feels the effects of the verb
	answers the question "What" in many cases (for example: Tom broke his leg. What did he break?)
	is controlled by the verb (which is controlled by the subject)

- Explain that not every verb is followed by an object.
- Explain that a verb that is followed by an object is called a transitive verb, because the action of the verb goes from the subject (who / which does the action) to the object (who / which receives the action).
- Write and draw the following illustration on the board, and reiterate the point made above.

Transitive Verb

$S \Rightarrow\Rightarrow\Rightarrow\Rightarrow\Rightarrow\Rightarrow\Rightarrow O$
    V

Meg is holding her book

- Explain that with a transitive verb, the action moves (is *transferred*) from the subject to the object.
- Ask students if they know what *intransitive* means.
- Explain that if a verb is intransitive, the action stays with the subject. It does not move to an object.
- Write and draw the following illustration on the board, and reiterate the point made above.

Intransitive Verb

 S *V*

Ali   smiled.

- Give more examples of transitive and intransitive verbs to help students understand this distinction. Have students tell you which words play the roles of subject, verb, and object in each sentence.
- Point out that words may follow intransitive verbs but that these are not objects.
- Write illustrative examples on the board. For example:

Transitive Verb

| Subject | Verb | Object |
| Kieko | loves | chocolate. |

Intransitive Verb

| Subject | Verb | Adjective |
| Bella | is | happy. |

❑ **EXERCISE 2.** Looking at grammar.
Page 160
Time: 5–7 minutes

- Ask students to take turns reading the words in the list aloud.
- As each student reads a word, ask if it is a noun or not. If the word is not a noun, see if other students can say what kind of word it is.

❑ **EXERCISE 3.** Looking at grammar.
Page 160
Time: 10 minutes

- Explain the direction line.
- Ask students to circle the subject of each sentence, in addition to considering whether the sentence contains an object or no object and what the object is.
- Give students time to complete this exercise as seatwork.
- Review as a class, having students read aloud. Provide immediate correction.

❑ **EXERCISE 4.** Looking at grammar.
Page 160
Time: 10 minutes

- Give students time to complete this exercise as seatwork.
- Review as a class by having students read items aloud. Provide immediate correction.

Optional Vocabulary

school subjects	whiskers
juice	scratch
catch	memorize
purr	

❑ **EXERCISE 5.** Warm-up. Page 161
Time: 5–10 minutes

- Remind students that they have been using nouns as objects of prepositions since the previous chapter.
- Have students look at the picture, complete each item, and then read the completed items aloud.
- Reiterate that a noun that follows a preposition is also an object, but the object of the preposition itself, not the object of the verb.

CHART 6-2. Nouns as Objects of Prepositions. Page 161
Time: 10–15 minutes

- Write the chart title on the board.
- Ask students to tell you prepositions they already know, and write these on the board. For example:

at	under
on	between
in	near
over	

- Ask the class to help you make a sentence describing the location of an object that is visible to everyone in the class. For example:

The map   is   on   the wall.

- Have students tell you which noun is the subject and which word is the verb and label these. For example:

| Subject | Verb | | |
| The map | is | on | the wall. |

- Explain that the noun following the preposition is an object but it is an object of a preposition, not the object of a verb.

- Have a student read the diagrammed example sentence (a) aloud while you write it on the board.
- Ask students to read the label for each part of the sentence. Write the labels on the board below the corresponding words. Review the notes on the right side of the chart with the class.
- Repeat the sequence above for example sentence (b).

❏ EXERCISE 6. Looking at grammar.
Page 162
Time: 5–10 minutes

- Lead the class in completing this exercise on sight.
- Explain that a phrase is a group of related words and write this definition on the board.
- Explain that each numbered item in this exercise is a phrase but that not all of the phrases are prepositional phrases.
- Have students identify the prepositional phrases (preposition and object, as explained in the direction line).
- Ask students to describe the other phrases they see, in terms of their function.

❏ EXERCISE 7. Looking at grammar.
Page 162
Time: 5–10 minutes

- Read the direction line aloud and review the completed example item.
- Give students time to work through the items as seatwork.
- Review the items as a class, having students take turns reading aloud.
- Correct clearly and immediately and use the board to identify parts of speech further.

❏ EXERCISE 8. Looking at grammar.
Page 163
Time: 10 minutes

This exercise requires students to become familiar with the process of creating a sentence diagram in which the function of each word or phrase in the sentence is identified. Emphasize that not just single words but whole phrases (more than one word—for example, a verb phrase) can play a single function in a sentence.

- Explain that this exercise will help students identify the function of each word and phrase within a sentence.
- Tell students that identifying the function of each word and phrase in a sentence will help them better understand and use simple English sentence structure.
- Review the two completed examples with students by having them read the sentences aloud while you ask for the parts of the sentence.
- Give students time to complete the items as seatwork.
- Review by having students read the nouns aloud and label the words and phrases according to the prompts below each sentence, in the diagram format.

Optional Vocabulary
parachute
phrase
erase
shining
filmmaking

❏ EXERCISE 9. Warm-up. Page 164
Time: 5 minutes

- Have three students read the items aloud and tell you whether they circled *yes* or *no*.

Expansion: Ask students what *raw* means. Expand the discussion to include other food adjectives and invite students to tell you any adjectives they know.

Ask students to describe what *opposite* means and ask them to tell you other adjectives for food, and their opposites.

To help students activate their passive knowledge, name certain food items and see if students can describe the taste. For example:

What is the taste of ice cream?
What is the taste of plain white rice?
What is the taste of peppers?
What is the taste of potato chips?

hot—cold
fresh—stale
spicy (hot)—mild
raw—cooked
sweet—sour—salty—bitter

- Ask students to say what kinds of foods they like, using adjectives and nouns together.
- Write students' responses on the board, in the third person. For example:

Ming, Chang, and Lisette like spicy food.
Jessie and Andrew love sweet food.
Martina does not like stale bread.
Chuming and Zara like fresh fruit.

CHART 6-3. Adjectives with Nouns.
Page 164
Time: 10–15 minutes

The list of adjectives in the chart contains many words and pairs of words that beginners have some familiarity with. Use this as an opportunity to get students speaking and showing what they know.

- Write the chart title on the board.
- Tell students they have been using sentences with adjectives since Chapter 1. Write a sentence with the verb *be* + adjective on the board. For example:

We are intelligent.

- Elicit other similar statements with *be* + adjective.

- Ask students to say where the adjectives in these sentences appear—before or after the nouns they describe?
- Explain that adjectives can also come directly before the nouns they describe, or *modify* them.

Expansion: Ask students to make observations about other class members, and write these on the board, underlining the adjectives.

   Gino is a <u>tall</u> man.

   Tanya is an <u>intelligent</u> woman.

   Fariah is a <u>hardworking</u> student.

- Ask a student to read example sentence (a) from the chart aloud.
- Write the sentence on the board. Ask other students to say what parts of speech are included, and label these.
- Repeat the step above for the remaining example sentences, (b)–(d), and review the notes from the chart.

Expansion: Go through the list of adjectives and spot-check students' understanding of their meaning by asking them to give you specific examples of certain adjectives. For example:

   Name a beautiful thing.

   A flower.

   Name a small animal.

   A mouse.

   Name a bright thing.

   The sun.

   Name a dangerous activity.

   Rock climbing.

❏ **EXERCISE 10.** Looking at grammar.
Page 164
Time: 10 minutes

- Read the direction line and completed example aloud.
- Ask students to read the sentences on sight and say which noun each adjective describes.

❏ **EXERCISE 11.** Let's talk: small groups.
Page 165
Time: 15 minutes

- Put students into small groups of three or four.
- Explain the direction line and tell each group to use at least three adjectives for each item.
- Tell students to find out why their group members hold the opinions they do.
- Circulate and meet briefly with each group, asking all group members to say more about their likes and dislikes. For example:

   Mohammed and Sebastian don't like small cities. Why?

   They don't have their own airports.

❏ **EXERCISE 12.** Let's talk: small groups.
Page 165
Time: 15 minutes

Part I
- Have students remain in the same small groups. Alternatively, have one member rotate out of each group and into another small group, depending on whether the momentum is dragging or not.
- Explain the direction line and encourage students to fill in the blanks with countries and nationality adjectives they know.

Part II
- Ask each group to use the questions in this part to find out the most popular ethnic foods in their groups and in the class.
- Take an informal poll of which foods are favorites and write these on the board. For example:

   Most of the class loves Japanese food.

   An example of this kind of food is sushi.

Part III
- Lead the class in naming and writing on the board as many nationality adjectives as they know.

Expansion: Ask students the nationality adjectives for the following countries:

   Holland

   Iceland

   Thailand

Optional Vocabulary
Adjectives in Chart 6-3 (page 164)
modify
experience
ethnic
popular

❏ **EXERCISE 13.** Warm-up. Page 166
Time: 5–10 minutes

- Read the direction line and have students complete the exercise independently as seatwork.
- Explain that all the words in the shaded gray box are pronouns.
- Have students read their completions aloud. Discuss if they have included a subject pronoun instead of an object pronoun in item 1 or 2 (other than *it*, which can be either).

CHART 6-4. Subject Pronouns and Object Pronouns. Page 166
Time: 10–15 minutes

Some beginners are familiar with both sets of pronouns, but many may use the subject pronoun for objects as well as subjects. As this is a difficult habit to break, correct this common error overtly and immediately, but supportively. This will help students break themselves of the habit before it becomes fossilized.

- Write the chart title on the board.
- Ask a student to remind you of the differences between subjects and objects and write basic notes on the board. For example:

  Subjects: do the action
              come before the verb
  Objects: receive the action
              follow the verb

- Explain that pronouns also have subject forms and object forms, and warn students that it is easy for them to use the subject pronoun accidentally when they need the object pronoun, usually because subject pronouns are the pronouns they learned first.
- Have students read example sentences (a)–(h), reading both sentences for each. Write the pronouns for each item as they are read.
- Ask students to read example sentences (i)–(j) aloud. Point out in the additional information on the right that a pronoun refers to a noun and has the same meaning as the noun.
- Have a student read (k), and point out that *it* refers to the phrase *a red book*.

❏ EXERCISE 14. Looking at grammar.
Page 166
Time: 10 minutes

- Read the direction line and review the completed example.
- Give students an opportunity to work through this exercise independently as seatwork.
- Have different students read the completions aloud and correct clearly and immediately.

❏ EXERCISE 15. Looking at grammar.
Page 167
Time: 10 minutes

- Read the direction line and review the completed example.
- Stress that students need to replace both the subject and the object with subject and object pronouns.
- Give students an opportunity to work through this exercise independently as seatwork.
- Have different students read the circled completions aloud and correct clearly and immediately.

❏ EXERCISE 16. Let's talk: interview.
Page 167
Time: 10–15 minutes

- Explain the direction line and tell the students that they should get up and move around in order to talk to one another.
- Model Student A's, B's, and C's roles with students, and review the content.
- Tell students to ask each other the questions they see in items 1–8 and to replace each noun with an object pronoun once they receive a *yes* response.
- Review by asking these questions with the class and comparing responses.

Expansion: Ask additional follow-up questions. Engage students further in spontaneous speaking; help them to use the target grammar (object pronouns) in their responses. For example:

Where do you do your homework?
Where do you visit your friends? Do you visit them at their houses? Do you meet them at restaurants or bars?
Where do you watch TV? Do you watch it in your room? Do you watch it on your computer?
Where do you use your laptop? Do you use it in cafés?

❏ EXERCISE 17. Looking at grammar.
Page 168
Time: 10 minutes

- Have students complete this exercise on their own as seatwork.
- Correct by having students read their completed responses aloud.

❏ EXERCISE 18. Listening. Page 168
Time: 10 minutes

- Before starting the listening, have the CD player ready and the track prepared.
- Read the direction line to your students.
- Write the words *her*, *him*, and *them on the board* and model reduced pronunciation of these pronouns.
- Play the CD track through.
- Have students try to say each sentence aloud by using the pronunciation they hear.

❏ EXERCISE 19. Listening. Page 169
Time: 10 minutes

- Have the CD player prepped and the track ready.
- Tell students that they will complete the items with words they hear on the CD.
- Have students read their completions aloud.
- Read from the CD script if students have remaining questions about what they heard.

Optional Vocabulary

refer to	convertible
purse	formula
invitation	suburbs

❏ EXERCISE 20. Warm-up. Page 170
Time: 5 minutes

- Have students read each item on the left aloud.
- Ask students to determine whether the noun describes one item (singular) or two or more items (plural).

Expansion: Ask students where the nouns in the Warm-up are usually found. For example:

Where are cups, usually?	In kitchens.
Where are classes, usually?	In schools.

Continue with other examples:

Where are leaves, usually?　　*On trees.*
Where are keys, usually?　　*In pockets. In purses.*
Where are shoes, usually?　　*On feet.*

CHART 6-5. Nouns: Singular and Plural
Forms. Page 170
Time: 10–15 minutes

> Many beginners are familiar with adding -s to make most nouns plural. Some students may also try to make adjectives plural, so watch for this and help students autocorrect.

- Write the chart title on the board.
- Ask students to look around the room and tell you what they see, using plural nouns.
- Write the words they produce on the board. For example:

  I see desks.
  I see books.
  I see pens.
  I see students.
  I see cell phones and laptops.

- Have students read the singular and plural nouns in example (a).
- Put examples on the board and remind students that adding an -s is the simplest way to make nouns plural but that not every noun can be made plural this way.
- Have students read examples (b)–(f) aloud.
- Write examples on the board along with the corresponding spelling rules so that students can copy these notes. For example:

baby	babies	*ending in consonant + y = add -ies*
wife	wives	*ending in f or fe = change f to v and add -es*
dish	dishes	*ending in -sh, -ch, -ss, -x = add -es*
tomato	tomatoes	*ending in consonant + o = add -es*

- Be ready to correct students' pronunciation. Many of the nouns ending in consonant blends are challenging for students to spell and pronounce correctly.

❏ EXERCISE 21. Looking at grammar.
Page 170
Time: 10–15 minutes

- Explain the direction line, telling students they will need to change the appropriate words in each separate box for Parts I, II, and III from singular to plural.
- Give students time to complete the exercise as seatwork.
- Review by having students read the completed items aloud. Correct pronunciation and discuss spelling changes.

❏ EXERCISE 22. Listening. Page 172
Time: 10 minutes

- Have the CD player and track ready.
- Explain the direction line to students, telling them that they should circle the word they hear in each item.
- Correct the items with your students, using the script as needed.

❏ EXERCISE 23. Listening. Page 173
Time: 10 minutes

- Have the CD player and track ready.
- Explain the direction line to students, telling them that in this exercise they will hear entire sentences containing one of the words in each item. Explain that they should circle which of the two words in each item they hear.
- Correct the exercise with your students, using the script as needed.

❏ EXERCISE 24. Grammar and speaking.
Page 173
Time: 10–15 minutes

- Explain the direction line to students.
- Review the completed example with students and remind them that if no ending is needed, they should write Ø.
- Have students work through the exercise as seatwork and remind them to circle *yes* or *no*, depending on whether they agree with the statement.
- Correct by having students read their completions aloud and discuss whether they agree or disagree.
- Ask students questions related to the content of the items, to give students opportunities to speak spontaneously.

  What foods do you eat every day?
  What is your favorite animal?
  What animals are cute?
  What are the most comfortable ways to travel?
  Are English grammar exercises easy?

Optional Vocabulary

pocket	taxes
compositions	cockroach
citizens	scare

❏ EXERCISE 25. Warm-up. Page 174
Time: 5 minutes

- Read the direction line.
- Have students tell you which words can be preceded by *a*.

CHART 6-6. Nouns: Irregular Plural Forms.
Page 174
Time: 10–15 minutes

Stress that as they expand their vocabulary, students will encounter more nouns with irregular plural forms. Rather than worrying about learning all or most of these nouns at once, students should focus on recognizing that these irregular plural forms exist in English so that they can be ready to use them as they learn.

- Write the chart title on the board.
- Have students take turns reading examples (a)–(f) on the left side of the chart and the corresponding example sentences on the right aloud.
- Explain that certain nouns do not have a plural form; they keep the same form as the singular.
- Have students read examples (g) and (h) and the example sentences aloud.
- Explain that (i), *people*, is always plural.
- Write notes and examples on the board as appropriate.

❑ **EXERCISE 26.** Looking at grammar.
Page 175
Time: 10–15 minutes

- Explain the direction line to the students.
- Give students time to complete the items as seatwork.
- Correct by having students read the completed items aloud. Ask students to spell their completions and correct their pronunciation.
- Write any particularly challenging items on the board for additional review.

❑ **EXERCISE 27.** Reading and grammar.
Page 176
Time: 10–15 minutes

Part I
- Have students take turns reading parts of the story aloud.
- Ask students to explain vocabulary and paraphrase sentences to give them speaking practice.
- Review the new vocabulary items listed in the yellow flag as well as familiar vocabulary in the paragraph. Ask students to paraphrase parts of the text.

Part II
- Have students complete the sentences that follow the reading with the appropriate ending or Ø.
- Correct the completions while having students take turns reading them aloud.

❑ **EXERCISE 28.** Looking at grammar.
Page 176
Time: 10–15 minutes

- Have students read the explanations of *complete* and *incomplete sentences* aloud.
- Write the following notes on the board:

  complete sentence: has a subject + verb

  incomplete sentence: does not have a subject + verb

- Read the remaining direction lines to your students.
- Review the changes that have been made in items 1 and 3 to make these sentences complete.
- Have students discuss why item 2 is marked *NC*.
- Have students complete the remaining twelve items as a class.
- Ask students to come to the board to write the items on the board, by way of correction.
- Discuss all the changes needed for each possible complete sentence and highlight what is missing for those that remain NC (not complete).

❑ **EXERCISE 29.** Looking at grammar.
Page 177
Time: 10 minutes

- Lead this exercise on sight.
- Explain that students need to select the correct pronouns from choices a–d for each item.
- Ask students to take turns reading and completing aloud.
- When a student selects the wrong pronoun, discuss it and involve others in explaining why the pronoun would not work, in each case.

Optional Vocabulary

sore	cavity
blowing bubbles	fit
checking	

❑ **EXERCISE 30.** Warm-up. Page 178
Time: 5 minutes

Near beginners will know many possessive pronouns but may make mistakes using them. Be ready to help students correct errors when using these possessive pronouns so these errors don't become fossilized.

- Have students complete items 4, 5, and 6.
- Ask students to read each item and the completion aloud.

CHART 6-7. Possessive Pronouns: *Mine, Yours, His, Hers, Ours, Theirs.* Page 178
Time: 10–15 minutes

- Write the chart title on the board.
- Have students take turns reading the example sentences (a)–(c) on the left.
- Write the list of possessive adjectives and corresponding possessive pronouns on the board. For example:

my	*mine*
your	*yours*
her	*hers*
his	*his*
our	*ours*
your	*yours*
their	*theirs*

- Explain that possessive adjectives, like other adjectives, go before the noun.
- Explain that possessive pronouns replace the possessive-adjective-and-noun combination.

❑ EXERCISE 31. Looking at grammar.
Page 178
Time: 10 minutes

- Lead this exercise with the class as a whole.
- Have different students read each item and complete it aloud, on sight.
- Provide immediate correction.
- Help students pronounce the end sound of the possessive pronouns so that the -s is clearly heard. Remind students that *mine* does not end in -s.

❑ EXERCISE 32. Looking at grammar.
Page 179
Time: 10–15 minutes

- Read through the direction line aloud and review the completed examples, highlighting that students have to produce the object pronoun, the possessive adjective, and the possessive pronoun.
- Have students work through this exercise, individually.
- Circulate and help students as needed.
- Correct by having students read the completed items aloud. Remind students to emphasize the ending of each form when speaking so that others can distinguish the possessive adjective from the pronoun.

❑ EXERCISE 33. Looking at grammar.
Page 180
Time: 10–15 minutes

- Explain the direction line.
- Have students complete the items, individually.
- Correct the exercise by having students read completions aloud.
- Put any particularly challenging items on the board for further discussion.

Optional Vocabulary

belong to	thoughtful
possess	flip phone
bouquet	smart phone

❑ EXERCISE 34. Warm-up. Page 180
Time: 5 minutes

- Explain the direction line.
- Have students choose the grammatical items.
- Discuss why items 2 and 3 are not grammatical.

CHART 6-8. Possessive Nouns. Page 181
Time: 10–15 minutes

- Write the chart title on the board.
- Have students take turns reading the examples sentences (a) and (b) aloud.

- Explain that nouns can be made possessive by adding an apostrophe (') and -s at the end of the noun.
- Write examples of this on the board:

  The book belongs to Olga.   *It's <u>Olga's</u> book.*
  That dog lives with Hiro.   *It's <u>Hiro's</u> dog.*

- Have students take turns reading example sentences (c) and (d) aloud.
- Explain that for a plural noun (which already ends with an added -s), the apostrophe follows the final -s.

❑ EXERCISE 35. Looking at grammar.
Page 181
Time: 10 minutes

- Have students read the items aloud, on sight, and complete the sentences.
- Pick up a couple of items on students' desks and review *belongs to*.

❑ EXERCISE 36. Looking at grammar.
Page 181
Time: 10 minutes

- Give students time to complete this exercise as seatwork.
- Review by having students read their completed items aloud and correct immediately and clearly.

❑ EXERCISE 37. Looking at grammar.
Page 182
Time: 10–15 minutes

- Read the direction line to students.
- Encourage students to move around and look at one another in order to complete the items. Encourage them to have fun with their classmates.
- Correct by inviting different students to read and compare their completions.

❑ EXERCISE 38. Game. Page 182
Time: 10–15 minutes

> This is a challenging game for beginners, who may know family words but may mix them up.

- Put students into small groups or teams of three or four.
- Read and explain the direction line.
- Have teams work through the items as quickly as possible.
- Review by having students read their team's completions aloud. Write each team's score on the board.

Expansion: Have students bring one or two big photos of their extended family to class. Then have students go to the front of the class, show their photos, and explain who the people are. For example:

This is my grandmother. She is my mother's mom.
This is my uncle Harry. He is my father's brother.

❑ **EXERCISE 39.** Looking at grammar.
Page 183
Time: 10–15 minutes

• Give students time to work through this exercise as seatwork.
• Correct by having students take turns reading items aloud.
• Ensure that students pronounce the ending of each targeted structure in order to make the form clear.

❑ **EXERCISE 40.** Listening. Page 184
Time: 10 minutes

• Have the CD and track ready to go.
• Explain that students need to distinguish between the normal noun form and the possessive form and read the completed example.
• Play the CD track.
• Have students give the correct answers in turn.
• Review any disputed answers by referring to the script or playing the track again.

❑ **EXERCISE 41.** Looking at grammar.
Page 184
Time: 10–15 minutes

• Explain the direction line to students.
• Give students time to complete the exercise as seatwork.
• Have students write their correct sentences (with apostrophes) on the board.
• Review as a class and model correct pronunciation.

Optional Vocabulary

messy	aunt / uncle
office	mother / father-in-law
uniform	sister / brother-in-law
crowded	grandmother / grandfather
schedule	cousin
borrow	gets x miles to the gallon
niece / nephew	

❑ **EXERCISE 42.** Warm-up. Page 185
Time: 5 minutes

• Have students read the two items and possible answers aloud.
• Discuss as a class.

CHART 6-9. Questions with *Whose*.
Page 185
Time: 10–15 minutes

• Write the chart title on the board.
• Have students take turns reading the example questions (a) and (b) aloud.
• Write the chart's questions—or similar questions—on the board. For example:

Whose watch is this?

Whose watches are these?

• Have students give possible answers in possessive form.
• Explain that *whose* can come before a noun in a question and that it asks about possession.
• Have students read example questions (c) and (d) aloud.
• Explain that if the noun being referred to is clear, *whose* can be used without a noun.
• Have a student read question (e) aloud and explain that *who's* (the contraction of *who* + *is*) and *whose* sound exactly the same.

❑ **EXERCISE 43.** Looking at grammar.
Page 185
Time: 10 minutes

• Have students choose the correct answer to each item on sight, reading the preceding question aloud.
• Reiterate when a simple noun is needed and when a possessive noun is needed, while correcting students.

❑ **EXERCISE 44.** Looking at grammar.
Page 186
Time: 10 minutes

• Remind students that *Who's* already has the verb *be* in the contraction.
• Give students time to complete the sentences on their own.
• Correct and review as a class.

❑ **EXERCISE 45.** Listening. Page 186
Time: 10 minutes

• Have the CD player and track ready to go.
• Explain the direction line to students.
• Play the CD track while students circle *Whose* or *Who's*.
• Have students take turns writing the answers on the board.

❑ **EXERCISE 46.** Looking at grammar.
Page 186
Time: 10 minutes

• Read the direction line to students.
• Lead this exercise with the class, asking different students to complete items on sight.
• Correct immediately, reminding students that the number of the subject noun determines the singular or plural verb and the singular or plural demonstrative pronoun.

❑ **EXERCISE 47.** Let's talk: pairwork.
Page 186
Time: 10 minutes

• Put students into pairs.
• Review the direction line with students.

- Model the example exchange with a student to prepare the pairs.
- Encourage students to include in their practice any objects they can see.
- Circulate around the room, helping students to speak fluidly.

Optional Vocabulary
bakery
dirty

❏ EXERCISE 48. Warm-up. Page 187
Time: 5 minutes

- Have students look at the illustration and discuss the correct answer.
- Ask students if they know other irregular plurals (for example, *man-men*) and put these on the board.

Expansion: Ask students to look for signs that use the possessive as they travel to school. Ask them to take a photo of the sign they find to present in class or to write down what the sign says. Explain that sometimes signs will use the possessive incorrectly, so they should be on the lookout for any errors on the signs they find.

CHART 6-10. Possessive: Irregular Plural Nouns. Page 187
Time: 10 minutes

- Write the chart title on the board.
- Have students read example sentences (a)–(d) on the board while you write just the irregular plural possessives.
- Remind students that because these irregular plurals do *not* have a final -s automatically added (the way regular plurals do), the apostrophe can go between the final letter of the irregular plural and the -s.
- Review the notes in the chart.

❏ EXERCISE 49. Looking at grammar.
Page 187
Time: 5–10 minutes

- Lead this exercise with students.
- Have students complete each item on sight and ask them to spell the possessive form.

❏ EXERCISE 50. Looking at grammar.
Page 188
Time: 10 minutes

- Read the direction line to students and review the completed example.
- Give students time to complete all the items as seatwork.
- Correct by having students read their completions aloud and ask them to spell their responses.

❏ EXERCISE 51. Looking at grammar.
Page 188
Time: 5–10 minutes

- Lead this review exercise with the class as a whole.
- Have different students read the items aloud and specify which word they have chosen—a, b, or c.

❏ EXERCISE 52. Check your knowledge.
Page 189
Time: 10 minutes

- Give students time to complete the review as seatwork.
- Circulate and help individuals as needed.
- Correct by having individual students read the corrected versions of the original sentences aloud.
- For clarity's sake, have students put any particularly challenging items on the board.

❏ EXERCISE 53. Grammar and writing.
Page 190
Time: 10–20 minutes

Part I
- Have students read the passage independently and label the boldface nouns either *S* or *P*, singular or plural.
- Ask students to read the sentences from the passage aloud and to say what they labeled the boldface nouns.
- Ask students to explain or paraphrase vocabulary to engage them in the topic.

Part II
- Read the direction line to students.
- Read the question *Where do you like to shop?* and the suggested places for shopping in the direction line. Explain that these suggestions will give students ideas for writing a passage similar to the one in Part I.
- Have students complete the five sentences (items 1–5) and then combine the sentences into a paragraph.
- Remind students to add additional adjectives and details to make the story as interesting as possible.

Part III
- Have students exchange their paragraphs with a partner.
- Ask students to use the checklist in Part III to edit and improve their partner's writing.
- Have students give the paragraphs back to the original writers, who will finalize their changes.

Optional Vocabulary
biography   grocery store
sewing machine   ingredients
nickname   dishes (foods)
lawn mower   selection

Chapter 7
Count and Noncount Nouns

CHAPTER SUMMARY

OBJECTIVE: In this chapter, students learn to use noncount nouns in combination with common measurement and quantity terms. In addition, students become more adept at using count nouns with indefinite articles and quantity words. Finally, students learn to use nouns without any articles or quantifiers at all in order to make general statements.

APPROACH: The chapter first introduces noncount nouns, a concept that is not easy for beginners to grasp. By comparing common count and noncount nouns within the first chart, students immediately see two distinctions: Noncount nouns cannot be preceded by *a*, *an*, or *one*, and they cannot be made plural. Students gain practice with distinguishing between countable items and the noncount noun groups to which these items may belong. The text then presents practice with indefinite articles for count nouns and contrasts their use with the indefinite term *some*. The text goes on to teach quantity terms that can be used with count nouns and measurement terms that can be used with noncount nouns. Finally, the text discusses and provides practice in using both count and noncount nouns without any preceding articles or quantity words to make very general statements.

TERMINOLOGY: Once again, the text presents only enough grammar terminology to help students understand quickly. The book consistently uses the more descriptive terms *count* and *noncount* rather than using any other terms (*collective*, *mass*) for this type of noun. Throughout the chapter, the text uses the actual articles, measurement, and quantity words rather than referring to other classifications of these words. This simplifies the presentation and makes it easier for students to remember which articles go in front of count nouns and which words can precede noncount nouns.

❑ EXERCISE 1. Warm-up. Page 191
Time: 5–10 minutes

Beginners may know some noncount words. Because some of these words, particularly those that describe small particles or grains such as sugar and rice, may also have a noncount form in their own languages, students may understand these more readily. The noncount nouns that may prove more challenging to students are those that describe a collective group noun (such as *furniture*) of which countable nouns can be considered members (*chairs*, *beds*, *desks*, *tables*).

- Have one student read the direction line.
- Have another student respond.
- Discuss why sugar cannot be counted and put students' explanations on the board. Teach the words *piece*, *particle*, *grain*, and others.
- Ask students to tell you other nouns that are similar to sugar—because the "pieces" are too tiny to count physically.
- Put the names of nouns that share these physical properties on the board, as students produce them. For example:

    Sugar has too many small pieces. You cannot count each one.
    Rice is like this too.
    So is sand.
    So is flour.

CHART 7-1. Nouns: Count and Noncount.
Page 191
Time: 10–15 minutes

- Write the chart title on the board.
- Ask students to tell you how many X objects they see in the classroom. For example:

    How many desks are in this classroom?
    How many books are in this classroom?
    How many students are in this classroom?
    How many teachers are in this classroom?
    How many clocks are in this classroom?

- Write students' responses on the board:

    There are <u>17 desks</u> in this classroom.
    There are <u>14 books</u> in this classroom.
    There are <u>13 students</u> in this classroom.
    There is <u>1 teacher</u> in this classroom.
    There is <u>1 clock</u> in this classroom.

- Explain that they have just demonstrated how to use count nouns—by counting the count objects in the classroom.
- Now explain that noncount nouns are just what their name suggests: nouns that cannot be counted.
- Write on the board:

Count Nouns:	can be counted
	can be preceded by a / one or a number
	can be plural
Noncount Nouns:	cannot be counted
	cannot be preceded by a / one or a number
	cannot be plural

- Ask students if they can think of a noun that is in the classroom and cannot be counted.
- Students may or may not be able to think of a noun they cannot count but that is in the classroom. If they cannot think of one, offer them a few to choose from:

  air
  friendliness
  homework
  furniture

- Refer back to the chart and have students read the examples from the chart aloud while you write the corresponding notes on the board.
- Review the list of common noncount nouns with your students.
- Ask students to describe any that they know and write related words on the board.

❏ EXERCISE 2. Looking at grammar.
Page 192
Time: 10 minutes

- Lead this exercise with the class as a whole.
- Read the direction line to your students and remind them that if a noun is a count noun, it can have a number, *a*, *one*, or *a lot of* before it and it can be plural.
- Have students take turns reading each item on the left, telling you the noun they will underline and saying whether the noun is count or noncount.
- Ask students for specific clues for each item: *How did they know the noun was count? How did they know it was noncount?*
- Use the board to clarify / illustrate any particularly challenging items.

❏ EXERCISE 3. Vocabulary and grammar.
Page 192
Time: 10 minutes

- Explain the direction line to students.
- Review the completed examples.
- Give students time to complete the exercise as seatwork.
- Correct by having students explain the changes, if any, they made to each item.

❏ EXERCISE 4. Looking at grammar: small groups. Page 194
Time: 10–15 minutes

- Put students into groups of three or four.
- Read the direction line to students.
- Circulate while students are discussing which noncount nouns and count nouns are close in meaning and writing them in the blanks.
- Review by having some students name the noncount nouns while others name the count nouns, using *a / an* as appropriate.

❏ EXERCISE 5. Looking at grammar.
Page 194
Time: 10 minutes

- Explain the direction line to students.
- Have students add either an *-s* or nothing to the nouns they find.
- Review by having students read their completions aloud and provide clear and immediate correction.
- Stress that students need to pronounce the ending of these words very clearly to show whether the noun is singular or plural.

❏ EXERCISE 6. Game. Page 194
Time: 15 minutes

- Put students into groups or teams of three or four.
- Explain the direction line and encourage students to look around the classroom to find nouns for each item.
- Give groups ample time to work on this while you walk around the room and help those who seem to need more support.
- Discuss various nouns that students provided and invite students to decide if they fit into the categories.
- Finally, tally the number of correct nouns each team provided for each item.

❏ EXERCISE 7. Game. Page 195
Time: 15 minutes

- Put students into groups or teams of three or four or have them work individually.
- Explain the direction line to students and encourage them to think of a word for every letter in the alphabet.
- Give groups or students ample time to work on this while you walk around the room and help those students who seem to need more support.
- Discuss various terms that students provided and invite students to debate how well each one fits into its category.
- Finally, tally the number of items each team or person listed for each category and list these on the board.

Optional Vocabulary
noncount nouns (from Chart 7-1 on page 191)
some advice
an assignment
a lot of bracelets
a cloud
a fact
a suggestion

❏ EXERCISE 8. Warm-up. Page 196
Time: 5–10 minutes

- Have students take turns reading the items aloud.
- Explain to students that they need to pronounce *a* and *an* carefully and that they need to consider the beginning sound of the noun that follows when using *a* or *an*.

CHART 7-2. Using *A* vs. *An.* Page 196
Time: 10–15 minutes

Articles can be problematic for beginners because in addition to choosing between indefinite, definite, and no article at all, they must also consider the sound of the consonant or vowel that the noun begins with. Provide immediate correction and clarification as you work through this chart, as such temporary errors can easily become fossilized. You can remind students that there are many advanced students who have great command of tenses and vocabulary but still make mistakes with prepositions and articles. You can help them avoid this by paying attention to these structures at the outset.

- Write the chart title on the board.
- Ask a student to read example sentence (a) aloud to the class.
- Say the example sentence aloud yourself, stressing the articles in boldface, and write the example on the board.
- Review the explanation in the right column of the chart.
- Stress that it is not just the first letter of the noun but the actual sound that that letter makes that determines whether *a* or *an* is used.
- Repeat the three steps above for the remaining example sentences, (b)–(g), and emphasize how important it is that students learn this correctly from the beginning.
- Tell students that you will be interrupting them frequently to provide supportive correction as they practice using *a* and *an*.

❑ EXERCISE 9. Looking at grammar.
Page 196
Time: 5–10 minutes

- Call on different students to complete each item aloud.
- As students complete each item, provide immediate correction when needed and write *a* / *an* with noun combinations on the board.

❑ EXERCISE 10. Listening. Page 197
Time: 5–10 minutes

- Have the CD player and CD track ready.
- Review the direction line and completed example with students.
- Play the CD and have students circle *a* or *an*.
- Review as a class and refer to the CD script for further clarification, as needed.

Optional Vocabulary
healthy
regular
exercise
tutor

❑ EXERCISE 11. Warm-up. Page 197
Time: 5–10 minutes

- Remind students that singular count nouns can be preceded by *a* / *an*.
- Ask students if they can explain what *some* means.
- Have students respond to the items by reading the questions aloud and discussing the answers.
- Ask students what conclusion they have reached about when to use *some*.

CHART 7-3. Using *A / An* vs. *Some.*
Page 198
Time: 10–15 minutes

It will help your students if you stress that *some* can be used in front of both count and noncount nouns and that when *some* is used in front of count nouns, those nouns are plural.

- Write the chart title on the board.
- Show your students one everyday item.
- Have more than one of them with you. For example, show and write:

    Here is a coin (a dollar, a key, a book, a pen, a sheet of paper, a credit card).

- Next, take several of the same items in your hands and show them to the class. Say:

    Here are <u>some</u> *coins (dollars, keys, books, sheets of paper, credit cards).*

- Explain that *some* is just any amount but it is more than a singular item. Stress that the idea behind *some* is that the exact number (or amount for noncount nouns) is not important.
- Have a student read example sentence (a) aloud and review the accompanying notes.
- Repeat this for example sentences (b) and (c) and write the notes on the board to assist students.

❑ EXERCISE 12. Looking at grammar.
Page 198
Time: 10 minutes

- Read the direction line to students and review the completed examples (items 1–3) with students.
- Give students time to work through the exercise, circling *a*, *an*, or *some* and then checking the correct category in the chart on their own, as seatwork.
- Review the correct answers with students, encouraging students to explain their choices.

❑ EXERCISE 13. Looking at grammar.
Page 199
Time: 10 minutes

- Have students look at the list of words and explain that they need to decide which words can belong to which category (*a*, *an*, or *some*).
- Give students time to complete the exercise.

- Have students take turns reading the words belonging to the three different categories.

Expansion: Ask students to use the words from the categories, as written, in grammatically correct sentences of their own invention. Have them write their sentences independently, and then put their sentences featuring particular words on the board. Five or six students can go up at once, and the remaining students should act as judges, to see if the sentences are correct in every way.

❑ EXERCISE 14. Looking at grammar.
Page 199
Time: 10 minutes

- Lead this as a group exercise.
- Explain the direction line to students and review the completed example with them. Make sure they understand they need to pick *a*, *an*, or *some* and then circle *singular count* or *noncount*.
- Correct immediately as students take turns reading completed responses.

❑ EXERCISE 15. Let's talk: small groups.
Page 200
Time: 10–15 minutes

- Put students into groups of three or four.
- Read the direction line to students and explain that they will see distinct categories for each item (beginning with the word *things*).
- Ask students to think of as many nouns as possible that will be preceded by *a*, *an*, or *some*.
- Review the lists produced by each group and discuss how common, rare, or appropriate the noun choices are.

❑ EXERCISE 16. Looking at grammar.
Page 200
Time: 10 minutes

- Read and discuss the direction line.
- Give students time to complete this cloze exercise independently as seatwork.
- Correct by reviewing as a class, having students take turns reading their completions.

❑ EXERCISE 17. Let's talk: pairwork.
Page 201
Time: 10 minutes

- Put students into pairs.
- Explain the direction line and tell Partner B to turn to page 502.
- Direct students to change roles when they have completed the first set of items.
- Circulate around the room, providing assistance and support.

❑ EXERCISE 18. Looking at grammar.
Page 201
Time: 10 minutes

- Explain the direction line and have students review the completed examples.
- Tell students they will need to add *-s* to a count noun, or give the irregular plural form, and identify noncount nouns (which cannot be made plural) correctly.
- Give students a few minutes to complete this on their own as seatwork.
- Correct and review as a class.

❑ EXERCISE 19. Reading and grammar.
Page 203
Time: 10 minutes

Part I
- Engage students in the topic by asking what they know about discounts and whether it is common to use coupons or even to ask for discounts in their countries.
- Preteach vocabulary that will support students' understanding of the text.
- Ask students to share with you any words they know that are related to discounts and coupons.
- Put these words on the board and, if possible, make a word web of related ideas. For example:

discount	buy one get one free
coupon	bargain
free	a deal
reduced	a steal

Part II
- Have a few students take turns reading individual sentences from the passage aloud.
- Ask students to write the nouns that follow *a* and *some* in the appropriate spaces and explain why *a* or *some* is used.

Part III
- Have students take turns responding to the discussion questions and put any new vocabulary that arises on the board.
- Encourage students to discuss why people may buy unnecessary items when they have coupons.

Expansion: Additional discussion questions:
  Do you enjoy shopping online?
  If so, what are the advantages and disadvantages of shopping online?
  Is it polite to ask for a discount when you shop in your country?
  What does barter mean? Do people barter in your country?
  In your country, do people freely say how much money they saved or discuss how much money they spent?
  Is money and spending money considered a taboo topic?
  If you don't use coupons yourself, do you know anyone who does?
  Are there certain special offers that you always take because they will save you money?

☐ **EXERCISE 20.** Warm-up. Page 204
Time: 10 minutes

> **Expansion:** Ask students additional questions to engage them in the topic. For example:
> *What is a liquid?*
> *What does thirsty mean?*
> *What liquids do you drink every day?*
> *Health experts say people should drink eight glasses of water a day. Do you do so?*
> *Other than because you are thirsty, why do you drink liquids?*
> *Do you ever drink something to cool down or to warm up? Do you drink tea or coffee to be sociable?*

- Ask a student to read the question in item 1 aloud, and then have students check any drinks they have every day.
- Ask different students to read item 2 and then item 3 aloud and discuss the uses of cups, glasses, and so on.
- Review the Warm-up questions as a class and move to the chart.

CHART 7-4. Measurements with Noncount Nouns. Page 204
Time: 10–15 minutes

> If possible, bring in physical examples of water, sand, sugar, flour, tea, and / or coffee so that students can clearly see why the only definite quantities that can be used with such substances are measurements of volume. You can easily show that the glasses of water can be counted, but that the water itself remains uncountable, simply by filling glasses of water from a pitcher. If you cannot demonstrate with real objects, be ready to draw a certain number of full glasses of water (as opposed to just "some water") on the board.

- Write the chart title on the board.
- If you have brought in a pitcher of water and plastic cups, as suggested above, show students an indefinite amount — *some water* — by pouring a bit of water into one glass. (Or draw a partially filled glass of water.)
- Now pour (or draw on the board) three full glasses of water and have students count them.
- Write on the board:

  three glasses of water

- Pour the glasses back into the pitcher of water and / or erase the board.
- State that both the partially filled glass and the full glasses of water represent some water, but only the full glasses of water represent a specific quantity.
- Turn to the chart in the book and have students read example sentences (a)–(d) aloud.

- Write these sentences on the board and read the explanatory notes on the right.
- Ask students to look through the common expressions of measurement and identify phrases they know and to expand on this list, if possible.
- Write any additional phrases on the board:

  a bunch of grapes / carrots
  a can of soup / any liquid / somewhat moist solid
  a container of x
  a jar of peanut butter
  a piece (slice) of bread / pizza
  a sip of water

☐ **EXERCISE 21.** Vocabulary and grammar.
Page 205
Time: 10 minutes

- Review the direction line and completed example.
- Give students time to complete the items on their own as seatwork.
- Correct by having students read the completed items aloud.

☐ **EXERCISE 22.** Let's talk: pairwork.
Page 205
Time: 10–15 minutes

- Put students into pairs.
- Explain the direction line to your students and stress that they should describe their daily intake of the items below to their partner, as modeled in the example.
- Circulate around the room while students work on the exercise and assist pairs as needed.
- Review as a class.

> **Expansion:** Using the list of food and drink at the bottom of page 205, take a class poll of who eats and drinks what, in what quantities, and how often (each day and / or each week). For example:
>
> *How many people eat an egg each morning?*
>
> Write the results on the board and help students figure out percentages to show the class's dietary habits as a whole.
>
> For example:
> *Twenty-five percent of our class never eats chicken or meat of any kind.*
> *Thirty percent of our class eats ice cream every day.*
> *Ten percent of our class never eats cheese or any food made from milk.*

☐ **EXERCISE 23.** Looking at grammar.
Page 206
Time: 10 minutes

- Have students complete this exercise on sight as you lead them through it.
- Ask students to take turns reading aloud and completing with an item that makes sense.
- Provide immediate correction and further discussion of vocabulary as needed.

❑ **EXERCISE 24.** Game. Page 206
Time: 10 minutes

• Put students into teams or groups of three or four.
• Have students study the picture carefully. Explain that they should list as many items as they can, in the quantities they see.
• Remind students that they need to use the correct articles, numbers, and / or units of measure to describe the nouns they see.
• Have each group send one writer to the board to write the group's completed list of items.
• The group that presents the most accurate and complete list wins the game.

❑ **EXERCISE 25.** Let's talk: pairwork.
Page 206
Time: 10–15 minutes

• Have students return to earlier pairs or arrange new pairs.
• Read and explain the direction line to students.
• Be prepared to reiterate the difference between *need* and *want* and explain that each pair must pretend or imagine a situation that is not real.
• Have students work on their lists together, using *We need . . .* to introduce different essential items in different quantities.

Expansion: Use this as an opportunity to discuss what people really *need*, materially, as opposed to what they think they need. If you have access to the book *Material World: A Global Family Portrait*, Peter Menzel, Charles Mann (Berkeley: Sierra Club Books, 1995), bring it to class. This book shows families from many countries all over the world, with the entire contents of their homes laid out on the ground. Showing pictures from this book would give students further chances to name and quantify objects, such as in Exercise 24, above. It would also enhance any discussion of what people think they need for mere existence versus what they want in order to be comfortable.

❑ **EXERCISE 26.** Let's talk: pairwork.
Page 207
Time: 15 minutes

• Put students into pairs or have them select their own partner.
• Because each partner needs to look at different pages in the book at the same time, read and explain the direction line very carefully.
• Walk around the room to ensure that each partner is on the correct page and help students produce targeted grammar.
• Take notes on any mistakes that you hear.
• Have students change roles as described.
• Review the exercise with the class as a whole and review any mistakes or inaccuracies you heard by writing these on the board.

Optional Vocabulary

phrases	fresh
units of measure	nap
quantity	

Note: You can also use "common expressions of measure" on page 204.

❑ **EXERCISE 27.** Warm-up. Page 207
Time: 5–10 minutes

Expansion: To engage students in the subsequent chart fully, ask them questions about what kind of foods they should eat a lot of and what kind of foods they should eat only a little of, according to common sense. For example:

Is it good to eat a lot of sweets?
Is it good to eat a lot of fatty foods?
Should you eat a lot of vegetables?
Should you drink only a little water?

• Have different students read the two exchanges in the Warm-up aloud and elaborate, if possible.
• Ask students to make sentences describing what other students do eat *a lot / a little* of. Write student-generated sentences on the board. For example:

Martha eats a lot of carbohydrates.
Ama eats a lot of fruit but not a lot of vegetables.
Kim doesn't drink milk, but she does drink a lot of water.

CHART 7-5. Using *Many, Much, A Few, A Little.* Page 208
Time: 10–15 minutes

Beginners are probably familiar with these terms, but they may make errors with them. The most important distinction to make is that *many* and *a few* are used for count nouns and *much* and *a little* are for noncount nouns. You cannot stress this difference enough, and you should correct errors immediately and overtly to avoid their becoming fossilized.

• Write the chart title on the board.
• Ask students to take turns reading the example sentences (a)–(d) aloud.
• Write the example sentences on the board and explain the accompanying notes. You may want to point out that *many* is used in statements and *much* is more often used in negative sentences and questions.
• Ask students to make new sentences using the following count and noncount nouns and the verb *have*:

grammar exercises	grammar homework

• Write the resulting student-generated sentences on the board.

Pablo has <u>many grammar exercises</u>.   *Jo doesn't have <u>much grammar homework</u>.*
Caren has <u>a few grammar exercises</u>.   *Ahmad has <u>a little grammar homework</u>.*

❏ EXERCISE 28. Looking at grammar.
Page 208
Time: 10 minutes

- Read the direction line to students and have them consider the two completed examples.
- Have students complete the questions independently as seatwork.
- Remind students they need to identify the noun as count or noncount before choosing *much* or *many*.
- Review and correct by having one student say the completed question to another student, who should respond with the correct information.

❏ EXERCISE 29. Grammar and speaking:
pairwork. Page 208
Time: 10 minutes

- Read and explain the direction line to students.
- Remind them to concentrate on whether the noun is count or noncount when deciding between *much* or *many*.
- Tell students to complete each question and then ask their partner the questions. They should mark their partner's answers, circling either *Yes, I do* or *No, I don't*.
- Have students compare their responses with a partner's and then review as a class.

❏ EXERCISE 30. Looking at grammar.
Page 209
Time: 10 minutes

- Have a student read the paragraph below the direction line aloud.
- Ask a few key questions to ensure that students understand that Andrew is lacking supplies for the party. For example:

    What is the problem with Andrew's party?
    Does he have a lot of food?
    Why are his friends surprised?

- Have students complete each noun phrase with either *a little* or *a few*, independently as seatwork.
- Ask students to read the completed items aloud, and provide immediate correction, as needed.

❏ EXERCISE 31. Looking at grammar.
Page 209
Time: 10 minutes

Part I
- Lead this exercise on sight, with students.
- Explain the direction line to students and highlight the change made in the completed example.
- Have various students make transformations from *a lot of* to *much* or *many* on the spot, and correct immediately.

Part II
- Repeat the steps from Part I in changing *some* to *a few* or *a little*.
- Correct by having students read each item aloud.

❏ EXERCISE 32. Let's talk: pairwork.
Page 210
Time: 10–15 minutes

- Put students into pairs.
- Read through the direction line with students and model the example exchanges with one student.
- While students are working through the items in this list, circulate and help partners engage each other.
- Keep notes on various mistakes with target grammar, associated vocabulary, or pronunciation that you hear and review with the class as a whole.

❏ EXERCISE 33. Let's talk: small groups.
Page 210
Time: 10–15 minutes

- Have students in pairs combine with other pairs to form groups of three or four.
- Have a student read the direction line aloud and review the instruction with students.
- Make sure students start with either *We need* or *We don't need any* and mention ingredients from the list.
- Have each group report on their dessert back to the class, sharing the name for it.

Expansion: After the imaginary chef groups have shared their recipes' names and what they consist of, ask students to vote on which recipe sounds the best. You can also change this Expansion to have students create the least tasty-sounding dessert they can from the ingredients listed.

Optional Vocabulary

spices	ingredients
cabinets	dessert
create	

❏ EXERCISE 34. Warm-up. Page 211
Time: 5 minutes

Some beginners will probably know the difference between *the book* (their grammar book for this class) and *a book* (any book) instinctively. Below, you will demonstrate this difference with them.

- Have a student read the direction line aloud.
- Have two other students read items 1 and 2 aloud and discuss the answers as a class.

CHART 7-6. Using *The*. Page 211
Time: 10–15 minutes

- Write the chart title on the board.
- Ask your students to pick up *the book*, and write this direction on the board. For example:

  Please pick up the book.

- When all (or most) students pick up their red Azar grammar books, ask them how they knew which book to pick up.
- Explain that they knew because they already understand a lot about when and how to use *the* correctly.
- Have students read example sentences (a)–(c) aloud.
- Write the example sentences on the board and explain that when *the* is used before a noun, the speaker understands that everyone is speaking about the same person or thing.
- Read and discuss the accompanying notes with your students.
- Give students additional examples of nouns that are generally preceded by *the*. Reiterate that *the* is used because people are talking about one noun—the one, same noun.
- Write additional examples of the correct use of *the* on the board:

the sky	*the moon*
the ceiling	*the Eiffel Tower*
the Internet	*the Statue of Liberty*
the earth	*the Great Wall of China*
the sun	*the Egyptian pyramids*

- Have students read example sentences (d)–(f) aloud.
- Review the explanatory notes on the right with students.
- Write the following sentences on the board to illustrate using *the* with the second mention of a noun:

  We are studying a grammar point.

  The grammar point is how to use the.

❏ EXERCISE 35. Looking at grammar.
Page 211
Time: 10 minutes

- Read and explain the direction line.
- Give students time to complete the items as seatwork.
- Correct by having students read their completions aloud.

❏ EXERCISE 36. Looking at grammar.
Page 212
Time: 10–15 minutes

- Read and explain the direction line.
- Emphasize that students have to understand which nouns are being referenced in each item in order to decide whether *a / an* or *the* is correct in each case.
- Give students time to complete the items as seatwork.
- Correct by having students read their completions aloud.
- If there is any doubt, have students state the noun being referred to and discuss whether it is one of many or one definite noun.

❏ EXERCISE 37. Let's talk: pairwork.
Page 213
Time: 10–15 minutes

- Put students into pairs.
- Stress that this exercise focuses on using *the* for a second mention of a noun and that students will follow the Speaker A–Speaker B direction to change roles as they read the conversations aloud.
- Circulate around the room as students are responding.
- Remind students that when they first look at the picture, their descriptions constitute the first mention of the nouns in the picture. Thus, it is correct that they start with *I see a chair, a desk*, and so on.
- Review and correct the entire exercise as a class. Refer to and explain the use of particular nouns as needed and clarify these corrections by writing them on the board.

❏ EXERCISE 38. Looking at grammar.
Page 214
Time: 10–15 minutes

- Read the direction line to students.
- Ask them to complete each sentence with the correct article on sight.
- Have pairs read the items aloud, asking questions to help them. For example, for item 1:

  You are going shopping to get _____ coat.

  Do you already know which coat it will be?

  Is this the second mention of the noun? No. So, you are right. The correct sentence is I need to buy a coat.

- By coaching and leading students toward the correct completions, you can help them learn to correct autonomously.
- Continue with the remaining completions and put any challenging items on the board.

❏ EXERCISE 39. Game. Page 214
Time: 5–10 minutes

- Put students into groups of three or four and explain that each group will act as a team.
- Explain the direction line and review the completed example item 1 with the class.
- Remind teams that their sentences must be grammatical and complete, in naming as many items as possible.
- Have one member of each team write the team's responses on the board.
- Other students should assess whether the sentences on the board are correct.
- Discuss mistakes in the target grammar and refer back to the chart to correct these.

Optional Vocabulary

hiding	figures
in mind	circle
mention	triangle
faucet	square
ceiling	rectangle
leak	

❏ EXERCISE 40. Warm-up. Page 215
Time: 5–10 minutes

> Many beginners will instinctively understand that when nouns are presented with no article at all, a very general reference is implied. As they read the Warm-up exercises, students should respond naturally and thus activate their own passive knowledge.

- Read the direction line.
- Have a student read item 1 and discuss as a class whether sentence a or b is true.
- Have another student read item 2 and discuss as a class whether statement a or b is true.

CHART 7-7. Using Ø (No Article) to Make Generalizations. Page 215
Time: 10–15 minutes

- Write the chart title on the board.
- Have your students take turns reading example sentences (a)–(d) aloud.
- Write these example sentences on the board and review the explanatory notes to the right.
- Explain to students that with both plural count nouns and noncount nouns, when the article is omitted a very general meaning is implied.
- Ask students to make general sentences about foods and write student-generated sentences on the board.
- Remind students that these are general nouns, not specific ones, and thus no article is required. For example:

  Vegetables are good for you.
  Kale is very nutritious.
  Lettuce is a vegetable, but it is not very nutritious.
  Ice cream is a treat.

- Have students read example sentences (e) and (f) aloud.
- Write the sentences on the board and review the explanatory notes.
- Ask students to make a few sentences about the quality of specific foods using *the*. Write the student-generated sentences on the board. For example:

  The sushi in Japan is more delicious than the sushi in Boston.
  The barbecue in Brazil is wonderful.
  The food in the United States is not spicy.

❏ EXERCISE 41. Looking at grammar.
Page 215
Time: 5–10 minutes

- Read the direction line and lead students through the exercise.
- Have students take turns reading these sentences aloud.
- As students finish reading each sentence, have them tell you if the boldface noun is specific or general.

❏ EXERCISE 42. Looking at grammar.
Page 215
Time: 10 minutes

- Read the direction line to students and review the one completed item.
- Give students time to complete the cloze items independently as seatwork.
- Correct this exercise by having students read each completed item aloud and discussing each as a group.

❏ EXERCISE 43. Listening. Page 216
Time: 10 minutes

- Have the CD player and track ready.
- Explain the direction line to the students.
- Ask them to decide whether each item, as heard in each sentence, represents a specific or general use.
- Have the script ready to refer to for correction and put any challenging items on the board for further clarification.

❏ EXERCISE 44. Let's talk. Page 216
Time: 10 minutes

> Assess how well students seem to be grasping the target grammar before deciding whether to lead this exercise as a class activity or have students work in small groups. If students seem to be using the new grammar easily, have them work in groups and circulate. If they seem to be struggling, lead the discussion from the center, writing on the board frequently to clarify and highlight.

- Have students take turns reading each situation aloud.
- Ask students to look at both a and b options beneath each statement and discuss which option is correct.
- Whenever possible, have students explain why a or b is appropriate and write additional notes on the board.

❏ EXERCISE 45. Listening. Page 217
Time: 10 minutes

- Have the CD player and track ready.
- Read the direction line to students and ensure that they know they will be writing *a / an* or *the*.
- Have students complete the items while listening.
- Review as a class, referring to the script as necessary for clarification.

Optional Vocabulary
caffeine
shelf
counter
woodpecker
head of department
battery

❑ EXERCISE 46. Warm-up. Page 217
Time: 5–7 minutes

> As with other grammar points in this chapter, many beginners can often tell which amount words (*some*, *any*) are correct and which are incorrect simply by trying out certain combinations. Encourage this ability in your students and use this opportunity to remind them that they do know more English than they think they do.

- Have students take turns reading each item aloud.
- Ask students to decide which words sound right in which sentences.
- Discuss their responses and clearly define the correct completions.

CHART 7-8. Using *Some* and *Any*. Page 217
Time: 10–15 minutes

> Think about what students have or don't have with them, physically, in class. Ask questions using *some* or *any* to get real student responses using *some* or *any*. For example, *Do you have some extra pens with you? Do you have any extra pens with you?*

- Write the chart title on the board.
- Start by making statements that utilize *some* and write these statements on the board, underlining the target grammar. For example:

  I have <u>some</u> coffee in my coffee cup.
  I have <u>some</u> tissues in my bag.
  I have <u>some</u> aspirin.

- Explain that *some* can be used for an amount or number of plural count nouns or with noncount nouns.
- Write the word *Statement* on the board and the following explanation:

  Use <u>some</u> to state that someone has an unspecific number or amount.

- Next, ask a student if he or she has *some* amount of an unusual item.

  Marco, do you have <u>some</u> marshmallows with you?
  Francine, do you have <u>some</u> apple juice in your handbag?

- The students will most likely not have the requested item and will say no.
- Write the word *Negative* on the board and explain how students can phrase their responses.

  Negative: Use <u>any</u> in a negative statement with <u>I don't have</u>.
  Marco doesn't have <u>any</u> marshmallows with him.
  Francine doesn't have <u>any</u> apple juice in her handbag.

- Next, explain that a question can use either *some* or *any*.
- Ask a couple of questions to demonstrate this.

  Do you have any brothers or sisters?
  Do you have some siblings?

- Write the following on the board:

  Questions: Use either some or any.

- Have students read the examples in the chart and discuss the accompanying notes.

❑ EXERCISE 47. Looking at grammar.
Page 218
Time: 10–12 minutes

- Read the direction line aloud.
- Have students take turns reading the completed example items 1–3 aloud.
- Give students time to work through the exercise as seatwork.
- Correct by having students read their completed answers and review any more challenging items by writing them on the board.

❑ EXERCISE 48. Let's talk: interview.
Page 218
Time: 15 minutes

- Read through the model in the book.
- Write Student A's and Student B's parts on the board.
- Have students move around the classroom and talk to one another.
- Help students follow the model correctly by interrupting and guiding them when they use *any* or *some* incorrectly.
- Correct and review by having students share with one another.

Expansion: Have students write full responses to the interview questions on the board for their peers to correct.

❑ EXERCISE 49. Let's talk: small groups.
Page 219
Time: 10–15 minutes

- Put students into groups of three or four.
- Explain to students that they should imagine that they are at a mall and have gift cards amounting to the cost of a new computer.
- Have students first discuss what that amount might actually be in dollars and define it.
- Then ask each group to decide what to buy for their group until the money is gone.

Expansion: Make this activity more interesting by giving each group a specific and different event or situation to prepare for. They must decide what they need to spend the group's money on with this event in mind. Students should expand the list of items, accordingly.

Suggestions:
a big party
a trip climbing a mountain
a trip to a tropical resort
a seminar to help foreign students feel comfortable in the United States
a cooking class
a picnic

❏ EXERCISE 50. Looking at grammar.
Page 219
Time: 10–15 minutes

• Read the direction line to students and make sure they understand that they may need to use a plural form of the words in the gray box.
• Have a volunteer student read item 1 aloud.
• Give students time to complete the exercise on their own, as seatwork.
• When students have finished, correct the exercise by having students take turns reading the completions aloud.
• If students give unexpected answers, have them explain and justify them. Put them on the board and discuss these as a class.

❏ EXERCISE 51. Check your knowledge.
Page 220.
Time: 10–15 minutes

• Explain the direction line and review the completed example.
• Tell students that they will complete this cumulative review on sight, with you leading them as a class.
• Have students take turns correcting the errors on the spot and make sure they can explain the corrections.
• Write any challenging items on the board for additional clarification.

❏ EXERCISE 52. Let's talk. Page 221
Time: 15–20 minutes

This exercise allows students to practice all target grammar in Chapter 7 in a very productive and spontaneous way. However, because the direction line has several parts to it, spend ample time with students to ensure that they fully understand the instructions before they start.

• Read the direction line carefully, explain the situation, and remind students of the establishments that will certainly be part of the shopping center: a drugstore, a bank, and a grocery store.

Part I
• Tell students to work alone to decide what other businesses should be included and where they should go on the available blueprint (page 221).
• Circulate around the room, helping students with vocabulary they are unfamiliar with.
• Discuss the merits of different establishments with them.

Part II
• Have students each choose a partner.
• Tell them not to show their blueprints to each other.
• Tell students to ask questions of their partner regarding their plans for the blueprint and fill in their

establishments on Blueprint #2. They will need to give directions using prepositional phrases so their partner will know where to locate the stores and businesses they have chosen.
• Tell students to follow the model questions in order to get as much information as possible.
• Eventually, have partners compare the two blueprints and compare theirs with others in your class.
• Discuss and decide why certain businesses work best in certain locations and discuss the perfect or ideal shopping center plan.

❏ EXERCISE 53. Reading, grammar, and writing. Page 222
Time: 15–20 minutes

Part I
• Have students take turns reading parts of the passage aloud.
• Stop and interrupt students with spontaneous questions about vocabulary and comprehension.
• Ask students to paraphrase certain parts of the passage.

Part II
• Have students work through this part independently as seatwork.
• Read the direction line so students are aware of what words may precede each noun, according to the passage.
• Review and correct as a class.

Part III
• Have students model their descriptive writing of the picture of the girl riding horseback (page 223).
• Remind students to use a / an and some.

Part IV
• At this stage, students should be familiar with the editing checklist. Encourage their autonomous use of it and help them see where details could be added.
• Have students exchange papers or allow them to check their own.
• Have students place check marks next to all points that are appropriately completed and / or addressed.
• Encourage students to use these checklists to rewrite their pieces appropriately.

Optional Vocabulary

affirmative	valley
negative	composition
statement	puzzle
get along fine	comfortable
pencils with erasers	cafeteria
stepchildren	aquarium
worries	blueprint
advice for me	a dry cleaner's
strawberry	a Laundromat
tray	a video rental store

Chapter 8
Expressing Past Time, Part 1

CHAPTER SUMMARY

OBJECTIVE: In this chapter, students learn to use the simple past tense to describe past actions. They are given clear charts to help them become comfortable using *be*, regular verbs, and irregular verbs in statements, negative statements, and questions in the simple past. They also learn to recognize and use the adverbs that accompany the simple past tense so that they can autonomously move from tense to tense.

APPROACH: The chapter introduces the simple past tense of *be* and provides ample opportunities for students to transform the simple present of this verb into the simple past. These exercises highlight additional changes that are made (adverbs of time), and the book follows with negative forms and questions. Regular verbs are presented, and then irregular verbs that share the same patterns in the past tense are introduced one by one. Students are given both highly controlled written exercises to allow them to become confident with the target grammar and freer oral exercises, which require them to use the grammar intuitively.

TERMINOLOGY: The chapter does not focus much of students' attention on grammar terms. Most grammar texts present the base form, the simple past form, and the past participle of irregular verbs all at once, which can be overwhelming. This book departs from that established pattern and simply presents the base form and the simple past form of irregular verbs as simple tense and past tense. By relating the name of the actual tense to the part of the verb, students are better able to use and remember tenses correctly.

❑ EXERCISE 1. Warm-up. Page 224
Time: 5–10 minutes

> Beginners are probably familiar with many simple past verbs. As much as possible, engage students by using any language they generate for board work.

- Have one student read the direction line aloud.
- Have students respond to each item as seatwork.
- Write all four items on the board and have students share their yes / no responses.
- Ask students to tell you *what time it was **two hours ago*** and write this time next to the appropriate item on the board.
- Ask students to tell you *what day it was **yesterday*** and write the day next to the appropriate item.

- Tell students where you were yesterday and write your sentence on the board. For example:

  Yesterday, I was at home.

- Ask students to contribute where they were yesterday and write their sentences on the board.

  Mei-Wei was at the cinema yesterday.

  Bengt was at the mall yesterday.

CHART 8-1. Using *Be*: Past Time. Page 224
Time: 10–15 minutes

> Emphasize that there are only two forms of *be* in the simple past—*was* and *were*. As it is very easy for beginners to perpetuate fossilized errors, correct students quickly and overtly. Tell them that you are doing so to help them be well understood by speakers beyond the classroom setting.
>
> Use the context of the class to generate example sentences that "star" students and help engage all class members. Remember, students usually like seeing their names on the board so always try to incorporate actual students into board work examples.

- Write the chart title on the board.
- Write two column headings:

  Present Time   *Past Time*

- Have students read example sentences (a) and (b) aloud to the class and write the sentences under the correct columns.

Present Time	*Past Time*
a) I <u>am</u> in class <u>today</u>.	
b) Alison is sick today.	

- Discuss the importance of the words that are boldface. They tell us *when* and indicate present time (*am*, *is*).
- Continue having students read example sentences (c) and (d) aloud, and write each one under the correct heading above.
- Discuss the boldface words. They tell us *when* and indicate present time (*are*) and past time (*was*).
- Finally, have students read example sentences (e) and (f) aloud while you write each one under the correct heading above.
- As a class, come up with a new sentence featuring *be* in the simple present tense and write it on the board.

  Mehmet is a grammar genius!

- Have your students conjugate *be* in the present tense and then change it to the simple past.
- Write the conjugation on the board, with appropriate headings.

Present Tense	Past Tense
Today, I <u>am</u> a grammar genius.	*Yesterday*, I <u>was</u> a grammar genius.
Today, you <u>are</u> a grammar genius.	*Yesterday*, you <u>were</u> a grammar genius.
Today, he / she <u>is</u> a grammar genius.	*Yesterday*, he / she <u>was</u> a grammar genius.
Today, we <u>are</u> grammar geniuses.	*Yesterday*, we <u>were</u> grammar geniuses.
Today, you <u>are</u> grammar geniuses.	*Yesterday*, you <u>were</u> grammar geniuses.
Today, they <u>are</u> grammar geniuses.	*Yesterday*, they <u>were</u> grammar geniuses.

❏ **EXERCISE 2.** Looking at grammar.
Page 224
Time: 5–10 minutes

- Read the direction line and completed example to your students.
- Give students time to complete all the items as seatwork.
- Have students take turns reading their completed sentences aloud.
- Provide clear and immediate correction, and write items on the board, as needed.

❏ **EXERCISE 3.** Looking at grammar.
Page 225.
Time: 10 minutes

- Review the direction line and example sentences with students.
- Give the students time to write the new past-time sentences.
- Ask students to go to the board, as they finish, and take turns writing the new sentences on the board.
- Review as a class, asking students who didn't write sentences to correct the work of those who did.

❏ **EXERCISE 4.** Let's talk. Page 225
Time: 10 minutes

Part I
- Have a student read the direction line aloud.
- Ask students to check all the words that applied to them as children and also to include additional adjectives that could also describe them as three-year-olds.

Part II
- Put students into pairs.
- Explain the direction line and instruct students to begin with the boldface clause.
- After students have met with one another, have partners describe each other to the group. As an alternative, students can write one sentence about each class member on an index card.

- Collect these cards and read them aloud but replace the students' actual names with *This student . . .*
- Based on the sentence, the class has to guess whom the card describes. For example:

  This student was shy and quiet but also very curious.

EXPANSION: Invite students to think of extra words and phrases to describe children and / or themselves as small children.

Additional nouns and adjectives could include:

a daredevil	*grumpy*
an early / late walker	*fearless*
an early / late talker	*peaceful*
a handful	*physical*
a poor sleeper	*serious*
active (hyperactive)	*wild*
angry	*willful*
calm	

Optional Vocabulary
tired
absent
shy
curious
a troublemaker

❏ **EXERCISE 5.** Warm-up. Page 226
Time: 5–10 minutes

Whenever students disagree on actual facts or subjective impressions (as is possible with weather), a teachable moment occurs. If your students disagree about whether the weather was nice last month, get details from them and have them give examples. For example:

No, it was not nice. It was too hot, and there were many thunderstorms.

One of the most important tasks for a teacher in a language class is to allow actual spontaneous conversation to flourish. Therefore, teachers should never shut down an opportunity for a friendly disagreement, but rather, use it as a chance for engaged conversation.

- Read the direction line to students.
- Have students choose the correct verb (affirmative or negative).
- Have students take turns reading the completed items aloud.

CHART 8-2. Simple Past Tense of *Be*:
Negative. Page 226
Time: 10–15 minutes

Remind students that they have already learned how to make negative contractions with the present of *be* and that using the past will be even easier, as the past of *be* has only two forms.

- Write the chart title on the board.
- Ask students where they were yesterday and write their answers on the board. For example:

  Marco was at home.
  Emma was at her brother's house.
  Fei Fei and Sandra were at the beach.

- Ask students to dictate negative versions to you as you write them on the board. For example:

  Marco wasn't at school.
  Emma wasn't at the mall.
  Fei Fei and Sandra weren't at school.

- Have students read example sentences (a) and (b) aloud.
- Correct students' pronunciations of the contracted and noncontracted versions.
- Have other students read example sentences (c) and (d) aloud.
- Correct students' pronunciations of the contracted and noncontracted versions.

☐ **EXERCISE 6.** Looking at grammar.
Page 226
Time: 5–10 minutes

- Read the direction line to students.
- Have a student read the sentence about Joe and JoAnn aloud and review the completed example.
- Give students time to complete the items as seatwork.
- Correct by having students take turns reading the completed items aloud.

☐ **EXERCISE 7.** Grammar and speaking.
Page 226
Time: 10 minutes

- Explain the direction line to the class and be sure they understand that each sentence should refer back to *Yesterday at noon, I was / wasn't . . .*
- Give students time to make sentences.
- Have students take turns writing their sentences on the board and have those who are seated review the board work and offer corrections.

☐ **EXERCISE 8.** Listening. Page 227
Time: 10 minutes

- Have the CD player and track ready.
- Review the example with your students and make sure they understand the task before you begin.
- After students have chosen *was* or *wasn't*, review and correct with the script as necessary.

Optional Vocabulary
expensive
crowded
outdoors

☐ **EXERCISE 9.** Warm-up: pairwork.
Page 227
Time: 5 minutes

> Expansion exercises allow students who work at different paces to continue to do so. Monitor students' progress whether they are working individually or in pairs so that you can offer those who finish first a few more practice questions.

- Put students into pairs and read the direction line aloud.
- Have students ask each other the questions.
- Have them take notes on each other's responses and share their partner's responses with the class.

Expansion: Expand the Warm-up questions so that students can gain additional practice. Write the following questions on the board:

This morning at 7:30 A.M.,

1.	awake	Were you
2.	hungry	Were you
3.	on your way to school	Was it crowded / easy / normal
4.	in your pajamas	Were you

Have students ask and answer these questions. Then have students ask questions that they create, with other students answering in long or short answers.

CHART 8-3. Past of *Be*: Questions. Page 227
Time: 10–15 minutes

> Remind students that they already know how to form questions with *be* in the present, and that forming them with the past will be easier because the past of *be* has only two forms. Also, ask students to remind you of the expected short answers to yes / no questions in the simple present.

- Write the chart title on the board.
- Have a student read example question (a) and the possible short answers aloud.
- Write these on the board and highlight the past of the verb *be* and related time words.
- Have another student read example question (b) and the possible short answers aloud.
- Write these on the board and highlight the past of the verb *be* and related time words.
- Generate a few more examples with the class and put these on the board. For example:

  Was Atsuko sick yesterday?   *Yes, she was. / No, she wasn't.*

  Were Ramon and Kenji on time last night?   *Yes, they were. / No, they weren't.*

- Ask students to remind the class how information questions are formed.
- Write their responses on the board. For example:

  Wh-question word + verb be + subject

- Have a student read example question (c) aloud and review the answers.
- Have a student read example question (d) aloud and review the answers.

❑ **EXERCISE 10.** Looking at grammar.
Page 228
Time: 10 minutes

- Review the direction line and locations listed with students.
- Have a student read the completed example.
- Give students time to complete the questions and answers independently.
- Review as a class.

❑ **EXERCISE 11.** Let's talk: class activity.
Page 229
Time: 10 minutes

- Read the direction line to students.
- Ask students to contribute other adjectives that could be used to describe their feelings on the first day of class. Write these on the board:

anxious	frustrated
calm	interested
concerned	peaceful
confused	sad
curious	tired

- Model the example with a student as shown in the book.
- Review as a class.

Expansion: Have students also explain their feelings in class now. For example:

I was anxious on the first day of class. Now, I am very calm.

❑ **EXERCISE 12.** Let's talk: pairwork.
Page 229
Time: 10 minutes

- Put students into pairs.
- Have students first describe the situation in the illustration.
- Complete the questions by using the correct form of the verb *be*.
- Have students read their completed questions aloud.

❑ **EXERCISE 13.** Looking at grammar.
Page 230
Time: 10–15 minutes

- Read the direction line to students.
- Give students time to complete the items as seatwork. Have students work in pairs, if you wish.
- Review as a class by having students in pairs read their completions aloud.
- Put any particularly challenging items on the board.

❑ **EXERCISE 14.** Let's talk: find someone who . . . . Page 231
Time: 10–15 minutes

- Read the direction line to students.
- Model the example given with a student.
- First, ask each student to decide which characteristics apply to him or her.
- Have students get up and walk around the class, talking to their classmates.
- Have students compare their own characteristics in elementary school days with one another and complete each characteristic listed with the name of one student who can be described by it.
- Review by discussing which students in the class best fit each adjective and invite students to elaborate on these characteristics.

Optional Vocabulary

talkative	athletic
outgoing	active
hardworking	well-behaved

❑ **EXERCISE 15.** Warm-up. Page 232
Time: 5 minutes

> Beginners may be familiar with the *-ed* ending on regular verbs. Encourage students to tell you more activities that they completed earlier and put these activities into simple past sentences.

- Read the direction line aloud.
- Ask students to contribute additional activities completed, if they can.
- Put any additional student sentences on the board.
- Ask students to pronounce each simple past regular verb and underline all *-ed* endings in board work. For example:

Mei-Yun walk<u>ed</u> to school.
Abdul talk<u>ed</u> with his mother.
Jean-Michel ask<u>ed</u> for a coffee.

CHART 8-4. Simple Past Tense: Using *-ed*.
Page 232
Time: 10–15 minutes

> As you discuss the chart, stress that the simple past is very easy because each form is the same, even for third person singular. Underline the *-ed* ending and explain that this *-ed* ending is not a separate syllable. Most students don't know the phonetic alphabet, so when writing what the verb sounds like, simply use the known alphabet.

- Write the chart title on the board.
- Have a student read sentences (a) and (b) aloud while you write them on the board.
- Ask another student to read sentences (c) and (d) aloud while you write them on the board.

- Ask students to tell you what they did last weekend and write these student-generated sentences on the board. For example:

    Tatiana danc<u>ed</u> in a competition.
    Bengt wash<u>ed</u> all his clothes.
    Rose travel<u>ed</u> to New York.

❏ **EXERCISE 16.** Looking at grammar.
Page 232
Time: 10 minutes

- Explain the direction line.
- Go around the room and have students complete each item in turn.
- If students add in a pronounced -ed syllable, correct immediately and write the simplified phonetic pronunciation on the board. For example:

    Last night, you exercis<u>ed</u>. ~ Last night, you exercizd.

❏ **EXERCISE 17.** Let's talk: pairwork.
Page 233
Time: 10 minutes

- Put students into pairs.
- Explain the direction line.
- Write the beginning of each sentence on the board: *Yesterday, I . . .*
- Walk around the room and help pairs as they work through the items.
- Correct any added -ed syllables immediately and help individual students with pronunciation while also engaging them in natural conversation about the items. For example:

    You cooked dinner, Carlos. What did you cook?
    You talked on your cell phone, Kyoko. Did you talk on your cell phone in class?

- When students have worked through the exercise with their partner, have them explain to the class what each did and write sentences on the board.

❏ **EXERCISE 18.** Looking at grammar.
Page 233
Time: 10–15 minutes

- Explain the direction line.
- Give students time to complete the exercise on their own, as seatwork.
- Have students take turns reading their completions aloud.
- Correct overtly and clearly, emphasizing -ed pronunciation.

❏ **EXERCISE 19.** Vocabulary and listening.
Page 234
Time: 10–15 minutes

Explain how this listening exercise will help students. When reviewing the direction line, model examples of

simple past endings that are hard to distinguish and write these on the board, the way they sound. Tell students that it can help them to hear the endings and say them themselves if they focus on the final *d / t* sound. Use new vocabulary as an opportunity to get students speaking, and whenever possible, put words they produce on the board.

- Have the CD player and the track ready.
- Explain the direction line to students.
- Put simple past forms on the board and pronounce their endings, punching the final *d / t* sound appropriately.
- Ask students if they know the vocabulary highlighted in the yellow box and invite their explanations, writing them on the board as appropriate. For example:

    Say: Good, Carlos. You are right. Let's get it on the board.

    Write: A tournament is an event that has many matches or games played to end up with one champion. Wimbledon is a tennis tournament.

- Play the track through once.
- Correct items with students.
- For challenging items, refer to the script and emphasize the endings heard.

Optional Vocabulary

shave	coach
erase	score
instead of	goals
beard	

❏ **EXERCISE 20.** Warm-up. Page 235
Time: 10 minutes

- Ask students to choose the past-time words that sound most natural to them.
- Put the current day's name, date, and time on the board. For example:

    It is Monday, April 29, at 9:00 A.M.

- For each of the possible time phrases in red, ask students when in the past these phrases refer to. For example:

    Yesterday morning was Sunday, April 28, before noon.

CHART 8-5. Past Time Words: *Yesterday, Last,* and *Ago.* Page 235
Time: 10–15 minutes

Most beginners are already familiar with *yesterday*. *Last* and *ago* will require more explanation and demonstration. *Last* refers to the most recent occurrence of the same time period or term. Be very explicit. Explain to students that if today is Monday, last Monday was one full week before. When you explain *ago*, tell students that *ago* means *before* when used with previous periods of time. These concepts can be more challenging than you imagine, so give lots of examples and write them on the board.

- Write the chart title on the board.
- Have a student read the time phrases under the column heading *Present* aloud.
- Write the words in the *Present* column on the board.
- Turning to the class, write a new column for the past.
- Have students close their books and try to give you the equivalent of each present time phrase in the past.
- Leave the completed columns on the board and have students try making sentences with these before you move on to *last* and *ago*.
- Write the term *Last* on the board.
- Explain that *last* specifies past time as the most recent occurrence of a given time word (*last week*, *last month*, *last year*).
- Explain that if it is spring now, *last spring* was one year ago, the "last" time we were in the spring season.
- Ask students to say what they did by using *last* + a time word.
- Write their responses on the board in correct sentences. For example:

  Michiko moved to the United States last fall.

  Ari worked last weekend.

- Review the time expressions under the *Last* column.
- Write *Ago* on the board.
- Explain that *ago* means "in the past" and uses specific lengths of time to tell us how long before the present moment.
- Ask students where they were *two hours ago*. To help them produce sentences, tell students to use *was*.

  Anna was at home two hours ago.

  Peter was at the library two hours ago.

  I was in the shower two hours ago.

- Review the phrases under the *Ago* column with your students.
- Highlight the notes for each column at the end of the chart.

❑ EXERCISE 21. Looking at grammar.
Page 236
Time: 5–10 minutes

> Tell students that *yesterday* is either the name of the previous day or precedes a part of the previous day (*yesterday morning*, *yesterday afternoon*, *yesterday evening*), while *last* is used with *night*—*last night.*

- Read the direction line.
- Give students time to complete the items.
- Review as a class.

❑ EXERCISE 22. Looking at grammar.
Page 236
Time: 10 minutes

- Read the direction line and tell students to use only *wasn't* or *weren't* as the verb, to keep their sentences simple.
- Give them time to complete the exercise as seatwork.

- Correct the exercise by having students read their sentences aloud. Alternatively, have students write their work on the board and have the class correct.

❑ EXERCISE 23. Looking at grammar.
Page 237
Time: 10 minutes

- Have a student read the direction line aloud.
- Tell students they should refer to Chart 8-5 (on page 235) so that they can use a variety of expressions to complete the sentences.
- Correct as a class and be prepared to discuss additional possibilities not chosen by students.

Expansion: Have students prepare calendars of their own. Pass out blank calendars and ask students to fill in their schedules for last week (five activities). Then have them pass their calendars to a partner. Tell the partners to write a sentence for each of their partner's activities (five sentences). Have volunteers write their sentences on the board.

❑ EXERCISE 24. Looking at grammar.
Page 238
Time: 10 minutes

> When leading an exercise in the moment, without giving students time to prepare, begin with the strongest student and allow those who struggle to hear a few correct completions before moving on to them. This will help them to hear the pattern and feel less inhibited when they are responding.

- Lead this exercise without having students prepare their answers.
- Write the word *ago* and the completed example on the board.
- Have students take turns completing the sentences on sight. Help students if they struggle with vocabulary or word order.

❑ EXERCISE 25. Listening. Page 238
Time: 10 minutes

- Have the CD player and track ready.

Part I
- Tell students they must write the date.
- Play the track.
- Correct as a class, referring to the script when needed.

Part II
- Tell students they must write the time.
- Play the track.
- Correct as a class, referring to the script when needed.

Optional Vocabulary
evening (*versus* night)   activities
seasons   elementary school
calendar

❏ EXERCISE 26. Warm-up. Page 239
Time: 10 minutes

- Explain the direction line to students.
- Tell students that the highlighted verbs are the past forms of irregular verbs they know well.
- Have a student read the completed version of "Every Night" aloud.

CHART 8-6. Simple Past Tense: Irregular Verbs (Group 1). Page 239
Time: 10–15 minutes

Because so many irregular verbs are basic and important for everyday conversations, students may have a greater passive knowledge of them than you anticipate. Involve students maximally in the presentation itself and acknowledge how close students are to the actual forms when they are able to even approximate them. Beginners know more than they think they do, and by your helping them gain confidence, you will make them more willing to try out words they are not sure of. Becoming comfortable with the trial-and-error process is critical to being an effective language learner, so encourage this process. Explain that the irregular verbs in the chart do not share an irregular pattern in the past; however, they are common and much-needed verbs.

- Write the chart title on the board.
- Have a student read the simple present forms under the column heading *Present* aloud.
- Write these present forms on the board.
- Write the column heading *Past* on the board.
- Enlist students to help you complete the past tense forms that correspond with the present forms you already have on the board.
- Encourage students to try what they think the past form may be, even if they are wrong.
- Have students take turns reading example sentences (a)–(f) aloud.

❏ EXERCISE 27. Vocabulary and speaking. Page 239
Time: 10 minutes

- Explain the direction line to students.
- Tell students to close their books but leave the notes from the previous chart on the board for them to refer to.
- Lead this as an oral exercise with individual students first.
- Model the example with one student, perhaps someone who struggles a bit more overtly.
- Work through the exercise, calling on various students or inviting the whole class to respond.
- Correct immediately and overtly.

❏ EXERCISE 28. Let's talk: pairwork.
Page 240
Time: 10–15 minutes

- Put students into pairs.
- Read the direction line aloud.
- Model the examples with two different students.
- Have students begin working.
- Circulate around the room, checking in with pairs as frequently as possible to help them engage with one another, clarify any vocabulary questions, recast questions, and model pronunciation.
- When students have finished working through the items, have the class, as a whole, provide simple past versions of the items under both *Partner A* and *Partner B*.

❏ EXERCISE 29. Looking at grammar.
Page 241
Time: 15–20 minutes

- Read the direction line to students and instruct them to look at time words carefully before deciding which tense is needed.
- Give students ample time to complete the items as seatwork.
- Correct by having students read their completions aloud.
- Review mistakes in the actual form needed or in the pronunciation of the form immediately and overtly.

❏ EXERCISE 30. Listening. Page 242
Time: 10 minutes

- Have the CD player and track ready.
- Ask a student to read the direction line aloud.
- Ask another student to read the completed example aloud.
- Emphasize that students must choose grammatically correct and contextually sensible endings.
- Play the CD track. Remind the class that more than one completion may be correct.
- Review with students.
- For any challenging items, refer back to the script.

Optional Vocabulary
downtown
best friend
journal
front row
briefcase
butter

❏ EXERCISE 31. Warm-up. Page 242
Time: 10 minutes

- Have a student read the direction line aloud.
- As a class, complete the two items and discuss the answers.

Expansion: Ask students to think of other significant changes in everyday life from the time of their grandparents until now. Ask students to describe these changes by using the following phrases:

My grandparents didn't have _____.

My grandparents weren't familiar with
_____.

Encourage students to provide a variety of completions to these phrases and write them on the board. Example completions:

My grandparents didn't have cell phones.

My grandparents weren't familiar with Lady Gaga.

My grandparents didn't have the Internet.

My grandparents weren't aware of global warming.

CHART 8-7. Simple Past Tense: Negative.
Page 243
Time: 10–15 minutes

Because the helping verb *do* is the one that changes to the past, mistakes with the negative of the simple past tense are a typical fossilized errors for higher-level students. Remind students supportively to change *don't / doesn't* to *didn't* for all persons and correct errors quickly, using the board for extra emphasis as needed.

- Write the chart title on the board.
- Have students take turns reading sentences (a)–(d) aloud.
- Write these examples or student-generated examples on the board.
- Stress that both regular and irregular verbs use *did not* or *didn't* with the base form of the verb to form the negative.
- Emphasize that there are *no -ed* endings in the simple past negative.
- Review the *incorrect* sentences with students.
- Have another student read sentences (e) and (f).
- Remind students that they know contractions well and that the *didn't* contraction is exactly like *don't,* in terms of general form and placement in the sentence.

❏ EXERCISE 32. Looking at grammar.
Page 243
Time: 10 minutes

- Lead this exercise from the center, as an oral exercise, asking either the whole class to answer at once or individuals to respond.
- Read the direction line to students.
- Review the completed example.
- Have students transform sentences to negative forms without prior preparation.
- Correct production immediately and overtly.
- Write challenging items and / or their pronunciations on the board as needed.

❏ EXERCISE 33. Let's talk: pairwork.
Page 244
Time: 10–15 minutes

As students become more familiar with pairwork—as they move through the text—the time spent getting students into pairs decreases. You can continue to assign pairs or encourage students to pick partners. Be prepared to direct students working with the same partner repeatedly to change partners and remind them that doing so improves their English by exposing them to a greater number of accents.

- Get students into pairs.
- Read the direction line.
- Model Partner A's and Partner B's turns with students.
- Have students begin working.
- Walk around the room.
- Check in with pairs. Help with vocabulary and pronunciation. Take notes on common errors in target structures for explicit board correction later.

❏ EXERCISE 34. Looking at grammar.
Page 244
Time: 10–15 minutes

- Read the direction line aloud or ask a student to do so.
- Review the completed example with students.
- Give students time to complete the exercise as seatwork.
- Correct by having students read the completed items aloud, in turn.
- Address both pronunciation and target grammar while correcting.

❏ EXERCISE 35. Let's talk: game. Page 245
Time: 15 minutes

- Get students into groups of six or eight.
- Read the direction line aloud.
- Have three students model the roles of Student A, Student B, and Student C in the completed example.
- Circulate as students begin.
- Encourage students to say more than one negative statement, thus increasing the number of negative past forms that need to be repeated, to see if the last person in the group can repeat everyone's information successfully.

Expansion: Have students return from their group configurations to their seats. Try the exercise as a class, changing the time frame to last week. Have each student contribute and appoint yourself the last person in the group. Repeat all the negative past statements. Encourage students to help if you make any mistakes.

EXERCISE 36. Reading and grammar.
Page 245
Time: 15 minutes

- Explain the direction line, emphasizing that students must make any false statements in the sentences below the reading true.
- Review the completed examples.
- Have students read the passage silently.
- Give students time to work through items 3–8 as seatwork.
- Review as a class, having students read corrected statements aloud.

Optional Vocabulary

radio	got dressed
magazine	recognize
hurried	misread
prepared	

EXERCISE 37. Warm-up. Page 246
Time: 5 minutes

- Have students answer the questions.
- Ask additional questions (first in the simple present and then in the simple past) to engage others in the class further.

CHART 8-8. Simple Past Tense:
Yes / No Questions. Page 246
Time: 10–15 minutes

Call on students to remind the class of the basic yes / no question-and-answer form used in the simple present. Using this information, show how similar the past tense version is.

- Write the chart title on the board.
- Ask students if they email friends every day and write their responses on the board.

  Say: Do you email friends every day?
  Possible answers: Yes, I do. or No, I don't.
  Ask: Does Iqbar email friends every day?
  Answers: Yes, he does.
  He emails friends every day.

- Now have your students put your simple present question into the simple past and write the new question on the board, underlining the helping verb. For example:

  Did you email your friends yesterday?
  No, I didn't.
  I didn't email my friends yesterday.

- Have a student read question (a) aloud along with the possible answers while you write the question and answers on the board.
- Have a second student read question (b) aloud along with the possible answers and write the question and answers on the board.

EXERCISE 38. Let's talk: class activity.
Page 246
Time: 15 minutes

- Ask students to close their books for this activity and lead the exercise from the center.
- Write the following sentences on the board and tell students they will be asking and answering yes / no questions using simple past.

  Yes, I did.
  No, I didn't.

- Using the completed example in the book, ask one student (Student A) the yes / no question and correct his or her short-answer form.
- Have that student ask the same question of a second student (Student B) and correct all the answers and questions produced.
- Go around the room for a few more exchanges before moving to a new question in the book.
- Work through all the items.

  Expansion: At the end of the exercise, go back to the items in the book and ask students questions about one another, based on what was learned through the content. For example:
  Did Sara drink coffee this morning?

  Students should respond with either:
  Yes, she did.
  No, she didn't.
  She didn't say.

  If students respond with *She didn't say,* the student in question should respond by using the target grammar.

EXERCISE 39. Looking at grammar.
Page 247
Time: 10 minutes

- Ask a student to read the direction line aloud.
- Have two students read the completed examples aloud.
- Give students time to complete the exercise as seatwork.
- Review as a class by having students read items aloud and providing clear and immediate correction.

EXERCISE 40. Listening. Page 248
Time: 10 minutes

- Have the CD player and track ready.
- Tell students they will hear complete sentences and will need to fill in the missing verbs and subjects.
- Review the completed example.
- Correct by having students take turns reading their completions aloud.
- Read from the script to clarify any misheard items.

❏ EXERCISE 41. Let's talk: find someone who . . . . Page 248
Time: 15–20 minutes

- Explain the direction line to students and remind them that they have done this type of exercise before.
- With students taking turns, review the example.
- Have students get up and move around, using their books both to ask questions and to write in names of students who can respond with *yes*.
- Help less easily engaged students by working with them directly and facilitating their interaction.
- Correct question-and-answer forms as you hear them produced, while circulating.
- Have students return to their seats for review.
- Ask questions of the class (*Who ate rice yesterday?*) and compare common responses.

❏ EXERCISE 42. Listening. Page 249
Time: 10 minutes

Tell students about reduced pronunciation and explain that many helping verbs and their subjects sound connected and less carefully enunciated than the distinct words they are learning. Model both standard pronunciation and reduced pronunciation. Explain that being able to understand this casual pronunciation will help students feel more autonomous in their use of English.

Part I
- Have the CD player and track ready.
- Play the track and stop it as needed to repeat the reduced pronunciations students hear.
- Review the reduced pronunciations in this part again by modeling them for students.

Part II
- Explain the direction line—that students will hear reduced pronunciation and will be asked to expand what they hear to the full form of helping verbs and subjects.
- With a student's help, review the completed example.
- Play the track and have students write the actual words heard.
- Correct as a class, referring to the script as needed.

❏ EXERCISE 43. Reading and grammar. Page 250
Time: 10–15 minutes

Having students read aloud serves many purposes. It gives you a chance to ensure that more reluctant students are participating in the class. It helps students become more confident sounding out and pronouncing less familiar words. And it gives you an opportunity to engage students around vocabulary and the paraphrasing of ideas, both of which require them to use unscripted English.

- Read the direction line to students.
- Give students time to read the story and complete the items below it as seatwork.
- Circulate, helping students as needed.
- Review by having students take turns reading lines from "Kevin's Unhealthy Habits" aloud.
- Have students read the questions, including the completed example, and their responses aloud.
- Correct target grammar and pronunciation immediately and use the board to clarify any challenging items.

Optional Vocabulary
text	complete the project
play video games	stand in line
wash the dishes	take a long time
make your bed	lifestyle
out of town	habits
assignment	

❏ EXERCISE 44. Warm-up. Page 251
Time: 5 minutes

- Ask students which sentences are true for them.
- Ask students to tell you more about their habits by asking questions related to these sentences. For example:

  Carolina, you don't drink water with dinner. Do you drink anything with dinner?

- Write students' habits and past actions on the board in order to involve students in the Warm-up and engage them in the next group of irregular verbs. For example:

  Carolina doesn't drink water with dinner. Last night, she drank tea after dinner.

CHART 8-9. Simple Past Tense: Irregular Verbs (Group 2). Page 251
Time: 10–15 minutes

Students should be able to discern common patterns in the irregular verbs in Group 2. However, these patterns are not consistent, and you should point out this lack of consistency to students. Memorizing the parts of common irregular verbs, as presented here, is very useful, but you should also stress that they will become familiar with what sounds right and what sounds wrong simply by using the language.

- Write the chart title on the board.
- Have students read the simple present and simple past pairs aloud.
- Highlight the overt similarities between verb endings in the simple present and similar endings in the simple past, as you see them.
- Warn students that they cannot assume that all verbs ending in *-ing*, like *bring*, have a simple past form ending in *-ought*.

❏ EXERCISE 45. Vocabulary and speaking.
Page 251
Time: 10–15 minutes

- Lead this activity from the center.
- Have students close their books.
- Write each simple present–simple past pair on the board before engaging students so that they can see the parts as they respond to you.
- Read each item aloud and ask the whole class to respond to the question at each item's end.
- In item 5, give students a chance to remember what they have just done and produce the past forms aloud.
- Facilitate correct production, and correct mispronunciation or incorrect usage right away.

❏ EXERCISE 46. Looking at grammar.
Page 252
Time: 10–15 minutes

- Ask a student to read the direction line aloud.
- Give students time to complete the exercise autonomously.
- Review by having students read completed items aloud.
- Correct clearly and immediately and put any challenging items on the board for further explanation.

❏ EXERCISE 47. Let's talk: pairwork.
Page 253
Time: 10–15 minutes

- Put students into pairs.
- Read the direction line.
- Model Partner A's and Partner B's turns with students, using the example in the book.
- Have students begin working.
- Walk around the room.
- Check in with pairs. Help with vocabulary and pronunciation. Take notes on common errors in target structures for explicit board correction later.
- Correct by having the class read aloud their Partner A and Partner B questions and answers.

❏ EXERCISE 48. Listening. Page 253
Time: 10 minutes

- Have the CD player and track ready.
- Read the direction line to students.
- Ask a student to read the completed example aloud.
- Emphasize that students must choose grammatically correct and contextually sensible endings.
- Play the track and have students complete each item.
- Review as a class by having students call out their completions.
- Refer to the script to clarify any challenging items.

❏ EXERCISE 49. Writing. Page 253
Time: 15–20 minutes

- Review the direction line with students and instruct students to use the phrases in each item in the simple past along with time phrases to write sentences about themselves.
- Have a student read the example and possible sentence.
- Have other students offer other possible sentences and write these on the board. For example:

  Last week, I did not go downtown with anyone.
  Yesterday, I went downtown by myself.

- Circulate around the room, giving students feedback and suggestions on their sentences.
- When students have had time to write sentences for all the items as seatwork, invite students to write a sentence for each item on the board.
- Correct as a class and give immediate feedback to the authors.

Optional Vocabulary

app	catch a cold
go fishing	out of breath
catch fish	

❏ EXERCISE 50. Warm-up. Page 254
Time: 5 minutes

- Ask students to mark the sentences that are true for them.
- Ask students to elaborate more in order to give more students a chance to use the present and past of *sing* and *speak*.
- Write student-generated sentences on the board. For example:

  Carlos sings karaoke almost every month.
  He sang karaoke last Friday night.

CHART 8-10. Simple Past Tense: Irregular Verbs (Group 3). Page 254
Time: 10–15 minutes

In Group 3, students should be able to discern some common patterns. However, these patterns are not consistent, and you should point out this lack of consistency to students. Explain that learning the parts of common irregular verbs, as presented here, is very useful, but also stress that students will become familiar with what sounds right and what sounds wrong simply by using the language.

- Write the chart title on the board.
- Have students read the simple present and simple past pairs aloud.
- Highlight the overt similarities between verb endings in the simple present and similar endings in the simple past, as you see them.
- Underline the final consonants in irregular verbs ending in -t, such as *left* and *sent*.

❏ EXERCISE 51. Vocabulary and speaking.
Page 254
Time: 10–15 minutes

- Lead this activity from the center.
- Have students close their books.
- Write each simple present–simple past pair on the board before engaging students so that they can see the parts as they respond to you.
- Read each item aloud and ask the whole class to respond to the question at the end of each item.
- Facilitate correct production, and correct mispronunciation or incorrect usage right away.

❏ EXERCISE 52. Looking at grammar.
Page 255
Time: 10 minutes

- Read the direction line and explain that students should complete the conversations by using the verbs in the box.
- Give students time to complete the exercise as seatwork.
- Circulate and assist students as needed.
- Correct by having students read each item (both question A and answer B) aloud.
- Correct target grammar and pronunciation immediately.

❏ EXERCISE 53. Let's talk: pairwork.
Page 256
Time: 10 minutes

- Put students into pairs.
- Review the Partner A–Partner B example with students.
- Encourage students to be imaginative in their vocabulary work.
- Have students begin working, and walk around the room, providing encouragement and connection.
- Review as a class by inviting students to share what their partner said in response to each question. You can also ask pairs to model their exchange.

❏ EXERCISE 54. Listening. Page 257
Time: 5–10 minutes

- Have the CD player and track ready.
- Play the track for "A doctor's appointment."
- Give students time to complete each item.
- Correct by having students read the sentences and answers aloud.
- Refer to the script as needed.

Optional Vocabulary
director's office
secretary
burglar
dawn
check (noun)

❏ EXERCISE 55. Warm-up. Page 257
Time: 5–10 minutes

- Ask students to mark the sentences that are true for them.
- Ask students to elaborate more in order to give more students a chance to use the present and past of *lose* and *wear*.
- Write student-generated sentences on the board. For example:

    Kotaro loses his voice when he gets a bad cold.
    He lost his voice last Monday.

CHART 8-11. Simple Past Tense: Irregular Verbs (Group 4). Page 257
Time: 10–15 minutes

In Group 4, students should be able to discern common patterns. However, these patterns are not consistent, and you should point out this lack of consistency to students. Learning the parts of common irregular verbs, as presented here, is very useful, but also stress that students will become familiar with what sounds right and what sounds wrong simply by using the language.

- Write the chart title on the board.
- Have students read the simple present and simple past pairs aloud.
- Highlight the overt similarities between verb endings in the simple present and similar endings in the simple past, as you see them.

❏ EXERCISE 56. Vocabulary and speaking.
Page 257
Time: 10–15 minutes

- Lead this activity from the center.
- Have students close their books.
- Write each simple present–simple past pair on the board before engaging students so that they can see the parts as they respond to you.
- Read each item aloud and ask the whole class to respond to the question at each item's end.
- Facilitate correct production, and correct mispronunciation or incorrect usage right away.
- Remind students that memorizing the specific parts of these common verbs is useful and that they will gain more familiarity the more they hear and use the simple past of irregular verbs.

❏ EXERCISE 57. Looking at grammar.
Page 258
Time: 10 minutes

- Read the direction line and explain that students should complete the conversations by using the verbs in the box.
- Give students time to complete the exercise as seatwork.
- Circulate and assist students as needed.

- Correct by having students read the completed items aloud.
- Correct target grammar and pronunciation immediately.

❏ EXERCISE 58. Let's talk: pairwork.
Page 259
Time: 10 minutes

- Put students into pairs.
- Review the Partner A–Partner B example with students.
- Have students begin working, and walk around the room, providing encouragement and connection.
- Review as a class by inviting students to share what their partner said in response to each question. You can also ask pairs to model their exchanges.

❏ EXERCISE 59. Listening. Page 260
Time: 5–10 minutes

- Have the CD player and track ready.
- Play the track for "A wedding ring."
- Give students time to choose the correct answer.
- Correct by having students read the sentences and answers aloud.
- Refer to the script as needed.

❏ EXERCISE 60. Looking at grammar.
Page 260
Time: 5–10 minutes

- Have students complete this exercise on sight.
- Ask a student to read the direction line.
- Write *did*, *was*, and *were* on the board.
- Call on students in order or jump around the class.
- Students complete the sentences with *did*, *was*, or *were*.
- Correct immediately and overtly.

Expansion: Birthday traditions vary somewhat from country to country. In some countries (like Greece) name days are celebrated instead of birthdays, and in other countries the birthday person should buy sweets or small gifts for friends, rather than the other way around. Ask students to describe, using the simple present, what they do in their countries for birthdays. Then ask individual students what they did on their last birthday, using the simple past. Write student-generated sentences and vocabulary items on the board.

❏ EXERCISE 61. Looking at grammar.
Page 260
Time: 10 minutes

- Have a student read the direction line and the completed example aloud to the class.
- Give students time to complete the items as seatwork.
- Correct by having students read the completed items aloud.
- Put any particularly challenging items on the board.

❏ EXERCISE 62. Looking at grammar.
Page 261
Time: 10 minutes

- Have a student read the direction line and the completed examples aloud to the class.
- Give students time to complete the items as seatwork.
- Correct by having two students read the completed questions and answers aloud.
- Put any particularly challenging items on the board.

❏ EXERCISE 63. Let's talk. Page 262
Time: 10–15 minutes

- Explain the direction line to the students.
- Have students get into pairs or small groups.
- Have students read and discuss the six items that serve as clues.
- Circulate, discussing the clues and which person lives in which apartment.
- Correct as a class, after all groups have identified the apartment dwellers. Have a volunteer put the chart on the board and explain the clues.

Expansion: Write the names of well-known but extinct creatures or people on index cards. For example:

dinosaurs, gladiators, the Roman emperors, Vikings

Pass index cards out to groups of students. Students have to create sentences describing the past habits of these beings using the simple past. Based on the content of these sentences, the class as a whole has to guess the group. For example:

They ate entire trees.
They ate other animals.
They died before the ice ages.
They were extremely large.

❏ EXERCISE 64. Check your knowledge.
Page 263
Time: 10 minutes

- Explain the direction line.
- Lead the exercise as an on-sight review.
- Ask students to identify mistakes and to make corrections as you call on them.
- Write any particularly challenging items on the board.

❏ EXERCISE 65. Reading and writing.
Page 263
Time: 10–20 minutes

Part I
- Have students take turns reading parts of the passage aloud.
- Stop and interrupt students with spontaneous questions about vocabulary and comprehension.
- Ask students to paraphrase certain parts of the passage and discuss which of the week's events were the most embarrassing and which they have experienced in their own lives.

Part II

- Read the Part II direction lines to students and discuss what events are considered embarrassing in a person's life.
- Review possible titles, and, if appropriate, share one of your most embarrassing moments with the class, writing a few descriptive sentences in the simple past to detail it.
- Remind students to use simple past extensively as they will be describing one incident in the past.
- Give students time to write as seatwork.

Part III

At this stage, students should be familiar with the editing check. Encourage their autonomous use of it and help them see where details could be added.

- Have students exchange papers or allow them to check their own.
- Have students check that all points are appropriately completed and / or addressed.
- Encourage students to use these checklists to rewrite their work appropriately.

Optional Vocabulary

jacket	shade
upset	messy
shell	went off
closet	rented
pieces	knocked on
interview	turned it down
slippers	embarrassing
garden	experience
fire alarm	upset

Chapter 9
Expressing Past Time, Part 2

CHAPTER SUMMARY

OBJECTIVE: In this chapter, students expand their knowledge and mastery of the simple past tense. They learn how to ask and answer *wh*-questions pertaining to the simple past and learn to anticipate whether a thing or person is required as they answer these information questions. *When* is introduced in combination with the simple past tense referring to one specific time in the past. It is also used to introduce the past progressive, to show the specific, simple past interruption of an ongoing past action already in progress.

APPROACH: The text first introduces simple past *wh*-questions that require either an adverb clause or phrase as a response. These questions ask *when / what* time, *where*, and *why* things happen. The text then asks students to provide both subjects and objects in questions posed in the simple past. Additional groups of irregular verbs are included as students gain mastery over the tense. Next, students move on to *before* and *after* time clauses, which allow students to string together sequential events in multiclause sentences. Finally, the past progressive tense is introduced, and the charts emphasize how to distinguish these two past tenses by both form and function.

TERMINOLOGY: As is typical throughout the text, terminology is used minimally and only to support students' ready comprehension of the material further. The most important terms used are *simple past* and *past progressive*, both of which connote important and useful meaning.

❏ EXERCISE 1. Warm-up. Page 265
Time: 5–10 minutes

> As was true of target structures in the previous chapter, many simple past tense questions are probably already familiar to some beginners. Ask additional questions of students and encourage them to tell you more about their past experiences by building on initial simple past questions. (For example: *When did you go downtown? Yesterday? Where did you go?*) As much as possible, engage students by writing up any language they generate as board work.

- Read the direction line.
- Ask students to read and respond to the items.
- Ask students if they know what questions the nonchosen responses would answer, and if they can give you such questions.

- Write additional questions on the board as well as other student-generated sentences. For example:

  Downtown is a place so the question is where.
  At midnight is a time so the question is when.

CHART 9-1. Simple Past Tense: Using *Where, Why, When,* and *What Time.* Page 265
Time: 10–15 minutes

> Explain that the question words in this chart all require either adverb phrases of time or place or *because* clauses, which explain why something happened. Beginners will have at least heard if not attempted these structures themselves. Remind students that they already know the basic question form with the helping verb *do* and that here they simply change to the past of *do* but use the same word order.

- Write the chart title on the board.
- Write two column headings:

  Question   *Short Answer*

- Have students read example sentences (a) and (b) aloud to the class while you write the sentences under the appropriate headings.
- Line up the words *did you go* underneath one another and stress that the word order (helping verb + subject + base verb) is the same in both versions.

Question	*Short Answer*
(a) Did you go downtown?	(a) Yes, I did. / No, I didn't.
(b) Where did you go?	(b) Downtown.

- Ask students to read example sentences (c) and (d) aloud to the class while you write the sentences under the appropriate headings.
- Continue having students read example sentences (e) and (f) aloud while you write the sentences under the correct heading.
- Write example sentences (g) and (h) by again lining up the related words to highlight the same word order.
- Continue presenting in this deliberate manner until you have reviewed all the example sentences in the chart and written them on the board.
- Discuss the difference between *When____?* and *What time____?* and write additional examples on the board.
- Because Exercise 2 involves freer production so soon after initial presentation, provide your students with additional practice before moving on to it.

- Without erasing the board, go through the various question forms one more time, asking different questions that are similar to each example and eliciting answers from different students.

❏ **EXERCISE 2.** Looking at grammar.
Page 266
Time: 5–10 minutes

- Read the direction line and completed example to your students.
- Have a student read the item 1 example aloud and refer back to Rosa's plan.
- Lead the exercise by asking students to create a simple past question using the phrases in 2 and 3.
- Write students' questions and responses on the board.

❏ **EXERCISE 3.** Looking at grammar.
Page 266
Time: 10 minutes

- Review the direction line and example sentences with students.
- Give students time to write appropriate questions for each answer.
- Correct as a class, asking students to read both their questions and the existing responses aloud.
- Address grammar and pronunciation errors immediately, and use the board for further emphasis or clarification.

❏ **EXERCISE 4.** Let's talk: interview.
Page 267
Time: 10–15 minutes

- Have a student read the direction line aloud.
- Review the example, having one student model Student A's role and another student read Student B's responses aloud.
- Walk around while students are interviewing one another and take notes on common errors.
- When students have completed most items with one another, gather again as a group and have students read the completed questions aloud, encouraging other students to respond.
- Review any common errors, using the board for clarification.

❏ **EXERCISE 5.** Listening. Page 267
Time: 10 minutes

- Have the CD player and track ready.
- Read the direction line aloud.
- Ask students to read the example aloud and discuss why b is the only appropriate response.
- Play the track and have students complete all items on the datebook pages.
- Correct as a class, referring to the CD script as needed.

❏ **EXERCISE 6.** Looking at grammar.
Page 268
Time: 10 minutes

- Have a student read the direction line and completed example.
- Lead this exercise on sight, asking different students to complete the negative question that goes with each response.
- Correct pronunciation and target grammar immediately, using the board to clarify as needed.

❏ **EXERCISE 7.** Listening. Page 268
Time: 10 minutes

- Have the CD player and track ready.
- Read the direction line aloud and write the *did-ja* pronunciation of *did you* on the board, to highlight the real sounds students will hear.
- Play the CD track and give students time to complete the exercise.
- Then play the track again, pausing for students to give their answers.

Optional Vocabulary
downtown
various
arrived
choose
decide

❏ **EXERCISE 8.** Warm-up. Page 268
Time: 5–10 minutes

Stress with students that any question beginning with *what* will have a thing as an answer. Any question beginning with *who* will have a person as a response.

- Read the direction line and write the Warm-up question on the board.
- Have students explain why b and c are not possible.
- Have students explain why d is not possible.
- Ask students for other possible responses to this question and write them on the board. For example:

  What did you want?
  Some help.
  A new book.
  An answer.
  Some food.

CHART 9-2. Questions with *What.* Page 269
Time: 10–15 minutes

- Write the chart title on the board.
- Write two column headings:

  Question   *Short Answer*

- Have students read example sentences (a) and (b) aloud to the class while you write the sentences under the appropriate headings.

- Line up the words *did Carol buy* underneath one another and stress that the word order (helping verb + subject + base verb) is the same in both versions.

Question	Short Answer
(a) *Did Carol buy a car?*	(a) *Yes, she did. / No, she didn't.*
(b) *What did Carol buy?*	(b) *A car.*

- Ask different students to read example sentences (c) and (d) aloud.
- Write these sentences beneath the correct column headings and line up the verbs as in the illustration above.

(c) *Is Fred holding a book?*	(c) *Yes, he is. / No, he isn't.*
(d) *What is Fred holding?*	(d) *A book.*

- Have other students read example sentence (e) and then (f) aloud.
- Write these sentences on the board.
- Explain that in sentence (e), the object of the verb follows the verb.
- Stress that in question (f), the object of the verb is the word *what* and it comes before the verb.
- Encourage students to create their own questions based on these models and write them on the board. For example:

  Did Shiko want a new cell phone? Yes, he did.
  What did Shiko want? A new cell phone.

❏ EXERCISE 9. Looking at grammar.
Page 269
Time: 10 minutes

- Have students work in pairs to read items 1 and 2 aloud in their completed forms as a question and answer.
- Give the pairs time to complete each item on their own as seatwork.
- Have pairs read their completions aloud and provide immediate correction.
- Write corrected items on the board, for clarification.

❏ EXERCISE 10. Let's talk: class activity.
Page 270
Time: 10–15 minutes

> Remind students that they first used the imperative form (for giving directions) in Chapter 1. Explain that this form does not have a written subject but the understood subject is always *you* (singular or plural).

- Lead this exercise from the center, giving directions and asking questions of students.
- Model the examples using Student A and Student B at the beginning of the exercise while students have their books open.
- Instruct students to close their books.
- Using the items in the exercise, tell students you choose to be Student A to follow your directions.

- As shown in the model, ask other students (Student B) to explain what each Student A did and ask the student who took your direction to explain what he or she did.

Expansion: This is a great exercise for expansion as you can give directions to, and ask questions of, individual students and groups, alike. Expand by writing more action verbs on the board. Ask a student to come to the board and instruct others to perform an action and then ask others to say what the "actor" did, using the simple past. Additional action verbs include:

hop on one foot
jump up and down on two feet
do five push-ups
do ten sit-ups
walk backward
walk to the door with eyes closed
meditate quietly for two minutes
make an animal noise
pretend to fall asleep

❏ EXERCISE 11. Vocabulary and grammar.
Page 271
Time: 10 minutes

- Have a student read the direction line.
- Ask students how they can ask others the meaning of a word, eliciting "What does X mean?"
- Ask another student to read the example question with you reading the answer.
- Ask students to take turns with the items, assigning different items to different students.

Expansion: Instead of responding to the question for each item, encourage students to supply meanings and definitions to their peers.

❏ EXERCISE 12. Let's talk: class activity.
Page 271
Time: 10–15 minutes

- Prepare by having the information for this activity open and accessible.
- Have a student read the direction line and situation description.
- Read the example with two different students.
- Have students ask for information as illustrated in the examples and give them specific answers based on the information from the *Let's talk: class activity* answers on page 503.
- As students gain the information to complete the chart, review and correct as a class.

❏ EXERCISE 13. Listening. Page 271
Time: 10 minutes.

- Have the CD player and track ready.
- Explain the direction line and review the completed example.
- Play the CD track and have students write what they hear to complete each item.

- Using the script as support, correct students' completions and be prepared to reread items as needed.

Optional Vocabulary

want	century
hold	humid
object of the verb	awful
suitcase	pretty difficult
mice	murder
salad	school tuition
activity	

❏ **EXERCISE 14.** Warm-up. Page 272
Time: 5 minutes

- Read the direction line to students.
- Have students match the illustration to the correct item.
- Discuss the difference between the two items.

CHART 9-3. Questions with *Who* and *Whom*.
Page 272
Time: 10–15 minutes

> Explain to students that *whom* is used in formal and written English but rarely in ordinary spoken English. Encourage students to be familiar with the difference but tell them that it is not a critical difference and that it is more important that they be able to understand the basic difference between subjects and objects, rather than use distinct terms for each when a person is in question.

- Write the chart title on the board.
- Write two column headings:

    Question   Answer

- Have students read example sentences (a) and (b) aloud to the class and write these example sentences (or similar ones you and your students generate) under the appropriate headings.
- Emphasize that *what* is used to ask questions about things and *who* is used to ask questions about people.
- Explain that questions (c) and (d) differ only in their use of *who* and *whom*.
- Have students read questions (c) and (d) aloud.
- Write questions (c) and (d) on the board and label every part of speech in both questions.

O	HV	S	V	O
(c) Who	did	they	see?	Jay.
(They saw Jay.)				
O	HV	S	V	O
(d) Whom	did	they	see?	Jay.
(They saw Jay.)				

- Have students read questions (e) and (f) aloud.
- Explain that *whom* can only be used for objects of the verb, but that *who* is also used in the same way.

- Write questions (e) and (f) on the board and label each part of speech.

O	HV	S	V	O
(e) Who(m)	did	they	see?	Jay.
(They saw **Jay**.)				
S	V	O	S	
(f) Who	saw	Jay?	Ella.	
(**Ella** saw Jay.)				

- Emphasize that when *who* is the subject of the sentence, no helping verb is needed.
- Review questions (g) and (h) and the notes to the right of the chart.

❏ **EXERCISE 15.** Looking at grammar.
Page 273
Time: 10–15 minutes

- Review the direction line and example questions with students.
- Have students work with a partner to create appropriate questions for each item.
- Correct as a class, asking students to read both their questions and the existing responses aloud.

❏ **EXERCISE 16.** Looking at grammar.
Page 273
Time: 10 minutes

- Explain the direction line to students.
- Remind students that *who* can refer to both the subject and the object of the verb.
- Give students time to complete the exercise as seatwork.
- Correct as a class, having students read their completions aloud.

❏ **EXERCISE 17.** Looking at grammar.
Page 274
Time: 10 minutes

- Explain the direction line to students.
- Remind students that *who* can refer to both the subject and the object of the verb.
- Give students time to complete the questions as seatwork.
- Correct as a class, having students read their completions aloud.

❏ **EXERCISE 18.** Let's talk: pairwork.
Page 275
Time: 10 minutes

- Read the direction line aloud.
- Ask students to brainstorm about the kinds of things that parents and teens typically talk or even argue about.
- Put some of these brainstorming ideas on the board. For example:

    Parents and teens often discuss_____.

    the time they come home—curfew

activities outside the home
friends
girlfriends / boyfriends
study habits
grades
their room—is it clean or dirty?

• Encourage students to share their own experiences and observations as either teens or parents.
• Have students describe typical relationships between parents and teens, depending on their background, nationality, religion, and so on.
• Have students get into pairs.
• Give pairs time to complete the dialogue between the parent and the teenager.

Expansion: The exercise seems like a conversation between an American parent and teenager. Have students work in pairs or small groups from their own countries, if possible, to prepare a conversation between a parent and a teenager. How would it be different? How would it be similar?

❑ **EXERCISE 19.** Listening. Page 276
Time: 10 minutes

• Have the CD player and track ready.
• Explain to students that they will have time to listen to the CD and choose the best answer to each question. Stop the CD between items, if necessary.
• When the CD has finished, ask students to correct the listening by reading their answers aloud as you read out the scripted question.
• Put any challenging items on the board for further clarification.

❑ **EXERCISE 20.** Game. Page 276
Time: 10–15 minutes

• Have students get into groups or teams.
• Explain the direction line to students and emphasize that the questions they write must be both grammatical and logical.
• Give students time to work on this task and circulate around the room, helping as needed.
• Review as class, encouraging peer correction.

Expansion: When most groups have completed the task, gather everyone's attention and ask a member of each group to write only the group's questions, not the locations, on the board. Others at their desks must both correct the grammar and guess what the original locations are, based on the details included in the questions.

Optional Vocabulary
arrivals
formal English
everyday English
grounded

❑ **EXERCISE 21.** Warm-up. Page 276
Time: 5 minutes

Expansion: To get more students speaking, expand item 1 to ask about other items that cost more now than they cost when students were younger. Additional items could include:

a gallon of milk   *flying to another country*
a pair of jeans   *going to the movies*
a tank of gasoline   *a bus or subway ride*

• Ask students to complete and read both items aloud.
• Discuss the past forms of the irregular verbs *cost* and *make*.

CHART 9-4. Simple Past Tense: Irregular Verbs (Group 5). Page 277
Time: 10–15 minutes

In Group 5, students should be able to discern common patterns. However, these patterns are not consistent, and you should point out this lack of consistency to students. Learning the parts of common irregular verbs, as presented here, is very useful, but you should stress that they will become familiar with what sounds right and what sounds wrong simply by using the language.

• Write the chart title on the board.
• Have students read the simple present and simple past pairs aloud.
• Stress that several verb pairs in this group have the same form for simple present and simple past.
• Let students know that memorizing the specific parts of these common verbs is useful and that they will gain mastery by hearing and using the simple past of irregular verbs.

❑ **EXERCISE 22.** Vocabulary and speaking. Page 277
Time: 10–15 minutes

• Lead this activity from the center.
• Have students close their books.
• Write each simple present–simple past pair on the board before engaging students so that they can see the verb pairs as they respond to you.
• Read each item aloud and ask the whole class to respond to the question at each item's end.
• Facilitate correct production, and correct mispronunciation or incorrect usage right away.

❑ **EXERCISE 23.** Looking at grammar. Page 278
Time: 10–15 minutes

• Read the direction line.
• Have students complete items independently as seatwork.
• Correct by having students in pairs read their completions aloud.

- Address mistakes in pronunciation and target forms immediately.
- Write simplified pronunciations of simple past verbs on the board to emphasize correct forms and help students avoid fossilized errors.

□ EXERCISE 24. Listening. Page 279
Time: 10 minutes

- Have the CD player and track ready.
- Explain to students that they will hear only the first part of a sentence, and then they should select as many completions as make sense.
- After students have completed the exercise, review by reading each item aloud from the script and having students explain the possible completions.

Optional Vocabulary
pack of gum
rock concert
telephone pole
calculator
barber

□ EXERCISE 25. Warm-up. Page 279
Time: 5 minutes

Expansion: To involve more students in using the verb *feel* in item 1, ask students to provide more adjectives to describe how they feel now and how they felt on the first day of classes. Additional adjectives include:

amused	*excited*
anxious	*exhausted*
curious	*frightened*
eager	

- Have students complete both items and expand on item 1, to engage a greater number of students.
- Discuss students' favorite sports teams with them and ask students if they know the names of any American sports teams.

CHART 9-5. Simple Past Tense: Irregular Verbs (Group 6). Page 279
Time: 10–15 minutes

In Group 6, students should be able to discern common patterns (*blow-blew*). However, these patterns are not consistent, and you should point out this lack of consistency to students. Learning the parts of common irregular verbs, as presented here, is very useful, but also stress that students will become familiar with what sounds right and what sounds wrong simply by using the language.

- Write the chart title on the board.
- Have students read the simple present and simple past pairs aloud.

- Let students know that memorizing the specific parts of these common verbs is useful and that they will gain mastery by hearing and using the simple past of irregular verbs.

□ EXERCISE 26. Vocabulary and speaking.
Page 279
Time: 10–15 minutes

- Lead this activity from the center.
- Have students close their books.
- Write each simple present–simple past pair on the board before engaging students so that they can see the parts as they respond to you.
- Read each item aloud and ask the whole class to respond to the question at each item's end.
- Facilitate correct production, and correct mispronunciation or incorrect usage right away.

□ EXERCISE 27. Looking at grammar.
Page 280
Time: 10 minutes

- Explain the direction line to students.
- Give students time to complete each item independently as seatwork.
- Correct by having students read their completions aloud. Attend to pronunciation and write any challenging items on the board.

□ EXERCISE 28. Listening. Page 281
Time: 10 minutes

- Have the CD player and track ready.
- Read the direction line aloud and emphasize that there may be more than one correct response.
- As you play the sentence beginnings, have students paraphrase what they heard and provide their completions.
- Review the entire exercise by reading required parts of the script aloud.

Optional Vocabulary
leaves
sleepy
baseball
ice
sidewalk
frog in your throat

□ EXERCISE 29. Warm-up. Page 281
Time: 5 minutes

- Ask students to read the sentences aloud and make them true for themselves.
- Compare other students' responses to the first true sentences you receive and expand upon students' answers to engage them further.
- For example, if students say they did feed animals at the zoo, ask them which animals they fed. Ask if they even fed the lions.

CHART 9-6. Simple Past Tense: Irregular Verbs (Group 7). Page 282
Time: 10–15 minutes

By this point, students should be used to the fact that there may be no obvious pattern among a certain group of irregular verbs. As with the previous groups of irregular verbs, stress that students will become familiar with what sounds right and what sounds wrong simply by using the language.

- Write the chart title on the board.
- Have students read the simple present and simple past pairs aloud.
- Let students know that memorizing the specific parts of these common verbs is useful and that they will gain mastery by hearing and using the simple past of irregular verbs.

❑ EXERCISE 30. Vocabulary and speaking. Page 282
Time: 10–15 minutes

- Lead this activity from the center.
- Have students close their books.
- Write each simple present–simple past pair on the board before engaging students so that they can see the parts as they respond to you.
- Read each item aloud and ask the whole class to respond to the question at each item's end.
- Facilitate correct production, and correct mispronunciation or incorrect usage right away.

❑ EXERCISE 31. Looking at grammar. Page 282
Time: 10 minutes

- Have a student read the direction line aloud.
- Have students complete each sentence on sight, without prior preparation.
- As students respond in turn (or in a random order, as called upon), correct pronunciation and usage.
- Ask students about nontarget structures and vocabulary, in order to engage them in the material further.

❑ EXERCISE 32. Listening. Page 283
Time: 10 minutes

- Have the CD player and track ready.
- Read the direction line aloud and emphasize that there may be more than one correct response.
- Have students paraphrase what they think they heard and provide their completions.
- Review the entire exercise by reading required parts of the script aloud.

Optional Vocabulary
storms
petted

diseases
umbrella
bookcase
wood
peacefully
What's the matter?

❑ EXERCISE 33. Warm-up. Page 284
Time: 5 minutes

- Ask students to read through all possible completions in both items 1 and 2 and decide which completions are true for them.
- Compare students' responses to the first completions you receive and write student completions on the board. For example:

  Before Marco ate breakfast this morning, he took a shower and combed his hair.

  After Hye Chang got to school today, he finished his homework and talked to his friends.

CHART 9-7. *Before* and *After* in Time Clauses. Page 284
Time: 15–20 minutes

Because this is the first sophisticated combining of clauses in a sentence that students have encountered to this point, it is very important to present the grammar clearly and deliberately so students can see that there are two separate clauses (both with subjects and verbs) but only one of those clauses contains the main action of the sentence. You can explain this by saying that a time clause beginning with *before* or *after* can also be replaced by a specific time phrase.

Some beginners will have heard such *before* and *after* time clauses on many occasions, but they may not know how to use and control them. Others will need even more support.

In order to keep students at all ranges within the general level both challenged and engaged, call on students to contribute what they can, based on their levels. Going slowly, writing carefully labeled examples on the board, and checking in with your students to ensure they have understood what has been presented are critical to their mastery of this grammar.

- Write the chart title on the board.
- Using either example sentence (a) from the chart or a student-generated example, write a main clause on the board and clearly label the subject and verb accordingly. For example:

  S   V
  main clause = Hiro called his girlfriend.

- Illustrate the function of *before* and *after* time clauses by initially writing a specific time phrase to show when the main clause took place. For example:

  S   V
  At 10:30 A.M.,   Hiro called his girlfriend.

- Underline the specific time phrase and explain that this is one way to show time—by writing the time or time period that an event happened.

- Explain that another way to show time is to use a *before* or *after* time clause.
- Replace the time phrase above with a *before* or *after* clause and explain that in this way, you have described the same time but used other events rather than the time itself.

         S   **V**

Before he arrived, Hiro called his girlfriend.

- Explain that *Before he arrived* is a time clause, and that as such, it also has a subject and a verb, as all clauses do.
- Label the subject and verb in the time clause and emphasize that the main action is in the main clause and the time clause (like a time phrase) tells us when. For example:

     S   **V**   **S**   **V**

Before he arrived, Hiro called his girlfriend.

- Explain that when the time clause comes before the main clause, a comma is needed.
- Have students read through all the example sentences, (a)–(h), aloud and review the notes to the right with the class.
- Write the example sentences or other examples on the board, as necessary.

❏ EXERCISE 34. Looking at grammar.
Page 284
Time: 10 minutes

- Ask a student to read the direction line aloud.
- Review the completed example with students so they are sure of their task.
- Give students time to complete the items independently while you walk around the room, assisting those who need it.
- Correct the exercise by having four students write items 2–5 on the board.
- Ask those students who remain at their seats to correct the board work and discuss as a class.

❏ EXERCISE 35. Looking at grammar.
Page 285
Time: 10 minutes

- Read the direction line to your students.
- Have a student read through the completed example and discuss the logic of it.
- Explain that in order for this example to be logical and meaningful, watching a movie would have to occur before sleeping.
- Remind students that they need to apply the same logic to the other items in the exercise and think about what the verbs mean, and what happened first.
- Give students time to complete the items. Put them into pairs, if you wish. (Pairs that speak different languages would be ideal—then they will discuss the items in English.)
- Review by having students read the correct combinations aloud.

❏ EXERCISE 36. Game. Page 285
Time: 10–15 minutes

- Put students into teams of three or four.
- Read the direction line to students and explain that some of the sentences are complete and some are incomplete.
- Emphasize that students need to invent the main clause for those sentences that are incomplete and that each main clause must be grammatical and make sense.
- Give teams five to seven minutes to complete all the items.
- Have teams read their completions aloud and give one point for each completely grammatical sentence.

❏ EXERCISE 37. Let's talk: small groups.
Page 286
Time: 10–15 minutes

- Put students into small groups.
- Read the direction line to students and have them read the example sentences aloud.
- Have students decide who will write down the combined sentences.
- While students work through the items, walk around the room and help each group.
- Ask the writer in each group to read the first set of sentences aloud and do the same with the remaining items in this exercise.
- Correct clearly and immediately, using the board as needed.

Optional Vocabulary
combed
brackets
chased

❏ EXERCISE 38. Warm-up. Page 287
Time: 5 minutes

The two sentences have the same meaning, but occasionally a student may suggest that in item 1, the student arrived home and then, as a next step, had a snack, but that in item 2, the actions happened almost simultaneously. Discourage students from focusing on such subtle differences, as they are somewhat subjective.

- Ask students to tell you some things they do when they go home and write these suggestions on the board. For example:

take off my coat   *eat*
put my books on the table   *turn on the TV*
work out

- Using the word *when*, ask students to make a few sentences that describe their activities upon arriving home and write these on the board:

When Mariano got home, he took his coat off.
Wan Yi put her books on the table when she got home.
When Maria got home, she ate dinner.

CHART 9-8. *When* in Time Clauses.
Page 287
Time: 15–20 minutes

> Because *when* is also a basic question word, many beginners will be familiar with it. However, using it to introduce a time clause will be new for many of them. Introduce the grammar carefully and write many examples on the board.

- Write the chart title on the board.
- Write both sentences included in example (a) on the board.
- Emphasize that the clause order does not change the meaning.
- Ask students to label the subjects and verbs in both the main and time clauses. Write these on the board. For example:

       S V   S V

When the rain stopped, we took a walk.

S V   S V

We took a walk when the rain stopped.

- Ask students to read example (b) aloud.
- Remind students that as with *before* and *after* clauses, if the adverb clause comes first, a comma is needed before the main clause.
- Ask students to read examples (c) and (d) aloud and compare their meanings.
- Model question intonation in example (c).
- Repeat the time clause in example (d) and demonstrate that this thought seems unfinished without the main clause.
- Stress this last point with students to help them understand that some clauses cannot stand alone, and show them that they should be waiting for the main clause to complete a sentence begun with a time clause.

Expansion: Prepare index cards beforehand with equal numbers of *when* clauses to begin sentences (capital *W* in *when* and a comma after the clause) and main clauses. Distribute the cards to students. Instruct them to walk around and find their match. If they have a *when* clause, they should look for a main clause and vice versa. Remind students that they need to pay attention not only to the grammar (subjects must either match or complement each other) but also to the sense and logic of the match.

Sample *When* clauses and corresponding main clauses:

When I finished running,	*I took a shower.*
When I completed my homework,	*I watched TV.*
When Antonia's mother called,	*she answered.*
When we arrived at the airport,	*our flight had taken off.*
When they walked to the store,	*it started to rain.*
When Jung Seok traveled to New York,	*he visited the Statue of Liberty.*
When Malak ran the race,	*he twisted his ankle.*
When Pat and Joanna met,	*they fell in love.*
When the lightning struck,	*the dogs hid under the bed.*
When we rang the doorbell,	*no one answered.*

❑ EXERCISE 39. Looking at grammar.
Page 287
Time: 10 minutes

- Read and explain the direction line to students.
- Write completed item 1 on the board.
- Emphasize that *when* in a question requires capital *W* and a question mark, that the subject and verb are inverted, and that the verb changes to the question form—*do*, *does*, *did* and the simple form of the verb.
- Remind students that in *when* time clauses, there is no inversion of subject and verb and that these are not complete sentences.
- Give students time to complete the remaining items on their own.
- Correct as a class, using the board as necessary.

❑ EXERCISE 40. Looking at grammar.
Page 288
Time: 10 minutes

- Have a student read the direction line aloud.
- Explain that as in the Expansion above, students need to consider the logic and context as well as the grammar in choosing the correct matches from both columns.
- Give students time to complete the exercise autonomously.
- Correct by having students read their completed (matched) sentences aloud, using both word orders.

❑ EXERCISE 41. Looking at grammar.
Page 288
Time: 10 minutes

- Read and explain the direction line.
- Review the completed examples in item 1.
- Remind students they need to complete the sentence begun with a *when* time clause by supplying a main clause.
- Have students write their *when* questions and completed sentences on the board.
- Those not writing on the board should correct the sentences that classmates write.
- Invite other students to share their completions.

Optional Vocabulary

snack	snowman
introduce	homesick
clapped	electricity
mirror	

❏ **EXERCISE 42.** Warm-up. Page 289
Time: 5–10 minutes

> All progressive tenses can be challenging to beginners. Before leading the Warm-up with students, give them some examples from your own life. Use the progressive and then a very specific time in the past so that they understand that the specific past time occurred during a past action already in progress. Because this grammar is challenging in both meaning and form, use the very same example when presenting the chart, and draw time lines accordingly.

- Tell students what you were doing the previous day at one very specific time.
- Explain that the action you were doing began before the time named and continued after. For example:

  Now, I am teaching grammar.
  Yesterday, at this time, I was teaching grammar.

- Read the direction line and stress the specificity of the time.
- Have students complete the two Warm-up items and discuss them.

CHART 9-9. Present Progressive and Past Progressive. Page 289
Time: 15–20 minutes

> This chart introduces a new concept and uses a verb form students don't often use, the present participle. Encourage students to think of this as either the present participle or the *-ing* form, whichever is most meaningful to them. Refer students to Chapter 4 for review as needed.
>
> Remind students of how simple present (for regular, scheduled actions) differs from present progressive (an action actually taking place at the moment of speaking). Emphasize that because other people can usually see what we are doing at any given moment, the present progressive is not used as often as the past progressive. Explain that very often we want to explain what we *were doing* when the action in progress was interrupted.
>
> Write on the board as much as is helpful and draw time lines to illustrate the concepts here. Call on those students who seem to grasp the concepts first to read the examples and model items in the exercises.

- Write the chart title on the board.
- Explain what you are doing right now, and write this on the board along with the very specific moment in time. For example:

  It is 9:37 A.M., and I am teaching grammar.

- Illustrate this with a time line, indicating that the intersection of the x-y axis is right now by writing the time.

  _____|_____

  now
  9:37 A.M.
  I am teaching.

- Using this same example, refer to the previous class at the same time, and use past progressive.

  Yesterday at 9:37 A.M., I was teaching grammar.

- Illustrate this with a time line, indicating that the intersection of the x-y axis is right now by writing the time.

  _____X_____|_____

  now
  Yesterday at 9:37 A.M.
  I was teaching grammar.

- Move to the sentences in the chart.
- Have a student read example sentence (a) aloud.
- Stress that example sentence (a) is happening right now.
- Have another student read example sentence (b) aloud.
- Read and reiterate the explanations on the right side of the chart.
- Have other students read example (c) aloud. Write the book examples or additional examples on the board.
- Ask other students to read the items included in example (d) aloud. Write the book examples or additional examples on the board.
- Remind students that the only change needed is in the form of the helping verb and that the present participle (*-ing* form) does not change at all.
- Review the illustrations and check with individual students, encouraging them to give you examples from their lives that you can write on the board.

❏ **EXERCISE 43.** Grammar and speaking: class activity. Page 290
Time: 10 minutes

- Review the direction line with students.
- Discuss the phrase *in progress*. State that anything in progress started before the moment of speaking or observation and will continue after.
- Have students look at the illustrations and discuss the times on the clocks and the actions taking place.
- Lead students through completing item 1.
- Continue working through the remaining items.

❏ **EXERCISE 44.** Let's talk: class activity.
Page 292
Time: 10 minutes

- Review direction line with students.
- Have a student read the sentences describing the situation aloud.
- Ask students to describe what the various guests in the house were doing at the time of the robbery.
- Have students write sentences describing these actions on the board and correct as a class.

Optional Vocabulary

in progress	invited
particular	thief
program	jewelry
arrived	stole
robbery	

□ EXERCISE 45. Warm-up. Page 292
Time: 10 minutes

- Read the direction line to students.
- Have students check all possible events.

CHART 9-10. Using *While* with Past Progressive. Page 293
Time: 15–20 minutes

> Explain that *while* is used to emphasize how long something lasts. Because *while* expresses duration, it precedes the past progressive tense and stresses the time an action was taking place.
>
> The chart presents an action that was already in progress but interrupted by another action (of less duration). Emphasize this connection to students and give them additional examples, as needed.

- Write the chart title on the board.
- Explain that *while* precedes an action in the past that was in progress when another action took place.
- Have a student read example (a) aloud.
- Ask students to state which action was in progress (*I was sleeping*) and which action interrupted this (*the phone rang*).
- Have a student read example (b) aloud.
- Ask students to state which action was in progress (*I was sleeping*) and which action interrupted this (*the phone rang*).
- Remind students that when the time clause comes first, a comma is required.
- Draw a time line to illustrate these concepts.
- Draw the time line first and bold a portion of it in the past.
- Write *While I was sleeping* . . .
- Mark the X on the time line and write *the phone rang*.

_____X_____|_____

While I was sleeping, the phone rang.

□ EXERCISE 46. Let's talk: class activity. Page 293
Time: 10 minutes

- Read the direction line to students.
- Lead this exercise from the center, asking various students to combine the sentences in each item.
- Remind students that their first task is to identify which action was already in progress (in the past progressive) when interrupted by an action of shorter duration (in the simple past).
- Ask students to put their completed combinations on the board and correct carefully, using time lines to illustrate the sequence of events.

Optional Vocabulary

fire alarm	burned
ring	raised
spider	windstorm
crawled	suddenly
caught fire	

□ EXERCISE 47. Warm-up. Page 293
Time: 10 minutes

- Read the questions in the direction line to students.
- Have students read the items aloud and identify the time words.

CHART 9-11. Simple Past Tense vs. Past Progressive. Page 294
Time: 15–20 minutes

> In order to explain the way these tenses are combined and which time words go with each tense, you need to pay attention to what the verbs actually mean and how long it takes the action of each verb to take place.
>
> Stress that, as students saw previously, *while* precedes actions that were in progress and have significant duration. In order to use *while* with the past progressive correctly, the action has to take some time. Actions that take only a short amount of time cannot, logically, be preceded by *while*. A good way to illustrate this is by closing the door. Normally, it takes a second to close a door, and thus, there is not enough time inherent in the activity to use *while* appropriately. Show students that if something were to happen *while* you were closing the door, you would need to be closing the door more slowly than is normal. Usually for an action like closing a door, *when* is the appropriate time word and the tense is the simple past. For example: *The teacher was talking when Max closed the door.*
>
> The points above are best illustrated by actions that students know and can see and picture. Use the physical space and context of the classroom to distinguish between actions of some duration (*The students were completing an exercise*) and actions that happen very quickly (*Kyoko dropped her pen*).

- Write the chart title on the board.
- Have students take turns reading example sentences (a)–(c) aloud and stress the characteristics of the simple past tense.
- Write examples and these characteristics on the board.
- Ask other students to read example sentences (d) and (e) aloud.
- Ask students to remind you of what they just learned—when to use the past progressive—and write this on the board.
- Review the notes to the right aloud with students.
- Have a student read example sentence (f) aloud while you write this new combination (or a student / teacher-generated version) on the board. For example:

2   1
Sayeed closed his notebook   when the teacher turned the lights off.

- Explain that if two clauses are both in the simple past, the action in the time clause happened first and the action in the main clause happened second.
- Have students read example sentences (g) and (h) aloud while you write these examples (or student / teacher-generated examples) on the board. For example:

   1   2

   When the teacher turned the lights off, Sayeed closed his notebook.

   When the teacher turned the lights off, Sayeed was studying.

- Have students compare these last two examples.
- Ensure that they understand that the first sentence is two consecutive actions; the time clause action (*turned off the lights*) happened first.
- Explain that the second example shows one action already in progress (*Sayeed was studying*) that was interrupted by the second action (*the teacher turned the lights off*).

❏ EXERCISE 48. Let's talk: class activity.
Page 294
Time: 10 minutes

- Have a student read the direction line.
- Start by demonstrating the example with a number of students and clearly instruct Students A, B, and C while the other students are still looking at their books.
- Ask students to close their books and work through the remaining items.
- Go slowly and have students write what they describe on the board so that their classmates can see the grammar they are hearing.

❏ EXERCISE 49. Looking at grammar.
Page 295
Time: 10 minutes

- Read the direction line to students.
- Remind them to identify the action already in progress and to think carefully about the duration (or lack thereof) of each action.
- Give students time to complete the exercise independently.
- Correct by having students read their completed items aloud.
- Write items on the board for further clarification.

❏ EXERCISE 50. Speaking and writing: pairwork. Page 296
Time: 10–15 minutes

Part I
- Put students into pairs.
- Explain the direction line to students and review the completed examples.
- Give pairs time to write sentences combining tenses (and events in Bill Gates's life) while you circulate and assist them.
- Have pairs write their sentences on the board.

Part II
- Have partners ask each other for events from their lives to list, in time line fashion.
- Ask students to combine these events and write sentences about one another, in the same manner as above.
- Invite students to share one another's histories with the class.

❏ EXERCISE 51. Reading and listening.
Page 296
Time: 10–15 minutes

Part I
- Read the direction line.
- Have students take turns reading the paragraphs about Steve Jobs's life aloud.
- Discuss the new vocabulary and the vocabulary included in the paragraphs.

Part II
- Read the direction line aloud.
- Give students time to complete the sentences independently.
- Review as a class by having students read the completed sentences aloud and provide immediate correction as needed.

Part III
- Read the direction line.
- Have the CD player and track ready.
- Play the CD track and have students complete the sentences accordingly.
- Review and correct as a class, using the script as needed.

❏ EXERCISE 52. Looking at grammar.
Page 298
Time: 10 minutes

- Read the direction line.
- Remind students to think carefully about tenses and duration.
- Give students time to complete the sentences with the verbs in parentheses.
- Correct as a class by having students read the completed items aloud.

❏ EXERCISE 53. Looking at grammar.
Page 298
Time: 10 minutes

- Explain the direction line and lead this exercise from the center.
- Have students take turns reading items aloud and choosing the correct completions on sight.
- Review any more challenging items by using the board.

❏ EXERCISE 54. Looking at grammar.
Page 299
Time: 15 minutes

- Read the direction line and tell students that this exercise covers grammar from both Chapters 8 and 9.
- Give students time to complete the items autonomously.
- Repeat the steps above with Parts II, III, and IV.
- Correct as a class by having students take turns reading items aloud.
- Ask students to justify and explain answers when there is any disagreement over tenses.

❏ EXERCISE 55. Check your knowledge.
Page 301
Time: 5–10 minutes

- Read the direction line.
- Lead this exercise from the center, having students identify and correct mistakes on sight.
- Put any challenging items on the board as needed.

❏ EXERCISE 56. Reading and writing.
Page 302
Time: 20–25 minutes

Part I
- Read the direction line to students.
- Explain that they should underline all past verbs and ensure they understand why either simple past or past progressive was used.

- Have students take turns reading the sentences of the paragraph aloud.
- Ask students impromptu questions requiring them to both paraphrase and explain vocabulary in their own words.

Part II
- Read the direction line and ask students to pick a very memorable day or event, as this will be easier to write about.
- Have students use the seven questions to prompt their writing and ask them to consider all seven questions carefully as they compose their first draft.

Part III
- Have students exchange paragraphs and use the editing check included to ensure that grammatical forms and correct writing format have been used.

Optional Vocabulary

suit and tie	artistic handwriting
slippers	successful
puppy	attending
entered	greet
computer program	surfing the Internet
software company	concerts
design	upset
active	ankle
foundation	bill
electronics	builders
fired	roof
cancer	earthquake
medical treatments	grabbed
cure	gas station
turned (+ age)	fortunately
calligraphy	

Chapter 10
Expressing Future Time, Part 1

CHAPTER SUMMARY

OBJECTIVE: In this chapter, students learn to express future plans, promises, and predictions. While becoming familiar with these structures, students also learn more time phrases and how to combine them appropriately with tenses. This chapter also presents a complete summary of the forms of *be* presented thus far.

APPROACH: The text first introduces *be going to*, which is commonly used for expressing future plans. Because each use of this structure involves a number of parts, students are provided many opportunities to produce it in both controlled and less controlled fashions. The text next introduces the use of the present progressive to discuss future plans that have already been made and that describe an event close to the present time. The text reviews and introduces new time words to stress how these are used with the tenses presented. Finally the *will* future is introduced, and a summary of the forms of *be* completes the chapter.

TERMINOLOGY: As is typical throughout the text, grammar terminology is used only to support students' ready comprehension of the material further. This chapter refers to the actual words used to form the future format most commonly used for plans (*be going to*).

❑ EXERCISE 1. Warm-up. Page 303
Time: 5 minutes

As was common with target structures in the previous chapter, many beginners are probably familiar with some versions of the future tense. Use the Warm-up as a way to maximally engage students in comparing the past and their immediate and scheduled plans.

- Read the direction line.
- Ask students to read and respond to the items.
- Write additional examples on the board, using students' actual lives as much as possible. For example:

    Mahmoud exercised yesterday after classes. Tomorrow he is going to exercise at 4 P.M.

CHART 10-1. Future Time: Using *Be Going To*. Page 303
Time: 10–15 minutes

Explain that the future time expressed in this chart shows plans that are going to be executed. Write clear examples and underline all the parts of the verbs so that students can easily see all the elements of *be going to* future verbs. Stress that because of the verb *be*, yes / no questions can simply be responded to with *Yes, I am (going to work at 6:00 A.M.)* or *No, I am not (going to work at 6:00 A.M.).*

- Write the chart title on the board.
- Have students read example sentences (a)–(c) aloud.
- Write either the exact sentences from the text or similar sentences using students' names and the contexts of their real lives on the board.
- Underline the target grammar.
- Remind students that they need to make changes to each use of *be going to*, depending on the number and person of the subject. For example:

    I am going to make dinner for my housemates tomorrow night.

    Lei Ping is going to make dinner for her housemates tomorrow night.

    Lei Ping and Armando are going to make dinner for their housemates tomorrow night.

- Explain to students that the *be going to* future is made negative simply by inserting *not* between the verb *be* and *going*.
- Have other students read sentences (d)–(f) aloud.
- Next, have students make the affirmative statements on the board into negative ones by putting *not* in the correct location and then making correct contractions. For example:

    *I am **not** / I'm **not** going to make dinner for my housemates tomorrow night.*

    *Lei Ping is **not** / isn't going to make dinner for her housemates tomorrow night.*

    *Lei Ping and Armando are **not** / aren't going to make dinner for their housemates tomorrow night.*

- Have students read the questions and short answers in (g)–(i) aloud.

- Write these questions on the board or, with the help of the class, create specific questions based on students' actual lives. For example:

  Is Alana going to travel to New York this weekend?
  Yes, she is.
  Are we going to have a test on Monday?
  No, we aren't.
  Are Pedro and Hiroko going to bring cookies to our last class?
  Yes, they are.

- Ask students to read sentences (j) and (k) aloud.
- Explain that this pronunciation is one they may hear but stress that it is not appropriate to write these reduced pronunciations.

❑ EXERCISE 2. Looking at grammar.
Page 303
Time: 5–10 minutes

- Lead this exercise from the center.
- Ask individual students to respond to different items.
- Correct structure and pronunciation immediately.

❑ EXERCISE 3. Let's talk: pairwork.
Page 304
Time: 10–15 minutes

Part I
- Have students pick partners or assign partners.
- Review the direction line.
- Give students the opportunity to read through the example.
- Instruct Partner A to ask questions of Partner B, according to the book prompts.
- Remind Partner B to give Partner A short answers, followed by complete sentences.
- Circulate, assisting pairs.
- Have students change roles and continue.

Part II
- Ask students to write three activities their partner is going to do and three they, themselves, are *not* going to do.

Expansion: Have students expand on this activity by writing their partner's plans on the board or on an index card, but without identifying the partner by name. In order to make this into a guessing game, encourage students to write additional clues about their partner. For example:

She is going to do some laundry. She likes wearing clean clothes.
She is going to get some exercise. She loves running.
She is going to do some ironing. She always takes good care of her clothes.

Then, based on the information presented, students have to guess who the clues are about. For example:

That's Jung Soo. She likes to run, and she always has clean clothes!

❑ EXERCISE 4. Looking at grammar.
Page 305
Time: 10 minutes

As students develop their abilities to apply new grammar structures in controlled exercises, engage them around other nontarget items. The more conversational you can make grammar exercises, the more meaningful they will be to students as they will become adept at responding to unscripted questions posed by you (just as they will need to do in actual spontaneous conversations). The notes below provide some sample questions, but part of teaching well is simply bringing the margins of an exercise into the fore and promoting real conversation while focusing on specific grammar.

- Review the direction line with students.
- Encourage students to come up with their own completions if they prefer.
- Give students time to complete these items autonomously.
- Have students read their completed items aloud, and provide immediate correction of structure and pronunciation.
- Ask questions to engage students further on the spot. For example:

  Are you going to stay home if you think you are getting sick?
  Are you going to take over-the-counter medicine?

❑ EXERCISE 5. Let's talk: interview.
Page 306
Time: 10–15 minutes

- Explain the direction line to students.
- Have everyone get up, move around, and speak with a variety of classmates while taking notes and writing their classmates' names and answers in the chart.
- Walk around the room, yourself, and assist students in engaging one another appropriately. Help students phrase questions as needed and ensure they can get responses from one another.
- Ask students to write some of their classmates' names and responses on the board.

❑ EXERCISE 6. Game. Page 306
Time: 10–15 minutes

- Put students into groups or teams.
- Tell students that they will be participating with their books closed, and so they will need to listen very carefully and respond by using *be going to* in a way that makes sense.
- Put the team / group names on the board so that you can award a point to the first team to answer sensibly and grammatically.
- Read each prompt aloud and assign one point for the first correct answer.
- Review additional possible answers and correct pronunciation.

Optional Vocabulary

short answer	burglar
worry	plumbing
make a mess	cash a check
mail a package	

❑ EXERCISE 7. Warm-up. Page 307
Time: 5 minutes

- Have different students take turns reading the items aloud.
- Have students check all the sentences that have a future meaning.
- Before presenting the grammar, ask students how soon they think the future events are going to happen.

CHART 10-2. Using the Present Progressive to Express Future Time. Page 307
Time: 10–15 minutes

Explain that when the present progressive is used to express future time, plans have been made and are generally in the near future. Stress that there is no significant difference between the *be going to* future and the present progressive. Some native speakers use present progressive when the plans are even more certain or imminent, but many students at this level are not prepared to detect this subtle difference.

- Write the chart title on the board.
- Have students take turns reading example sentences (a)–(d) aloud.
- Write the sentences from the book, or sentences that you and the class create together.
- Underline the present progressive portion of the sentence and stress that the meaning is future. For example:

    Sultan *is picking up* his mother at the train station tonight.
    She *is arriving* on the 7:30 train from New York.
    They *are taking* the subway back to his house.

- Review the notes on the right side of the chart with students.
- Go over the list of verbs commonly used with the present progressive with a future meaning.
- Ask students what these verbs have in common, eliciting the response that most have to do with traveling—arriving, staying, flying, and so on.

❑ EXERCISE 8. Looking at grammar.
Page 307
Time: 10 minutes

- Explain the direction line to students.
- Give students time to rewrite each sentence by using the present progressive.
- Ask students to take turns reading their completions aloud.
- Correct immediately for target grammar and pronunciation when students are reading aloud.

❑ EXERCISE 9. Listening. Page 308
Time: 10 minutes

- Have the CD player and track ready to go.
- Explain the direction line to students and review the completed example.
- Stress that they will not circle something they actually hear but instead must decide whether the meaning of each present progressive sentence is present (actually happening this moment) or future (plans have already been made).
- Play the listening track.
- Review students' responses by using the script.
- Be prepared to write the sentences on the board, explain why the meaning is present or future, and highlight other clues heard by students.

❑ EXERCISE 10. Let's talk: interview.
Page 308
Time: 10–15 minutes

- Read and explain the direction line to students.
- Tell students that this exercise is very similar to Exercise 5 on page 306.
- Have everyone get up, move around, and speak with a variety of classmates while taking notes and writing their responses in the chart.
- Walk around the room, yourself, and assist students in engaging one another appropriately. Help them phrase questions as needed and ensure that they can get responses from one another.
- Complete the exercise by asking students to write some of their classmates' names and responses on the board.

❑ EXERCISE 11. Listening. Page 308
Time: 10 minutes

- Have the CD player and track ready.
- Read and explain the direction line.
- Tell students that they need to listen carefully for the verb form they actually hear and circle it.
- Correct by reading items from the script aloud and having students confirm the verbs they hear.
- Put any challenging items on the board for further clarification.

❑ EXERCISE 12. Let's talk: small groups.
Page 309
Time: 10–15 minutes

When working with beginners, your ability to help students to engage with other small-group members or partners is critical to the success of an activity. Approach small groups that do not seem be interacting maximally, and direct specific questions to specific students. Reference the countries your students come from and any interests they have mentioned. Compare their responses to your experiences and others' experiences openly and engagingly. Do not expect beginners to have the confidence simply to follow directions to engage one another. Getting students to talk to one another requires the same social skills required by a good host. It is necessary to be social yourself.

- Put students into small groups.
- Have students read sentences from the direction line aloud.
- To ensure students understand the task, have the class define the agreed-upon significant amount. Write it on the board. Explain the idea of the task further and offer alternatives. For example:

  The money is to help the city you are studying in become safer and more convenient.

  The money is to help children in the city you are studying in.

  The money is to help older people in the city you are studying in.

  The money is to help people who cannot afford to take English classes.

  The money is to help the environment.

  The money is to help endangered animals.

- Circulate among the groups and encourage students, enlisting specific students' ideas and facilitating a lively conversation in whatever ways you can.
- Correct students' pronunciation encouragingly and overtly, and take notes on common mistakes to present to the class as a whole.
- Put students' ideas on the board and discuss and compare ideas generated by the different groups.

Optional Vocabulary
sightseeing
contest
amount
improve
wonderful

❏ **EXERCISE 13.** Warm-up. Page 309
Time: 5 minutes

- Have students decide which time phrase correctly completes each of the three items.
- Discuss all the time phrases in red.
- For each time phrase, ask students which word or words is most important in telling them what tense to use.
- For example, students should identify that *ago* is used only with the simple past tense and that *last* is also only for the past.

CHART 10-3. Words Used for Past Time and Future Time. Page 309
Time: 10–15 minutes

Students will not be able to memorize every exact time phrase that is included in this list. The chart is well designed to contrast past time words with future ones.

Therefore, *yesterday* is contrasted with *tomorrow*, *last* is contrasted with *next*, and units of time + *ago* are contrasted with *in* + units of time. Get students to focus on learning these contrasting pairs rather than every complete time phrase.

- Write the chart title on the board.
- Draw students' attention to the list of contrasting time words listed on the left side of this chart, and then have students take turns reading various example sentences on the right.
- With students, put sentence starters on the board, and based on these, have students provide any completions that make sense, tense-wise. For example:

  One hour ago, Chia-Cheng was asleep.

  In one hour, Abdulla is leaving for New York City.

- Explain that by focusing on the most important word in every time phrase (not the unit or name of time itself, but the words indicating future or past), students will be able to use the correct tenses.

❏ **EXERCISE 14.** Looking at grammar.
Page 310
Time: 10–15 minutes

- Read the direction line and the completed example sentences aloud.
- Give students time to work through the items independently as seatwork.
- Then have students read the completed sentences aloud.
- If a student's response is incorrect, ask which word made him or her choose that time phrase and engage students in a discussion of the correct choice.

❏ **EXERCISE 15.** Grammar and speaking.
Page 311
Time: 10–15 minutes

Part I
- Read the direction line to the class.
- Give students time to complete the questions in Part I independently.

Part II
- Put students into pairs or have students pick their own partner.
- Have students work with their partner, asking and answering each other questions.
- Share some of the pairs' answers with the class, and compare plans and recent activities among classmates.

❏ **EXERCISE 16.** Looking at grammar.
Page 311
Time: 10–15 minutes

- Have a student read the direction line aloud.
- Ask two other students to read the two completed example sentences aloud.

- Give students time to complete the rest of the items as seatwork.
- Correct by asking students to read completed sentences aloud, using the time phrases appropriately.

❏ EXERCISE 17. Let's talk: pairwork.
Page 312
Time: 10–15 minutes

> This exercise provides an opportunity to explain to students the concepts of paraphrasing. Explain that they are to retell each sentence by using a time phrase rather than the actual date. Tell students that we often say "Tell me in your own words" in order to get students to explain text in their own voices, choosing their own vocabulary.

- Read the direction line to students.
- Explain that they will replace the actual date (month and date) with a phrase using *ago* or *in*.
- Circulate around the room and help pairs to formulate replacements for the actual dates.
- After students have had a chance to restate each item using time phrases to one another, invite individual students to write their sentences on the board.
- Correct all the sentences as students write them on the board.

❏ EXERCISE 18. Listening. Page 312
Time: 10 minutes

- Have the CD player and track ready to go.
- Read the direction line to students.
- Read the example items aloud and explain that students will hear the main part of the sentence (including the verb tense) and then will need to complete it by choosing the right time phrase.
- After you have played the track and students have chosen the correct items, correct by using the script as much as needed.

❏ EXERCISE 19. Let's talk: interview.
Page 312
Time: 10–15 minutes

- Read the direction line to students.
- Have every student get up and walk around the room, using the chart on page 313 to form questions.
- Circulate, assisting students and helping them form correct questions.
- Have students write the names and answers of those who responded to their questions in the chart.
- Review as a class and encourage additional questions and answers.

❏ EXERCISE 20. Looking at grammar.
Page 313
Time: 10–15 minutes

- Read the direction line and completed example sentence to students.

- Give students time to complete the sentences with the correct time words.
- Correct by having students read their completed sentences aloud.
- Review any challenging items and have students cite key words that informed their choices.

Optional Vocabulary
take a break
take a trip
used car
enter the university
graduated
competition
high school sweetheart
have company for dinner
freshman

❏ EXERCISE 21. Warm-up. Page 314
Time: 5 minutes

- Read the direction line aloud.
- Have a student read each item, and discuss the correct number choices.

CHART 10-4. Using *A Couple Of* or *A Few* with *Ago* (Past) and *In* (Future). Page 314
Time: 10–15 minutes

> Many beginners will be familiar with *a couple* and *a few*. Explore the meaning of *a couple* (two) and *a few* (not a precise number—could be two to five).

- Write the chart title on the board.
- Ask students when they use these number phrases and ask them to use them in simple sentences.
- Write student-generated sentences on the board. For example:

    Ali has <u>a few</u> cousins here in Boston.
    Tomas has <u>a couple of</u> questions for you.

- Ask students to remind you of the meaning and use of *ago*.
- Discuss the meaning of *ago* with specific units of time with students and write sample sentences on the board. For example:

    Jin Ok left Korea <u>three days ago</u>.
    Ariel bought his new car <u>one month ago</u>.

- Ask various students to read example sentences (a)–(c) aloud and discuss their meanings.
- Have other students take turns reading example sentences (d)–(g) aloud, and write either these exact sentences on the board or (better) student-generated ones. For example:

    We studied the simple present <u>a few weeks ago</u>.
    We're going to end class <u>in a couple of minutes</u>.

- Invite students to tell you what the date *a few weeks ago* was.

- Show students a calendar and have them pick possible dates that match the meaning of this time phrase (*a few weeks ago* = *two to five weeks ago*).
- Ask students to look at a clock and tell you what time *in a couple of minutes* is.
- Have a student read example sentence (h) aloud and explain that *more* is used to emphasize additional time.

❏ EXERCISE 22. Reading and speaking.
Page 315
Time: 10 minutes

- Read the direction line aloud to students.
- Have different students take turns reading parts of the passage aloud.
- Ask students questions about the meanings of words as they arise and / or ask them to paraphrase the meanings of whole sentences.
- Ask students who did not have an opportunity to read earlier to take turns reading the questions aloud, and involve still other students in selecting the correct responses.

❏ EXERCISE 23. Let's talk: small groups.
Page 315
Time: 10–15 minutes

- Ask a student to read the direction line.
- Assign students to small groups or invite them to choose their own.
- Have students read the completed examples aloud.
- Give groups time to complete each item.
- Circulate around the room, providing support to students.

❏ EXERCISE 24. Looking at grammar.
Page 316
Time: 10 minutes

- Read the direction line to students.
- Encourage students to be as specific as they feel comfortable being.
- Give students time to write each item and circulate to provide them with vocabulary, and so on.
- Review by having students read their completed items aloud.

Expansion: Have students write their completions on index cards. Instruct them to be specific enough so that their classmates can make a guess about who wrote the sentences.

Collect the index cards and redistribute them among the class. Have the students now holding the cards read them aloud and have others guess which students wrote the original index card sentences.

❏ EXERCISE 25. Listening. Page 316
Time: 10 minutes

- Have the CD player and track ready.
- Read the direction line to students.

- Review the example with them.
- Play the CD while students complete the exercise.
- Correct as a class and replay items as needed.

Optional Vocabulary
expressions
fell in love
changed her mind
got married
was born

❏ EXERCISE 26. Warm-up. Page 316
Time: 10 minutes

> To engage as many students as possible in the Warm-up exercises, you can write more examples on the board. Doing so provides more students with opportunities to preview the grammar point they will soon be presented with.

- Read the direction line to students.
- Have students pick the sentence with a present meaning and ask them how / why they chose it.
- Ask students to identify the two other tenses used with *this morning*.
- If helpful, write additional examples on the board. For example:

  I am going to watch TV this morning.
  I am watching TV this morning.
  I watched TV this morning.

- Give students the exact time and demonstrate how the present time determines when "this morning" is. For example:

  I am eating breakfast this morning. (Now it is 8:00 A.M.)
  I am going to eat breakfast this morning. What time are you going to eat breakfast?
  I ate breakfast this morning. What time did you eat breakfast?

CHART 10-5. Using *Today, Tonight,* and *This + Morning, Afternoon, Evening, Week, Month, Year.* Page 317
Time: 10–15 minutes

> Most beginners will understand that *this* relates to the present time. Stress that when using words for time periods, students must look at the verb to decide whether it was earlier in the same (*this*) time period or whether it is going to be later during the same (*this*) time period.

- Write the chart title on the board.
- Explain that time periods that are as long as an afternoon or a morning or a month or a year can have earlier and later parts within each one.
- Ask a student to read example sentence (a) aloud and discuss it. Ask students to tell you what time this morning. (They should look at the clock.)

- Ask another student to read example sentence (b) aloud and discuss it. Ask students what time earlier this morning. (Students should pick a time earlier in the same morning.)
- Ask another student to read example sentence (c) aloud and discuss it. Ask students what time later this morning. (Students should pick a time later in the same morning.)
- Write *Present* on the board with an additional example sentence. For example:

    Present: I am eating a sandwich this morning.

- Have students give you a time reference for what time *this morning* refers to in the present sentence.
- Then have them write the past and future sentences and tell you what time *this morning* refers to.

❑ EXERCISE 27. Looking at grammar.
Page 317
Time: 10 minutes

- Lead this exercise from the center.
- Have a student read the direction line and completed example aloud.
- Call on students to respond. You can ask different students to respond to the same questions, as their answers will be personalized.
- Correct overtly and point out the tense used in the question if students respond incorrectly.
- Write some student responses on the board and welcome students to compare their responses with others. For example:

    Marie and Abdulla are going to spend two weeks skiing in December.

    Jose, Carlos, and Hyung-Seo are going to take the international TOEFL in their countries later this year.

❑ EXERCISE 28. Looking at grammar.
Page 317
Time: 10–15 minutes

- Read the direction line aloud.
- Give students time to complete the items autonomously.
- Review by having students tell you which phrases are possible in each case.
- Correct overtly and clearly and use these cues to further engage students who may not have participated openly In the previous exercise.

❑ EXERCISE 29. Let's talk: small groups.
Page 318
Time: 10–15 minutes

- Read the direction line to students.
- Put students into small groups or invite them to put themselves into small groups.
- Model the example with two students so that students can understand the distinct tasks for Students A, B, and C.
- Have students begin working while you circulate.
- Go first to any small groups that appear not to be connecting optimally.

- Take the role of Student A as needed and ask questions directly, as appropriate.
- When most groups have worked through the twelve items, review as a class.
- Correct by asking various groups to give you sentences and write some of these on the board. For example:

    Shinko and Mari are going to go downtown this weekend.

❑ EXERCISE 30. Let's talk: pairwork.
Page 318
Time: 10–15 minutes

- If practical, have students work in pairs within their small groups so that you can minimize having them move around.
- Read the direction line aloud.
- Ask students to review short answer forms with the *going to* future and simple past and write these on the board. For example:

    Yes, I am. / No, I'm not.
    Yes, I did. / No, I didn't.

- Model the examples in the book with a couple of students.
- Have students work in pairs while you circulate, engaging, correcting, and helping them with pronunciation and needed vocabulary words.
- To correct, ask students if their partner is going to do something or not, and if their partner did or did not do something. They should answer in the short answer format. They will respond about their partner by using third person. For example:

    Did Sergio eat pizza last night, Marie?
    Marie: Yes, he did. / No, he didn't.
    Is Marie going to visit friends in a couple of hours?
    Sergio: Yes, she is. / No, she isn't.

❑ EXERCISE 31. Listening. Page 319
Time: 10 minutes

- Have the CD player and track ready.
- Read the direction line to students and have a student read the completed example aloud.
- Remind students that they need to focus on the tense they hear by listening especially for helping verbs and the endings of the verb forms themselves.
- Correct by having students read their responses.
- Review with the CD script as needed for any problems or questions.

❑ EXERCISE 32. Warm-up. Page 319
Time: 5–8 minutes

Most beginners have already met the *will* future, perhaps even before they met the *be going to* future in this chapter. At this point, the emphasis is on how similar both future forms are. Later, in their learning, students will begin to distinguish which one to use when, but for now, as beginner learners, they can use them interchangeably.

- Ask a student to read the direction line aloud.
- Have a different student read each of the items aloud.
- Ask students to decide, after each item is read, whether the sentence has a future meaning.

CHART 10-6. Future Time: Using *Will*.
Page 319
Time: 10–15 minutes

> Stress the similarity between *will* and *be going to* while presenting this chart.

- Write the chart title on the board.
- Draw a time line to show when *will* is used.

```
_____|_____X
        present time    future time
```

- Put a present progressive tense sentence beneath present time and put both a *will* and *be going to* sentence beneath future time.

```
_____|_____X
        present time    future time
    I am teaching now.  I will teach tomorrow.
                        I am going to teach
                        tomorrow.
```

- Ask a student to read example sentences (a) and (b) aloud. Point out that the two sentences have the same meaning.
- Ask another student to read example sentences (c)–(e) aloud. Remind students that they should not add an -*s* on third person singular.
- Write the incorrect forms that you see in sentences (c)–(e) on the board. Correct them with the class, crossing out incorrect final -*s* in (c) and (d) and *to* in example (e).
- Ask another student to read the example sentences in (f) to show contractions.
- Write the contracted forms on the board, and with students, discuss how to pronounce the contracted *'ll* form and write new examples on the board. For example:

  He'll go to the store later.

  We'll learn more about future tense in a few months.

- Have a different student read example sentences (g) and (h) aloud and write the negative contraction *will* + *not* = *won't* on the board. Write additional *will / won't* examples on the board to engage students further.

  They won't arrive at 4:00. They will arrive at 6:00.

❏ EXERCISE 33. Let's talk: class activity.
Page 320
Time: 10 minutes

- Read the direction line to students and have a student read the completed example aloud.
- Give students time to complete each item autonomously, as seatwork.
- Review as a class, correcting each item by having students read the *will* version aloud.

❏ EXERCISE 34. Let's talk: small groups.
Page 320
Time: 10–15 minutes

> Before beginning this exercise, ask about predictions and what predictions students have seen come true in the world in their lifetimes.

- Put students into small groups or have them form their own groups.
- Read the direction line aloud and ask students to define the word *prediction*. Write their ideas on the board. For example:

  Predictions are ideas about what will happen.

  Predictions are guesses about the future.

  People predicted that we would all have our own computers, and that is now true.

  Some people predicted the world would end in 2012, and that wasn't true.

- Ask students who made predictions, historically, and who in society makes predictions. Write more student-generated ideas on the board.

  Nostradamus made predictions. Stockbrokers make predictions.

  Weather forecasters make predictions.

- Tell your students they are going to make predictions about their classmates.
- Stress that in order to make predictions about their classmates' futures, they will need to observe their classmates' present situations carefully.
- Once students have started working, circulate, helping students who need prompting with ideas and vocabulary.
- Complete the exercise by asking groups to share their predictions with the class.

  Expansion: Have classmates vote on the best, most accurate predictions. Have students write their predictions for one another on the board, and then ask students to vote, by a show of hands, on whether they think the prediction will come true. Finalize each prediction by asking the person about whom the prediction was made whether he or she thinks it will come true.

❏ EXERCISE 35. Listening. Page 320
Time: 10–15 minutes

> The *will* and *'ll* sounds are very hard for students to distinguish from one another. Present the two pronunciations as clearly as possible and write each one on the board as you say it.

- Have the CD player and track ready.
- Explain that in Part I students will only listen and that in Part II they will have to complete the sentences.

Part I
- Read the sentences aloud for students.
- Enunciate the *will* and *'ll* very clearly.

- Discuss how similar the *will* and *'ll* sounds are and caution students to listen to the words that precede these sounds.
- Then have students listen carefully while you play the pairs of sentences on the CD.

Part II
- Tell students they should complete the sentences with *will* or *'ll*.
- Play the track.
- Review and correct by using the CD script as needed.

Optional Vocabulary
basically
research scientists

❑ EXERCISE 36. Warm-up. Page 321
Time: 5 minutes

- Read the direction line and have students take turns reading and responding to each item aloud.
- Say and write additional questions on the board to engage more students in this Warm-up. For example:

Will you speak English   Yes, I will.   No, I won't.
next year?

Will you travel next year?   Yes, I will.   No, I won't.

CHART 10-7. Asking Questions with *Will*.
Page 321
Time: 10–15 minutes

- Write the chart title on the board.
- Ask a student to tell you what he or she will do next year. Write the response in the third person on the board. For example:

Luzette will travel to Spain next year.

- Explain to students that the rule for changing a sentence with *will* to a yes / no sentence is similar to what they have already learned about simple present sentences.
- Tell students they should invert the subject and the *will* part of the verb.
- Ask students to dictate the new *will* question to you, and write this new question on the board.

Will Luzette travel to Spain next year?

- Next, ask students to give you short answer options based on what they have learned so far.

Yes, she will.
No, she won't.

- Have a student read example questions (a) and (b) aloud, along with the possible short answers.
- Ask students to give you some *wh*-question words and write these on the board as they say them. For example:

what   where
what time   who
when   why

- Remind students that the subject and verb remain inverted after these question words.

- Ask a student to form a question about a classmate, starting with *What time*, and write this question on the board. For example:

What time will Isabella come home?

- Ask what the short answer should be and stress that it should be only the information asked for. For example:

At 11:00 P.M.

- Have other students take turns reading example questions (c)–(e) aloud, along with the corresponding short answers.

❑ EXERCISE 37. Looking at grammar.
Page 321
Time: 5–10 minutes

- Read the direction line and the completed example questions and short answers to students.
- Give students time to complete the items autonomously.
- Review the exercise by having students read the completed items aloud and correcting immediately.

❑ EXERCISE 38. Let's talk: pairwork.
Page 322
Time: 10–15 minutes

- Put students into pairs or have them choose partners.

Part I
- Read the direction line aloud and ask your students to talk about the Paris sites mentioned in Part I.
- Have students check what they would do and ask them to think about why they would choose some sites and activities rather than others.

Part II
- Model the example with a student.
- Tell students to begin taking turns with their partner and circulate around the room.
- Help students respond in correct short answer form and engage students by asking them to explain their choices further.
- Ask the questions partners have already asked of each other to the class as a whole. Ask students to answer on behalf of their partner.

Expansion: Ask students to vote on which Parisian sites and activities are most popular. Have students identify why certain sites and activities are more popular than others.

❑ EXERCISE 39. Listening. Page 323
Time: 10 minutes

- Have the CD player and track ready.
- Read the direction line to students.
- Ask students to share their dream vacation spots with you and share yours with them.
- Tell students what factors you consider in selecting a dream vacation locale: warm / cool, rural / urban, oceanfront / island / mountain / forest, activities to choose from, crowded / isolated, and so on.

- Write a few students' dream vacation spots on the board. For example:

  Tokyo, Rio, a deserted island, Miami Beach, the Alps, and so on.

- Once students have written this place at the top of Exercise 39, play the CD track. Tell them they will need to respond to questions while referring to their ideal places.
- To correct and review, have students share their responses, referring back to their ideal spots.

❏ **EXERCISE 40.** Reading, listening, and speaking. Page 324
Time: 15–20 minutes

Teachers should be sensitive when leading discussions about bad habits and resolutions. If there is a very overweight person in the class, it could be embarrassing for that student. Therefore, if it doesn't feel comfortable to invite students to discuss their own bad habits and potential resolutions, it is best to give them more information about you or a universally famous person and ask students to make resolutions for this person.

Part I
- Have the CD player and track ready.
- Ask students if they know what a New Year's resolution is and if they have ever made one.
- Ask a student to read the situation aloud.
- Ask students to read the paragraph quietly to themselves.
- Tell students to listen to the questions and, based on the paragraph, decide whether Samantha will or won't do the actions described in the questions.

Part II
- Discuss common bad habits that people may wish to change.
- Ask students if they have any bad habits they, personally, would like to change and then ask them to make resolutions about these habits.
- Have students share these resolutions with the class, if they are willing.
- Write some resolutions on the board. For example:

  Next year, Seok Young is going to stop smoking.

❏ **EXERCISE 41.** Listening. Page 324
Time: 10 minutes

- Have the CD player and track ready.
- Read the direction line to students.
- Ask a student to make a sentence with *want* and write it on the board.

  Some people <u>want</u> only money.

- Now ask another student to make a sentence with *won't* and write that on the board.

  My sister <u>won't</u> break up with her boyfriend.

- Play the CD track and have students circle the words they hear.
- Correct by reading through the script and having students respond as a group.

CHART 10-8. Verb Summary: Present, Past, and Future. Page 325
Time: 10 minutes

- Use this chart to remind students of all the tenses they now know and can use.
- Have students read through all the tenses of the verb *eat* presented in the chart.

Expansion: Write the chart categories (rows and columns) on the board and ask students to complete either the whole chart or a single column or row by using one assigned verb. Give them board markers to do so. Students who do not participate in the board work should correct the writers from their seats.

It may help students if you lead this Expansion with a regular verb first.

❏ **EXERCISE 42.** Looking at grammar. Page 325
Time: 10 minutes

- Read the direction line aloud.
- Give students time to complete each item autonomously as seatwork.
- Correct by asking individual students to read their completed sentences aloud.

❏ **EXERCISE 43.** Listening. Page 326
Time: 10 minutes

- Have the CD player and track ready.
- Read the direction line to students and stress that they are listening for the missing verbs in each sentence.
- Correct by having students read their completed sentences aloud and referring to the script as needed.

CHART 10-9. Verb Summary: Forms of *Be*. Page 327
Time: 10 minutes

- Use this chart to remind students of all the *be* tenses they now know and can use.
- Have students read through all the tenses of the verb *be* presented in the chart.

❏ **EXERCISE 44.** Looking at grammar. Page 327
Time: 10 minutes

- Read the direction line aloud.
- Give students time to complete each item autonomously as seatwork.
- Correct by asking individual students to read their completed sentences aloud.

❏ EXERCISE 45. Looking at grammar.
Page 328
Time: 5–8 minutes

- Lead this review from the center.
- Read the direction line aloud.
- Call on students randomly and correct overtly and immediately, as needed.

❏ EXERCISE 46. Looking at grammar.
Page 328
Time: 5–8 minutes

- Lead this review from the center.
- Read the direction line aloud.
- Call on students randomly and correct overtly and immediately, as needed.

❏ EXERCISE 47. Looking at grammar.
Page 328
Time: 10–15 minutes

- Read the direction line aloud.
- Give students time to complete each item autonomously as seatwork.
- Correct by asking individual students to read their completed sentences, questions, and short answers aloud.

❏ EXERCISE 48. Check your knowledge.
Page 329
Time: 10–15 minutes

- Lead this exercise from the center.
- Call on students to correct the mistakes on sight.
- Ask students to explain and justify their corrections by referring back to previous charts, if needed.

❏ EXERCISE 49. Listening, reading, writing, and speaking. Page 330
Time: 20–25 minutes

- Have the CD player and track ready.

Part I
- Read the direction line.
- Ask students what fairy tales are and if they know any fairy tales that are common among English-speaking cultures.

- Prompt them by asking about "Sleeping Beauty" or other fairy tales.
- Ask students what the name for this type of story is in their languages and countries.
- Write any related vocabulary on the board to build interest in the script.
- Play the CD.
- After playing through the track once, ask students to take turns reading the roles aloud.
- Discuss the highlighted vocabulary as it arises.
- Ask students what the message of the story is.

Part II
- Put students into small groups or have students place themselves into groups.
- Tell students that together they have a chance to rewrite this fairy tale as "Jill and the Dragon."
- Have groups complete the lines in their own fashion.
- Have one student act as secretary and write the lines down.
- Circulate and help groups find needed vocabulary words or have them bounce ideas off you.

Part III
- Have students use the editing check within groups to ensure clarity and accuracy.
- Continue to circulate, stopping to help groups edit.

Part IV
- Have each group vote whether to choose Option 1 or Option 2.
- Designate a time for the performances.

Optional Vocabulary
community college
street artist
designer shop
lifestyle
chat online
mammal
scared
unfortunate
retire
bean stalk
giant
harp
eat you alive
chopped down
fire-breathing dragon

Chapter 11
Expressing Future Time, Part 2

CHAPTER SUMMARY

OBJECTIVE: In this chapter, students learn to express degrees of certainty in the future. Students also learn to use future time clauses with main clauses as well as *if* conditional clause combinations. The chapter goes on to show the difference between *if* conditional sentences and *if*-clauses that introduce a habitual present. The chapter concludes with a presentation of *what + do* as used in ordinary speech and provides ample review of all the grammar presented in this chapter.

APPROACH: The text first introduces *may* and *might*, which are commonly used to show degrees of certainty with regard to future plans. The text continues to focus on usage rather than strict grammatical definitions in stressing the difference between *may be* and *maybe*. Students' prior study of time clauses is reinforced in the presentation of time clauses used for future time, which also paves the way for the use of *if*-clauses, for both future happenings and present habits. *What + do* also gives students more structures for expressing common ideas. Throughout this chapter, the emphasis is on teaching students structures that allow them to expand the kinds of conversations they can have; the introduction of *if*-clauses allows students to talk about things that happen only under certain circumstances.

TERMINOLOGY: Again, grammar terminology is used only to support students' ready comprehension of the material further. This chapter refers to the actual words that express degrees of certainty and show conditions instead of teaching modals, per se, or introducing the *if*-clause combinations as *conditionals*.

❑ EXERCISE 1. Warm-up. Page 334
Time: 5 minutes

> As was common with target structures in the previous chapter, many beginners have heard *might* or *may* to express uncertainty. Use the Warm-up to engage students with what they already know about *might* and *may*.

- Read the direction line.
- Ask students to read the items and decide which have the same meaning.
- Write additional pairs of sentences on the board and ask if students can describe the differences between them. For example:

  It might rain later.
  It will rain later.

We may go to the movies tonight.
We will go to the movies tonight.
Kiko might get a tattoo.
Kiko will get a tattoo.

CHART 11-1. *May / Might* vs. *Will.* Page 334
Time: 10–15 minutes

> Give students opportunities to say what they *may / might* do throughout the exercise. Encourage students to think about what things they *will* do and why they *will* do them as opposed to things they *may* or *might* do.

- Write the chart title on the board.
- Have students read example sentences (a) and (b) aloud to the class.
- Invite students to give you a similar *may* example to write on the board. For example:

  After class, we <u>may</u> get coffee.

- Emphasize that the possibility expressed in *may* can be either future or present.
- Underline the target grammar.
- Ask other students to read sentences (c) and (d) aloud.
- Invite students to create new sentences with *might*. Write these on the board and underline the target grammar. For example:

  We <u>might</u> visit the Statue of Liberty in New York.
  Yuri <u>might</u> work for his brother in Philadelphia after this course.

- Ask other students to read sentences (e) and (f) aloud.
- Explain the comparison in the notes on the right and invite students to tell you what they *may / might* do and what they *will* do.
- Review negative sentence (g) and the explanations of common mistakes with the target grammar at the bottom of the chart.

❑ EXERCISE 2. Looking at grammar.
Page 335
Time: 5–10 minutes

- Lead this exercise from the center.
- Ask individual students to respond to different items.
- Correct structure and pronunciation immediately.

- If students choose to use *will / won't*, ask them why they are sure. If students use *may / might* or *may not / might not*, ask them why they are not sure.

❏ EXERCISE 3. Let's talk: small groups.
Page 336
Time: 10–15 minutes

- Read the direction line aloud.
- Facilitate small-group arrangements.
- Ask students to look at the people / roles named in the list and discuss actual people who are movie stars, world leaders, and famous athletes.
- Circulate around the room, helping students produce grammatically accurate and sensible completions.
- Correct by having each group read the completed items aloud and compare responses.

❏ EXERCISE 4. Writing and speaking.
Page 336
Time: 10–15 minutes

- Read the direction line aloud and explain that students should complete Paragraph 1 in the past and Paragraph 2 in the future.
- Have a few students read their completed paragraphs aloud.
- Correct structure and pronunciation immediately. Put any common errors on the board so that students can learn from one another's mistakes.

Optional Vocabulary

presence	cloudy
essentially	planets

❏ EXERCISE 5. Warm-up. Page 337
Time: 5 minutes

- Read the direction line to your students.
- Ask students when they use *maybe*.
- Have students first answer which sentences are true or not true for them and then say what they will or may do the following morning and following night.
- Write students' contributions on the board and underline the verbs.

  Atsuko <u>will rent</u> a car tomorrow morning.

  Shan Yue <u>may call</u> his girlfriend tomorrow night.

  Maybe Ahmed and Pablo <u>will go</u> to the movies tomorrow night.

CHART 11-2. *Maybe* (One Word) vs. *May Be* (Two Words). Page 337
Time: 10–15 minutes

Stress that *maybe* is not a verb. *Maybe* is an adverb that lets us know that the verb will *possibly* happen but not *certainly* happen. Many students will be familiar with *maybe* as a response to a yes / no question. Stress the connection. *Maybe* is an answer given when

we can't say yes and we can't say no. Similarly, when *maybe* is used as an adverb to modify a verb, it means "possibly"—neither yes nor no.

- Write the chart title on the board.
- Have students read the exchange in example (a) aloud.
- Explain that *maybe* is an adverb that changes the meaning of the verb.
- Elicit and write contrasting examples using *maybe* on the board and underline the verbs.

  Ricardo <u>will travel</u> to Korea next week.

  Maybe Ricardo <u>will travel</u> to Korea next week.

- Remind students that *maybe* comes in front of both the subject and the verb.
- Have a student read example sentence (b) aloud.
- Finally, ask a student to read example sentence (c) aloud and write it, or a similar student-generated sentence, on the board.
- Stress that when using *may* + *be* (two distinct words), *may* makes the main verb *be* less certain. For example:

  Stephane <u>may be</u> at his mother's house tomorrow. He doesn't know yet.

❏ EXERCISE 6. Looking at grammar.
Page 337
Time: 5–10 minutes

- Read the direction line to your students.
- Have a student read the completed examples aloud. Discuss how students know that *maybe* is an adverb in item 1. (For example, it comes before both the subject and the verb, it is one word, and the verb immediately before the base form is *will*.)
- Ask students to complete the exercise as seatwork and circulate while they work on it.
- Correct by having students explain which part of speech *may / maybe* is and have students explain how they determined this.

❏ EXERCISE 7. Looking at grammar.
Page 338
Time: 5–10 minutes

- Read the direction line aloud.
- Ask two students to read the exchanges in completed items 1 and 2 aloud.
- Have two students read and complete the exchange in each item on sight, taking turns as a class.
- Provide immediate correction of pronunciation and grammar.

❏ EXERCISE 8. Let's talk. Page 338
Time: 10–15 minutes

Though this exercise also lends itself to group work, it may be most effective to lead it from the center. In this way, you can ensure everyone participates by asking each class member at least one question.

- Write the following cues on the board to help students.

  Maybe I will_____. / I may_____. / I might _____.

❑ EXERCISE 9. Looking at grammar.
Page 339
Time: 5–10 minutes

- Read the direction line.
- Have a student read the two completed examples aloud.
- Give students time to complete each item as seatwork.
- Review by having students read their completed sentences aloud and provide immediate correction.

❑ EXERCISE 10. Listening. Page 339
Time: 5–10 minutes

- Have the CD player and track ready.
- Read the direction line to the students.
- Have a student read the example aloud.
- Tell students that they need to decide what form of *may* they hear in each item.
- Review by having students tell you their responses.
- If there are any questions or discrepancies, refer to the script.

❑ EXERCISE 11. Looking at grammar.
Page 340
Time: 10 minutes

- Read the direction line aloud.
- Have students read the completed example aloud.
- Lead the rest of the exercise from the center, calling upon different students to complete each item.
- Correct pronunciation and usage right away.

❑ EXERCISE 12. Let's talk: pairwork.
Page 340
Time: 10–15 minutes

- Put students into pairs.
- Read the direction lines to the students.
- With a student, model the Partner A–Partner B examples.
- While students work through the items in pairs, circulate and help students to formulate complete answers.
- Review by having students read their responses and their partner's responses aloud.
- Correct and put any challenging items on the board.

❑ EXERCISE 13. Listening. Page 341
Time: 10 minutes

- Have the CD player and track ready.
- Read the direction line aloud.
- Read the examples aloud and remind students that they will need to pick the sentence that best restates what they heard.

- Correct by having students provide the right answers.
- Refer to the script for any particularly challenging items.

❑ EXERCISE 14. Let's talk: pairwork.
Page 341
Time: 10–15 minutes

- Read the direction line aloud.
- Put students into pairs.
- Have a student read the examples aloud to model possible sentences.
- Have students check off their own planned or possible activities for tomorrow and then show their answers to their partner.
- Then have students make sentences about their partner's activities and share them with the class.

Optional Vocabulary
get some exercise
take a nap
shop online
visit a social networking site
chat online

❑ EXERCISE 15. Warm-up. Page 342
Time: 5–10 minutes

- Read the direction line to the students.
- Have students read the red clauses and discuss their meanings.
- Explain that while the verbs of the red clauses are in the present, their meanings are in the future.

CHART 11-3. Future Time Clauses with *Before, After,* and *When.* Page 342
Time: 10–15 minutes

> The combination of clauses presented here is also called "the first conditional" in many grammars. The verb in the time clause is in the present tense, but the main clause is in the future tense. The meaning of the whole sentence is in the future, and the first clause shows the time when the main clause action will take place.

- Write the chart title on the board.
- Remind students that they have worked with time clauses when using the past tense.
- Ask a student to read sentence (a) aloud.
- Write the sentence from the chart (or one suggested by students) on the board and underline the verbs in both the time clause and the main clause. For example:

  Before Ann goes to work tomorrow, she will eat breakfast.

  Before Tatiana comes home, she will go to the grocery store.

- Review the *incorrect* examples given in the chart, and remind students that only the main clause (and *not* the time clause) is in the future tense.

- Have a student read sentence (b) aloud while you write it or a student-generated example on the board. Underline the verbs and stress that only the verb in the main clause is in the future. For example:

    I'm going to finish my homework after I eat dinner tonight.

    Britta will call her family after she gets home.

- Ask a student to read sentence (c) aloud while you write it or a student-generated example with *when* on the board.

    When I go to New York next week, I'm going to stay at the Hilton Hotel.

    When I finish university, I will apply for a job in my field.

- Emphasize that in a time clause, *before*, *after*, and *when* have future meanings when followed by a present tense verb.

❑ EXERCISE 16. Looking at grammar.
Page 342
Time: 5–10 minutes

- Read the direction line to the students.
- Have students take turns telling you which is the time clause, on sight.
- Remind students that when the time clause is first, there must be a comma before the main clause.

❑ EXERCISE 17. Looking at grammar.
Page 342
Time: 10–15 minutes

- Read the direction line to students and expand on it.
- Remind students to decide carefully which is the time clause (introduced by *before*, *after*, or *when*) and which is the main clause.
- Ask students to write two complete sentences, one that uses *after* and one that uses *before*.
- Remind students that in both cases, only the main clause should be in the future tense.
- Have a student read the example in item 1.
- Give students time to complete the items as seatwork.
- Review each completed item by calling on different students to share their sentences.
- Put any challenging items on the board for class correction.

❑ EXERCISE 18. Looking at grammar.
Page 343
Time: 10–15 minutes

- Lead this activity from the center.
- Have a student read the direction line aloud.
- Discuss which action happened first (1) and which happened second (2) and have students write *1* and *2*.
- Tell students that their responses must be complete sentences combining time clauses with main clauses.
- Remind them that only the main clauses will be in the future tense.
- Read through the example with one or two students.
- Instruct students to close their books.

- After completing the eight sentences with different students orally, invite other students to offer their completions.
- Write any particularly challenging items on the board for further discussion.

❑ EXERCISE 19. Let's talk: class activity.
Page 344
Time: 10 minutes

- Read the direction line and example aloud, and then lead this activity from the center.
- Have students close their books and take turns answering your questions.
- Expand this conversation to include as many speakers as possible.

❑ EXERCISE 20. Let's talk. Page 344
Time: 10 minutes

Expansion: Before beginning this exercise, have students come to a working definition of *fluently*. Put the words *fluency*, *fluent*, and *fluently* on the board, and ask students to tell you any words that they think are related. Put their ideas on the board and compare personal definitions of *fluently*. Examples of useful connotations are:

naturally

without mistakes

with a broad vocabulary

without translating

with no accent or almost no accent

so everyone who also speaks English can understand me

so people won't be able to guess my nationality

so people will think I am a native speaker

- Read the direction line to students.
- Have students get into small groups or pairs, or lead the exercise from the center.
- As students give you their sentences, write them on the board.
- Correct students' usage and pronunciation immediately.

❑ EXERCISE 21. Speaking and writing: pairwork. Page 345
Time: 10–15 minutes

- Put students with a partner or have them arrange themselves in pairs.
- Read the direction lines included in Part I and Part II aloud.
- Have one or two students read the paragraphs given as the writing sample aloud.
- Emphasize the various uses of the future tense and the time clauses.
- Have each pair member complete the chart with his or her plan and the years he or she plans to do these things.
- Have students trade plans and write about each other's plans, as explained in Part II.

- Ask a few students to share their writing with the class and use this as a springboard for the Expansion below.

Expansion: Distribute index cards. Ask students to write one future plan on the cards by using an *I* statement but instruct students not to write their names on the cards. Collect all the cards. Change the *I* statements to third person expressions (i.e., *this person, this student*) and read the plans aloud. Ask the class to guess *whose* plan each one is.

Optional Vocabulary
cheap airfares
spell-check
go through security
feel relaxed
to train
underwater

❏ EXERCISE 22. Warm-up. Page 345
Time: 5 minutes

- Read the direction line.
- Have students select the correct verb forms.
- Help students hear that *If I will have* is incorrect. Explain that the *if*-clause uses the present tense to express the future in the same way that time clauses do.

CHART 11-4. Clauses with *If*. Page 346
Time: 10–15 minutes

> This structure is often called the first conditional. The *if*-clause verb is in the present tense, and the main-clause verb is in the future. The meaning of the whole sentence is future, and the *if*-clause shows the condition under which the main-clause action will take place.

- Write the chart title on the board.
- Explain to students that *if*-clauses are very similar to the time clauses they just worked with. The main difference is that the *if*-clause gives the conditions under which the main-clause action will occur.
- Ask a student to read sentence (a) aloud.
- Write the sentence from the chart (or one suggested by students) on the board and underline the verbs in both the if-clause and the main clause. For example:

    If it _rains_ tomorrow, we _will stay_ home.

    If we _finish_ the chapter, we _will have_ time for more review.

- Have another student read sentence (b) aloud and write this or another student-generated example on the board.
- Explain that the comma is only used when the *if*-clause comes before the main clause.

    We _will stay_ home if it _rains_ tomorrow.

    We _will have_ time for more review if we _finish_ the chapter.

- Have a student read sentences (c) and (d) aloud while you write them on the board.

- Ask students to generate new *if*-sentences relating to the class and write these on the board.

    If José _completes_ all his homework, he _will meet_ us at the beach on Saturday.

    If Zara _has_ time, she _will make_ food for the picnic.

    We _will go_ bodysurfing if the waves are not too strong.

❏ EXERCISE 23. Looking at grammar.
Page 346
Time: 5–10 minutes

- Read the direction line and the situation description.
- Lead this exercise from the center.
- Ask various students to read each sentence on sight, choosing the correct verb form.
- Correct students immediately and put examples on the board, as needed.
- Reiterate that the *if*-clause cannot use a future verb tense.

❏ EXERCISE 24. Let's talk: pairwork.
Page 346
Time: 10–15 minutes

- Read the direction line and directions for Partner A and Partner B to the students.
- Model the example with a student by playing the role of Partner A.
- Have students pair up and begin working through the items orally.
- Circulate around the room and assist partners in responding to each other.
- Have partners change roles and continue assisting each pair.
- When students have worked through all the items, play the role of Partner A and call on random students to answer as Partner B.
- Correct immediately, and if students continue to struggle with the tenses, write notes and examples on the board again.

Expansion: Before class, write or type a number of *if*-sentences on index cards or strips of paper. Cut these sentences "in half," separating the *if*-clauses from the main clauses. Hand out half sentences to everyone in the class so all parts are evenly distributed. Have students memorize what is on their cards and move around the classroom, searching for the appropriate beginnings or endings to go with their clauses. You can pick a particular topic for the sentences or make them random statements that students will understand. Once students have found their matches, have them read the completed sentences aloud. For example:

If you heat water to 212 degrees,	it will boil.
If you don't put sunscreen on,	you are going to get a sunburn.
You will get sick	if you drink unclean water.
You are going to feel exhausted	if you don't get enough sleep.
If you put an egg in a microwave,	it will explode.
Children will be happy	if their parents love them.

❏ EXERCISE 25. Looking at grammar.
Page 347
Time: 10–12 minutes

- Read the direction line aloud.
- Ask a student to read the completed example aloud.
- Ask students to complete items 2–7 on their own as seatwork.
- When students have finished the exercise, ask them to read their completed sentences aloud.
- Provide immediate correction of usage and pronunciation.

❏ EXERCISE 26. Listening. Page 347
Time: 10–12 minutes

- Have the CD player and track ready.
- Read the direction line to students and reiterate that they should answer each question in a complete sentence.
- Remind students that *going to* may sound more like *gonna* and that they should listen for that.

❏ EXERCISE 27. Reading and speaking.
Page 348
Time: 15–20 minutes

Part I
- Read the direction line to your students.
- Preview the highlighted vocabulary with students.
- Have students take turns reading the paragraphs aloud.
- Ask students to paraphrase parts of the story to ensure understanding.
- Give students time to answer the questions and review them.

Part II
- Have students get into small groups.
- Have students write predictions using *will*, *maybe*, *may*, and *might*.
- Ask students to write some of their predictions on the board.
- Discuss them as a class.

Optional Vocabulary
loan
journal
article
streetcar

❏ EXERCISE 28. Warm-up. Page 348
Time: 5 minutes

- Read the direction line to students.
- Have students discuss the difference between the two sentences.
- Discuss the correct time word choice for each sentence.

CHART 11-5. Expressing Future and Habitual Present with Time Clauses and *If*-Clauses.
Page 349
Time: 10–15 minutes

> Remind students that the simple present is used to show everyday habits and practices.

- Write the chart title on the board.
- Ask a student to read sentences (a) and (b) aloud and write a student-generated version on the board. For example:

  After students <u>take</u> their tests, they <u>are going to meet</u> with their tutors. (a specific date)

  After students <u>take</u> their tests, <u>they meet</u> with their tutors. (as a habit, regularly)

- Have other students read sentences (c) and (d) aloud and write student-generated versions on the board.

  If it <u>is</u> sunny tomorrow, we <u>are going to run</u> outside. (a specific date)

  If it <u>is</u> sunny, we <u>run</u> outside. (as a habit, regularly)

- Review the notes on the right of the chart with students and discuss particular future conditions and habitual-present practices with them.

❏ EXERCISE 29. Looking at grammar.
Page 349
Time: 10 minutes

- Read the direction line.
- Have students decide whether each sentence is a present habit or future activity.
- Review any sentences by using the board.

❏ EXERCISE 30. Looking at grammar.
Page 349
Time: 10–15 minutes

- Read the direction line.
- Give students time to complete the items as seatwork.
- When most students have completed the exercise, ask individual students to read the items aloud.
- Correct immediately and put any challenging items on the board.

❏ EXERCISE 31. Looking at grammar: small groups. Page 351
Time: 10–12 minutes

- Read the direction line aloud to students.
- Put students into small groups.
- Have a student read the completed item aloud.
- Walk around the room, helping groups match the phrases in Column A with those in Column B and clarifying any vocabulary questions.
- When groups have worked through the items, have various members write their combinations on the board.
- Students at their seats can correct the sentences produced.

❏ **EXERCISE 32.** Listening. Page 351
Time: 10 minutes

• Have the CD player and track ready.
• Read the direction line to the students.
• Ask a student to read the completed example aloud.
• Stress that students need to determine whether the clauses they hear introduce specific future situations or habitual present ones.
• Play the track.
• After students have completed the exercise, correct by having students read the correct choices.
• If there are any questions, refer to the script and read the clauses aloud so students can easily hear which main clauses provide correct completions.

❏ **EXERCISE 33.** Looking at grammar.
Page 352
Time: 10–15 minutes

• Read the direction line aloud.
• Encourage students to respond as completely and specifically as they can.
• Give students time to complete each item in their own words.
• Ask various students to read their completions aloud.
• Other students should listen carefully to correct the sentences produced.

Optional Vocabulary

in-laws	skips breakfast
yawn	oversleeps
stretch	sore throat
ferry	scratch

❏ **EXERCISE 34.** Warm-up. Page 352
Time: 5 minutes

• Read the direction line.
• Have students take turns reading the items aloud.
• Discuss which conversation asks, "What is your job?"

Expansion: Ask students if this is a typical question asked in their countries. Discuss typical introductory questions and their appropriateness in different countries / cultures. Ask if it is okay to ask questions about a person's profession, marital status, history, and age as "small talk." In the United States, "What do you do?" is a very common question asked to begin a conversation around someone's profession.

CHART 11-6. Using *What* + a Form of *Do*.
Page 353
Time: 10–15 minutes

• Write the chart title on the board.
• Remind students how to form *what*-questions with auxiliaries.
• Ask various students to read questions and answers (a)–(c) aloud.

• Compare the types of present tenses used among these first three sentences, and ask students to explain in what context these questions would be heard.
• Have students read question and answer (d) aloud.
• Have students read questions and answers (e) and (f) aloud.

❏ **EXERCISE 35.** Let's talk: class activity.
Page 353
Time: 10–12 minutes

• Have a student read the direction line aloud.
• Lead this exercise from the center.
• Work through the example with two students before having students close their books.
• Ask the same questions to a few students and remind them to give sentences in complete answers, including repetition of the original time clause.

❏ **EXERCISE 36.** Looking at grammar.
Page 353
Time: 10–12 minutes

• Read the direction line aloud to students.
• Have a student read the question and answer in item 1.
• Ask students to formulate questions using *what* with various forms of *do* for each sentence in the exercise.
• Give students time to do this as seatwork.
• Correct by having students read their questions aloud. Write any particularly challenging question forms on the board for clarification.

❏ **EXERCISE 37.** Let's talk: pairwork.
Page 354
Time: 10–15 minutes

• Read the direction line aloud.
• Have students get into pairs.
• Take the role of Partner A and have a student be Partner B.
• Ask students to look at their books first for the time cues and to formulate their questions.
• Have students work through the first set of items before changing roles.
• Circulate and help students correct their use of *What* + *do* for the particular contexts needed.
• When students have worked through all the items in the exercise, ask students a few of the Partner A questions to compare the verb tenses they chose with Partner B responses.

❏ **EXERCISE 38.** Looking at grammar.
Page 354
Time: 10–15 minutes

• Read the direction line to students.
• Ask two students to read A and B in the completed item 1 aloud.

- Give students time to complete the remaining items as seatwork. You may want to have them work in pairs to complete the exchanges.
- Correct and review by having students (or pairs of students) read their completions aloud.
- Provide immediate correction of usage and pronunciation and write particularly challenging items on the board.

❏ EXERCISE 39. Listening. Page 356
Time: 10 minutes

- Have the CD player and track ready.
- Read the direction line aloud.
- Have students listen for the missing words in each item.
- Play the track for students while they fill in the missing words.
- Correct the exercise by having students read their completed items.
- Review the script as needed to resolve any disputed completions.

❏ EXERCISE 40. Looking at grammar.
Page 356
Time: 10 minutes

- Read the direction line aloud.
- Lead this review from the center.
- Have students read sentences aloud and complete with the appropriate words or phrases.
- Correct as you work through the items with the class.

❏ EXERCISE 41. Looking at grammar: past, present, future. Page 357
Time: 10–15 minutes

- Have a student read the direction line aloud.
- Remind students that this review covers Chapters 3, 4, and 8–11.
- Give students time to complete each item as seatwork.
- Review by having pairs read their completed exchanges and give explanations for their completions.

❏ EXERCISE 42. Check your knowledge.
Page 358
Time: 10 minutes

- Read the direction line aloud.
- Give students time to correct the mistakes as seatwork.
- Correct by having students write their corrected versions on the board.
- Those who aren't writing the answers can check for errors.

❏ EXERCISE 43. Reading and writing.
Page 359
Time: 15–20 minutes

Part I
- Read the direction line to your students.
- Preview the highlighted vocabulary with students.
- Have students take turns reading paragraphs aloud.
- Ask students to paraphrase parts of the story to ensure understanding.

Part II
- Read the direction line to your students.
- Have students model their writing on the five-paragraph comparative model given in the exercise.
- Ask students to get started on the writing in class, and if they need more time, the writing can be completed as homework.

Part III
- Read and discuss the editing check.
- Depending on students' comfort with other students reading their work, have them exchange papers and check the items in the editing checklist.

Optional Vocabulary
accountant
janitor
server
plumber
sales manager
deposit
cash machine
account
dormitory
snorkeling
penguins
details

Chapter 12
Modals, Part 1: Expressing Ability

CHAPTER SUMMARY

OBJECTIVE: In this chapter, students learn to express ability. Students learn a variety of ways to express ability in both present and past tenses and recognize that a modal comes before the base form of the main verb (the infinitive form without *to*) but that other verb phrases include *to*. The objective is for students to recognize the common functions among various structures and to see for themselves that modals work in similar ways to other phrases.

APPROACH: The text first introduces *can* / *can't*. Through the use of very clear charts, it demonstrates that these modals are used immediately before the base form of the verb (the infinitive without *to*). The chapter stresses the critical importance of pronouncing *can* and *can't* and provides opportunities for students to listen for the differences in these modals. The text also provides an introduction to other verb phrases that show ability (*know how to* and *be able to*). Finally, the text presents *could* used to indicate a past ability. In addition, students learn how to use special phrases (*too _____ to _____*) to describe situations that influence choices.

TERMINOLOGY: Again, grammar terminology is used only to support students' ready comprehension of the material further. This chapter introduces the term *modal* and offers an introduction to how modals, in general, function. The chapter focuses on what modals do rather than what words are modals. This functional approach, presented with minimal terminology, serves students' whole language needs well.

❏ EXERCISE 1. Warm-up. Page 361
Time: 5 minutes

As is common with target structures throughout the text, many beginners are likely to be very familiar with *can* / *can't*. This Warm-up is easily expandable as students enjoy talking about what they *can* do. Ask students additional questions about what they *can* and *can't* do to provide opportunities for all to participate.

• Read the direction line and have students circle which answers are true for them.
• Ask students to offer alternative sentences and write these on the board. For example:

  Joao can water-ski.
  Mei-Chen can touch her tongue to her nose.
  Akiko and Ahmed can walk on their hands.

CHART 12-1. Using *Can*. Page 361
Time: 10–15 minutes

Give students opportunities to say what they *can* do throughout the chart presentation.

• Write the chart title on the board.
• Write a sentence highlighting one of your abilities and using *can* on the board.
• Underline the modal *can* and the base form of the verb that immediately follows it. For example:

  I can run fast and far. I can run a marathon.

• Stress that both possibility (opportunity) and ability are expressed by using *can*.
• Ask students to take turns reading example sentences (a)–(c).
• Emphasize that the base form of the verb (the infinitive without *to*) follows modals.
• Have students take turns reading example sentences (d)–(f) aloud. Ask them to point out the errors in (e) and (f).
• Remind students that as they improve their English, they will be able to hear mistakes as they read aloud.
• Have students read the various negative forms presented in example (g) aloud.
• Write additional sentences on the board, using your own or your students' lives to inform the negative structures. For example:

  I can not run 40 miles.
  I cannot run 40 miles.
  I can't run 40 miles.

❏ EXERCISE 2. Let's talk. Page 362
Time: 10–15 minutes

• Put students into pairs.
• Model the examples with a student or students aloud and write examples showing both *can* and *can't* on the board.
• Demonstrate the correct pronunciation for both the positive and negative modals.
• Circulate while students work in pairs, helping students form sentences and correcting *can* / *can't* pronunciation.
• Correct by asking questions of individual students for each item. For example:

  Can a bird fly?
  Yes, a bird can fly.

❑ EXERCISE 3. Let's talk: class activity.
Page 362
Time: 10–15 minutes

- Have a student read the direction line aloud.
- Give students a few minutes to make sentences about themselves from the cues given.
- Ask different students to respond to different items. Have more than one student give his or her sentence for the same item.
- Encourage those who can perform physical feats (for example, wiggle ears) to do so in class, in keeping with their levels of comfort.
- Ask students to present and discuss other unusual skills they may have.

❑ EXERCISE 4. Game: small groups.
Page 363
Time: 10–15 minutes

- Have ready access to the correct answers.
- Ask a student to read the direction line aloud.
- Put students into groups and remind them to discuss each statement carefully to arrive at the correct response.
- After students have worked through each item, correct by asking one student to read each item aloud and ask each group to respond with *yes / no*.
- Keep score on the board and announce the winning group.

Optional Vocabulary
newborn
float
lift
wiggle
hold (their) breath

❑ EXERCISE 5. Warm-up: listening.
Page 363
Time: 5 minutes

- Have the CD player and track ready.
- Read the direction line aloud to students.
- Play the track for students and have students respond.
- Review by having students tell you what they *can* and *can't* do.

CHART 12-2. Pronunciation of *Can* and *Can't*. Page 364
Time: 10–15 minutes

> Though students may not always be able to distinguish between *can* and *can't* when listening to native speakers, they can help themselves be better understood by exaggerating the final *-t* sound.

- Write the chart title on the board.
- Ask a student to read example sentence (a) aloud.

- Read the notes included on the right of the chart aloud and repeat *can* by making simple sentences about students and writing these on the board. For example:

  Tae-Weong <u>*can*</u> *also speak Spanish.*
  Carlo <u>*can*</u> *ride a unicycle.*

- Ask another student to read example sentence (b) aloud.
- Read the notes included in the chart regarding the pronunciation of *can't*. Remind students that the *a* sound is stressed and that this stress will help students distinguish *can* from *can't*.

❑ EXERCISE 6. Listening. Page 364
Time: 10 minutes

- Have the CD player and track ready.
- Read the direction line aloud to students.
- Have students read through the two examples given and emphasize that students will need to be listening carefully for the modal in this exercise.
- Play the track for students and have them circle the modal they hear, affirmative (*can*) or negative (*can't*).
- Correct by having students tell you, individually, which modal they heard.
- Use the script as needed to clarify any disputes, and write original student sentences on the board.

❑ EXERCISE 7. Listening. Page 364
Time: 10 minutes

- Have the CD player and track ready.
- Read the direction line aloud to students.
- Ask a student or students to read the ad aloud.
- Discuss why a job announcement like this may not contain subjects before the verbs (cost per letter or word) and discuss the use of the word *Needs* in the ad.
- Play the track.
- Lead discussion of why Matt is or is not a good candidate for the job advertised.
- Have students form their sentences with *can* and / or *can't*.

Optional Vocabulary
skills
job opening
manner
available

❑ EXERCISE 8. Warm-up. Page 365
Time: 5–10 minutes

- Read the direction line aloud.
- Have students answer the Warm-up questions.

Expansion: Ask more questions using *can* in combination with other *wh*-question words. Write these on the board as you go and include students' answers.
  Where can you find fresh fruit?
    We can find fresh fruit at a farm stand or a fruit stand.

When can you phone your family?
  I can phone my family very early in the morning.
What can you do here on the weekends?
  I can go downtown. I can run along the river.
  I can shop in Harvard Square.
Who can help you if you are sick?
  A nurse or doctor can help me if I am really sick.

CHART 12-3. Using *Can*: Questions.
Page 365
Time: 10–15 minutes

> *Can* is often found in question-answer exchanges
> and is particularly important when students are using
> English as the language of travel. Emphasize that
> because students know basic question forms already
> (both yes / no and *wh*-questions), they should be able
> to use *can* correctly in question forms in everyday
> speech. It is common for beginners to say simply, "I
> can leave early?" with exaggerated question intonation
> to ask a *can* question. Push your students to use
> correct question structure with *can / can't* when they
> are asking questions in class.

• Write the chart title on the board.
• Ask a student to read example questions (a) and (b)
  aloud, along with their answers.
• Have students give you additional questions using
  the target grammar and write them on the board. For
  example:

  Can Ahmed water-ski?
    Yes, he can. No, he can't.
  Can Freda paint well?
    Yes, she can. No, she can't.

• Have students read questions (c) and (d) aloud.
• Discuss what kind of answers follow a *wh*-question.
• Have students read the responses to (c) and (d).
• Ask students to formulate *wh*-questions with *can*.
• Write student-generated questions with *can* and
  encourage other students to respond. Write
  responses underneath.

  What can you make with apples?
    I can make apple pie.
  Where can you find snakes?
    *We can find snakes in warm climates, often in the
    desert.*
  Who can order the army to fight?
    The president can order the army to fight.

❑ EXERCISE 9. Question practice. Page 365
Time: 10–15 minutes

• Read the direction line aloud.
• Ask students to read the completed examples aloud.
• Give students (in pairs, if you wish) time to complete
  all the items on their own.
• Correct by asking student pairs to read their questions
  and short answers aloud.

❑ EXERCISE 10. Let's talk: pairwork.
Page 366
Time: 10–15 minutes

• Read the direction line aloud.
• With a student, read through the example aloud.
• Have students pick a partner (or put them into pairs)
  and have them decide who will be Partner A and
  Partner B.
• Circulate while students work through the items.
• Make note of mistakes in pronunciation or usage to
  review at the end of the exercise.
• Review by asking questions with various items to
  different class members.
• Ask questions with the same item of more than one
  student in order to promote comparison.

❑ EXERCISE 11. Listening. Page 366
Time: 10 minutes

• Have the CD player and track ready.
• Read the direction line aloud.
• Have students fill in missing words as they hear them
  when you play the CD track.
• Correct by having students read the completed
  sentences aloud.
• Refer to the script as necessary during review.

❑ EXERCISE 12. Reading. Page 367
Time: 10–15 minutes

• Before reading the passage, write *color blindness* on
  the board and ask students if they know anyone who
  has this condition and what they know about it.
• It is known that men tend to have more incidences
  of color blindness than women. Ask your students if
  they have heard this.
• Ask students what kind of professions would be
  difficult for someone who is color-blind, facilitating
  responses such as pilot, electrician (colored wires),
  member of the military, and so on.
• Have students take turns reading sentences from the
  passage aloud.
• Then ask various students to take turns reading and
  correctly completing the items.

Optional Vocabulary
hardware store
stick shift
return a call
confuse

❑ EXERCISE 13. Warm-up. Page 368
Time: 5–8 minutes

• Think of something that most people can't do but that
  you can.
• Write this on the board and ask students if they *know
  how to* do it. For example:

  I <u>know how to</u> juggle.

• Read the direction line aloud.

- Put students into pairs and give them time to discuss the phrases and make true statements about themselves. Then they should ask each other questions using *know how to*.

CHART 12-4. Using *Know How To*. Page 368
Time: 10–15 minutes

Explain to your students that *know how to* is used to stress that the abilities were learned. Tell students that *know-how* is even used as a phrase to describe skilled and learned knowledge.

- Write the chart title on the board.
- Have students read example sentences (a) and (b) aloud.
- Discuss the difference in meaning between *can* and *know how to*.
- Ask other students to read example sentences (c) and (d) aloud.
- Invite students to share things they *know how to* do because they have learned these skills.
- Write these student contributions on the board. For example:

   Fabiana knows how to crochet and knit.

   Siham and Akiko know how to ski.

   Viktor and I know how to build a fire in the woods.

❑ EXERCISE 14. Let's talk: pairwork.
Page 368
Time: 10 minutes

- Read the direction line.
- Put students into pairs.
- While students ask and answer questions of one another, circulate and interact with each pair.
- Review by having students share what their partner *knows how to* do.

❑ EXERCISE 15. Speaking and writing: pairwork. Page 369
Time: 10 minutes

- Read the direction line aloud to students.
- Put students into pairs.

Part I
- Have students work with a partner and complete the chart.
- Ask students to form questions using *know how to*.

Part II
- Ask students to write questions and answer them, according to the chart information.

❑ EXERCISE 16. Let's write: small groups.
Page 369
Time: 10 minutes

- Read the direction line aloud to students.
- Put students into small groups.
- Ask students to complete each item with their groups.
- Correct by having students from each group read their completions aloud and compare these with other students' responses.
- Encourage discussion and debate about items 1 and 2 and write completions on the board. (Students may not agree on exactly what three-year-olds *know how to* do or *don't know how to* do.)

Optional Vocabulary
replace
hard drive

❑ EXERCISE 17. Warm-up. Page 369
Time: 5–10 minutes

- Read the direction line to students.
- Have students read the items and select the verbs that are correct for them.
- Ask students to share their completed items and write them on the board, using information given by students to generate sentences about the class as a whole. For example:

   Two years ago, Marco, Celeste, and Pei Ying couldn't drive a car.

   Two years ago, Alfonso, Pema, and Abdullah could drive a car.

CHART 12-5. Using *Could*: Past of *Can*.
Page 370
Time: 10–15 minutes

Explain to your students that *could* is used both for the past of *can* and to indicate future possibility. However, when students are talking about one completed action in the past, *could* is not used. It is used to show past ability, and students should be reminded of this.

- Write the chart title on the board.
- Ask a student to read example sentences (a) and (b) aloud.
- Review the notes included in the right of the chart.
- Ask students to share things they *could* do when they were younger and things they *couldn't* do.
- Write these on the board. For example:

   When they were younger, Mahmoud and Yuki could stand on their heads.

   When she was younger, Gabriella couldn't dive off the high dive.

- Ask a student to read example question (c) aloud.
- Review the word order used in a *could* question, as explained in the notes.
- Ask students a few questions about what they *could* and *couldn't* do ten years ago. For example:

  Could you speak any English ten years ago?
  Could you ski ten years ago?

❏ EXERCISE 18. Let's talk: pairwork.
Page 370
Time: 5–10 minutes

- Read the direction line to students.
- Have students get into pairs and ask and tell each other what they *could* and *couldn't do*.
- Circulate around the room, engaging with pairs and correcting pronunciation and usage as needed.
- Review by having students take turns reading the sentences and saying whether they and / or their partner could do the actions described.

Expansion: Prepare index cards with the following phrases. Each one is people living at a particular historical time.

  Cave people.
  People living before the year 1000 A.D.
  People living in the Middle Ages.
  People living in the 1700s.
  People living in the 1800s.
  People living at the turn of the last century (1900).
  People living in the 1940s.
  People living in the 1970s.

In class, put students into groups and / or pairs and distribute the prepared index cards. Have each pair or group compose sentences that include completions and variations of the following sentence:

  They couldn't _____, but they could _____.

The task is for each group to write descriptive sentences that will allow other students to guess the time frame given, based on what people *couldn't do*. The goal is for students to include enough revealing clues to help other groups guess the time frame. For example:

  People living in ancient Greece

  They couldn't travel far, but they could see entertainment in a big outdoor theater.
  Many people could vote, but slaves, foreign people, and women couldn't.
  They could see the beginnings of democracy, but they couldn't drive cars.

❏ EXERCISE 19. Looking at grammar.
Page 370
Time: 10 minutes

- Read the direction line to students.
- Have a student read the completed example aloud.
- Give students time to complete the exercise on their own, using the phrases given or their own words.

- Review the completed exercise by having students read their completions aloud.
- Correct pronunciation and usage immediately and use the board to clarify mistakes as they arise.

❏ EXERCISE 20. Let's talk: pairwork.
Page 371
Time: 10–15 minutes

- Read the direction line to students.
- Explain that the cues the exercise gives are to connect the *could / couldn't* sentence with a particular reason.
- Have students read the situation and examples aloud.
- Put students into pairs.
- Give students time to expand the cues into full sentences and explain what Mr. Kostis couldn't do and why.
- Have pairs read their sentences aloud and write challenging items on the board to clarify correction.

❏ EXERCISE 21. Let's talk: class activity.
Page 372
Time: 15 minutes

- Read the direction line aloud.
- Emphasize that students need to distinguish whether they need to use *can't* or *couldn't*.
- Read the example aloud.
- Have students close their books.
- Read the sentences aloud and have students give the negative results of each situation.
- Correct pronunciation and usage immediately, and put useful student responses on the board.

❏ EXERCISE 22. Check your knowledge.
Page 372
Time: 10 minutes

- Read the direction line.
- Give students time to complete the items independently.
- To review, ask students to read their corrections aloud and justify / explain them to the class by using the grammar rules they have focused on in this chapter.
- Put any more challenging items on the board for review.

Optional Vocabulary

communicate	poverty
cartwheels	turn up
hearing aid	

❏ EXERCISE 23. Warm-up. Page 373
Time: 10 minutes

- Read the direction line to students.
- Ask students to match the form of *can* in Column A with the appropriate *be able to* sentence in Column B.
- Review the items as a class and reiterate that forms of *can* and *be able to* are interchangeable in meaning.

CHART 12-6. Using *Be Able To.* Page 373
Time: 10–15 minutes

> Explain to your students that *be able to* describes both ability and possibility. Stress that *be able to* is not a modal, but it has the same meaning as *can / could.*

- Write the chart title on the board.
- Ask a student to read example sentences (a) and (b) aloud.
- Reiterate that both sentences have the same meaning.
- Invite students to contribute additional sentences using *be able to* in the present. Write these on the board:

  Federico is able to play the piano.

  Vilma is able to scuba dive.

- Ask a student to read example sentences (c) and (d) aloud.
- Invite students to contribute additional sentences using *be able to* in future. Write these on the board:

  Bertrand will be able to climb Mount Kilimanjaro next spring.

  Chun Wua will be able to snowboard when she returns to Korea.

- Ask a student to read example sentences (e) and (f) aloud.
- Reiterate that both sentences have the same meaning.
- Invite students to contribute additional sentences using *be able to* in the past. Write these on the board:

  When he lived in Rio, Kenji was able to surf every weekend.

  When Marcia was young, she was able to walk on her hands.

❑ EXERCISE 24. Looking at grammar.
Page 373
Time: 10 minutes

- Read the direction line to students.
- Have students read the completed examples aloud.
- Give students time to transform each item into a similar sentence using a form of *be able to.*
- Review the items as a class by having students read their *be able to* sentences aloud.
- Correct mistakes in structure (not changing the tense of *be*), pronunciation, and or usage right away.
- Have students write items on the board for further clarification.

❑ EXERCISE 25. Reading and grammar.
Page 374
Time: 10–15 minutes

Part I
- Read the direction line.
- Ask students to take turns reading the passage aloud.
- Ask comprehension and vocabulary questions as they naturally arise.

Part II
- Read the direction line.
- Have students underline the *could, couldn't,* and *can* verbs.
- Give students time to rewrite the *could, couldn't,* and *can* sentences using the correct forms of *be able to.*
- Correct by having students read the new *be able to* sentences aloud.

❑ EXERCISE 26. Listening. Page 375
Time: 10 minutes

- Have the CD player and track ready.
- Read the direction line aloud and prepare students to complete the sentences with what they hear.
- Correct after you have played the track through and students have completed the sentences with what they have heard.
- If there are any questions, read from the script so that students can readily hear the words missed.

Optional Vocabulary
bending	enrolled
thief	cashier
multilingual	encourages
basic	lectures
common	wondering
frustrated	

❑ EXERCISE 27. Warm-up. Page 375
Time: 5–10 minutes

- Tell students to look at the illustration and then choose the correct response.
- Ask students to explain why b is the correct response to what is presented in the picture.

CHART 12-7. Using *Very* and *Too* + Adjective. Page 376
Time: 10–15 minutes

> Explain to students that *very* strengthens an adjective but does not necessitate a negative consequence. *Very* is different from *too.* When *too* precedes an adjective, a negative consequence follows.

- Write the chart title on the board.
- Ask a student to read example sentences (a) and (b) aloud.
- Refer to the notes at the right.
- To model this for students on the board, invite students to help you make new sentences using observable facts.
- Write the sentences on the board and stress where the meanings are neutral or negative. For example:

  Javier is very tall. → *neutral meaning → no negative result*

  Javier is too tall. → *negative result → Javier is too tall. He can't sleep on a plane.*

- Have students read sentences (c) and (d) aloud.
- Write the sentences on the board, underlining *very* and *too*.
- Ask students to read example sentences (e) and (f) aloud, and stress that with *too* we anticipate that a negative result will follow.
- If your students are having trouble using *two, too,* and *to*, show them the following chart and discuss the different meanings of the words and their pronunciations.

Using *Two, Too,* and *To*		
two	(a) I have **two** children.	***Two, too,*** and ***to*** have the same pronunciation. In (a): ***two*** = a number.
too	(b) Timmy is **too** young. He can't read. (c) Ann saw the movie. I saw the movie **too**.	In (b): **too** young = impossible to do because of his youth. In (c): **too** = **also**.
to	(d) I talked **to** Jim. (e) I want **to** watch television.	In (d): **to** = a preposition. In (e): **to** = part of an infinitive.

❏ EXERCISE 28. Let's talk. Page 376
Time: 10 minutes

- Read the direction line aloud.
- Put students into pairs.
- Have students look at the two illustrations and discuss the example sentences.
- Then tell pairs to formulate two sentences, using *very* or *too* and *can* or *can't*, that make sense for each pair of illustrations.
- Ask students to read their sentences. Correct and review as a class.

❏ EXERCISE 29. Looking at grammar.
Page 378
Time: 10 minutes

- Read the direction line to students.
- Give students time to complete the items by using the phrases given.
- Correct and review by having students read their completions aloud.
- Compare students' completions and write any challenging items on the board.

❏ EXERCISE 30. Looking at grammar.
Page 378
Time: 10 minutes

- Read the direction line aloud.
- Have students complete the sentences by using *too* + adjectives from the box.
- Give students time to complete as seatwork and correct as a class.

❏ EXERCISE 31. Looking at grammar.
Page 379
Time: 5–10 minutes

- Read the direction line aloud.
- Lead this activity from the center.
- Have students read the completed examples aloud.
- Ask students to complete the sentences on sight by calling on them individually.
- Provide immediate correction.

❏ EXERCISE 32. Reading and listening.
Page 380
Time: 15–20 minutes

Part I
- Read the direction line aloud.
- Look through the reading with students and discuss highlighted vocabulary.
- Have students take turns reading the passage aloud.
- Ask students comprehension and vocabulary questions that prompt them to restate or paraphrase what they have read.

Part II
- Read the direction line aloud.
- Give students time to complete the statements, referring back to the passage as needed.
- Ask students to read their completions aloud and point to specific sentences in the passage to justify them.

Part III
- Have the CD player and track ready.
- Read the direction line aloud to students.
- Have students read their completions aloud and correct by referring to the script, as needed.

❏ EXERCISE 33. Check your knowledge.
Page 381
Time: 5–10 minutes

- Read the direction line.
- Give students time to correct the mistakes they find.
- Ask students to read the corrected sentences aloud and explain what they changed to make the sentences correct.

❏ EXERCISE 34. Writing. Page 382
Time: 15–20 minutes

Part I
- Read the direction line to students.
- Have students begin thinking about a fictional character they would like to describe.
- Ask students to take turns reading the passage aloud.
- Give students time to write a paragraph about their chosen characters. Remind them to include the information listed below the "Superman" passage.

Part II
- Read the direction line aloud.
- Ask students either to share their passage with a partner or simply to use the editing checklist to proof their own work.
- Discuss writing with individual students.

Optional Vocabulary

result	rows
solve	objects
take a break	weak
dorm	justice
gained weight	catches criminals
stand up straight	rescue
complete	hero
create	admire
strangers	

Chapter 13
Modals, Part 2: Advice, Necessity, Requests, Suggestions

CHAPTER SUMMARY

OBJECTIVE: In this chapter, students learn to use modals to carry out many important functions. Modals allow speakers to give advice, talk about what is needed, make requests, and offer suggestions. Students are reminded how to form modal structures, and they continue to explore their many uses.

APPROACH: One aspect of modals is that they can be imagined as increasing in strength or urgency. Thus, this chapter first focuses on giving advice to students with *should*. Advice is not something anyone is required to take, and thus, modals for advice can be conceived as less urgent than what follows. The modals that follow express requirements (*have to* and *must*). Presenting these modals on a continuum often helps students understand the difference. The chapter then presents polite questions and requests as well as commands and imperative statements. The charts explicitly state degrees of formality, which is important for students who are just beginning to learn how to modify register according to different situations. The chapter concludes with making suggestions and a review.

TERMINOLOGY: As is the case throughout the text, grammar terminology is used when the terminology actually helps students better understand use. This chapter builds on the term *modal*. The chapter focuses on what modals do rather than which words are modals. This functional approach, presented with minimal terminology, best serves students' whole language needs and helps students internally categorize new structures.

❑ **EXERCISE 1.** Warm-up. Page 383
Time: 5–10 minutes

> As is common with target structures throughout the text, beginners will certainly be familiar, intuitively, with the function of giving advice but may have had no experience using *should*.

- Read the direction line aloud.
- Ask a student to read Ella's problem aloud.
- Write the word *problem* on the board and ask students what words they already know that are related to *problem*. In this way, create a word web on the board containing related words that students may know. For example:

problem	answer
difficulty	solution
challenge	advice
question	

- Focus students' attention on the terms *problem* and *solution*.
- Explain to students that advice consists of possible solutions, and that the modal *should* is used to show advice.
- Have students discuss which of the solutions listed would best solve Ella's problem.
- Have students discuss which pieces of advice are most likely to be useful to Ella.
- Ask students which solutions they think Ella *should* choose.

CHART 13-1. Using *Should*. Page 383
Time: 10–15 minutes

> Everyone loves giving advice. As students are mastering control of the structure, give them natural opportunities to say what people *should* do throughout the chart presentation.

- Write the chart title on the board.
- Have students take turns reading example sentences (a)–(c) aloud and write these on the board.
- Stress, by reading the example sentences in (d) aloud, that *should* does not change form and that like other modals, it is followed directly by the base form of the verb.
- Ask students to read example sentences (e) and (f) aloud and review the contraction of *should not* to *shouldn't* with students.

❑ **EXERCISE 2.** Looking at grammar.
Page 384
Time: 10 minutes

- Read the direction line to students.
- Have a student read the completed example conversation aloud.
- Emphasize that speaker A is asking for advice and that each speaker B response must begin with *You should*.
- Give students time to complete the exercise as seatwork.

- Correct by having two students read the completed exchanges aloud. Respond immediately to any errors in structure or pronunciation.

❏ EXERCISE 3. Let's talk: small groups.
Page 385
Time: 10–15 minutes

- Put students into small groups.
- Read the direction line aloud.
- Give each group enough time to discuss each situation and make sentences using *should* or *shouldn't*. Circulate while they are doing so.
- Check in with the quietest groups first to ensure that they are on task and are able to carry out the directions successfully.
- Review by having students read their sentences (or write them on the board).
- Provide clear and immediate correction, using the board as much as possible.

Expansion: Tell students that in addition to making sentences with *should / shouldn't*, they should rank the sentences the groups make in terms of best to worst suggestion. Try to get a class consensus on the best and worst piece of advice for each situation.

❏ EXERCISE 4. Looking at grammar.
Page 386
Time: 10 minutes

- Read the direction line and completed examples aloud.
- Lead the exercise on sight, having students complete sentences aloud as you randomly call on them to do so.
- Correct the form—and, importantly, the pronunciation—of both affirmative and negative modals immediately as students give responses.
- Ask students if there are any "correct" answers that they disagree with or that are at least debatable (for example, items 3 and 10).

❏ EXERCISE 5. Let's talk: small groups.
Page 387
Time: 10–15 minutes

- Have students choose new small groups.
- Ask a student to read the direction line aloud.
- Circulate around the room to ensure that students are taking turns presenting each of the five situations to their group.
- After students have had time to give advice in response to each situation, review by having groups read their completed sentences aloud.
- Ask students from each group to write a few sentences on the board and have other students correct the grammar and usage.

Expansion: Prepare white labels with simple problematic situations presented in the second person. Explain to students that you will put a sticker describing a problem on each student's back so that

each student is not able to see his or her situation. Instruct students to stand up, walk around, and show their backs to other students. Students should give each other advice based on the specific problem given to each student (and stated on their labels).

You may want to prepare students by modeling this yourself. You can turn your back to the class, give the stack of white labels with problematic situations written on them to a student, and have the student put one on your back. Your students will then give you advice (for example, "You should go to the police." "You should cancel your credit cards.") based on your particular situation.

Possible problematic situations include:
Your girlfriend / boyfriend is flirting with another friend.
Someone stole your wallet.
You lost your passport.
You are going to babysit for your sister's children.
You are going to take care of a neighbor's dog.
You have a bad cold, but you also have an important test tomorrow.
Someone you don't know well is angry at you.
Your parents are angry at you.
You want to learn English very fast.
You want to get in good shape.
You have never traveled before, but you want to travel to another country alone.
You want to learn to be a good cook.
You have a very noisy upstairs neighbor.
Your best friend smokes cigarettes, and you are worried about his or her health.
You have a lot of studying to do, but you also want to go to a party.
Someone broke your heart.

❏ EXERCISE 6. Listening. Page 387
Time: 10 minutes

- Have the CD player and track ready.
- Read the direction line aloud.
- Repeat that students need to both circle the word they hear (*should* or *shouldn't*) and decide whether they agree with the advice they hear.
- Stress that students should decide whether they agree right away, before they forget what the advice was.
- Correct by having students tell you what words they heard and whether they agreed.
- If there are any discrepancies or challenges, refer to the script.
- Correct usage, pronunciation, and vocabulary as students justify their responses.

Optional Vocabulary

heel	hoarse
missed	hitchhike
glue	chance
Band-Aid	skip class
get some cash	waste
toothache	intersection
cavity	jaywalk
blister	

❏ EXERCISE 7. Warm-up. Page 387
Time: 5 minutes

> Don't spend too much time teasing out whether items 2 and 3 have exactly the same meaning. Rather, facilitate that these two items are closest in meaning. In order to help students discover this, ask them to think about *why* for each situation.

- Read the direction line to students.
- Have students discuss the meaning of each sentence, which sentences are closest in meaning, and *why* each could be true.
- Compare students' responses and highlight similarities (and common *why*-explanations) for items 2 and 3.

CHART 13-2. Using *Have* + Infinitive (*Have To* / *Has To* / *Had To*). Page 388
Time: 10–15 minutes

> When presenting forms of *have to* as synonymous with *need to*, point out that they are both followed by the infinitive. Explain that with *should*, the subject has a choice to accept or reject the advice that is given. Here the subject doesn't have a choice and necessity is present.

- Write the chart title on the board.
- Have students take turns reading example sentences (a)–(d) aloud while you write these on the board.
- Stress, by reading example sentences aloud, that *need to* and *have to* share a common meaning.
- Read the notes explaining the similarities (at the right of the chart) aloud to students.
- Ask students to provide the past of *have* and write *had* on the board.
- Have a student read example sentence (e) aloud while you write this on the board.
- Ask students to provide the question form and auxiliary verbs needed for questions with *have*.
- Ask a student to read example sentences (f)–(h) aloud while you write these on the board.
- Write the question forms of *have to* on the board and read the additional notes to the right aloud.
- Ask students how to put *have* into the negative.
- Ask students to read example sentences (i) and (j) aloud.
- Review notes on the negative form.
- Ask random students to tell you what they *want to* do and then what they *have to* do.
- Write students' sentences on the board and underline the verb phrases for comparison. For example:

    Suzette wants to go to Quebec.
    Suzette has to return to Paris and return to her job.
    Wei-Ling wants to become a poet.
    Wei-Ling has to pay her bills.

❏ EXERCISE 8. Looking at grammar.
Page 388
Time: 10 minutes

- Read the direction line aloud.
- Ask a student to read the completed example aloud.
- Give students time to complete the exercise as seatwork.
- Correct by having students read the *need to* sentences transformed into *have to* sentences aloud.
- Provide immediate correction of all aspects of their production.

❏ EXERCISE 9. Let's talk: class activity.
Page 388
Time: 10 minutes

- Lead this exercise from the center.
- Read the direction line.
- Direct questions to different students and ask students to share the reasons *why* they *want to* and *have to* do certain things.
- Write responses on the board and compare them with other students' responses to the same questions.
- If students provide responses in the wrong tense, correct them as they are speaking.

❏ EXERCISE 10. Let's talk: class activity.
Page 389
Time: 10–15 minutes

- Continue by also leading this exercise from the center.
- Read the direction line aloud.
- Model the example by involving two strong students in its completion.
- Direct particular items to particular students and correct as students speak.
- Use the board to clarify production and explanations as needed.

❏ EXERCISE 11. Looking at grammar.
Page 389
Time: 10–15 minutes

- Read the direction line aloud.
- Review the completed example with the class before they begin to work.
- Give time for students to complete the exercise as seatwork.
- Correct by having students read the completions aloud.
- Provide immediate and explicit correction for any errors in structure, usage, and / or pronunciation.

❏ EXERCISE 12. Listening. Page 391
Time: 5–10 minutes

- Have the CD player and track ready.
- Read the direction line aloud to students.

- Explain and model the reduced pronunciation students are likely to hear in actual conversations.
- Play the track and have students circle what they hear.
- Correct by having students read their answers aloud.
- Refer to the script to clarify any discrepancies.

Optional Vocabulary

responsibilities	immigration office
cross	postpone

❑ EXERCISE 13. Warm-up. Page 391
Time: 5 minutes

> Help students understand that *must* is one of the strongest and most emphatic modals. It is used in those situations where no other choice is possible and where the speaker strongly wants the reader or listener to adhere to a requirement. It is used exactly as it is here—in written instructions and especially when restating rules to children.

- Read the direction line to students.
- Ask students to match sentences and discuss / correct their choices.

CHART 13-3. Using *Must, Have To / Has To,* and *Should.* Page 392
Time: 10–15 minutes

> The most important consideration here is the freedom from obligation versus the prohibition against doing something. Stress that *don't have to* simply means that there is no necessity or obligation. However, *must not* is a prohibition against doing something and *should not* is advice *not* to do something. Work through the chart carefully. By using the terms *no necessity / you have a choice* and *prohibition against / you don't have a choice* consistently, students will be able to hang on to the main distinction.

- Write the chart title on the board.
- Ask a student to read example sentences (a) and (b) aloud.
- Write these sentences on the board.
- Explain and reiterate the notes describing how *must* is used (primarily in writing and when speaking to children) and give additional examples.
- Ask a student to read example sentence(s) (c) aloud and conjugate it on the board with students' assistance.
- Write the subheading *Negative: Must vs. Have To* on the board, calling students' attention to the fact that this is the crux of the difference.
- Stress, by reading example sentences (d) and (e) aloud, that *must not* and *don't have to* are not at all the same.
- Read the notes explaining the difference (included at the right of the chart) aloud to students and write these on the board.

- Explain the differences between *must* (no choice) and *should* (good idea but not required) clearly.
- Ask students to read example sentences (f) and (g) and then (h) and (i) aloud.
- Ask students to think of things they *must do* as foreign students studying in another country and ask them to think of things they *should do*.
- Have students share their ideas with the class and write sentences from those that all agree are true. Underline the target grammar. For example:

  > We *must have* valid passports.
  > We *should study* hard.

❑ EXERCISE 14. Let's talk: small groups.
Page 392
Time: 10 minutes

- Read the direction line aloud to students.
- Either assign small groups or have students arrange themselves.
- Before students begin, have them discuss which rules are universal and which may differ, depending on the country to which they apply.
- Give students time to work in groups, and circulate, asking leading questions to get students talking.
- After students have had time to come up with two more rules for each situation, have each group read the situations and the given rules aloud and then add their group's rules.
- Correct structure, usage, and pronunciation.
- Have other groups comment on one another's rules and decide whether the rules are truly universal.

❑ EXERCISE 15. Looking at grammar.
Page 393
Time: 10 minutes

- Read the directions aloud.
- Give students an opportunity to complete the exercise independently as seatwork.
- When most students have completed the exercise, correct by having students read their completions aloud.
- If there is any disagreement on which phrase successfully completes each blank, discuss as a group and write the sentences on the board.

❑ EXERCISE 16. Looking at grammar.
Page 394
Time: 10–15 minutes

- Read the direction line aloud.
- Give students an opportunity to complete the exercise independently as seatwork.
- Once they have completed the exercise, have students read the sentences with the correct choices.
- Provide immediate correction of structure as well as pronunciation.
- Ask students to explain why their choices are correct.

❑ EXERCISE 17. Let's talk: small groups
Page 395
Time: 15 minutes

- Read the direction line aloud.
- Have students get into small groups, encouraging them to work with classmates they have not recently partnered up with.
- With one student, model the example and expand on it, inviting more completions.
- While students are working in groups, circulate and challenge students to explain why students *should / have to / don't have to* for each item.
- Have students from each group share their completions and discuss as a class.

Expansion: Particularly when working with a group of students from many different backgrounds, there will be some discrepancies regarding behaviors expected and not expected of students. Have students compare student behaviors in certain countries with others and ask students to consider other factors that could impact such expectations. For example, there are different expectations for students of different ages as well as students in different historical time periods. There are also differences that have to do with the subject and context in which one is a student. There are different expectations for a student in a yoga class than one at a military academy. In order to expand this discussion, ask students to consider the following settings and write the phrases on the board.

Students in kindergarten, primary school, elementary school, high school, college, postgraduate programs

Students from Europe, the Americas, the Middle East, Asia, Africa

People who were students in the middle of the previous century, the 1800s

Students in a military academy, martial arts school, yoga class, ballet school, auto repair shop, police academy, aesthetician school, college

❑ EXERCISE 18. Listening. Page 395
Time: 5–10 minutes

- Make sure the CD player and track are ready.
- Read the direction line aloud to students.
- To ensure that students know what to anticipate, model the completed example by having students decide which they agree with.
- Play the track and have students decide which sentences they agree with.
- As there are no correct responses, have the script ready so you can use each item to promote discussion as you review with the class.

Optional Vocabulary

text and drive	matches
apply	polluted
in person	charge
income tax	taking off
tablet	memorize
uniforms	

❑ EXERCISE 19. Warm-up. Page 395
Time: 5 minutes

Because many beginners may have been exposed to a more formal register of English than is actually used in the United States currently, they may be able to readily determine which form is the most polite. Help them by giving actual contexts for each request.

- Read the direction line aloud.
- Have students discuss the two more polite requests and ask which one they consider more polite.

CHART 13-4. Polite Questions: *May I, Could I,* and *Can I.* Page 396
Time: 10–15 minutes

There are some subjective considerations when it comes to register and politeness. Help students understand that their subjective experiences inform their choice of modals for each social situation. First have students consider different social situations and explain that while some may think a formal dinner requires more politeness than a job interview, others may not. This is fine, but discuss the subjective nature so that students know not to expect to use or hear these questions the same in every situation.

Further, with your explaining the continuum on which these questions can be imagined, students will better understand how to adjust their questions to be maximally communicative. Students will gain by understanding that there are not exact rules of social register in conversation. Remind students that you can never go wrong by adding *please*.

- Begin by asking students about which situations they need to be most polite in.
- Write the following situations on the board:

  job interview
  doctor's appointment
  formal dinner party
  cookout / picnic / barbecue
  class
  business presentation

- Invite a couple of students to rank these situations in terms of how polite a person is required to be, from most polite (1) to least polite (6).
- Compare and discuss the situations that require the most politeness.
- Ask a student to read example sentences (a)–(c) aloud.
- Review the notes to the right and draw a line to illustrate this continuum.

  can_____could_____may
  least polite   *most polite*

- Ask different students to read example sentences (d)–(f) aloud.

- Reiterate that including *please* in any situation where you hope to be served or helped is always a good idea.
- Ask students to read typical responses (g)–(k) aloud and to decide which responses go with which polite question.

❑ EXERCISE 20. Let's talk: pairwork.
Page 396
Time: 10 minutes

- Encourage students to work with a new partner.
- Read the direction line aloud.
- Have pairs begin writing appropriate conversations, both the polite questions and the responses.
- Circulate and ensure students are working productively together.
- After pairs have written a conversation for each illustration, have students read their conversations aloud and / or write them on the board.

❑ EXERCISE 21. Let's talk: pairwork.
Page 397
Time: 10 minutes

- Ask students to switch partners.
- Read the direction line aloud.
- Model the example with a student, taking the role of Partner A.
- Have students begin the dialogues, using the appropriate questions.
- Walk around the room, helping pairs speak as fluidly and correctly as possible.
- When the pairs have worked through both sets of situations, ask them to share their dialogues with the class and invite other students to both correct them and comment on the politeness level employed.

Optional Vocabulary
snack	eraser
borrow *versus* lend	server
calculator	

❑ EXERCISE 22. Warm-up. Page 397
Time: 5 minutes

- Read the direction line aloud.
- Ask students to discuss the meanings and help them understand that the meanings are very similar.

CHART 13-5. Polite Questions: *Could You* and *Would You*. Page 397
Time: 10–15 minutes

Could you and *Would you* both mean that the speaker wants the listener to perform an action on the speaker's behalf. Though both *could* and *would* have alternative meanings in the past, they both refer to a not-yet-real (but asked-for) future.

- Ask a student to read example sentences (a) and (b) aloud.
- Stress that both questions are very polite and share the same meaning.
- Write the following on the board:

    Could you _____? = *Would you* _____?

- Explain that both are true modals and are followed by the base form of the verb, not the *to*-infinitive.
- Review the typical responses included in the chart and model typical conversations.

❑ EXERCISE 23. Let's talk: pairwork.
Page 398
Time: 10 minutes

- Ask students to choose a partner.
- Read the direction line aloud.
- Have students discuss what they see in each illustration.
- Circulate and interact with each pair to ensure that they are able to produce appropriate questions with *Could you* or *Would you* and typical responses.
- Invite students to share their exchanges with the class. Write these on the board to promote discussion.

❑ EXERCISE 24. Let's talk: pairwork.
Page 398
Time: 10–15 minutes

- Have students remain with their current partner.
- Read the direction line aloud.
- Remind students that both *Could you* and *Would you* are used to get another person to do what you want.
- Model the example with a student.
- Now have students use the items 1–8 to promote a minidialogue. Encourage them to write down their miniconversations for later reference.
- Have students share their dialogues with the class and encourage peers to provide immediate correction, if possible. If peer correction is not practical, make sure to correct clearly and immediately.

❑ EXERCISE 25. Let's talk: pairwork.
Page 399
Time: 10–15 minutes

- Have students work with a new partner.
- Read the direction line aloud.
- Model the example with a few students.
- Have students begin working with their partner and ensure that they use specific, polite questions and vocabulary to clearly demonstrate the situations.
- Review as a class by having students "perform" these dialogues or simply describe what was said.
- Compare with what other pairs invented as dialogues and provide correction to all immediately.

Optional Vocabulary
glad	translate
typical	hand you
pass	

❏ EXERCISE 26. Warm-up. Page 399
Time: 10–15 minutes

• Read the direction line.
• Have students discuss what the wisest course of action is for each situation.
• Ask students why the suggested answers are not questions.

CHART 13-6. Imperative Sentences.
Page 400
Time: 10–15 minutes

There are two considerations for the imperative: how urgent the situation is and what the relationship between the speaker and the listener is. Emphasize these aspects in each chart example, and highlight the way they change from situation to situation.

• Write the title of the chart on the board.
• Ask a student to read example sentence (a) aloud.
• Write it on the board.
• Ask students about other relationships in which it is normal for one person to simply direct or order another person to do something, and have students compare these cross-culturally and even within families. (Some parents and spouses use the imperative more with each other than others do.)
• Ask students to read sentences (b) and (c), and write these on the board.
• Ask students to imagine situations in which you would use the imperative, no matter what the relationship. (It is usually used in urgent situations where a negative consequence [such as an injury] could follow if the direction is not immediately followed.)
• Emphasize that the subject in all imperatives is always understood to be *you*, as is explained in the accompanying note.
• Ask a student to read example sentences (d) and (e) aloud.
• Ask students to give other examples of negative commands and write them on the board. For example:

Don't put your coffee there. It might spill.
Don't cross the street in the middle of the block.
Don't slam the door.

• Have various students read example sentences (f)–(i) aloud. Write each category for the imperative on the board and have students come up with original examples of each.
• Write these examples on the board. For example:

Orders: Be quiet, kids.
Directions: Go straight till the end of the road.
Advice: Don't work too hard.
Requests: Please give me your name.

❏ EXERCISE 27. Let's talk. Page 400
Time: 10 minutes

• Read the direction line aloud.
• Lead this activity from the center.

• Give students just a few minutes to decide which commands go with which pictures.
• Have students read the commands aloud and explain why they have chosen each one for each picture.
• Correct any confusion immediately and remind students to tell you who the subject is and when the action takes place (the immediate future).

❏ EXERCISE 28. Looking at grammar.
Page 401
Time: 10 minutes

• Read the direction line aloud.
• Give students time to underline all the imperative verbs.
• Have students read the underlined (imperative) verbs aloud and ask students to identify what the precise use is (order, direction, advice, request).

❏ EXERCISE 29. Looking at grammar.
Page 401
Time: 10 minutes

• Read the direction line aloud.
• Ask students to write an imperative sentence for each illustration.
• If a student finishes early, have him / her write alternative sentences.
• When everyone has completed the exercise, have students read their imperatives aloud.

Expansion: Discuss the elements of a good imperative sentence and why the elements are important. Write these on the board. For example:

The sentence has to be very clear.
The sentence has to be very short.
The sentence has to have an immediate impact.
To be effective, the listener has to know immediately what to do.

Then, going back to Exercise 29, have students vote on which precise imperative sentences would be most effective in each situation.

❏ EXERCISE 30. Reading and writing.
Page 402
Time: 15–20 minutes

Part I
• Go through the highlighted vocabulary with students before they read the conversation.
• Have a couple of students read the conversation aloud.
• Ask other students to paraphrase the meaning of what they have just heard.

Part II
• Ask students to complete the question by choosing a common location, known to most students in the class.
• Then have students write directions, using imperative verbs.

- Ask students to share their directions with other students and have classmates decide on their clarity. You may want to have students actually follow the directions and mark any commands that don't work.

❏ **EXERCISE 31.** Let's talk: class activity.
Page 402
Time: 10–15 minutes

- Read the direction line to students.
- Model the example with five students.
- Ask students to close their books and listen to the descriptions of each situation.
- Write students' imperatives in response to each setting on the board and discuss as a class.
- Provide immediate correction if students use the conjugated form or say the subject.
- Review responses to all six situations and decide which are the most effective imperatives.

Optional Vocabulary

command	wastebasket
march	scholarship
relax	tourist
hiccups	

❏ **EXERCISE 32.** Warm-up. Page 403
Time: 5 minutes

- Read the direction line aloud.
- Have students complete all the possible sentences, using the verbs given.
- Ask students which verbs are followed by *to* and which are not.

CHART 13-7. Modal Auxiliaries. Page 403
Time: 10–15 minutes

This chart draws a clear distinction between modal auxiliaries, which come right before the base form of a verb, and other verb phrases that include *to*.

- Write the title of the chart on the board.
- Ask a student to read example sentence(s) (a) with all the auxiliaries aloud.
- Remind students that like other auxiliaries (*do, have*), a modal auxiliary comes in front of the base form of a main verb.
- Ask another student to read example sentence(s) (b) aloud.
- Remind students to consider whether the verb is followed by the base form of a verb or the complete infinitive. If the verb is followed by only the base form, then it is a true modal.

❏ **EXERCISE 33.** Looking at grammar.
Page 403
Time: 10 minutes

- Read the direction line.
- Explain that students will be choosing whether they need to add *to*.
- Ask a student to read the completed example items 1 and 2 aloud.
- Give students time to complete the remainder of the items as seatwork.
- Ask students to take turns reading the correct sentences aloud.
- Provide immediate correction and write any challenging items on the board.

CHART 13-8. Summary Chart: Modal Auxiliaries and Similar Expressions. Page 404
Time: 10–15 minutes

- Write the chart title on the board.
- Give each student a different letter in the chart to read aloud. They should read the modal auxiliary, the meaning, and the example.
- Ask students to identify which of these are very similar in meaning [(a) and (i); (g) and (j)].

❏ **EXERCISE 34.** Let's talk: small groups.
Page 405
Time: 15–20 minutes

- Assign students small groups to work in.
- Read the direction line aloud.
- Ask three students to model the example given.
- Ask the members of each group to follow the direction in each item.
- Circulate around the room, helping small groups and ensuring that the time is used productively.
- Have a few students share their answers with the class.

❏ **EXERCISE 35.** Looking at grammar.
Page 405
Time: 10 minutes

- Read the direction line aloud.
- Give students time to choose the correct completion for each blank.
- Correct by having students take turns reading the completed items aloud and explaining why they chose the options they did.

❏ **EXERCISE 36.** Listening. Page 406
Time: 10 minutes

- Have the CD player and track ready.
- Read the direction line to students.

- Remind students that sometimes the sentence closest in meaning is not particularly close in form or hearing. They need to pick the one sentence that is closest in meaning to what they just heard.
- Review by having students read aloud the sentences they chose.
- Turn to the script for any particularly difficult items and correct by referring to it.

❏ **EXERCISE 37.** Reading and grammar.
Page 407
Time: 15–20 minutes

Part I
- Read the direction line aloud.
- Preview the highlighted vocabulary and discuss the meanings.
- Ask a few students to read parts of the passage aloud.
- Ask other students to paraphrase the meanings of what they have just heard.

Part II
- Give students time to complete each item according to what they have just read.
- Review and correct by asking different students to read a completed item aloud. If there are any questions, ask the reader to point to the exact place in the passage where the information was found.

❏ **EXERCISE 38.** Warm-up. Page 408
Time: 5 minutes

- Read the direction line aloud.
- Ask one student to read Speaker A's part.
- Ask another student to read all of Speaker B's suggestions.
- Ask the class to discuss and decide which suggestions go with Speaker A's description.

CHART 13-9. Using *Let's*. Page 409
Time: 10 minutes

- Write the chart title on the board.
- Explain that though *Let us* is the verb phrase that *Let's* is contracted from, we do not say *Let us* to make such suggestions.
- Ask two students to read the exchanges in (a) and (b).
- Review the notes to the right of the chart.
- Explain that *Let's* is usually a spontaneous decision, made when one is aware of a change or a question about what to do.

❏ **EXERCISE 39.** Looking at grammar.
Page 409
Time: 10 minutes

- Read the direction line.
- Ask two students to read the completed example aloud.

- Have students complete the remaining eight items in the exercise independently or with a partner.
- When students have completed the exercise, have pairs take turns reading their completed exchanges and discussing whether they are correct.

❏ **EXERCISE 40.** Let's talk: pairwork.
Page 410
Time: 10–15 minutes

- Ask students to find a new partner.
- Read the direction line aloud.
- Model the example as Partner A with a student as Partner B.
- Give students time to work together while you circulate.
- Once students have worked through most of the items, ask them to take turns reading their suggestions for each situation aloud.
- Write these suggestions on the board and have students correct and compare suggestions.

❏ **EXERCISE 41.** Check your knowledge.
Page 410
Time: 5–10 minutes

- Read the direction line aloud.
- Have students take turns correcting on sight.
- For further clarification, have students explain their corrections.

❏ **EXERCISE 42.** Reading and writing.
Page 411
Time: 10–15 minutes

Part I
- Read the direction line aloud.
- Preview the highlighted vocabulary items.
- Ask students to take turns reading paragraphs aloud.
- Ask other students to paraphrase the different paragraphs.

Part II
- Read the direction line aloud.
- Have students read the questions included as prompts aloud and discuss these.
- Discuss the options that follow the direction "Begin this way".
- Give students time to write.

Part III
- Read the direction line aloud.
- Have students either swap paragraphs or use the editing check to review their own work.
- Ask students to write second drafts following the editing check.

Optional Vocabulary

free time	wait times
interrupt	hometown
amazing	

Chapter 14
Nouns and Modifiers

CHAPTER SUMMARY

OBJECTIVE: In this chapter, students learn to categorize and modify nouns in order to use them more fluently and accurately. Included in the chapter are different types of modifiers, expressions of quantity, and indefinite pronouns.

APPROACH: The text begins by examining types of noun modifiers (including other nouns) and then goes on to look at adjectives and related adverbs. Later, the text explores expressions of quantity that modify nouns and pronouns that take the place of nouns.

TERMINOLOGY: As is the case throughout the text, minimal grammar terminology is used. The grammatical terms employed (for example: *modifier*, *expressions of quantity*, *subject-verb agreement*, and *indefinite pronoun*) are used frequently in presentations because they are both descriptive and common.

❏ **EXERCISE 1.** Warm-up. Page 413
Time: 5–10 minutes

> This Warm-up illustrates that nouns can be used to modify other nouns. Beginners may know this in practice, but would not be able to explain their use. Emphasize that though adjectives commonly precede nouns, nouns can also be modified by other nouns.

• Read the direction line aloud.
• As students match the pictures to the phrases, ask students to tell you what kind of a word *mouse* is and what kind of a word *keyboard* is (adjective, noun, or verb).
• As you explain that nouns can be used as adjectives, ask students if they know any other compound nouns in which the first noun is used as an adjective. Help students think of these and write some on the board. For example:

  picture book
  dinner table

CHART 14-1. Modifying Nouns with Adjectives and Nouns. Page 413
Time: 10–15 minutes

• Write the chart title on the board.
• Ask a student to read example sentences (a) and (b) aloud while you write these examples on the board.

• Ask students what they notice about adjectives before plural nouns and help them understand that these words do not have plural forms.
• Ask another student to read example sentences (c)–(e) aloud.
• Write these on the board and explain that the nouns used as adjectives do not become plural when the main noun is plural.
• Have yet another student read example sentence (f) aloud while you write it on the board.
• Explain to your students that adjective order is something that will become obvious to them the longer they study English. Eventually, learners will be able to "hear" the correct order. For now, tell students that a descriptive adjective (*old*, *new*, *funny*, *interesting*, *boring*) goes before a noun describing another noun.

❏ **EXERCISE 2.** Looking at grammar.
Page 414
Time: 5–7 minutes

• Lead this exercise from the center.
• Ask a student to read the directions and the completed example aloud.
• Call on students in a random order. Ask them first to read the sentence aloud and then to identify the adjective and the noun it modifies.
• Students should be able to do this easily, so correct their pronunciation as well.

❏ **EXERCISE 3.** Looking at grammar.
Page 414
Time: 5–10 minutes

• Read the direction line to students and stress that this exercise is like the previous one, but instead of descriptive adjectives, the words modifying the nouns are also nouns.
• Ask a student to read the completed example aloud.
• Give students time to complete the exercise autonomously as seatwork.
• Correct by having students read the sentences, the nouns acting as adjectives, and the nouns they modify aloud.

❏ EXERCISE 4. Listening. Page 414
Time: 5–10 minutes

- Have the CD player and track ready.
- Read the direction line to students along with the given example.
- Restate that the task is to decide whether the given word is acting as a noun or an adjective.
- Correct by having students read their selections aloud.
- Refer to the script if there are any questions regarding what was heard.

❏ EXERCISE 5. Let's talk: small groups.
Page 415
Time: 10–15 minutes

- Put the students into small groups.
- Read the direction line aloud and emphasize that the right noun is the one that can be used after all three nouns acting as adjectives.
- Ask a student to read the completed example aloud.
- Circulate and assist students with any questions they may have.
- Correct by giving groups an opportunity to share their answers with the entire class.

❏ EXERCISE 6. Looking at grammar.
Page 416
Time: 10–15 minutes

- Read the direction line aloud.
- Ask students to read the completed examples aloud.
- Lead the remainder of the exercise from the center.
- Call on various students to complete each item or encourage all students to answer spontaneously.

❏ EXERCISE 7. Looking at grammar.
Page 417
Time: 10–15 minutes

> Before having students attempt this exercise, it is useful to discuss the difference between adjectives that are subjective and those that are objective. For example, elementary students would consider a homework assignment of fifteen pages *long*, but graduate students would not. Therefore, a *long homework assignment* represents a subjective experience or an opinion combined with a noun, adjective, and a noun.

- Read the direction line aloud.
- Ask a student to read the completed example aloud.
- Give students time to complete the exercise on their own.
- Correct and review by having students read completed items aloud.
- Encourage students to say various options aloud so they can train their ears to hear mistakes.

Optional Vocabulary

official	bricks
locker	narrow
vases	

❏ EXERCISE 8. Warm-up. Page 418
Time: 5–10 minutes

> To help students become familiar with the topic and to encourage them to listen for what sounds correct and natural, ask them to tell you as many adjectives as they can think of for random items around the classroom. For example:
>
> *There is a clock. It is new. It is white. It is round.*
> *There are desks. They are old. They are wooden.*
> *They are brown.*
>
> Before teaching students the actual adjective order, help put each set of adjectives into the order a native speaker would naturally use. You can do this by simply trying out various adjective orders as students find the one that sounds correct.

- Read the direction line aloud.
- Have students answer each question and write the description.

CHART 14-2. Word Order of Adjectives.
Page 418
Time: 10–15 minutes

- Write the chart title on the board.
- Ask a student to read example (a) aloud.
- Explain that size comes before color when there is a list of adjectives.
- Ask another student to read examples (b)–(d) aloud.
- Ask students to explain what an opinion adjective is and be sure they understand that an opinion adjective is subjective whereas an objective adjective represents a factual description.
- Review the notes in the right of the chart aloud and give another example of each of the types of adjectives preceded by opinion adjectives:

  a handsome young man

  an ugly gray truck

  an interesting Korean city

- Ask a student to read the adjectives in example list (e) aloud.
- Encourage students to try to define those adjectives they cannot readily define. Ask students to "define" an adjective by saying what it is not.
- Write the category of each adjective on the board in the order presented under the heading "Usual Word Order of Adjectives."
- Ask students to invent and share sentences about nouns, using the adjectives in the correct order. Tell students it is unusual that they will see so many adjectives preceding a noun.
- Ask a student to read example phrases (f)–(h) aloud and review the notes in the right of the chart.

- Ask a student to read example phrase (i) aloud. Again, emphasize that they are much more likely to see sentences that use some of the adjectives in the order described, rather than one adjective from each of six categories.

❏ EXERCISE 9. Looking at grammar.
Page 419
Time: 10–15 minutes

- Read the direction line aloud.
- Ask a student to read the completed example aloud, starting with *"It is a(n) . . ."*
- Have students work on completing the next five items autonomously. Remind students that they may come up with different adjectives than their peers but all adjectives should make sense and be listed in the order now becoming familiar to students.
- Once students have completed all remaining five items, ask various students to read their completions aloud and compare the variety of adjectives that are possible.
- Make sure that all adjective word orders are standard, according to what has just been presented.
- When there is any doubt, ask students to try reading the completed items aloud, using another order so they can hear their mistakes.

❏ EXERCISE 10. Looking at grammar.
Page 421
Time: 10–15 minutes

- Read the direction line aloud.
- Ask a student to read the completed example aloud.
- Give students time to complete each item autonomously.
- Correct by having students take turns reading their completions aloud.

❏ EXERCISE 11. Looking at grammar.
Page 421
Time: 10–15 minutes

- Lead this exercise from the center.
- Call on students in no particular order. Ask them to put the adjectives in the correct order before the noun in the sentence and read the completion aloud.
- Review any challenging items by trying out alternative orders as a class.

❏ EXERCISE 12. Looking at grammar.
Page 422
Time: 10–15 minutes

Ask students to consider how they will know which category of adjective to choose in completing the task here. Lead them to the conclusion that they should consider the adjectives that precede the blanks and which come immediately after them. Based on this information, their choice in each item is limited to a category of adjective that comes between the two.

- Read the direction line aloud.
- Give students time to complete the exercise autonomously.
- Correct and review by having students read their completed items aloud.
- Compare how students have completed items and discuss the criteria for which kind of adjective to use.

❏ EXERCISE 13. Looking at grammar.
Page 423
Time: 10 minutes

Emphasize that as students progress in English, they will not need to refer back to the actual rules of grammar. Their ears will hear what is correct and what is incorrect. Explain to students that in this way, their learning of a foreign language will come to resemble the way in which they learned their native languages.

- Ask a student to read the direction line.
- Lead the exercise from the center, asking students to choose the correct completions.
- Whenever possible, have students choose as fast as possible the completion that sounds right.

❏ EXERCISE 14. Let's talk: pairwork.
Page 423
Time: 10–15 minutes

- Put students into pairs.
- Ask a student to read the direction line aloud.
- With a student, model the prompt and the exchange between Partner A and Partner B.
- Remind students to give all the nouns to which they think the adjective can apply.
- Correct and review by asking students to offer the most logical combinations they came up with.

❏ EXERCISE 15. Listening. Page 424
Time: 10–15 minutes

- Have the CD player and track ready.
- Read the direction line aloud and emphasize that more than one answer may fit.
- Play the track and have students circle the best completions.
- Correct and review as a class.
- Refer to the script for any challenging or disputed items.

❏ EXERCISE 16. Game. Page 424
Time: 10–15 minutes

Prepare for this game by bringing a wide variety of unusual items to class. The use of realia can stimulate students to engage more fully with the task at hand, and, therefore, a variety of objects will produce more fluent descriptions.

- Read the direction line aloud to students.
- Put students into teams.
- Describe to students exactly what their task is and how they will be scored in teams.
- When students have told you the objects and any adjectives that apply, give the teams one point for each object and one point for each adjective and keep teams' scores on the board.
- Review by bringing out each item and encouraging students to combine adjectives, in the correct order, to describe each item fully.

Optional Vocabulary

opinion	containers
material	landmark
blanket	prompt
leftover	

❏ EXERCISE 17. Warm-up. Page 424
Time: 5–10 minutes

- Read the direction line aloud.
- Emphasize that while many people share the same opinions about how the items listed seem to us, the sentences are still subjective opinions.
- Ask students to complete each item.
- Have students compare by reading aloud each item and invite students to add additional opinion adjectives to each one.

CHART 14-3. Linking Verbs + Adjectives. Page 425
Time: 10–15 minutes

- Write the chart title on the board.
- Ask a student to read example sentence (a) aloud.
- Present this sentence on the board by writing the following:

  . *The flowers were beautiful.*
  or
  The flowers = beautiful.

- Remind students that they are used to the verb *be* being followed by an adjective.
- State that the purpose of this chart is to teach students other verbs that also are non-action verbs, like *be*.
- Ask students to take turns reading example sentences (b)–(f) aloud.
- Ask students to explain the meaning of the linking verb in each sentence.
- While it may be very challenging for students to explain the meaning of each linking verb, they will quickly see (and you can help them to do so) that the meaning of each linking verb is very similar to that of *be*.
- Explain to students that the linking verbs listed here are sense verbs (*look, smell, feel, taste, sound*).
- Tell students that they can always test whether a verb is a linking verb by substituting the verb *be* for that particular verb.

- Students can also test the meaning of a linking verb by considering whether they can replace the verb with an equal sign.

❏ EXERCISE 18. Let's talk: pairwork. Page 425
Time: 10–15 minutes

- Put students into pairs.

Part I
- Read the direction line aloud.
- While pairs are working with each other, circulate around the room, assisting and encouraging.
- Have students make sentences that accurately describe how they feel at the moment of speaking, to share with their partner.
- Ensure that there is time for all partners to describe themselves.

Part II
- Read the direction line aloud.
- Explain to students that taste is a subjective sense, and thus it is possible or even probable that students will hold different opinions about what tastes or smells a certain way.
- While students are working with one another, circulate around the room, assisting and encouraging.

Part III
- Read the direction line aloud.
- While students are working with one another, circulate around the room, assisting and encouraging.
- Review all three parts as a class, putting lists on the board and comparing differing student opinions.

❏ EXERCISE 19. Let's talk. Page 425
Time: 10–15 minutes

- Lead this in groups or as a class.
- Read the direction line.
- Ask one student to take the role of Student A and show an angry face, demonstrate angry actions, and say angry things.
- Ask another student to be Student B. Student B should participate by saying how Student A looks, feels, seems, and so on.
- Proceed by following this model through all emotions listed in the items.

❏ EXERCISE 20. Looking at grammar. Page 426
Time: 10–15 minutes

- Read the direction line aloud.
- Ask a student to read the completed example sentence aloud.
- Give students time to work autonomously and remind them that they may use adjectives included at the top of the exercise as well as their own adjectives.
- When most students have completed all items, review by having students read the completed items aloud.
- Discuss each item and compare all suitable answers.

❏ EXERCISE 21. Let's talk. Page 427
Time: 10–15 minutes

- Invite students to put themselves into pairs or small groups, as they prefer.
- Have students close their books.
- Read the direction line aloud and tell students that the class will vote on whether the adjectives they supply can meaningfully apply to each noun given.
- Read the first noun item and ask students to write as many adjectives as possible that describe the noun in one minute.
- After a minute, stop students and read them a new noun.
- Correct and review by having students compare lists of adjectives.

Optional Vocabulary
expression
Internet security
flat tire
darling
alley

❏ EXERCISE 22. Warm-up. Page 427
Time: 5–10 minutes

> Before starting the Warm-up, demonstrate adverb use by asking a student to perform an action *slowly*, *quickly*, *loudly*, and / or *softly*. For example:
>
> *Arturo, please stand up quickly.*
>
> Write the sentence on the board and ask students what they already know about adverbs of manner, based on their responses to the simple direction above.

- Read the direction line aloud.
- Ask a student to read the completed examples aloud.
- Now, have students complete the remaining items with your guidance.

CHART 14-4. Adjectives and Adverbs.
Page 428
Time: 10–15 minutes

- Write the chart title on the board.
- Have students give you a simple sentence describing another student and write this on the board. For example:

  Julio is a quick runner.

- Explain to students that in this sentence, the adjective *quick* tells us what kind of a runner Julio is.
- Tell students that another way to express the same idea but give focus to the verb is to use an adverb, which can be made easily from an adjective.
- Ask students to look at the sentence above and decide what verb suggests itself (*run*).
- Explain to students that they can create an adverb from the adjective *quick* by adding -*ly* and putting the adverb after the verb.

- Write the subject *Julio* and ask students to tell you the new sentence that has the same meaning as *Julio is a quick runner*.
- Write the sentence:

  Julio runs quickly.

- Ask a student to read example sentences (a) and (b) aloud while you write these on the board.
- Discuss the chart notes with students.
- Ask other students to read example sentences (c) and (d) aloud. Point out that not every adverb ends in -*ly*.
- Stress that some adverbs have exactly the same forms as the adjectives. Point out that the adverb *fast* has the same form as the adjective *fast*.
- Ask another student to read example sentences (e) and (f) aloud and emphasize that though most adjectives become adverbs by adding -*ly*, this is another exception.

❏ EXERCISE 23. Looking at grammar.
Page 428
Time: 10–15 minutes

- Read the direction line to students.
- Emphasize that one way to decide whether they need an adjective or an adverb is to see if the word in red precedes a noun or follows *be* or a linking verb. If so, an adjective is needed.
- Give students time to complete the exercise autonomously.
- Correct by having students read their completions aloud.
- Provide immediate correction and feedback on pronunciation and usage.

Expansion: Play "In The Manner of the Adverb." In this game, you will give each student an index card that has one simple adverb written on it. You will then ask one student to come to the front of the class. Classmates will ask this student a variety of questions, and in every case the student must answer "in the manner of the adverb." Thus, if classmates ask what the student did yesterday and the adverb is *angrily*, the student in the hot seat must respond angrily. Sometimes it is hard for students to separate the content of a response from the manner in which it is delivered, so be ready to coach students appropriately. Possible adverbs include:

angrily	hungrily
calmly	quickly
emotionally	purposefully
energetically	shyly
happily	slowly

❏ EXERCISE 24. Looking at grammar.
Page 429
Time: 10–15 minutes

Part I
- Read the direction line to students.
- Remind students that some adverb forms are the same as the adjective forms.

Part II

- Read the direction line aloud.
- Give students time to complete each sentence on their own by using adjective or adverb forms of the words from Part I.
- Correct as a group, having students read their responses aloud.

☐ EXERCISE 25. Looking at grammar.
Page 429
Time: 10–15 minutes

- Lead this exercise on sight.
- Ask a student to read the direction line and the completed example aloud.
- Call on various students to complete the items and discuss each one.

Expansion: To further engage students who may find this exercise easy, ask students if they can name the opposite adjective or adverb, depending on what is required. For example, ask students whether the opposite adverb and adjective for items 9 and 10 are the same word. (The opposite adverb is *easily* and the opposite adjective is *easy*.) Finding ways to teach in the margins and asking students about other aspects of each exercise gives students opportunities to speak spontaneously and use English they already know. Moreover, it requires that they pay attention even when they may find the target material relatively simple.

☐ EXERCISE 26. Reading, grammar, and speaking. Page 430
Time: 15–20 minutes

- Read the direction line aloud to students.
- Give them time to read through the passage on their own, marking adjectives and adverbs as instructed.
- Ask students to read parts of the passage aloud and address the highlighted vocabulary as well as any words that would provide students a chance to speak autonomously.
- Similarly, ask students to restate and paraphrase in order to give them opportunities to engage with the material.
- Ask students to read the discussion questions aloud and provide time for thorough discussion of each one.
- Put students' thoughts and opinions on the board.

Expansion: Ask students to answer additional questions. Questions are included here, but feel free to include your own. You can write the questions on the board or simply ask the class, but encourage those who do not speak regularly to do so.

Did you know about Elvis Presley before now?

Do you know of other famous pop musicians from the last century (the Beatles, the Rolling Stones, etc.)?

Did your family often play music in your house when you were a child?

If so, what kind of music and what performers did your family listen to?

Do you play a musical instrument or sing?

What are other situations where you enjoy listening to music? Do you like background music? What types of music and performers do you like?

Do you often download music onto a smart phone or MP3 player? What are the advantages of doing so?

What do you think is a classic song of your generation? Why do you think it represents your generation?

Optional Vocabulary

whispered	slow down
pronounces	accent
carelessly	composition
generous	has trouble hearing
thoughtful	

☐ EXERCISE 27. Warm-up. Page 431
Time: 5–10 minutes

- Ask a student to read the direction aloud.
- Have students decide which of the three statements best describes the illustration.
- Ask a student to explain why item 3 is the most accurate.

CHART 14-5. Expressions of Quantity: *All Of, Most Of, Some Of, Almost All Of.* Page 431
Time: 10–15 minutes

- Write the chart title on the board.
- In order to demonstrate the meanings of these expressions of quantity, create sentences about the students in your class. (The example sentences below will need to be adapted to reflect your actual class makeup.)
- Write three true examples illustrating the meanings of *all of*, *most of*, and *some of* on the board . The meanings of each expression should be very clear to students, based on the examples you have chosen. For example:

  All of the students in this class are studying English.

  Most of the students in this class have dark hair.

  Some of the students in this class are women.

- Now, have students count the total number of students in the class and the number of students that fall into each category. As students give you the information, write fractions representing those numbers on the board. For example:

All of the students in this class are studying English.	*20 / 20*
Most of the students in this class have dark hair.	*15 / 20*
Some of the students in this class are women.	*11 / 20*

- Turn to the chart and ask a student to read example sentence (a) aloud.
- Review the note on the right explaining example sentence (a) aloud and write the following on the board:

  all of = 100%

- Ask another student to read example sentence (b) aloud.

- Review the note for (b) with students and write the following on the board:

    most of = > 75%

- Ask a third student to read example sentence (c) aloud and review the note for (c).

    some of = 1%–75%

- Explain that *all of*, *most of*, *some of*, and *almost all of* go before a specific group of people in a specific setting like the group of students in the class in the example above.

- Tell students that *of* must be followed by a determiner (*the*, *his*, *her*, etc.).

    Incorrect: all of money, most of money, some of money, almost all of money.

    Correct: all of the money, most of his money, some of her money, almost all of our money.

- Ask another student to read example sentence (d) aloud.

- Explain that *almost* modifies the *all*, and explain the meaning and notes.

- Write the following on the board:

    almost all of = 90%–100%

❑ EXERCISE 28. Looking at grammar.
Page 432
Time: 5–10 minutes

> Even advanced students tend to make many mistakes with these expressions of quantity. Your students will benefit greatly from your emphasizing that we cannot put a preposition immediately before a noun (for example, *all of people*). In order to use this expression, there must be a definite article, a demonstrative adjective, or a possessive adjective following the preposition *of* (for example, *all of these numbers*). Correct students immediately and clearly, and write the corrections on the board so students can see that there *must* be one of these words before the noun. Because your students are beginners, you can help them avoid this fossilized error.

- Read the direction line aloud.
- Ask a student to read the completed example aloud.
- Give students time to complete the exercise autonomously, as seatwork.
- Correct the exercise by having students read responses aloud.

Optional Vocabulary
omitted

❑ EXERCISE 29. Warm-up. Page 433
Time: 5–10 minutes

- Read direction line to students.
- Tell students that *all of* is either plural or singular, depending on whether the noun following *of* is a count (plural) or noncount (singular) noun.
- Ask students which noun the verb *be* agrees with in both sentences, and ask them to explain their answers.

CHART 14-6. Expressions of Quantity:
Subject-Verb Agreement. Page 433
Time: 10–15 minutes

> When the subject includes an expression of quantity, the verb agrees with the noun that comes immediately after *of*.
>
> *All of the cake is gone.*
> *All of my friends are sick today.*
> *Some of my homework is not finished.*
> *Some of my friends are sick today.*
>
> These expressions of quantity are singular or plural depending on whether the nouns following them are count (plural) or noncount (singular). To help students prepare for more sophisticated subject structures, explain that this is because these expressions (*some of*, *all of*) take their meaning and their number from the noun that follows.

- Write the chart title on the board.
- Ask a student to remind you of the difference between count and noncount nouns and ask that student to write a couple of examples of count and noncount nouns on the board.
- Ask a student to read example sentences (a) and (b) aloud.
- Emphasize that in example sentence (a), *work* is noncount, and thus requires a singular verb.
- Ask another student to read example sentences (c) and (d) aloud.
- Stress that the word *homework* in sentence (c) is noncount and, therefore, the verb following it must be singular.
- Ask students to create sentences about the class using these expressions of quantity.
- Write these sentences on the board, underlining the parts of the sentences that agree. For example:

    A lot of our class enjoys baseball.

    Half of the students speak more than two languages.

❑ EXERCISE 30. Looking at grammar.
Page 433
Time: 10–15 minutes

- Ask a student to read the direction line and the completed example aloud.
- Give students time to complete the exercise as seatwork.
- Correct by having students read their completions aloud.
- Provide very clear direction about pronunciation and usage to avoid future fossilized errors.

❑ EXERCISE 31. Listening. Page 434
Time: 10 minutes

- Have the CD player and track ready.
- Read the direction line aloud.
- Review the completed example with students and explain they will need to hear the expressions

of quantity correctly in order to select the right percentages.

- Correct by having students read their percentages for each item.
- If there are any questions, refer to the script for verification.

❏ EXERCISE 32. Let's talk: class activity.
Page 435
Time: 10–15 minutes

- Read the direction line aloud.
- Read through the example to model the form for students.
- Have students close their books.
- Take turns asking the questions of students. You can redirect the same question to others to give many students the opportunity to respond.
- Correct students' structure and pronunciation immediately.
- Encourage students to discuss with one another, particularly if there is any disagreement about which expression of quantity works best.

❏ EXERCISE 33. Looking at grammar.
Page 435
Time: 10–15 minutes

- Read the direction line to the class.
- Tell students to be ready to explain why their choices are correct when they respond.
- Give students time to select the correct sentences.
- Correct by having students give and justify their choices.

Optional Vocabulary
polluted
coins
valuable

❏ EXERCISE 34. Warm-up. Page 435
Time: 5 minutes

- Read the direction line aloud.
- Ask students what they already know about the word *every*.
- Have students read their completed and logical sentences aloud.

CHART 14-7. Using *Every, Everyone, Everybody, Everything*. Page 436
Time: 10–15 minutes

Though almost all beginners have heard the word *every* or its variants before, this can be a challenging concept to teach. Explain that *every* and *all* have essentially the same meaning, but *every* is always followed by a singular noun. When using *every*, the fact that each *one* is a separate person, item, or place is very important because the verb is always singular.

Because students tend to make mistakes with *every*, it will help if you show them the common errors included in the chart, and with great flourish, stress that these structures are never okay. In this way, students may avoid these common errors becoming fossilized.

- Write the chart title on the board.
- Ask a student to read example sentences (a) and (b) aloud while you write these on the board.
- Explain that *every* can never be followed by a plural noun or a preposition followed by a plural noun.
- Write the *incorrect* examples on the board and then draw a line through them, emphasizing that they are never correct.
- Have a different student read example sentences (c) and (d) aloud while you write these on the board.
- Ask another student to read example sentences (e) and (f) aloud while you write these on the board.
- Have students generate sentences about your class using *every* and write these on the board. For example:

  Every student loves grammar.
  Everyone has a grammar book.

- Finish by asking what *every* student has learned about *every*. Remind students that *every* is always followed by a singular noun and a singular verb.

❏ EXERCISE 35. Looking at grammar.
Page 436
Time: 10–15 minutes

- Have a student read the direction line and completed example aloud.
- Remind students that *every* is always followed by a singular noun and verb and that *all of* can be followed by either a count or a noncount noun, which determines whether the verb is plural or singular.
- Give students time to complete this exercise as seatwork.
- Have students read their completions aloud and listen very carefully for the correct verb usage as other students give their answers.
- Provide immediate and clear correction.

Optional Vocabulary
regularly
bedtime stories
transportation system

❏ EXERCISE 36. Warm-up. Page 437
Time: 10 minutes

Most beginners will be familiar with the idea of indefinite pronouns and many will also have heard *someone*, *anyone*, and others. Often, the most challenging thing for students is the difference between *someone* and *anyone*. This Warm-up is very useful because although the person is unknown, and, therefore, indefinite, the fact that there is a person is known.

You can refer back to this Warm-up when teaching the indefinite pronouns beginning with *any* as those pronouns would not be suitable in affirmative statements here. For example, in *He knew that **someone** was coming up behind him*, only *someone* can be used because the sentence is affirmative. *Anyone* is not possible here.

- Read the direction line aloud.
- Have students take turns reading A's and B's lines aloud.
- Discuss the mystery and explain the answer.
- Have students underline *someone*, *somebody*, *anyone*, and *anybody* in the dialogue and discuss how they are used.
- Point out that *any* can be used only in a question or negative statement.

CHART 14-8. Indefinite Pronouns: *Something, Someone, Somebody, Anything, Anyone, Anybody.* Page 438
Time: 10–15 minutes

- Explain to your students that you will be vigilant about correcting their use of these indefinite pronouns to help them avoid making common mistakes that English speakers around them might be making.
- Write the chart title on the board.
- Ask students to give you an example of an affirmative statement and a negative one.
- Explain that *some_____* words are used for affirmative statements and questions. They are not used for negative ones.
- Ask a student to read example sentences (a)–(c) aloud.
- Write the sentences on the board and review the notes.
- Ask a student to read example sentences (d)–(f) aloud.
- Write the sentences on the board and review the notes.
- Ask a student to read example questions (g)–(l) aloud.
- Write the sentences on the board and review the notes.
- To help students remember the basics, write the following on the board:

  *I know **somebody**, but I don't know **anybody**.*

❑ EXERCISE 37. Looking at grammar.
Page 438
Time: 10–15 minutes

- Read the direction line aloud.
- Ask a student to read the completed example.
- Emphasize that both forms may be possible.
- Give students time to complete the items as seatwork.
- Correct by having students read their completions aloud and be very directive and explicit in reminding students why certain forms are needed.

❑ EXERCISE 38. Looking at grammar.
Page 439
Time: 10–15 minutes

- Read the direction line aloud.
- Give students time to complete the items as seatwork.
- Correct by having students read their sentences aloud.
- Ask students to explain why their responses were the only acceptable ones.

❑ EXERCISE 39. Looking at grammar.
Page 440
Time: 10–15 minutes

- Have a student read the direction line aloud.
- Explain that students should close their books and then lead the questions from the center.
- Students may be tempted to say *I see nothing*. Ask them to rephrase their responses by using negative verbs.
- Highlight the kind of situations in which speakers use *anything*, often in denial of an accusation, as in items 6 and 7.

❑ EXERCISE 40. Listening. Page 441
Time: 10 minutes

- Have the CD player and track ready.
- Read the direction line and example aloud to your students.
- Correct by having students give you their yes / no responses, according to the listening.

❑ EXERCISE 41. Looking at grammar.
Page 441
Time: 10–15 minutes

- Ask a student to read the direction line aloud.
- Give students time to complete the review as seatwork.
- Have students read the correct completions and review challenging items by asking them to state the rules that informed their decisions.

❑ EXERCISE 42. Let's talk. Page 442
Time: 15–20 minutes

- Read the direction line aloud.
- Have students get into pairs or small groups.
- Ask a student to read the facts aloud and then have students work together to use the clues to complete the chart.
- Circulate around the room and assist pairs and groups.
- As students are finishing their charts, draw one big chart on the board.
- Ask students from each group to go to the chart and complete one piece of information, based on what they have determined.
- Correct the chart as needed and encourage further discussion of any disagreement among students.

❏ EXERCISE 43. Check your knowledge.
Page 442
Time: 10–15 minutes

- Lead this exercise from the center.
- Ask a student to read the direction line aloud.
- Ask another student to read the completed example and explain the grammar practice behind it.
- Have students take turns reading and correcting each item on sight.
- Ask students to refer to particular grammar rules and / or a chart to explain their responses.

❏ EXERCISE 44. Reading and writing.
Page 443
Time: 15–20 minutes

> Whenever possible and particularly in reading passages, after students have read something aloud, ask them about random words, phrases, and expressions that they already know. Ask students to explain what they have just read and ask related questions of your own devising. Remember that engaging students in this way permits them to respond spontaneously while studying the target structures. Doing this prevents any grammar exercise from being only a decontextualized, rote experience.

Part I
- Read the direction line aloud.
- Engage students by having them take turns reading aloud from the passage.
- As students read aloud, ask them to paraphrase meanings and define vocabulary, or simply give synonyms.

Part II
- Read the direction line aloud.
- As not every student is prepared to write, warm them up to the task by discussing the topic—a way to create special memories—with them.
- Ask students the three questions to help them formulate their ideas for their paragraphs.
- Based on how students respond, engage them further by encouraging them to share more.
- Have students then read the writing sample aloud, taking turns.
- Discuss its contents with students and ask them to share their impressions of the sample.
- Give students time to write the assigned paragraphs about creating special memories, either in class, or more appropriately, as homework.

Part III
- Read the direction line aloud and have students decide how they wish to work, whether in pairs or alone.
- Have students edit their own or their partner's work by referring to the items in the editing checklist.
- Invite students to share their own work by reading it aloud to the class and discussing their writing.

Optional Vocabulary
anniversary
vending machine
secretly engaged
the mall
psychologists
create
sports event
souvenirs
deli

Chapter 15
Making Comparisons

CHAPTER SUMMARY

OBJECTIVE: In this chapter, students learn a variety of ways to compare people, things, and statements. Students learn to use comparative and superlative forms to compare nouns. The chapter also introduces other ways to make comparisons, including using comparative phrases (*the same as*, *similar to*, *different from*) and directly contrasting clauses by using *but*.

APPROACH: The text first looks at comparative adjectives and introduces rules and practices for forming and using them (comparing two people or things) before providing opportunities for increasingly freer production. The concept of the superlative is introduced and students are given exercises to facilitate their ability to compare three items or more. The chapter then introduces the comparison of adverbs and the direct comparison of whole clauses. Throughout the chapter, there are many open-ended exercises requiring students to produce the target structures in discussions. This is particularly important for this target grammar as it is all about comparing things and situations, and thus exchanging opinions. Support and facilitate lively discussions throughout the chapter, while also correcting structures, to give students the confidence to speak autonomously and spontaneously.

TERMINOLOGY: As is the case throughout the text, minimal grammar terminology is used. The terms *comparative* and *superlative* are used throughout the chapter, as they apply to both adjectives and adverbs. Teachers will need to revisit the concept of syllables in order to ensure students' success with comparative forms. The text does not teach the categories of certain adjective types and / or phrases (for example, *like*, *alike*, *the same as*) but focuses on their actual usage. Similarly, no mention is made of the grammatical names of words like *as*, *than*, and so on. While some grammarians refer to *than* as a comparative conjunction, others call it a preposition. The omission of such terms altogether highlights the fact that though linguists may find these distinctions interesting, English students need only to recognize and use the actual terms correctly.

❏ EXERCISE 1. Warm-up. Page 445
Time: 5 minutes

It is likely that even beginners have heard or seen comparative forms. However, it is equally likely that students are not confident about what word should

follow the *-er* form. Many beginners use *as* and *than* interchangeably and incorrectly. When introducing the comparative forms, be sure to emphasize that only one word— *than*—can correctly follow the adjective.

- Read the direction line aloud, and as a class, identify the true sentences.
- Have students read these aloud.
- Emphasize that the word immediately following the comparative form is *than*.

CHART 15-1. The Comparative: Using *-er* and *More*. Page 445
Time: 10–15 minutes

Before beginning the comparative presentation, ask students if they know what a syllable is and / or if they can describe it to you. The concept itself will likely be familiar, but because students have to think about syllables in such a concrete way, you will need to refresh their memories.

Although it can be time-consuming to re-create grammar charts on the board, doing so helps ensure that students are really attending to the rules and practices that will allow them to manipulate the grammar autonomously. In addition, many students need to see, hear, and have some visual and aural illustration in the form of an actual example, to take in new material. Though it can take time, you can make chart presentations a vibrant part of the class by using students' names and characteristics in examples. Try to give every student a chance to read some part of the chart or offer you an alternative adjective so that they participate in their own exposure to the material. Taking time with these charts provides students a better grounding as they make the structures their own.

- Write the chart title on the board.
- Ask students what a syllable is and if they can tell you how many syllables are in their names.
- Depending on how familiar students are with syllables, spend an appropriate amount of time explaining what they are and their importance in deciding the comparative form of adjectives.
- A good working definition of a syllable is "an independent sound unit (containing a distinct vowel sound)." Many students may know how to clap out

syllables and can count them in that way. In whatever way works for you and your students, ensure that they can distinguish adjectives with two or more syllables from those with one.

• Write the first two sentences on the board and then have a student read example sentences (a) and (b) from the chart aloud.

• Write example sentences (a) and (b) on the board after students read them aloud.

• Model the incorrect versions. Write these on the board but be sure to draw a line through them or emphatically erase them to help students see that these incorrect versions are never acceptable.

• Ask a student to state which word follows the comparative form and write *than* on the board. Stress that this word, *than, always* follows the comparative form.

• Work through the chart, having students read the examples from each heading while you write on the board.

• Alternatively, you can present the same categories (*Adjectives with One Syllable, Adjectives That End in -y, Adjectives with Two or More Syllables, Irregular Comparative Forms*) and have students give you examples, which you write on the board, expanding into comparative forms and actual sentences featuring students' names to engage them in the material further.

• Finish by involving any student(s) who did not take part in the presentation by asking them to help provide a couple of example sentences for the whole class. For example:

Meilan, can you tell us who is quieter in class, Bruno or Marisol?

Meilan: Marisol is quieter than Bruno.

Hiroko, who is taller, Ahmed or Zara?

Hiroko: Zara is taller than Ahmed.

❏ **EXERCISE 2.** Looking at grammar.
Page 446
Time: 5–10 minutes

• Ask a student to read the direction line and completed example aloud.

• Give students time to complete the remaining items as seatwork.

• Correct by having students take turns reading their completed items aloud.

• Provide overt and immediate correction and use the board to highlight mistakes, helpfully.

❏ **EXERCISE 3.** Looking at grammar.
Page 446
Time: 5–10 minutes

Teach students that in spoken and informal English, an object pronoun (rather than a subject pronoun + verb) often follows a comparative phrase. Explain that this is not acceptable in written and more formal English.

Engage students in optional vocabulary and content as you go. (For example, some people may find that a mattress is too soft, and though they may not find that a floor is more comfortable, they may find that a futon is more comfortable.) As students' opinions will differ on these completions, engage more than one student per item, and if students have a difference of opinion, ask them to justify their side by using more (unscripted) comparative forms. This exercise offers a lot of room for exploitation in terms of discussion or expansion, so make it as conversational as possible. Highlight the fact that some comparisons are simply objective and some are subjective. Discuss the difference.

• Ask a student to read the direction line and completed example aloud.

• Lead this exercise from the center and have students read completions as you go around the room.

• Correct all forms immediately and ask other students if the form they just heard a classmate read was correct.

• Put any challenging items on the board. Also, write any sentences that provoke discussion on the board and write discussion points as students raise them.

❏ **EXERCISE 4.** Let's talk: pairwork. Page 448
Time: 10–15 minutes

• Ask a student to read the direction line aloud.

• Ask another student to read the example aloud and write this on the board.

• Have students arrange themselves in pairs and decide who will be Partner A and who will be Partner B.

• Partner A will start the exercise by comparing the things in item 1 in his or her column.

❏ **EXERCISE 5.** Let's talk: class activity.
Page 448
Time: 15–20 minutes

• Bring additional books or items of a similar category to class.

• Ask a student to read the direction line aloud.

• Have another student read the example aloud.

• Ask students to come to where the books are and make comparisons that they can share with the class.

• Highlight again that some of the adjectives are subjective, and students will need to explain why they think one book is better than another.

• Put example sentences on the board, correct the target grammar immediately, and encourage extended discussion and justification.

Expansion: Bring food items to class for students to taste and compare. You can bring a variety of cheap snack foods or ask everyone to prepare for the comparison by bringing one of their favorite foods (in small quantities) to class.

Prepare students to participate in a comparison of food by creating a list of adjectives that apply particularly to food, along with some adjectives that are generally descriptive of preference. For example:

acidic	delicious
bad	salty
bitter	sour
bland	spicy
filling	strong
flavorful	sweet
good	tasty

❑ **EXERCISE 6.** Listening. Page 448
Time: 5–10 minutes

- Have the CD player and track ready.
- Read the direction line aloud.
- Read the example aloud, clearly distinguishing, "You will hear" from "You will choose" to ensure that students understand the task at hand.
- Play the track and have students choose the comparative forms they hear.
- Correct by having students read aloud the comparative forms they chose.
- If there are any doubts, refer to the script and read the original sentences aloud, emphasizing the comparative forms.

❑ **EXERCISE 7.** Looking at grammar.
Page 449
Time: 10–15 minutes

- Read the direction line aloud.
- Ask students to look through the list of adjectives to see if there are any unknown words.
- Explain that it is important that students know what the adjectives mean in order to complete each item meaningfully and review any unfamiliar words.
- Give students time to work through the remaining items as seatwork.
- Correct by having students read their completed items aloud.
- Correct pronunciation and structure immediately and ensure students say *than* after the comparative form distinctly enough so it is not misused (*as*), misheard, or omitted.

❑ **EXERCISE 8.** Let's talk. Page 450
Time: 10–15 minutes

Encourage students to defend their opinions and think critically. (For example, it is obvious that good health is more important than money, but it is also true that in a great many societies, without money, it is impossible to obtain good health.) Your role is to foster lively discussion while keeping students on track in terms of accuracy.

Sometimes students find themselves stuck on what to say and how to compare uninteresting things such as dust and sand. You can help them by encouraging them to think of where they find both items and what physical properties each has.

- Read the direction line aloud.
- Ask a student to read aloud the example with the comparative sentences.
- Have students decide how to work—whether in pairs, in small groups, or as a class—and have them arrange themselves accordingly.
- Encourage students to try new adjectives in comparative forms. If students are working in small groups or pairs, go to each one and lead students in discussing certain aspects of each set of items.
- Review by gathering the class and having different students provide comparative sentences for each set of items.
- Within the class, compare how many students chose the same aspects or properties of each set of items to compare. Discuss how many students chose subjective approaches to each set of items and how many chose objective approaches (such as the simple physical properties of each).

❑ **EXERCISE 9.** Let's talk: small groups.
Page 450
Time: 10–15 minutes

Remind students that comparative adjective forms are essential to good and lively discussions. Emphasize the great practice they are gaining in stating their opinions in grammatically correct sentences.

- If students are already in pairs, have the pairs join other pairs to form small groups.
- Have a student read the direction line aloud.
- Bring students' attention to the phrase *in general*.
- Ask students why *in general* is a useful direction in such discussions.
- Have students work through the eight items, deciding their individual answers and comparing them with their group members.
- As you circulate around the room, take note of commonly heard errors.
- Encourage students to expand their statements from the most general to particular justifications or rationales to support the most general form, using new comparative forms.
- Review as a class by having various students read the statements and offer their own responses and the consensus (if reached) of their groups.
- Discuss any commonly heard errors.
- Discuss at more length any provocative opinions, and ask those giving them for further reasoning.

❑ **EXERCISE 10.** Let's talk: pairwork.
Page 451
Time: 10–15 minutes

- Have the small groups split into new pairs.
- Read the direction line aloud.
- With a student or two, model the exchange in the example.

- Remind students that Partner A will first have his or her book open and that Partner B will have his or hers closed. Remind Partner B to respond in complete sentences, using the target comparative forms accurately.
- Circulate around the room and oversee the switch of partners, ensuring that the Partner Bs are now asking the questions and that the Partner As have their books closed.
- Take notes on any commonly heard errors, and note items that are hard to respond to.
- Review by having everyone close their books and ask both sets of questions to the class as a whole.
- Welcome spontaneous responses but provide clear and immediate correction of the target forms.
- Write any challenging items or oft-heard errors on the board and correct them by emphatically crossing out incorrect items and leaving only correct forms on the board.
- As you read out the directions in all the items and welcome responses, make note of how many students respond in the same way, which responses reflect objective facts, and which reflect opinions.
- Engage students in as much natural and spontaneous discussion as possible, while also correcting form and asking questions that will produce more student-generated constructions.

Optional Vocabulary

syllable	logically
vowel	arithmetic
consonant	algebra
difficult	orange
deep	lemon
ocean *versus* sea	lake
lazy	ocean
course	bedroom slippers
curly	dust
bride	sand
groom	strict
nervous	lenient
bright	relaxed
sour	serious
afford	

❑ **EXERCISE 11.** Warm-up. Page 451
Time: 5–10 minutes

> Just to do the Warm-up, students will need some understanding of the concept behind the superlative. Explain that by saying *in the world* you are stating that the comparison is among more than two.

- Read the direction line.
- Have students read and complete each item according to their own opinions and whether they agree or not.
- Ask various students to read the items, and answer *yes* or *no* aloud.
- Encourage students who don't agree with the statements given to tell you what they think the *prettiest*, *most expensive*, and *most exciting* cities in the world are.

- Write their opinions on the board and ask the class as a whole to comment.
- In every case and for every sentence, ask students to give you some support for their opinions, stating what it is that makes X the most ____ city in the world for them.

CHART 15-2. The Superlative: Using *-est* and *Most*. Page 452
Time: 10–15 minutes

> Before presenting the chart, have students remind you of the rules for comparative adjectives and discuss the role of syllables in forming them.

- Write the chart title on the board.
- Begin by having a student read example sentence (a) aloud.
- Write this sentence on the board or choose another sentence illustrating the comparative form to write on the board.
- Explain to students that whereas the comparative form is used when comparing the qualities of two nouns, the superlative form requires at least three nouns to be compared among one another.
- Ask another student to read example sentence (b) aloud to the class.
- Write example sentence (b) or another superlative example on the board.
- Explain that when using the superlative, students are saying that one noun has the most of a certain adjectival quality *of all*. Because one of all is being specified, a definite article is also required.
- Ask students to take turns reading aloud the simple adjective form, the comparative, and the superlative for each type of adjective.
- Write these forms on the board, using either the adjectives given in the chart or similar student-generated adjectives.
- Give students opportunities to change other adjective forms and locate them in the correct category in the chart. For example:

  You say: Okay, and what about happy? How would we change happy?

  A student can then say: happier than; the happiest

- Stress that the additional words used to make the comparative form can be considered part of the form itself and that learning to include *(more)* _____ *-er than* and *the (most)* _____ *-est* will help students always use these forms correctly.
- Complete the chart presentation by reviewing the irregular adjectives included at the bottom of the chart.

❑ **EXERCISE 12.** Looking at grammar.
Page 452
Time: 10 minutes

- Read the direction line aloud to students.
- Have a student read the completed examples aloud.

- Give students time to complete the items.
- Correct by having students read and even spell out the correct comparative and superlative forms.

  Expansion: Ask each student reading the comparative and superlative forms aloud to also create a logical sentence featuring each comparative and superlative form. Ask the remainder of the class to decide whether the sentences are correct or incorrect. This Expansion can be useful as it will illustrate to students that they often correctly change the adjective form itself but fail to include the required *than* or *the*.

❏ **EXERCISE 13.** Looking at grammar.
Page 453
Time: 10–15 minutes

- Ask a student to read both the direction line and the completed example item aloud.
- Give students time to complete the exercise autonomously, as seatwork.
- Correct by having students read the completed items aloud.
- Ask students to identify which set of nouns the superlative one is being compared to, and make sure they can identify this.
- Have fellow classmates correct pronunciation and usage on the spot.
- If an actual discussion should arise from this exercise, encourage it and help students participate fully. For example, students may debate what the most beautiful cities are, and your encouraging them to do so provides an opportunity for them to use the target grammar spontaneously.

❏ **EXERCISE 14.** Listening. Page 454
Time: 10 minutes

- Have the CD player and track ready.
- Read the direction line aloud as well as the circled example answer *no*. Make sure that students understand that their task is to listen to the sentences and look at the people at the same time.
- Play the ten items and give students time to circle *yes* or *no*.
- Correct by inviting students to share their responses.
- When / If there is a debate about the content of what was heard, read the script aloud and have students rethink their responses, if necessary.

❏ **EXERCISE 15.** Looking at grammar.
Page 455
Time: 10–15 minutes

- Lead this exercise from the center.
- Have students read the direction line and completed examples aloud.
- Have students complete each item on sight and call out their responses as you go around the room, inviting responses.
- Correct all aspects of what you hear. Make sure that you can readily hear the *the's* and *than's*. If not, have students read their completions aloud again until these are heard by all.

❏ **EXERCISE 16.** Looking at grammar.
Page 458
Time: 10–15 minutes

- Have a student read the direction line aloud.
- Reiterate that students need to use whichever form (comparative or superlative) is called for.
- Give students time to complete the exercise on their own, as seatwork.
- Correct the exercise by having students read their completions aloud.
- Make sure that students read and pronounce all the required words for each form clearly.
- Put any challenging items on the board and have students correct these together as a class.

❏ **EXERCISE 17.** Listening. Page 459
Time: 10 minutes

- Have the CD player and track ready.
- Ask a student to read the direction line aloud.
- Have another student read the completed example aloud.
- Play the track and be sure that students are completing the items as required.
- Correct each item by having students read their completions aloud.
- Compare students' completions with the script as necessary and discuss any particularly challenging items in detail.

Optional Vocabulary

opinion	population
landmark	sandals
continent	

❏ **EXERCISE 18.** Warm-up. Page 459
Time: 5–10 minutes

- Read the direction line to students.
- On the board, write a sample sentence generated by what you know of your class, using *one of the* + superlative + plural noun. For example:

  One of the youngest students in the school is in our class.

- Ask your students why this particular construction is useful for speakers.
- Explain that this structure allows a softer statement. Using this form, students don't have to be as absolute in their opinions (*one of the most* is a more qualified opinion than *the most*).
- Ask students to complete the Warm-up and discuss their answers.

CHART 15-3. Using *One Of* + Superlative + Plural Noun. Page 460
Time: 10–15 minutes

- Write the chart title on the board.
- Ask a student to read example sentence (a) aloud while you write it on the board.

- Write the incorrect versions of this example sentence on the board as well, but emphatically cross out the incorrect forms, explaining what is missing in each case.
- Have a student read example sentence (b) aloud while you write this on the board.
- Do the same with example sentence (c).
- Ask students to come up with a few sentences of their own, referring to their classmates or common topics. Have students write their sentences on the board and correct these as a class. For example:

  Mei-Ling is one of the smartest students in the class.

  Sheila is one of the tallest students in the school.

  Lobster is one of the most popular dishes in New England.

❑ EXERCISE 19. Looking at grammar.
Page 460
Time: 10–15 minutes

- Ask a student to read the direction line aloud.
- Have three different students read both the cues and the completed sentences for items 1–3.
- Continue with this exercise, leading it from the center.
- Ask students to read the cues for each item aloud, along with possible sentences.
- Ask students to write their sentences on the board and correct their grammar and usage accordingly.
- Because the structure allows for more than one noun to be discussed, ask other students to use the same cues to form different sentences. Write these on the board as well.
- Correct by ensuring that the sentences that remain on the board include every element necessary for this structure to be accurate.

❑ EXERCISE 20. Let's talk: class interview.
Page 460
Time: 15–20 minutes

- Read the direction line aloud to students.
- Ask all students to get up out of their seats, circulate, and ask as many classmates as they can questions using the items listed.
- Instruct students to take notes on their classmates' responses so that they can compare these as a group.
- Tell students to continue until they have completed the chart with a number of students' responses for each item.
- While students are doing this, walk around the room yourself, taking notes on oft-overheard errors in pronunciation and / or usage.
- Encourage students also to include you in their questions and use this as an opportunity to engage them in both the structures and content of the questions.
- When most students have completed the chart, ask them to return to their seats.
- Go around the room, having students share the responses they received from their classmates with the class.

- While comparing responses, have students write on the board various responses that they heard, to foster further discussion.
- Review any overheard errors you have jotted down and give students very clear instructions to correct these errors.

❑ EXERCISE 21. Let's talk. Page 462
Time: 10–15 minutes

- Put students into groups of three or four.
- Read the direction line aloud.
- Have students ask and respond to the questions in the exercise with others in their small groups.
- As a class, review all the questions with all the groups, encouraging students to give particular answers and comparing these with responses from other groups.
- Correct pronunciation and usage immediately.

Expansion: From what students in the class have now learned from one another, form statements that represent class opinions. These opinions can be based on the most common responses. Write these on the board and have students correct and / or refine these. For example:

One of the most famous movie stars in the world is Brad Pitt, in our opinion.

An earthquake is one of the most frightening natural events in the world.

❑ EXERCISE 22. Let's talk: small groups.
Page 462
Time: 10–15 minutes

- Ask a student to read the direction line aloud.
- Give students time to take the quiz and form their responses individually before getting into small groups.
- Once students are in small groups, have the groups compare answers. Individual group members should try to convince one another of their positions before turning to page 465 to find the correct answers.
- Have students respond to every item (Parts I–VI), and then check their answers against the Table of Statistics on page 465.
- Discuss as a class.

❑ EXERCISE 23. Reading and grammar.
Page 466
Time: 15–20 minutes

- First, read the direction line aloud to all students.
- Next, ask students to read the passage to themselves first.
- Have three or four students take turns reading parts of the whole passage aloud.
- Discuss the highlighted vocabulary with students.
- Ask students to explain other (nonhighlighted) vocabulary and to paraphrase what they have read aloud.
- Ask students to respond to the question by writing their reasons on the board.
- Discuss different students' opinions and compare them.

Optional Vocabulary

event	tsunami
scariest	invention
earthquake	service plan
cyclone	convenient
volcano	modern

❏ **EXERCISE 24.** Warm-up. Page 466
Time: 5–10 minutes

• Read the direction line to students.
• Ask students to respond to the three items.
• Then have students read these items aloud and compare responses.
• Have students discuss what is being compared and help them understand that it is how an action is performed that is the point of comparison.

CHART 15-4. Making Comparisons with Adverbs. Page 467
Time: 10–15 minutes

• Write the chart title on the board.
• Explain to students that when making comparisons with adverbs, they will notice the same basic structures as for adjectives, but that these are adapted to adverb usage.
• Ask students who in the class talks the most quickly, and write the names that students give you on the board. For example:

Marissa   Ahmed
Kwon   Georgina

• Now ask the students to make comparisons of those four fast talkers, using the verb *talk* and the adverb *quickly*.
• Tell students that to compare an adverb, they will need the comparative form of the adverb and the comparative term *than*.
• With your students' assistance, write a simple sentence comparing two speakers. For example:

Kwon speaks <u>more quickly than</u> Ahmed.

• Again, with your students' participation, create a sentence using the superlative and the same topic. For example:

Georgina speaks the most quickly of all.

• Have students take turns reading through examples (a) and (b), (c) and (d), and (e) and (f) in pairs.
• Write these sentences on the board and discuss them with students, and review the notes in the right of the chart with them.

❏ **EXERCISE 25.** Looking at grammar. Page 467
Time: 10–15 minutes

• Ask a student to read the direction line aloud.
• Ask another student to read the completed example item aloud.

• Give students time to complete the remaining items autonomously, as seatwork.
• Correct by having students read their completions aloud.
• Draw attention to any challenging or disputed items by writing these on the board and carefully writing out the correct forms for comparative / superlative adverbs.

❏ **EXERCISE 26.** Looking at grammar.
Page 468
Time: 10–15 minutes

• Read the direction line aloud to students.
• Ask a student to read the completed example aloud.
• Lead this from the center, and have students give you completed responses on sight, without time to prepare them.
• If students disagree about what a correct completion should be, write the item on the board and carefully complete it as a class, emphasizing structural requirements.
• Engage students further by asking them specific questions about the content and associated vocabulary for each item.

❏ **EXERCISE 27.** Listening. Page 468
Time: 10 minutes

• Have the CD player and track ready.
• Read the direction line aloud.
• Read the completed example aloud.
• Play the CD track and have students complete each item.
• Correct by having students read their completions aloud.
• If any doubts arise, review the script to clarify.

Optional Vocabulary
neat
clear
artistic
pronounces

❏ **EXERCISE 28.** Warm-up. Page 469
Time: 10 minutes

• Read the direction line aloud.
• Ask students to explain what *similar* means.
• Have students complete the three items.
• Discuss these items and the yes / no answers as a class.
• Invite students to tell you about sports they find similar to one another, whether or not they are included here.

CHART 15-5. Comparisons: Using *The Same (As)*, *Similar (To)*, and *Different (From)*.
Page 470
Time: 10–15 minutes

> These concepts will be very easy even for beginners to grasp as they are quite universal. Present the phrases and ensure that students remember to include the required prepositions. Because these concepts are so readily understood, don't belabor the chart itself and focus more on controlled usage.

- Write the chart title on the board.
- Ask students what they understand about *the same as* and *similar to*.
- Explain that in English, we use *the same as* when one thing is exactly like another. Teach the word *identical* here to further students' understanding.
- Explain that we use *similar to* when one item has many of the same qualities as another item but is not exactly the same as the first item.
- Explain that we use *different from* when the differences between two items are very obvious.
- Ask different students to read the sentences beneath each chart illustration.
- Ask students if they have any questions. Stress that though you know the concept is easy for them, the harder part is just remembering the required prepositions.

❏ EXERCISE 29. Let's talk: class activity.
Page 470
Time: 10 minutes

- Lead this exercise from the center.
- Read the direction line aloud.
- Have students read the questions aloud and respond to each one.
- Ask students to cite specific details to prove their responses to each item.

Expansion: Bring in index cards (the larger size works best) on which you have pasted photos of two items from a catalog. Catalogs such as the one from The Sharper Image company work well as there are a number of interesting gadgets featured in these. In any case, prepare each index card with two random items. They do not have to be very similar or very different, but students will be asked to express specific similarities and differences that they see between the two. Make sure you have enough cards for each student to have two or three (for two or three sets of items to be compared). Ask students to create sentences that explain the differences and similarities and use the target grammar.

For example, if given a card with a picture of an HD TV and a car, students can say:

These things are similar because they are both expensive.

These things are different because the TV is inside a home and the car is outside.

Students can also utilize the exact phrases *similar to* and *different from* by making one item the subject of the sentence. For example:

The TV is similar to the car because they both have electronic screens.

The TV is different from the car because the car is more necessary.

❏ EXERCISE 30. Looking at grammar.
Page 470
Time: 10–15 minutes

- Read the direction line to the students.
- Ask a student to read the two completed example items.
- Give students time to complete each item as seatwork.
- Correct by having students read their completions aloud to the class.
- Refer to specific qualities of each shape to justify the completions.

❏ EXERCISE 31. Listening. Page 471
Time: 10 minutes

- Have the CD player and track ready.
- Read the direction line aloud.
- Explain that students must refer to Exercise 30 to see the pictures A–G.
- Play the CD track.
- Have students select *yes* or *no* for each item.
- Correct by having students read their answers aloud.
- Refer to pictures A–G in Exercise 30 as well as the script to clarify responses.

❏ EXERCISE 32. Let's talk: class activity.
Page 471
Time: 10–15 minutes

- Read the direction line aloud.
- Ask students to take turns reading questions 1 and 2 aloud and deciding which shapes have the same designs.
- Tell students to be careful in looking at the various designs.
- Have students discuss the numbers of triangles in each design, per the directions in questions 3–5.

❏ EXERCISE 33. Let's talk: class activity.
Page 472
Time: 10–15 minutes

- Lead this activity from the center.
- Read the direction line to students.
- With one student, model the example given in the book.
- Have students close their books.
- Read each item aloud and have students respond spontaneously. Ask more than one student to respond to each item.
- Correct each response you receive from students and emphasize the correct use of the prepositions required for each comparing phrase.
- Encourage students to find points of comparison, even among those items that seem different.

❏ EXERCISE 34. Warm-up. Page 472
Time: 5–10 minutes

- Read the direction line question aloud.
- Have students discuss all the statements and give specific examples for why they agree with certain statements but not others.
- If students are not able to give you justifications for both statements, help provide them by suggesting ways in which items are both similar / alike and different / not alike.

CHART 15-6. Comparisons: Using *Like* and *Alike*. Page 473
Time: 10–15 minutes

This will be students' initial introduction to predicate adjectives, those that can only follow the verb *be*. Go through the chart carefully and slowly so that students will see the two patterns and avoid future errors.

- Write the chart title on the board.
- Ask a student to read the first two sentences aloud while you write these on the board.
- Ask another student to read example sentence (a) aloud.
- Write the form of this sentence on the board as *this + be + like + that*.
- Have another student read example sentences (b) and (c) aloud.
- Write their format on the board as *this and that + be + alike*.
- Stress to students that *alike* always comes after a plural subject and thus is preceded by the verb *be* in its plural form.

❏ EXERCISE 35. Let's talk: pairwork.
Page 473
Time: 10–15 minutes

- Read the direction line aloud.
- With a student or two, read through the completed example comparing a pencil and a bus to the items in Column B.
- Put students into pairs.
- Have each pair start by deciding which items from Column A compare with which items from Column B.
- Next, instruct each pair to create sentences that give specifics about why these items compare with other items, as was modeled in the example above.
- Circulate around the room, assisting pairs as much as possible and encouraging them to be creative in comparing items.
- Correct by asking students from different pairs to read their sentences aloud and compare these with what other students have generated.

❏ EXERCISE 36. Looking at grammar.
Page 474
Time: 10 minutes

- Ask a student to read the direction line and completed example item 1 aloud to the class.
- Lead this exercise from the center, asking students to complete the items on sight, without prior preparation.
- Correct structure and pronunciation on the spot and stress all elements of the correction.
- If students find any items particularly challenging, write these on the board.

❏ EXERCISE 37. Looking at grammar.
Page 474
Time: 10 minutes

- Read the direction line aloud to students.
- Have students complete each item.
- Correct by having students read aloud every combination for each item that is both sensible and grammatical.

Optional Vocabulary
honey
a suit coat
a dormitory
lemonade
fog
smog

❏ EXERCISE 38. Warm-up. Page 474
Time: 10 minutes

- Read the direction line aloud.
- Explain to students that they can use the conjunction *but* to show opposite ideas in one sentence.
- Ask students to complete the sentences by using information that is true in their opinions.

CHART 15-7. Using *But*. Page 475
Time: 10 minutes

This particular use of *but* may be new, but it should be very easy for students to understand. Stress that using *but* in this way shows complete contrast.

- Write the chart title on the board.
- Ask a student to read example sentence (a) aloud while you write it on the board.
- Ask another student to read example sentence (b) aloud while you write it on the board.

❏ EXERCISE 39. Looking at grammar.
Page 475
Time: 10–15 minutes

- Read the direction line aloud.
- Have a student read the completed example aloud.
- Give students time to complete this exercise independently as seatwork.

- Correct by having students read their completions aloud and provide them with immediate clarification of usage and / or pronunciation.

❏ EXERCISE 40. Listening. Page 476
Time: 10 minutes

- Have the CD player and track ready.
- Read the direction line aloud to students.
- Go through the example with students and explain they will need to complete the sentences they hear with appropriate (and opposite) adjectives.
- Play the track aloud while students complete each item.
- Correct by having students read their completions aloud.
- Stress that the words they choose must convey an opposite meaning and correct any that do not.
- Refer to the script for any particularly challenging items.

Optional Vocabulary
narrow (wide)

❏ EXERCISE 41. Warm-up. Page 476
Time: 10 minutes

- Read the direction line aloud to students.
- Have students answer each sentence according to what is true for them.

CHART 15-8. Using Verbs after *But*.
Page 476
Time: 10 minutes

Students should readily recognize that what follows *but* in this chart is the same as the short answer form they have already mastered. Stress that students already know this form and have used it in other situations. As before, they can use the auxiliary verb or *be* without the participle.

- Write the chart title on the board.
- Give students opportunities to read aloud the sentences included as part of the chart.
- Stress that when the affirmative clause comes first, a negative short form comes after and vice versa.

❏ EXERCISE 42. Looking at grammar.
Page 477
Time: 10 minutes

- Read the direction line aloud.
- Ask students to complete the sentences on their own as seatwork.
- Correct by having students read their completions aloud and give them clear direction as needed.

❏ EXERCISE 43. Listening. Page 478
Time: 10 minutes

- Have CD player and track ready.
- Read the direction line aloud to students and review the completed example so that students understand the task fully.
- Play the track.
- Have students complete the sentences with the appropriate auxiliaries.
- Have students take turns reading their completions aloud and correct any that are wrong immediately.
- Refer to script as needed to clarify corrections.

❏ EXERCISE 44. Let's talk: class activity.
Page 478
Time: 10–15 minutes

- Read the direction line aloud.
- With three students, model the examples as given.
- Instruct students to close their books.
- Read the questions and engage a number of students for each question. Have alternate students play the role of Student C, summarizing both responses and using *but*.
- If helpful, have the Student Cs write the complete summary sentences with *but* on the board.

❏ EXERCISE 45. Let's talk: pairwork.
Page 479
Time: 10–15 minutes

- Ask a student to read the direction line aloud.
- Have students get into pairs and work on identifying the differences between the two pictures.
- Ask each pair to make sentences contrasting the two pictures and utilizing *but*.
- Have each pair write its sentences on the board by way of correction. Other students should correct these sentences for grammar and content accuracy.
- The "winner" is the pair who was able to spot all the differences and articulate them correctly.

Optional Vocabulary
graduate on time
summarize

❏ EXERCISE 46. Let's talk: pairwork.
Page 480
Time: 10–15 minutes

- Have students get into new pairs.
- Read the direction line aloud.
- With a student, model the exchange in item 1.
- Remind students that Partner A will first have his or her book open and that Partner B will have his or hers closed. Remind Partner B that he or she is to respond in complete sentences using the target comparative forms accurately.

- Circulate around the room and remind students that they can consult the Table of Statistics on page 465.
- Oversee the switch of partners after item 10, ensuring that the Partner Bs are now asking the questions and the Partner As have their books closed.
- Take notes on any commonly heard errors, and note items that are hard to respond to.
- Review by having everyone close their books and asking both sets of questions to the class as a whole.
- Write any challenging items or oft-heard errors on the board and correct them by crossing out incorrect items and leaving only correct forms on the board.
- Engage students in as much natural and spontaneous discussion as possible, while also correcting form and asking questions that will produce more student-generated constructions.

❑ EXERCISE 47. Looking at grammar.
Page 480
Time: 5–10 minutes

- Have a student read the direction line aloud.
- Ask students to complete the exercise on their own.
- Correct the exercise by having students read their completions aloud.
- Put any challenging items on the board and have students correct these together as a class.

❑ EXERCISE 48. Check your knowledge.
Page 481
Time: 10–15 minutes

- Lead this exercise from the center.
- Call on students to correct the mistakes on sight.

- Ask students to explain and justify their corrections by referring back to previous charts, if needed.

❑ EXERCISE 49. Reading and writing.
Page 482
Time: 15–20 minutes

Part I
- Read the direction line aloud.
- Engage students by having them take turns reading aloud from the passage.
- As students read aloud, ask them to paraphrase meanings and define vocabulary, or simply give synonyms.

Part II
- Read the direction line aloud.
- As not all students are prepared to write, warm them up to the task by discussing the topic—the similarities and differences between themselves and a friend.
- Point out the list of comparison words that writers might use.
- Give students time to write the assigned comparison paragraph(s) either in class or, more appropriately, as homework.

Part III
- Read the direction line aloud and have students decide how they wish to work, in pairs or alone.
- Have students edit their own or their partner's work by referring to the items in the editing checklist.
- Invite students to share their own work by reading it aloud to the class and discussing their writing.

Index

Answer Key

Chapter 1: Using *Be*

Exercise 2, p. 1.
1. yes
2. yes
3. (*free response*)

Exercise 3, p. 2.
2. he
3. he
4. it
5. he or she
6. she
7. he or she
8. it
9. he
10. she

Exercise 4, p. 2.
2. are
3. is
4. is
5. am
6. is

Exercise 6, p. 3.
1. two, three, or more
2. one OR two, three, or more
3. two, three, or more

Exercise 7, p. 4.
2. we
3. we
4. you
5. they
6. you

Exercise 8, p. 4.
2. am
3. is
4. are
5. is
6. are
7. are
8. are
9. are
10. is
11. are
12. are

Exercise 9, p. 5.
2. They are absent.
3. She is sick.
4. I am homesick.
5. You and I are homesick.
6. We are late.
7. Jack is hungry.
8. You are early.
9. You are early.
10. Mr. and Mrs. Nelson are late.
11. Amy and I are late.

Exercise 10, p. 5.
1. yes
2. yes
3. yes

Exercise 11, p. 6.
2. a
3. an
4. a
5. a
6. an
7. an
8. a

Exercise 12, p. 7.

COUNTRY	LANGUAGE	CITY	ISLAND
Cuba	(Arabic)	(Beijing)	Cuba
France	Chinese	Lima	Hawaii
Mexico	French	Moscow	Taiwan
Russia	Japanese	Paris	
Saudi Arabia	Russian	Tokyo	
Taiwan	Spanish		

Exercise 13, p. 7.
1. a book
2. books
3. books

Exercise 14, p. 8.
1. two or more
2. one
3. one
4. two or more
5. one
6. two or more
7. one

Exercise 15, p. 8.

2. textbooks
3. pencils
4. erasers
5. pens
6. dictionaries

Exercise 16, p. 9.

2. a sport . . . sports
3. a city . . . cities
4. a language . . . languages
5. a country . . . countries
6. an animal . . . animals
7. an island . . . islands

Exercise 17, p. 9.

2. Peas are vegetables.
3. Dictionaries are books.
4. Airplanes are machines.
5. June and July are months.
6. Winter and summer are seasons.
7. Egypt and Indonesia are countries.

Exercise 21, p. 11.

2. she's
3. you're
4. we're
5. it's
6. they're
7. he's

Exercise 22, p. 12.

2. He is
3. It is
4. I am
5. She is
6. We are
7. You are

Exercise 23, p. 12.

2. He's
3. I'm
4. They're
5. She's
6. We're
7. They're

Exercise 24, p. 12.

2. I'm
3. I'm
4. We're
5. It's
6. We're
7. It's

Exercise 26, p. 13.

	FULL FORM	CONTRACTION
2.	is not	isn't not OR 's not
3.	are not	aren't OR 're not
4.	are not	aren't OR 're not
5.	is not	isn't OR 's not
6.	are not	aren't OR 're not

Exercise 27, p. 14.

1. Canada is a country. It isn't a city.
2. Argentina isn't a city. It is a country.
3. Beijing and London are cities. They aren't countries.

4. Asia isn't a country. It's a continent.
5. Asia and South America are continents. They aren't countries.

Exercise 28, p. 14.
Part I.

2. a
3. a
4. a
5. a
6. a
7. a
8. a
9. an
10. an
11. a
12. an
13. a

Part II.

1. isn't
2. is
3. is
4. isn't
5. are
6. are
7. aren't
8. aren't

Exercise 29, p. 15.
Part I.

2. Gloria
3. Lars
4. Rick
5. Jennifer
6. Sana
7. Omar
8. Joe

Part II.

2. isn't
3. is . . . (*Answers may vary.*)
4. isn't . . . is a plumber
5–7. (*Answers may vary.*)

Exercise 30, p. 16.

1. tall
2. old
3. short and young

Exercise 31, p. 16.

2. 's poor
3. 's short
4. 're clean
5. 're beautiful
6. 're expensive
7. 're fast
8. 's easy
9. 's tall
10. 're old
11. 's noisy

Exercise 32, p. 17.

2. are cold
3. is square
4. are round
5. is sweet
6. is large/big . . . is small/little
7. is wet . . . is dry
8. is funny
9. is important
10. are dangerous
11. is . . . flat
12. is sour

Exercise 35, p. 19.
3. isn't . . . It's
4. isn't . . . It's
5. are . . . They aren't
6. is . . . It isn't
7. is . . . It isn't
8. are . . . They aren't
9. isn't . . . It's

Exercise 38, p. 21.
1. yes
2. yes
3. yes

Exercise 39, p. 22.
2. under
3. on
4. next to
5. above
6. behind
7. between

Exercise 41, p. 23.
2. is a
3. They're in
4. is an
5. It's
6. aren't
7. They're happy
8. is
9. isn't
10. She's

Exercise 42, p. 23.
(*Answers may vary.*)
2. sick
3. husband and wife
4. a little nervous/happy
5. good

Exercise 43, p. 24.
4. are . . . noun
5. is . . . place
6. is . . . adjective
7. are . . . place
8. am . . . noun
9. is . . . place
10. are . . . adjective
11. are . . . noun
12. is . . . place
13. are(n't) . . . adjective
14. are . . . noun

Exercise 45, p. 25.
1. b
2. a
3. b
4. a
5. a
6. a
7. b
8. b
9. a
10. b

Chapter 2: Using *Be* and *Have*

Exercise 2, p. 28.
1. Are
2. Is
3. Are
4. Are
5. Is
6. Am
7. Are
8. Are
9. Is
10. Are

Exercise 3, p. 29.
2. Are carrots vegetables?
3. Is Mr. Wang absent today?
4. Are planets big?
5. Are Amy and Mika here today?
6. Is English grammar fun?
7. Are you ready for the next exercise?

Exercise 4, p. 29.
1. Is
2. Is
3. Are
4. Is
5. is

Exercise 6, p. 30.
3. A: Are you homesick?
   B: No, I'm not.

4. A: Is Kareem homesick?
   B: Yes, he is.

5. A: Is Kara here today?
   B: No, she isn't. / No, she's not.

6. A: Are the students in this class smart?
   B: Yes, they are.

7. A: Are the chairs in this room comfortable?
   B: No, they aren't. / No, they're not.

8. A: Are you single?
   B: No, I'm not.

9. A: Are you married?
   B: Yes, we are.

Exercise 9, p. 32.
B: No, they aren't.
B: On your head!

Exercise 10, p. 32.
1. b
2. b
3. a
4. b

Exercise 11, p. 33.
3. Is Cairo in Egypt?
4. Where is Cairo?
5. Are the students in class today?

6. Where are the students?
7. Where is the post office?
8. Is the train station on Grand Avenue?
9. Where is the bus stop?
10. Where are Ali and Jake?

Exercise 14, p. 35.
1. have
2. have
3. has
4. have
5. have
6. have
7. has
8. has
9. has
10. have

Exercise 15, p. 35.
2. has
3. has
4. have
5. has
6. have
7. have
8. have . . . has
9. has
10. has
11. have

Exercise 16, p. 36.
2. have toothaches
3. have a fever
4. has a sore throat
5. have a cold
6. have backaches
7. has a stomachache
8. have high blood pressure
9. has the chills
10. have coughs

Exercise 18, p. 37.

Dr. Lee

He is a doctor. He is 70 years old, so he has many
years of experience. He has many patients. Some
are very sick. He has a clinic downtown. He also has
patients at the hospital. It is hard work, and he is often
very tired. But he is also happy. He helps many people.

Exercise 19, p. 37.
Part I.
2. is
3. has
4. has
5. is
6. has
7. is
8. has
9. is
10. has
11. has
12. is

Part II.
1. have
2. have
3. are
4. are
5. are
6. are
7. have
8. are
9. have
10. have

Exercise 20, p. 38.
1. My
2. His
3. Her
4. Their

Exercise 21, p. 39.
2. her
3. their
4. her
5. my
6. their
7. your
8. our
9. his
10. her

Exercise 22, p. 40.
1. His . . . Palmer
2. His . . . John
3. His . . . B.
4. Their . . . 98301
5. Their . . . 888
6. Her . . . 4/12/80
7. Her . . . 4/12 or April 12
8. Her . . . Ellen

Exercise 24, p. 42.
2. His
3. My
4. Their
5. Your
6. Our
7. Your
8. Her
9. His
10. Their
11. His
12. My

Exercise 25, p. 43.
1. Her . . . have
2. She has
3. Her . . . has
4. They are
5. Her . . . has
6. She has . . . her
7. They are
8. She has
9. Her . . . have

Exercise 26, p. 43.
2. have . . . Your
3. have . . . My
4. has . . . His
5. has . . . Her
6. have . . . Their
7. have . . . Our
8. have . . . Their
9. have . . . My
10. has . . . Her

Exercise 27, p. 44.
Part I.
1. yes
2. no
3. yes
4. no

Part II.

1. Her
2. Her . . . Her
3. Her/Their
4. His

Part III.

1. is
2. has
3. has
4. are
5. have
6. are
7. are
8. is
9. is
10. is
11. has

Exercise 28, p. 45.

1. Picture B
2. Picture A

Exercise 29, p. 46.

3. This
4. That
5. That
6. This
7. This
8. That
9. That
10. This

Exercise 30, p. 47.

PARTNER A	PARTNER B
1. That is a credit card.	2. This is a wallet.
3. This is a credit card.	4. That is a checkbook.
5. This is a business card.	6. That is a computer bag.

Exercise 31, p. 48.

1. Picture A
2. Picture B

Exercise 32, p. 48.

1. These
2. Those
3. Those
4. These
5. Those
6. These

Exercise 33, p. 49.

2. is
3. are
4. are
5. is
6. is
7. are
8. is

Exercise 34, p. 49.

2. These . . . That
3. This . . . Those
4. These . . . Those
5. These . . . Those
6. This . . . Those
7. This . . . Those

Exercise 35, p. 50.

1. That is a debit card.
2. This is a wallet.
3. These are rulers.

4. Those are paper clips.
5. This is a notepad.
6. Those are checks.
7. These are checkbooks.
8. This is a folder.
9. That is a stapler.
10. These are staples.

Exercise 36, p. 52.

1. That is
2. This is
3. Those are
4. Those . . . are
5. These . . . are
6. That . . . is
7. This . . . is
8. That . . . is

Exercise 37, p. 52.

1. a beetle
2. Tim

Exercise 38, p. 53.

2. What are
3. Who is
4. What is
5. Who are
6. What is
7. Who is
8. Who are
9. What is
10. What are

Exercise 41, p. 55.

2. What are **those**? OR What is **that**?
3. **Is Roberto** a student in your class?
4. **I have** a backache.
5. This is **your** dictionary. **My** dictionary is at home.
6. Where **are** my keys?
7. **I have** a sore throat.
8. **His** father is from Cuba.
9. This book **is** expensive. OR **These** books are expensive.
10. Where **are** the teachers? OR Where is the **teacher**?
11. A: Are you tired?
    B: Yes, **I am**.

Exercise 42, p. 55.

2. c
3. b
4. b
5. a
6. c
7. c
8. b
9. a
10. c
11. a
12. b

Exercise 43, p. 56.

1. aren't
2. is
3. am
4. are
5. aren't
6. are . . . aren't
7. aren't . . . are
8. is
9. are
10. is not . . . is

Exercise 45, p. 57.

3. I am OR I'm
4. I am OR I'm
5. My
6. is
7. He is OR He's
8. My
9. is
10. She is OR She's
11. have
12. are
13. is
14. She is OR She's
15. is
16. She is OR She's
17. is
18. is
19. has
20. It is OR It's
21. is
22. His
23. He is OR He's
24. He is OR He's
25. are
26. my
27. They are OR They're

Chapter 3: Using the Simple Present

Exercise 1, p. 59.

1. take
2. takes
3. post
4. posts
5. share
6. shares

Exercise 2, p. 60.

1. speaks
2. speak
3. speaks
4. speaks
5. speak
6. speak
7. speak
8. speak
9. speak
10. speak
11. speak

Exercise 4, p. 61.

2. wakes
3. gets
4. go
5. does
6. watches
7. take
8. takes
9. take
10. talk

Exercise 5, p. 61.

2. drinks
3. take
4. takes
5. study
6. walk
7. begins
8. stops
9. eat
10. bring
11. go
12. go

Exercise 7, p. 63.

2. usually
3. often
4. sometimes
5. rarely
6. never

Exercise 8, p. 63.

	S	V	
2.	I	eat	I never eat carrots
3.	I	watch	I seldom watch TV
4.	I	have	I sometimes have dessert
5.	Kiri	eats	Kiri usually eats lunch
6.	We	listen	We often listen to music
7.	The students	speak	The students always speak English

Exercise 10, p. 64.

2. one time . . . rarely / seldom
3. six times . . . usually
4. five times . . . often
5. never
6. three times . . . sometimes

Exercise 12, p. 65.

3. Liliana is **often** late for class.
4. Liliana **often** comes to class late.
5. It **never** snows in my hometown.
6. It is **never** very cold in my hometown.
7. Hiroshi is **usually** at home in the evening.
8. Hiroshi **usually** stays at home in the evening.
9. Tomas **seldom** studies at the library in the evening.
10. His classmates are **seldom** at the library in the evening.
11. I **sometimes** skip breakfast.
12. I **rarely** have time for a big breakfast.

Exercise 15, p. 66.

1. one
2. one
3. one
4. two
5. one
6. two

Exercise 16, p. 67.

2. teaches
3. fixes
4. drinks
5. watches
6. kisses
7. wears
8. washes
9. walks
10. stretches . . . yawns

Exercise 17, p. 68.

2. teach
3. fixes
4. fixes
5. watch
6. watches
7. brush
8. brushes
9. wash
10. washes

Exercise 18, p. 68.

2. gets
3. cooks
4. sits
5. washes
6. turns
7. watches
8. takes
9. brushes
10. reads
11. falls

Exercise 19, p. 68.

CONSONANT + -*y*: fly, study
VOWEL + -*y*: buy, play

Exercise 20, p. 69.

2. studies
3. says
4. enjoys
5. worries
6. pays
7. stays
8. flies
9. buys
10. plays

Exercise 21, p. 69.

2. buys
3. employs
4. cries
5. stays
6. carries
7. pays
8. studies

Exercise 22, p. 70.

HAVE: he, she, it has
DO: he, she, it does
GO: he, she, it goes

Exercise 23, p. 70.

3. have
4. has
5. goes
6. does
7. do
8. goes . . . go
9. play

Exercise 24, p. 71.

3. is
4. has
5. goes
6. has
7. does
8. has
9. does
10. has
11. goes
12. is
13. is

Exercise 25, p. 72.

2. usually studies
3. bites
4. cashes
5. worry . . . never worries . . . studies
6. teach . . . teaches
7. fly . . . have
8. flies . . . has
9. always does . . . never goes
10. always says
11. always pays . . . answers . . . listens . . . asks

Exercise 28, p. 73.

2. walks
3. catches
4. shares
5. comes
6. (*no change*)
7. (*no change*)
8. speaks . . . speaks
9. (*no change*)
10. tries . . . gives
11. (*no change*)
12. enjoys . . . misses

Exercise 31, p. 74.

2. We want to go home.
3. Bill and I like to eat sweets.
4. You need to speak more quietly.
5. She likes to talk on the phone.
6. Her friends like to text.
7. They need to save money.
8. He wants to travel.

Exercise 32, p. 74.

1. is
2. likes to
3. invite
4. wash . . . help
5. like

Exercise 35, p. 76.

2. does not
3. do not
4. do not
5. does not
6. do not
7. doesn't
8. don't
9. don't
10. doesn't
11. don't
12. don't

Exercise 36, p. 77.

3. doesn't know
4. don't speak
5. don't need
6. don't live
7. doesn't have
8. don't have
9. doesn't have
10. doesn't snow
11. doesn't rain

Exercise 39, p. 79.

2. don't speak
3. doesn't shave
4. don't go
5. doesn't smoke
6. don't eat
7. don't do
8. doesn't drink
9. doesn't make
10. doesn't put on

Exercise 40, p. 80.

	BE	EAT
2.	are not	do not eat
3.	is not	does not eat
4.	are not	do not eat
5.	is not	does not eat
6.	are not	do not eat
7.	is not	does not eat
8.	is not	does not eat
9.	are not	do not eat

Exercise 41, p. 80.

2. do not
3. does not
4. are not
5. does not
6. does not
7. is not
8. do not
9. do not
10. are not

Exercise 44, p. 82.

2. Does Anita speak Italian? a.
3. Do Thomas and Sierra speak Arabic? a.
4. Does it rain in April? a.
5. Does he do his homework? a.
6. Do you do your homework? a.
7. Do they have enough money? a.

Exercise 47, p. 84.

Part I.

2. live . . . are
3. lives . . . is
4. live . . . are
5. lives . . . is
6. live . . . are

Part II.

8. do not/don't live . . . am not/'m not
9. does not/doesn't live . . . is not/isn't
10. do not/don't live . . . are not/aren't
11. does not/doesn't live . . . is not/isn't
12. do not/don't . . . are not/aren't

Part III.

14. Do . . . live . . . Are
15. Does . . . live . . . Is
16. Do . . . live . . . Are
17. Does . . . live . . . Is

Exercise 48, p. 85.

2. Does (no) [The earth goes around the sun.]
3. Do (yes)
4. Is (no) [It's a star.]
5. Are (no) [They're stars!]
6. Is (yes) [Around 900 degrees Fahrenheit]
7. Is (no) [You need a telescope.]
8. Is (yes) [The winds are stronger than the earth's winds.]
9. Do (yes)
10. Do (yes) [Saturn has at least 24; Uranus has at least 21.]

Exercise 49, p. 86.

1. c
2. b
3. a

Exercise 50, p. 86.

3. What does Hana eat for lunch every day?
4. Where does Alfonso work?
5. Does Alfonso work at the post office?
6. Do you live in an apartment?
7. Where do you live?
8. What does Hector like for a snack?
9. Where does Ming go to school?
10. What is her major?
11. Where do you go every morning?
12. Where are the students right now?

Exercise 54, p. 88.

1. 8:00 A.M.
2. 8:30 A.M.

Exercise 55, p. 89.

3. When/What time do you usually get up?
4. When/What time does Maria usually get up?
5. When/What time does the movie start?
6. When/What time do you usually go to bed?
7. When/What time do you usually eat lunch?
8. When/What time does the restaurant open?
9. When/What time does the train leave?
10. When/What time do you usually eat dinner?
11. When/What time do classes begin?
12. When/What time does the library close on Saturday?

Exercise 57, p. 91.

3. Does he teach Psychology 102? No, he doesn't.
4. Where does he teach Psychology 205? He teaches (Psychology 205) in Room 201.
5. Is he in his office every day? No, he isn't.
6. Is he in his office at 9:00? No, he isn't.
7. Does he teach at 7:00 A.M.? No, he doesn't.
8. What time does he leave the office on Tuesdays and Thursdays? He leaves at 4:00.
9. Is he a professor? Yes, he is.

Exercise 58, p. 91.

2. Do
3. is
4. Are
5. are
6. do
7. Do
8. Are
9. Does
10. Do
11. Does
12. does
13. Is

Exercise 59, p. 93.

2. Lisa **usually comes** to class on time.
3. Diego **uses** his cell phone often.

4. Amira **carries** a **notebook computer** to work every day.
5. She **enjoys** her job.
6. Miguel **doesn't** like milk. He never **drinks** it.
7. Tina doesn't **speak** Chinese. She **speaks** Spanish.
8. **Are you** a student?
9. Does your roommate **sleep** with the window open?
10. Where **do** your parents live?
11. What time **does** your English class **begin**?
12. Olga **doesn't** need a car. She **has** a bicycle.
13. I **don't** speak English.
14. Omar speaks English every day.
15. A: Do you like strong coffee?
    B: Yes, I **do**.

Chapter 4: Using the Present Progressive

Exercise 1, p. 96.
1. happy . . . laughing
2. sad . . . crying

Exercise 2, p. 97.
2. are
3. are
4. are
5. am
6. are
7. are
8. is

Exercise 3, p. 97.
2. are sleeping
3. is reading
4. am eating
5. are helping
6. are playing
7. is snowing

Exercise 7, p. 99.
1. yes
2. yes
3. no
4. no
5. no
6. yes
7. no
8. yes
9. no
10. no

Exercise 8, p. 100.
1. ride
2. count
3. sleep
4. stop

Exercise 9, p. 100.
2. coming
3. dreaming
4. biting
5. hitting
6. raining
7. hurting
8. planning
9. baking
10. snowing
11. studying
12. stopping

Exercise 10, p. 101.
1. smiling
2. reading
3. drinking
4. sitting
5. eating
6. clapping
7. writing
8. flying
9. sleeping
10. sneezing
11. cutting
12. crying

Exercise 11, p. 101.
2. is sending
3. is calling
4. are eating
5. is charging
6. is searching

Exercise 12, p. 101.
1. aren't
2. are
3. isn't

Exercise 13, p. 102.
1. isn't watching TV . . . is talking on the phone.
2. is listening to music . . . isn't playing soccer.
3. are reading . . . aren't eating lunch.
4. isn't making photocopies . . . is fixing the photocopy machine

Exercise 14, p. 104.
Part I.
Checked phrases: 3, 5, 6, 7, 8, 10

Part II.
3. He is changing the oil in a car.
4. He isn't watching a movie in the theater.
5. He is putting on a new tire.
6. He is answering the office phone.
7. He is giving a customer a bill.
8. He is repairing an engine.
9. He isn't eating at a restaurant.
10. He is replacing a windshield wiper.

Exercise 17, p. 106.
2. Is Ivan talking on his phone?
3. Are you sleeping?
4. Are the students watching TV?
5. Is it raining?
6. Is John riding a bike?

Exercise 19, p. 108.
2. Why are you reading your grammar book/it?
3. What are you writing?
4. Where is Yoshi sitting?
5. Where are you staying?
6. What is Jonas wearing today?
7. Why are you smiling?

Exercise 20, p. 108.
3. A: Is Magda eating lunch?
   B: she is.
4. is she eating lunch?
5. A: Is Sam drinking a cup of coffee?
   B: he isn't.
6. is he drinking?
7. A: Are the girls playing in the street?
   B: they aren't.
8. are they playing?
9. are they playing in the park?
10. Are the girls playing together?
11. Is a parent watching them?

Exercise 22, p. 110.
2. every day
3. today
4. now
5. today
6. every day
7. every day
8. right now

Exercise 23, p. 111.
1. . . . isn't talking
2. rains . . . isn't raining . . . is shining . . . Does it rain
3. are sitting . . . help . . . is helping
4. cooks . . . is cooking . . . Is he cooking . . . never eats . . . Do you eat . . . Are you

Exercise 24, p. 111.
1. every day
2. now
3. now
4. every day
5. every day
6. now
7. every day
8. now

Exercise 26, p. 113.
2. a. cook, dance, understand
   b. angry, a dancer, driving, ready
3. a. a problem, here, new, raining, ready, true
   b. help, work

Exercise 27, p. 113.
3. Does
4. Is
5. Are
6. Are
7. Do
8. Is
9. Do
10. Is
11. Does

Exercise 28, p. 114.
1. Are you working
2. I'm not
3. I'm writing
4. Do you write
5. don't write
6. Does she write
7. texts

Exercise 29, p. 114.
2. walk . . . don't take . . . Do you take

3. B: Is she talking
   A: is running
4. A: read
   B: Do you read
   A: don't read
5. A: are you reading
   B: am reading
6. A: Do you want . . . is this
   B: is hanging

Exercise 30, p. 115.
Part II.
2. Does
3. Do
4. Does
5. Is
6. Is
7. Is
8. Does
9. Do

Exercise 32, p. 116.
2. is snowing . . . like
3. know
4. is talking . . . understand
5. is eating . . . likes . . . tastes
6. smell . . . Do you smell
7. is telling . . . believe
8. is smoking . . . smells . . . hate
9. is holding . . . loves . . . is smiling

Exercise 34, p. 118.
1. a. am looking at
   b. am watching
2. a. am listening to
   b. hear

Exercise 36, p. 119.
Situation 1.
3. are doing
4. are speaking
5. know
6. speak
7. wants
8. is not working
9. is looking
10. is checking
11. is staring
12. is smiling
13. is tapping
14. is chewing

Situation 2.
1. works
2. has
3. often eats
4. usually brings
5. usually sits
6. sits
7. watches
8. often sees
9. relaxes
10. am looking
11. isn't
12. is
13. is sitting
14. is eating
15. is running
16. is sitting
17. is eating
18. is watching
19. always watches
20. are swimming
21. are flying
22. is riding
23. rides
24. is having
25. go

Exercise 41, p. 122.
1. F
2. F
3. T
4. F

Exercise 42, p. 123.
2. a
3. b
4. c
5. b
6. c
7. b
8. a
9. b

Exercise 43, p. 123.
2. I like New York City. I **think** that it is a wonderful city.
3. **Is** Abdul **sleeping** right now?
4. Why **are you** going downtown today?
5. I **like** flowers. They **smell** good.
6. Bill **is eating** at a restaurant right now. He usually **eats** at home, but today he **is eating** dinner at a restaurant.
7. Alex is **sitting** at his desk. He **is writing** a letter.
8. Where **are** they sitting today?

Chapter 5: Talking About the Present

Exercise 1, p. 125.
1. Picture C
2. Picture A
3. Picture B

Exercise 2, p. 126.
2. What's the date today?
3. What time is it?
4. What month is it?
5. What time is it?
6. What day is it?
7. What's the date today?
8. What year is it?
9. What time is it?

Exercise 4, p. 127.
1. b. from . . . to
   c. in . . . in
2. a. in
   b. at
3. a. in
   b. in
   c. on
   d. on
4. a. on
   b. from . . . to
   c. at

Exercise 6, p. 129.
Part I.
1. Ron
2. Marta
3. Shen
4. Lisa

Part II.
1. in . . . on . . . Shen
2. in . . . on . . . Marta
3. in . . . at . . . Lisa
4. Ron . . . in . . . on . . . in

Exercise 9, p. 130.
2. 0°C   cold, freezing
3. 38°C   hot
4. 24°C   warm
5. −18°C very cold, below freezing

Exercise 10, p. 131.
2. 36°F
3. 86°F
4. 60°F
5. −4°C
6. 21°C
7. 38°C

Exercise 13, p. 133.
3. are
4. is
5. are
6. is
7. are
8. are

Exercise 16, p. 134.
1. There're
2. There's
3. There're
4. There's
5. There's
6. There're
7. There's
8. There're

Exercise 24, p. 138.
The Prime Minister of England

Exercise 25, p. 139.
1. in
2. in
3. on
4. at . . . in
5. First Street
6. Miami / Florida OR Miami, Florida
7. 342 First Street
8–11. (*free response*)

Exercise 26, p. 140.
1. a. in
   b. on
   c. at
   Eiffel Tower
2. a. in
   b. at
   c. on
   Prime Minister of Canada

3. a. on
   b. at
   c. in
   Giza Pyramids
4. a. in
   b. on
   c. at
   Nike
5. a. on
   b. at
   c. in
   President of the United States
6. a. in
   b. at
   c. in
   Boeing

Exercise 27, p. 140.

1. in	6. in
2. in	7. in
3. at	8. in
4. in	9. in
5. at	10. in

Exercise 28, p. 141.

1. at	7. in . . . in
2. in	8. in . . . in
3. at . . . at	9. in
4. in . . . in	10. in
5. in	11. at . . . in
6. in	12. in . . . in

Exercise 30, p. 143.

2. under/in front of
3. above/behind
4. beside, near, next to
5. far (away) from
6. in/inside
7. between
8. around
9. outside/next to
10. front
11. back
12. the front/inside
13. the back/inside

Exercise 32, p. 145.

1. T	6. F	11. F
2. F	7. F	12. F
3. T	8. T	13. T
4. T	9. T	14. T
5. F	10. T	15. F

Exercise 34, p. 146.

Part I.

1. She is eating at/in a restaurant.
2. I see a cup of coffee, a vase of flowers, a candle, a bowl of salad, a glass of water, a plate, and a piece of meat.
3. She is holding a knife in her right hand. She is holding a fork in her left hand.
4. There's salad in the bowl.
5. There's meat / a piece of meat / a steak on the plate.
6. There's coffee in the cup.
7. A candle is burning.
8. No, she isn't eating breakfast.
9. No, she isn't at home. She's at/in a restaurant.
10. She's cutting meat / a piece of meat / a steak.

Part II.

1. at	5. at/in
2. on	6. isn't
3. in	7. isn't
4. is . . . in	

Exercise 35, p. 147.

Part I.

1. He is studying.
2. I see a clock, a sign, some books, some shelves, a librarian, a desk, a plant, a table, three chairs, and two students.
3. No, he isn't at home. He's at the library.
4. No, he isn't reading a newspaper.
5. The librarian is standing behind the circulation desk.
6. He is right-handed.

Part II.

1. at/in	6. on
2. at	7. on
3. in/on	8. isn't
4. under	9. is . . . behind
5. on	10. beside/near/next to

Exercise 36, p. 148.

Part I.

1. She is cashing a check.
2. No, she isn't at a store. She's at/in a bank.
3. I see a bank teller, a clock, a sign, a line of people, a check, a purse/handbag/pocketbook, a briefcase, a tie/necktie, eyeglasses/glasses, a suit, a T-shirt, a beard and a mustache, pants, jeans, and a dress.
4. A woman is standing behind Megan.
5. A man is standing at the end of the line.
6. There are three men in the picture.
7. There are two women in the picture.
8. There are five people in the picture.
9. There are four people standing in line.

Part II.
1. at/in/inside
2. are
3. at/in front of
4. behind/in back of
5. is . . . behind/in back of
6. isn't . . . at . . . of
7. is . . . at . . . of
8. is . . . between

Exercise 37, p. 149.
Answer: Would like is more polite.

Exercise 38, p. 150.
3. Hassan and Eva would like
4. They would like
5. I would like to thank
6. My friend would like to thank
7. My friends would like to thank

Exercise 41, p. 151.
1. 'd like
2. like
3. 'd like
4. likes
5. 'd like
6. likes
7. like
8. 'd like
9. like
10. 'd like

Exercise 44, p. 153.
Part I.
1. She is signing/writing a check.
2. Her address is 3471 Tree Street, Chicago, Illinois 60565.
3. Her full name is Mary S. Jones.
4. Her middle initial is S.
5. Her last name is Jones.
6. She wants fifty dollars.
7. Her name and address are in the upper-left corner of the check.
8. The name and address of the bank are in the lower-left corner of the check. OR Her account number is in the lower-left corner of the check.
9. The name of the bank is First National Bank.

Part II.
1. check
2. her
3. May 3, 2013
4. at
5. in
6. cash OR fifty dollars

Exercise 45, p. 154.
Part I.
1. He is cooking/making dinner.
2. I see a kitchen, a stove, a pot, a salt shaker, a pepper shaker, a clock, a refrigerator, a sign, a spoon, and a shopping/grocery list.
3. He is in the kitchen. He is next to/beside the stove.
4. Yes, he is tasting his dinner.

5. No, he isn't a good cook. [because he doesn't like the taste of the food]
6. The refrigerator is beside/near/next to the stove. (*also possible:* behind Dave)
7. A grocery list is on the refrigerator. OR There's a shopping/grocery list on the refrigerator.
8. The food on the stove is hot.
9. The food in the refrigerator is cold.

Part II.
1. in
2. on
3. next to/beside
4. on
5. to go
6. on
7. on . . . of
8. in

Exercise 46, p. 155.
Part I.
1. They are sitting on the sofa/couch. They're watching TV.
2. I see a TV set, a fishbowl, a fish, a rug, a dog, a cat, a lamp, a clock, and a sofa/couch.
3. No, they aren't in the kitchen. They're in the living room.
4. The lamp is on the floor. OR The lamp is beside/next to the sofa/couch.
5. The rug is on the floor in front of the sofa/couch.
6. The dog is on the rug.
7. The cat is on the sofa/couch. OR The cat is beside/next to Lisa.
8. No, the cat isn't walking. The cat is sleeping.
9. The dog is sleeping (too).
10. A fishbowl is on top of the TV set. OR There's a fishbowl on top of the TV set.
11. No, the fish isn't watching TV.
12. A singer is on the TV screen. OR There's a singer on the TV screen. OR They are watching a singer on TV.

Part II.
1. are . . . to
2. are . . . on
3. aren't
4. on
5. is . . . on
6. is . . . on

Exercise 48, p. 156.
2. b
3. a
4. c
5. b
6. c
7. c
8. c

Exercise 49, p. 157.
2. There **are** many problems in big cities today.
3. I'd like **to** see a movie tonight.
4. We **need** to find a new apartment soon.
5. Mr. Rice **would like** to have a cup of tea.
6. How many students **are there** in your class?
7. What day **is it** today?
8. I **would** like to leave now. How about you?
9. How **is** the weather in Kenya?
10. The teacher would like to **check** our homework now.

Chapter 6: Nouns and Pronouns

Exercise 2, p. 160.
Checked words: 4, 7, 8, 9, 10, 12

Exercise 3, p. 160.
3. cheese . . . cheese
4. people . . . people
5. whiskers
6. no object
7. furniture

Exercise 4, p. 160.
2. a, c: vocabulary
3. a: paper
   b: ink, paper
   c: problems
4. b: workers
5. (*no objects*)

Exercise 5, p. 161.
1. above
2. under
3. in

Exercise 6, p. 162.
Checked phrases: 2, 3, 4, 7, 8
2. noon
3. counter
4. closet
7. chair
8. broom

Exercise 7, p. 162.
1. a. A tutor helps Sari with her (homework.)
   b. A tutor helps Sari on (Tuesday afternoons.)
   c. A tutor helps Sari in the (library.)

2. a. The teacher erases the board.
   b. The teacher erases the board after (class.)
   c. The teacher is erasing the board with an (eraser.)

3. a. Elin cleans windows.
   b. Elin cleans in the (afternoons.)
   c. Elin cleans five days a week.

4. a. I do my homework in the (library.)
   b. I do my homework every weekend.
   c. I do my homework with my (friends.)

5. a. Birds fly during the day.
   b. Birds live in (nests.)
   c. Birds sit on (eggs.)

Exercise 8, p. 163.

1.	Kids	like	candy.	(none)	(none)
	subj.	verb	obj. of verb	prep.	obj. of prep.

2.	Dayo	lives	(none)	in	Africa.
	subj.	verb	obj. of verb	prep.	obj. of prep.

3.	The sun	is shining.	(none)	(none)	(none)
	subj.	verb	obj. of verb	prep.	obj. of prep.

4.	Lev	is reading	books	about	movies and filmmaking.
	subj.	verb	obj. of verb	prep.	obj. of prep.

5.	Dara	doesn't eat	chicken or beef.	(none)	(none)
	subj.	verb	obj. of verb	prep.	obj. of prep.

6.	Monkeys and birds	eat	fruit and insects.	(none)	(none)
	subj.	verb	obj. of verb	prep.	obj. of prep.

Exercise 10, p. 164.
2. My sister has a beautiful house
3. We often eat at an Italian restaurant
4. Valentina sings her favorite songs in the shower.
5. Olga likes American hamburgers.
6. You like sour apples but I like sweet fruit.

Exercise 13, p. 166.
1. him, her, it
2. him, her, it
3. He, She, It

Exercise 14, p. 166.
2. She . . . him
3. They . . . her
4. They . . . him
5. He . . . her
6. She . . . them
7. He . . . them
8. They . . . them

Exercise 15, p. 167.
2. them
3. they
4. She
5. him
6. her . . . She . . . I
7. them . . . They
8. us
9. It
10. We . . . it

Exercise 17, p. 168.
2. it . . . It
3. we . . . I . . . you
4. they . . . They . . . them
5. it. It
6. he . . . him

Exercise 19, p. 169.

1. A: I are going . . . with us
   B: I are going . . . We need to

2. B: It's
   A: her
   B: know her
   A: her

3. B: them . . . him

Exercise 20, p. 170.

1. one
2. one
3. two or more
4. two or more
5. one

Exercise 21, p. 170.

Part I.

2. countries
3. babies
4. keys
5. cities
6. parties
7. trays
8. dictionaries
9. ladies
10. Cowboys

Part II.

11. leaves
12. wives
13. lives
14. thieves
15. knives

Part III.

16. glasses
17. sexes
18. dishes
19. taxes
20. bushes
21. matches
22. tomatoes
23. potatoes
24. zoos
25. classes
26. sandwiches

Exercise 22, p. 172.

2. table
3. face
4. hats
5. offices
6. boxes
7. package
8. chairs
9. edge
10. tops

Exercise 23, p. 173.

2. places
3. sandwich
4. sentences
5. apple
6. exercise
7. pieces
8. roses
9. bush
10. college

Exercise 24, p. 173.

2. Ø
3. elephants
4. Ø
5. bab**ies**
6. exercise**s**
7. Ø
8. Ø
9. Ø
10. Cockroach**es**

Exercise 25, p. 174.

1. a. a child
2. b. a tooth
3. a. a foot

Exercise 26, p. 175.

1. foot . . . feet
2. fish . . . fish
3. teeth . . . tooth
4. children . . . child
5. sheep . . . sheep . . . sheep . . . sheep
6. woman . . . man
7. women . . . men . . . men . . . women OR
   men . . . women . . . women . . . men
8. mouse . . . mice

Exercise 27, p. 176.

1. site**s**
2. malls
3. websites . . . sales
4. husband Ø . . . child**ren**
5. jackets . . . skirts . . . shirts . . . dress**es** . . . coat**s**
6. shoes . . . **feet**
7. websites . . . return**s**

Exercise 28, p. 176.

4. This class ends at two o'clock.
5. *NC*
6. My mother works.
7. *NC*
8. My mother works in an office.
9. Does your brother have a job?
10. *NC*
11. My sister lives in an apartment.
12. *NC*
13. The apartment has two bedrooms
14. *NC*
15. *NC*

Exercise 29, p. 177.

2. b
3. c
4. c
5. c
6. a
7. d
8. b
9. b
10. a

Exercise 30, p. 178.

4. ours
5. theirs
6. mine

Exercise 31, p. 178.

1. yours
2. ours
3. hers
4. theirs
5. his
6. mine
7. his
8. hers
9. theirs
10. ours

Exercise 32, p. 179.

2. a. them
   b. their
   c. theirs

3. a. you
   b. your
   c. yours

4. a. her
   b. her
   c. hers

5. a. him
   b. his
   c. his

6. a. us
   b. our
   c. ours

Exercise 33, p. 180.

2. hers

3. A: your
   B: my . . . Mine

4. yours

5. theirs . . . Their

6. A: our . . . yours
   B: Ours

7. A: your
   B: his

8. my . . . Hers

Exercise 34, p. 180.

Correct sentences: 1, 4

Exercise 35, p. 181.

2. car . . . Dave
3. room . . . Samir
4. office . . . the doctor

Exercise 36, p. 181.

1. one
2. more than one
3. more than one
4. one
5. more than one
6. one

Exercise 38, p. 182.

1. brother
2. mother
3. brother
4. children
5. daughter
6. son
7. sister
8. mother
9. wife
10. mother . . . father OR father . . . mother

Exercise 39, p. 183.

2. a. ours
   b. theirs
   c. Our
   d. Theirs

3. a. Don's
   b. Kate's
   c. His
   d. Hers

4. a. mine
   b. yours
   c. Mine . . . my
   d. Yours . . . your

5. a. Ray's
   b. Ours
   c. His
   d. Ours

6. a. my
   b. yours
   c. Mine . . . my
   d. Yours . . . your

7. a. Our
   b. Theirs
   c. Our car
   d. Their

8. a. Gabi's
   b. Evan's
   c. Hers . . . her
   d. His . . . his

Exercise 40, p. 184.

1. Mack's
2. Mack
3. teacher's
4. teacher
5. friend
6. friend's
7. manager's
8. cousin

Exercise 41, p. 184.

3. (*no change*)
4. teachers'
5. teacher's
6. students'
7. girl's
8. girls'
9. Monica's
10. Ryan's

Exercise 42, p. 185.

1. b
2. a

Exercise 43, p. 185.

1. a
2. b
3. a
4. b
5. b
6. a

Exercise 44, p. 186.

1. Who's
2. Whose
3. Who's
4. Who's
5. Whose
6. Who's

Exercise 45, p. 186.

1. Who's
2. Whose
3. Who's
4. Who's
5. Whose
6. Whose
7. Who's
8. Whose
9. Whose
10. Who's

Exercise 46, p. 186.

2. are those
3. is that
4. is this
5. are these

Exercise 48, p. 187.

Women's Restroom

Exercise 49, p. 187.

2. my friend's
3. my friends'
4. the child's
5. the children's
6. the woman's
7. the women's

Exercise 50, p. 188.

2. women's
3. person's
4. people's
5. Students'
6. brother's
7. wife's
8. dog's
9. dogs'
10. men's
11. man's . . . woman's
12. children's

Exercise 51, p. 188.

2. b
3. a
4. a
5. c
6. b
7. a
8. a
9. c
10. b

Exercise 52, p. 189.

2. **Babies** cry.
3. Kurt helps Justin and **me**.
4. Our teacher gives **difficult tests**.
5. Charlie is cutting **the grass with a lawnmower**.
6. Do you know **Yuko's** roommate?
7. My **roommate's** desk is always a mess.
8. There are nineteen **people** in my class.
9. Veronica and Victor have three **children**.
10. Excuse me. Where is the **men's** room?
11. There **are** twenty **classrooms** in this building.
12. Mr. Torro is our teacher. I like **him** very much.
13. Does that store sell **children's** toys?
14. **Whose book is** on the chair?
15. It is **my** book.

Exercise 53, p. 190.

          S
My favorite **store** is City Market. It is a grocery store.

                                        P
I like this store because it has many kinds of **groceries**.

                       P
I can buy interesting **ingredients** there. I often cook

P   S
dishes from my **country**. City Market has a big

S   P
selection of rice and fresh **vegetables**. I like to buy

fresh, not frozen, vegetables and meat, but the meat at

City Market is expensive, so I don't buy much. The store

          S   P
is near my **house**, and I can walk to it. The **people** are

friendly and helpful.

Chapter 7: Count and Noncount Nouns

Exercise 1, p. 191.

Count: sugar bowl

Exercise 2, p. 192.

3. coin   (count)
4. money   (noncount)
5. traffic   (noncount)
6. cars   (count)
7. fact   (count)
8. information   (noncount)
9. homework   (noncount)
10. assignment   (count)
11. music   (noncount)
12. coffee   (noncount)
13. library   (count)
14. vocabulary   (noncount)
15. advice   (noncount)
16. job   (count)
17. work   (noncount)
18. bracelets   (count)

Exercise 3, p. 192.

5. s
6. Ø
7. Ø
8. Ø
9. s
10. s
11. Ø
12. a. s
    b. Ø
13. a. Ø
    b. s

Exercise 4, p. 194.

	NONCOUNT	COUNT
2.	advice	a suggestion
3.	furniture	a desk
4.	homework	an assignment
5.	information	a fact
6.	jewelry	a bracelet
7.	money	a coin
8.	music	a song
9.	weather	a cloud
10.	work	a job

Exercise 5, p. 194.

1. Ø, Ø, s, s, s
2. Ø, Ø s, s
3. Ø, Ø, Ø
4. Ø, s, s, s

Exercise 8, p. 196.
Correct

Exercise 9, p. 196.
1. an	5. a	9. A
2. a	6. a	10. an
3. an	7. an	11. a
4. an	8. An	12. an . . . a

Exercise 10, p. 197.
2. a	5. a	8. a
3. an	6. an	9. a
4. an	7. an	10. a

Exercise 11, p. 197.
1. COUNT: a bike, some cars, some motorcycles, a truck
2. NONCOUNT: some pollution, some traffic
3. SINGULAR COUNT: a bike, a truck
4. PLURAL COUNT: some cars, some motorcycles

Exercise 12, p. 198.
4. a	(sing. count)
5. some	(pl. count)
6. some	(noncount)
7. a	(sing. count)
8. some	(pl. count)
9. some	(pl. count)
10. some	(noncount)
11. some	(noncount)
12. an	(sing. count)
13. some	(pl. count)
14. an	(sing. count)
15. some	(pl. count)

Exercise 13, p. 199.
A: computer, day, word
AN: evening, idea, uncle
SOME: help, ideas, mail, vocabulary, words

Exercise 14, p. 199.
2. an	(sing. count)
3. some	(noncount)
4. a	(sing. count)
5. a	(sing. count)
6. some	(noncount)
7. some	(noncount)
8. a	(sing. count)
9. some	(noncount)
10. some	(noncount)
11. a	(sing. count)
12. some	(noncount)
13. a	(sing. count)
14. an	(sing. count)

Exercise 16, p. 200.
2. some . . . some
3. a . . . a
4. a . . . a . . . some
5. some furniture
6. some music
7. an orange
8. some . . . some
9. some
10. some

Exercise 18, p. 201.
4. flour	12. help
5. flowers	13. sandwiches
6. information	14. animals
7. jewelry	15. bananas
8. children	16. water
9. homework	17. weather
10. advice	18. pictures
11. suggestions	19. rice . . . beans

Exercise 19, p. 203.
2. stores
3. coupon
4. rice
5. coupon
6. coupon
7. coupons
8. coupon
9. money

Exercise 21, p. 204.
2. a piece of bread
3. a glass of/a cup of water
4. a cup of tea
5. a piece of cheese
6. a bowl of/a cup of soup
7. a piece of meat
8. a glass of wine
9. a piece of fruit
10. a bowl of/a cup of rice

Exercise 28, p. 208.
3. many	6. much
4. much	7. many
5. much	8. many

Exercise 29, p. 208.
2. many	7. much
3. much	8. much
4. much	9. many
5. many	10. many
6. much	

Exercise 30, p. 209.

1. a few	6. a few
2. a little	7. a little
3. a few	8. a little
4. a little	9. a few
5. a little	10. a few

Exercise 31, p. 209.

Part I.

2. much	6. much
3. much	7. much
4. many	8. many
5. much	

Part II.

2. a little	5. a few
3. a few	6. a little
4. a little . . .	7. a little
a few . . .	8. a few
a little	

Exercise 34, p. 211.

Conversation 2

Exercise 35, p. 211.

1. a. the	2. a. The
b. the	b. The
c. the	c. The
d. The	d. The
e. The	e. The

Exercise 36, p. 212.

1. (a notebook) . . . a grammar book. The notebook . . . The grammar book
2. a woman . . . a man. The woman. The man
3. a ring . . . a necklace. The ring
4. a magazine . . . a newspaper . . . the newspaper . . . the magazine
5. a circle . . . a triangle . . . a square . . . a rectangle. The circle . . . the triangle The square . . . the triangle . . . the rectangle
6. a card . . . a flower . . . The card . . . the card . . . the flower

Exercise 37, p. 213.

1. a	12. a
2. a	13. The
3. a	14. The
4. a	15. a
5. the	16. a
6. The	17. a
7. the	18. a
8. the	19. the
9. The	20. the
10. the	21. The
11. a	22. the

Exercise 38, p. 214.

1. A: a	6. A: an
B: an	B: a
2. B: The	7. the
A: the	8. the
3. a . . . a	
4. the	
5. a	

Exercise 40, p. 215.

1. b
2. a

Exercise 41, p. 215.

1. specific	4. general
2. general	5. general
3. specific	6. specific

Exercise 42, p. 215.

2. Ø	6. The
3. The	7. The
4. Ø . . . Ø	8. Ø . . . Ø
5. Ø	9. Ø . . . Ø

Exercise 43, p. 216.

2. general	6. specific
3. specific	7. specific
4. general	8. specific
5. general	

Exercise 44, p. 216.

1. a	3. a	5. b
2. b	4. a	6. b

Exercise 45, p. 217.

1. the . . . the
2. the . . . the
3. A: a
   B: a . . . a
4. A: the
   B: an
   A: the
5. B: an
   A: the
   B: a

Exercise 46, p. 217.

1. some fruit / some oranges
2. any fruit / any oranges
3. some fruit / some oranges / any fruit / any oranges

Exercise 47, p. 218.

4. some/any
5. any
6. some
7. any
8. any . . . any . . . any . . . any
9. any
10. some . . . some/any
11. any
12. any
13. some . . . some/any
14. any
15. any
16. some

Exercise 50, p. 219.

2. Leaves
3. sex
4. knives
5. information
6. paper
7. dishes
8. women
9. bushes
10. homework
11. pages
12. pieces
13. edges
14. valleys
15. weather
16. Thieves
17. Strawberries
18. trays
19. sizes
20. glasses
21. fish
22. centimeters
23. inches
24. feet

Exercise 51, p. 220.

2. I don't like hot **weather**.
3. I usually have **an** egg for breakfast.
4. **The** sun rises every morning.
5. The students in this class do a lot of **homework** every day.
6. How many **languages** do you know?
7. I don't have **much** money.
8. Ricardo and Lisa don't have **any** children.
9. **The** pictures are beautiful. You're a good photographer.
10. There isn't **any** traffic early in the morning.
11. I can't find **a** bowl for my soup. / I can't find **any** bowl**s** for my soup.

Exercise 53, p. 222.

1. a
2. Some
3. a
4. A
5. a
6. a
7. A
8. some
9. An
10. a
11. Some
12. A . . . a
13. a
14. The
15. The
16. some
17. Some
18. a
19. The

Chapter 8: Expressing Past Time, Part 1

Exercise 2, p. 224.

2. were
3. was
4. were
5. was
6. were
7. were
8. were
9. was
10. was

Exercise 3, p. 225.

3. Martina was at the library yesterday too.
4. We were in class yesterday too.
5. You were busy yesterday too.
6. I was happy yesterday too.
7. The classroom was hot yesterday too.
8. Elise was in her office yesterday too.
9. Tony was in his office yesterday too.
10. Noor and Eli were in their offices yesterday too.

Exercise 6, p. 226.

2. weren't
3. wasn't
4. weren't
5. weren't
6. wasn't
7. wasn't

Exercise 8, p. 227

1. wasn't
2. was
3. was
4. wasn't
5. was
6. was
7. were
8. weren't
9. were
10. weren't

Exercise 10, p. 228.

2. A: Was Mr. Gupta at work last week?
   B: he wasn't.
   A: was he?
   B: was in the hospital.

3. A: Were Oscar and Anya at the train station at midnight?
   B: they weren't.
   A: were they?
   B: were at the airport.

4. A: Was Gabriella at the gym yesterday afternoon?
   B: she wasn't.
   A: was she?
   B: was at the dentist.

5. A: Were you and your family in Canada last year?
   B: we weren't.
   A: were you?
   B: in Iceland.

Exercise 12, p. 229.

2. Was
3. Were
4. Was
5. Were
6. Was
7. Were
8. Was
9. Was
10. Were

Exercise 13, p. 230.

3. A: Were you tired last night?
   B: I was.

4. A: Are you hungry right now?
   B: I'm not.

5. A: Was the weather hot in New York City last summer?
   B: it was.

6. A: Is the weather cold in Alaska in the winter?
   B: it is.

7. A: Were Astrid and Mohammed here yesterday afternoon?
   B: they were.

8. A: Are the students in this class intelligent?
   B: they are.

9. A: Is Mr. Tok absent today?
   B: he is.
   A: is he?
   B: He is . . . . (*free response*)

10. A: Were Tony and Benito at the party last night?
    B: they weren't.
    A: were they?
    B: They were . . . . (*free response*)

11. A: Was Amy out of town last week?
    B: she was.
    A: was she?
    B: She was . . . . (*free response*)

12. A: Are Mr. and Mrs. Sanchez in town this week?
    B: they're not.
    A: are they
    B: They are . . . . (*free response*)

Exercise 16, p. 232.

2. worked
3. shaved
4. watched
5. exercised
6. smiled
7. rained
8. asked
9. talked
10. listened

Exercise 18, p. 233.

2. walk . . . walked
3. asks . . . asked
4. watched . . . watch
5. cooked . . . cooks
6. stay . . . stayed

7. work . . . worked
8. dream . . . dreamed/dreamt
9. waits . . . waited
10. erased
11. smiles
12. shaved . . . shaves

Exercise 19, p. 234.

1. works
2. plays
3. played
4. scored
5. helped
6. learned
7. watched
8. like
9. worked
10. works

Exercise 21, p. 236.

1. b. last
   c. last
   d. last
   e. last
   f. last

2. a. last
   b. yesterday
   c. yesterday
   d. yesterday
   e. last
   f. last

Exercise 22, p. 236.

Sample answers:

2. I wasn't here yesterday.
3. she wasn't busy yesterday.
4. they weren't at work yesterday afternoon.
5. he wasn't at the library last night.
6. you weren't here yesterday.
7. she wasn't in her office yesterday morning.
8. it wasn't cold last week.
9. we weren't tired yesterday evening.

Exercise 23, p. 237.

2. Four days ago . . . was
3. One week ago . . . was
4. Yesterday / One day ago . . . was
5. Two weeks ago . . . were
6. Yesterday / One day ago . . . were
7. Two days ago / The day before yesterday . . . were

Exercise 24, p. 238.

(*Answers may vary depending on date and time.*)

Exercise 26, p. 239.

1. eats
2. does
3. goes

Exercise 29, p. 241.

2. talked
3. is talking
4. talks
5. ate

6. eat
7. went
8. studied
9. wrote
10. writes
11. is sitting
12. did
13. saw
14. had . . . dreamed/dreamt . . . slept
15. happened
16. comes
17. came
18. is standing
19. stood
20. put
21. puts
22. sits . . . sat . . . is . . . was

Exercise 30, p. 242.

1. b	3. a, b	5. a, c
2. a, c	4. a, c	6. b, c

Exercise 32, p. 243.

2. didn't get	7. didn't do
3. didn't get	8. didn't do
4. didn't stay	9. wasn't
5. didn't stay	10. weren't
6. didn't do	

Exercise 34, p. 244.

2. went . . . didn't enjoy . . . wasn't
3. is reading . . . isn't watching . . . doesn't like
4. A: Were
   B: didn't feel
5. doesn't eat . . . doesn't have . . . didn't have . . . got

Exercise 36, p. 245.

3. He didn't cook a big breakfast.
4. He didn't wash the dishes.
5. (no change)
6. He didn't see his friends at the bus stop.
7. He wasn't late for work.
8. It wasn't time for work.

Exercise 39, p. 247.

3. A: Did you eat lunch at the cafeteria?
   B: Yes, I did.

4. A: Did Mr. Kwan go out of town last week?
   B: No, he didn't.

5. A: Did you have a cup of tea this morning?
   B: Yes, I did.

6. A: Did you and Ricardo go to a dance last night?
   B: Yes, we did.

7. A: Did Galina study English in high school?
   B: Yes, she did.

8. A: Did Kirsten and Ali do their homework last night?
   B: No, they didn't.

9. A: Did you see Gina at dinner last night?
   B: Yes, I did.

10. A: Did you dream in English last night?
    B: No, I didn't.

Exercise 40, p. 248.

1. Did we		6. Did he
2. Did you		7. Did she
3. Did it		8. Did they
4. Did I		9. Did you
5. Did they		10. Did she

Exercise 42, p. 249.

Part II.

1. Did you		6. Did he
2. Did it		7. Did she
3. Did you		8. Did you
4. Did they		9. Did I
5. Did I		10. Did he

Exercise 43, p. 250.

2. Did you change . . . No, I didn't.
3. Did you exercise . . . No, I didn't.
4. Did you sleep . . . No, I didn't.
5. Did you think . . . No, I didn't. OR Yes, I did.

Exercise 46, p. 252.

1. ran

2. A: rode
   B: drove

3. thought

4. A: Did you go
   B: bought

5. A: Did you study
   B: read . . . went

6. drank . . . was

7. brought

8. taught . . . taught

9. caught

Exercise 48, p. 253.

1. b		4. b, c
2. a, c		5. b
3. a, c		6. b, c

Exercise 52, p. 255.

1. broke
2. spoke
3. left
4. sent
5. met
6. heard
7. took
8. rang
9. sang
10. woke
11. paid
12. flew

Exercise 54, p. 257.

1. no
2. yes
3. no
4. no
5. no

Exercise 57, p. 258.

1. began
2. told
3. lost
4. hung
5. found
6. sold
7. said
8. stole
9. wore
10. tore

Exercise 59, p. 260.

1. no
2. no
3. yes
4. yes
5. yes

Exercise 60, p. 260.

1. Did
2. Were
3. Was
4. Were
5. Did
6. Was
7. Did
8. Did
9. Were
10. Did

Exercise 61, p. 260.

2. was . . . did

3. A: Was . . . Did
   B: was

4. A: Were . . . Did
   B: was . . . were

5. A: were
   B: was
   A: Did
   B: was . . . were . . . was . . . did

Exercise 62, p. 261.

3. Do you want a roommate?
4. Did you have a roommate last year?
5. Was it a good experience?
6. Was he messy?
7. Did he help you clean?
8. Were you glad when he left?

Exercise 63, p. 262.

1. Lara = 3 or 4

2. Josh = 2 or 3
3. This information doesn't help you solve the puzzle.
4. Kira = 1 or 4
5. This information doesn't help you solve the puzzle.
6. Max lives between Kira and Josh.
So Kira = 1, Max = 2, Josh = 3, Lara = 4

Exercise 64, p. 263.

2. Did you **go** to the party **last** weekend?
3. I **heard** an interesting story yesterday.
4. The teacher **was not/wasn't** ready for class yesterday.
5. Did Dennis **come** to work last week?
6. **Last night** I **stayed** home and **worked** on my science project.
7. Several students **weren't** on time for the final exam yesterday.
8. Your fax came ten minutes **ago**. Did you **get** it?
9. Did you **watch the movie?**
10. The store **didn't** have yellow bananas. I **got** some green ones. (*also possible*: The store **doesn't** have yellow bananas. I **am getting** some green ones.)
11. **Were** you nervous about your test last week?
13. I didn't **see** you at the party. **Were** you there?

Chapter 9: Expressing Past Time, Part 2

Exercise 1, p. 265.

1. c
2. b

Exercise 2, p. 266.

2. A: Why did Rosa go there?
   B: She went there for a vacation.

3. A: When/What time did Rosa leave?
   B: She left at 2:00 P.M.

Exercise 3, p. 266.

2. When did Mr. Chu arrive in Canada?
3. What time did their plane arrive?
4. Why did you stay home last night?
5. Why were you tired?
6. Where did Sara go for her vacation?
7. What time did Lia finish her homework?
8. When did you come to this city?

Exercise 4, p. 267.

Questions:
1. What time did you get up this morning?
2. When did you finish your homework last night?
3. Where were you at 10:00 last night?

4. Why did you choose this school?
5. Why did you decide to study English?
6. What time did you cook dinner?
7. Where did you cook dinner?
8. What time did you walk into this room?
9. Where did you buy this book?
10. When did you buy this book?

Exercise 5, p. 267.

1. b	4. c	7. b
2. c	5. b	8. a
3. a	6. c	9. c

Exercise 6, p. 268.

2. you finish your homework
3. you eat breakfast this morning
4. you clean your apartment last week
5. you turn on your cell phone yesterday

Exercise 7, p. 268.

1. did	5. didn't
2. didn't	6. did
3. didn't	7. did
4. did	8. didn't

Exercise 8, p. 268.

Correct answer: a

Exercise 9, p. 269.

3. Is Maya carrying a suitcase?
4. What is Maya carrying?
5. Do you see a plane?
6. What do you see?
7. Are you afraid of mice?
8. What is the teacher talking about?
9. What did Franco have for lunch?
10. Did Franco have some soup for lunch?
11. What does Franco usually eat for lunch?
12. Does Franco like salads?

Exercise 13, p. 271.

1. When did he
2. Why did you
3. What did she
4. Where did you
5. What did he
6. When did they
7. Where did they

Exercise 14, p. 272.

1. Picture B
2. Picture A

Exercise 15, p. 273.

1. a. Who called Yuko?
   b. Who visited Yuko?
   c. Who studied with Yuko?
   d. Who did Alan call?
   e. Who did Alan visit?
   f. Who did Alan study with?

2. a. Who talked to the kids?
   b. Who did Ron talk to?
   c. Who watched the kids?
   b. Who did Ron watch?
   e. Who played with the kids?
   f. Who did Ron play with?

Exercise 16, p. 273.

1. a. the baby
   b. Astrid carry

2. a. the firefighter save
   b. the woman

3. a. the students . . . Professor Ramic
   b. Professor Jackson teach . . . The students

Exercise 17, p. 274.

1. Who did you see at the party?
2. Who came to the party?
3. Who did you talk to?
4. Who did Barak help?
5. Who helped Abbey?
6. Who did you invite?

Exercise 19, p. 276.

1. a	4. a	6. c
2. b	5. c	7. a
3. b		

Exercise 23, p. 278.

2. cost	8. shut
3. gave	9. spent
4. hit	10. lent
5. forgot	11. cuts
6. made	12. cut
7. shuts	

Exercise 24, p. 279.

1. a, b, c	4. b, c
2. a	5. b, c
3. a, b	

Exercise 27, p. 280.

1. won	6. blew
2. fell	7. knew
3. kept	8. swam
4. drew	9. felt
5. grew	10. threw

Exercise 28, p. 281.

1. b, c
2. a, b
3. a, b, c
4. a, c
5. a, c

Exercise 31, p. 282.

2. broke
3. hid
4. built
5. fed
6. became
7. held
8. bit
9. shook

Exercise 32, p. 283.

1. a, c
2. c
3. a, b
4. a, b, c
5. a, c

Exercise 34, p. 284.

2. [We arrived at the airport]ᴹ
   [before the plane landed.]ᵀ

3. [I went to a movie]ᴹ [after I finished my homework.]ᵀ

4. [After the kids got home from school,]ᵀ
   [they watched T.V.]ᴹ

5. [Before I moved to this city,]ᵀ
   [I lived at home with my parents.]ᴹ

Exercise 35, p. 285.

2. 2, 1 (b)
3. 1, 2 (b)
4. 1, 2 (a, c)

Exercise 36, p. 285.

Incomplete sentences: 1, 4, 6, 7

Exercise 38, p. 287.

Same meaning

Exercise 39, p. 287.

2. a. *NC*
   b. When were you in Iran?

3. a. When did the movie end?
   b. *NC*

4. a. *NC*
   b. When were Khalid and Bakir at the restaurant on First Street?

5. a. *NC*
   b. When does the museum open?

Exercise 40, p. 288.

2. When I was in Japan, I stayed in a hotel in Tokyo.
   I stayed in a hotel in Tokyo when I was in Japan.

3. Elena bought some new shoes when she went shopping yesterday.
   When she/Elena went shopping yesterday, Elena/she bought some new shoes.

4. I took a lot of photographs when I was in Hawaii.
   When I was in Hawaii, I took a lot of photographs.

5. Adam was a soccer player when he was in high school.
   When he/Adam was in high school, Adam/he was a soccer player.

6. When the rain stopped, I closed my umbrella.
   I closed my umbrella when the rain stopped.

7. The mirror broke when I dropped it.
   When I dropped the mirror, it broke.

Exercise 41, p. 288.

(Answers in parentheses may vary.)

2. a. When did you leave?
   b. When you left, (I was sad).

3. a. When did Thomas feel homesick?
   b. When Thomas felt homesick, (he looked at pictures of his family).

4. a. When did the electricity go out?
   b. When the electricity went out, (we lit candles).

Exercise 43, p. 290.

1. was eating . . . came
2. called . . . was watching
3. was playing

Exercise 45, p. 292.

Checked sentences: 1, 3, 5

Exercise 46, p. 293.

2. Someone knocked on my apartment door while I was eating breakfast yesterday.
   While I was eating breakfast yesterday, someone knocked on my apartment door.

3. While I was cooking dinner last night, I burned my hand.
   I burned my hand while I was cooking dinner last night.

4. Yoko raised her hand while the teacher was talking.
   While the teacher was talking, Yoko raised her hand.

5. A tree fell on my car while I was driving in a windstorm.
   While I was driving in a windstorm, a tree fell on my car.

6. While I was studying last night, a mouse suddenly appeared on my desk.
   A mouse suddenly appeared on my desk while I was studying last night.

Exercise 47, p. 293.

1. a. While + past progressive
   b. while + past progressive

2. a. When + simple past
   b. when + simple past

Exercise 49, p. 295.

2. called . . . was washing
3. came . . . was eating
4. was eating . . . came
5. came . . . was streaming . . . invited
6. was streaming . . . came
7. was wearing . . . saw
8. was watching . . . relaxing . . . took

Exercise 51, p. 296.

Part II.
1. While*   4. Before
2. After   5. While*
3. While*   6. Before

Part III.
1. was
2. was growing . . . became
3. built
4. graduated . . . went
5. wasn't . . . stayed
6. learned . . . helped
7. fired . . . started
8. was working . . . met
9. became
10. was working . . . got
11. didn't . . . died

Exercise 52, p. 298.

1. were having . . . saw . . . introduced
2. heard . . . walked . . . opened . . . opened . . . saw . . . greeted . . . asked
3. were playing . . . called . . . was . . . was . . . bought . . . took
4. was walking . . . saw . . . said

Exercise 53, p. 298.

2. c   5. c   8. a
3. d   6. b   9. c
4. a   7. c   10. d

---

*When is also possible but not as common as while.

Exercise 54, p. 299.

Part I.
2. went   7. got
3. overslept   8. ran
4. didn't ring   9. was
5. woke   10. was
6. heard

Part II.
11. went   16. talked
12. was sitting   17. were talking
13. saw   18. stood
14. called   19. stepped
15. joined   20. broke

Part III.
21. drove   25. paid
22. went   26. left
23. took   27. took
24. put   28. helped

Part IV.
29. got   35. came
30. looked   36. ate
31. rang   37. went
32. was not   38. was sleeping
33. sat   39. dreamed/dreamt
34. waited

Exercise 55, p. 301.

2. Yesterday I **spoke** to Ken before he **left** his office and **went** home.
3. I **heard** a good joke last night.
4. **Pablo** finished his work. OR
   When Pablo finished his work, (**he went home**).
5. I **visited** my cousins in New York last month.
6. Where **did you** go yesterday afternoon?
7. Ms. Wah **flew** from Singapore to Tokyo last week.
8. When I **saw** my friend yesterday, he **didn't** speak to me.
9. Why **didn't** Mustafa **come** to class last week?
10. Where **did you buy** those shoes? I like them.
11. Mr. Adams **taught** our class last week.
12. Who **did** you talk to?
13. Who **opened** the door? Jack **opened** it.

Exercise 56, p. 302.

(2) was . . . was . . . were having
(3) was . . . were putting
(4) heard . . . began . . .
(5) didn't stop . . . was . . . grabbed . . . got
(6) told . . . was . . . felt . . . lasted
(7) felt . . . was traveling . . . wanted
(8) tried . . . was
(9) was . . . wasn't thinking
(10) remembered . . . checked . . . saw
(11) finished . . . called . . . was driving
(12) felt . . . stopped . . . waited . . . was
(13) fell . . . died

Exercise 2, p. 303.
2. are going to be
3. is going to be
4. are going to be
5. are going to be
6. are going to be
7. is going to be
8. are going to be

Exercise 4, p. 305.
2. is going to get something to eat.
3. am going to take them to the laundromat.
4. am going to try to see the dentist today.
5. is going to take it to the post office.
6. are going to go to the park.
7. are going to take dance lessons.
8. am going to call the police.
9. am going to take a sick day OR lie down.
10. are going to go to an Italian restaurant.
11. is going to call the manager.

Exercise 7, p. 307.
Checked sentences: 1, 2, 3

Exercise 8, p. 307.
2. We are flying to Athens.
3. We are spending a week there.
4. My father is meeting us there.
5. He is taking the train.
6. We are going sightseeing together.
7. I am coming back by boat, and they are returning by train.

Exercise 9, p. 308.
1. present
2. future
3. present
4. future
5. present
6. present
7. future
8. future

Exercise 11, p. 308.
1. b
2. c
3. b
4. a
5. a
6. b
7. b
8. c
9. a

Exercise 13, p. 309.
1. last week
2. in a few minutes
3. last night

Exercise 14, p. 310.
3. next
4. last
5. yesterday
6. Tomorrow
7. last
8. next
9. next
10. Last
11. next
12. last
13. tomorrow
14. Last
15. Tomorrow
16. yesterday

Exercise 16, p. 311.
3. an hour ago
4. in an hour
5. in two months
6. two months ago
7. a minute ago
8. in half an hour
9. in one week
10. a year ago

Exercise 17, p. 312.
2. He is going to start a new job . . . in five days.
3. He graduated . . . three months ago.
4. He is going to be in a cooking competition in two weeks / in fourteen days.
5. Tom began taking cooking classes (five years ago, etc.). (*Answers may vary.*)
6. He moved to Paris in 2010.
7. Tom is going to cook for a TV show in three weeks / in twenty-one days.
8. Tom is going to get married in three months.

Exercise 18, p. 312.
1. b
2. a
3. a
4. b
5. a
6. a
7. b
8. b
9. a

Exercise 20, p. 313.
2. ago
3. next
4. in
5. yesterday
6. tomorrow
7. last
8. tomorrow
9. ago
10. in
11. Tomorrow
12. Last
13. Yesterday
14. last
15. in
16. Next

Exercise 21, p. 314.
1. two
2. four

Exercise 22, p. 315.
1. F
2. T
3. T
4. F
5. F

Exercise 25, p. 316.

1. same
2. same
3. different
4. same
5. different

Exercise 26, p. 316.

Time phrase in each sentence: this morning
Checked sentence: 1

Exercise 28, p. 317.

1. a, b, c, d, e
2. a, b, c, d, e
3. a, b, c, d, e

Exercise 31, p. 319.

1. future
2. past
3. future
4. past
5. present
6. future
7. present
8. past
9. future
10. past

Exercise 32, p. 319.

Checked sentences: 1, 4

Exercise 35, p. 320.

Part II.

1. 'll
2. 'll
3. will
4. 'll
5. will
6. 'll
7. will

Exercise 37, p. 321.

4. A: Will the plane be on time?
   B: it will.
5. A: Will dinner be ready in a few minutes?
   B: it will.
6. When will dinner be ready?
7. When will you graduate?
8. Where will Elyse go to school next year?
9. A: Will Jenna and Scott be at the party?
   B: they won't.
10. A: Will Martin arrive in Chicago next week?
    B: he will.
11. Where will Martin be next week?
12. A: Will you be home early tonight?
    B: I won't.
13. When will Dr. Fernandez be back?
14. A: Will you be ready to leave at 8:15?
    B: we will.

Exercise 40, p. 324.

2. No, she won't.
3. No, she won't.
4. No, she won't.
5. No, she won't.
6. Yes, she will.
7. No, she won't.
8. Yes, she will.

Exercise 41, p. 324.

2. won't
3. won't
4. want
5. want
6. won't
7. want
8. won't

Exercise 42, p. 325.

2. is not doing / isn't doing . . . is chatting
3. chats
4. doesn't chat
5. don't expect
6. sent . . . started
7. rang
8. didn't finish . . . talked . . . went
9. is going to call / will call
10. isn't going to chat / won't chat
11. Do you chat
12. Did you chat
13. Are you going to chat / Will you chat

Exercise 43, p. 326.

1. doesn't like
2. doesn't eat . . . didn't eat
3. doesn't eat
4. doesn't enjoy
5. are going to try
6. opened . . . say
7. will . . . have
8. won't have . . . 'll . . . ask
9. Are they going to enjoy
10. Will they go

Exercise 44, p. 327.

1. am . . . was not/wasn't . . . was . . . Were you . . . Was Carmen
2. were . . . were not/weren't
3. will be / are going to be . . . will be / am going to be . . . Will you be / Are you going to be . . . Will Akira be / Is Akira going to be
4. is not/isn't . . . is . . . are not/aren't . . . are

Exercise 45, p. 328.

3. Do
4. Do
5. Are
6. Do
7. Are
8. Are
9. Do

Exercise 46, p. 328.

1. Were
2. Did
3. Did
4. Were
5. Were
6. Did
7. Did
8. Were
9. Did

Exercise 47, p. 328.

2. A: Did you walk
   B: didn't . . . rode

3. A: Will you be / Are you going to be
   B: will/am . . . won't be / am not going to be

4. A: do you usually study
   A: Do you go
   B: don't like

5. A: Did Abby call
   B: did . . . talked
   A: Did she tell
   B: didn't . . . she didn't say
   A: was
   A: ran . . . didn't see . . . hit
   B: Is he
   A: isn't . . . is

Exercise 48, p. 329.

2. Is Kiril **going to go** to work tomorrow? OR
   Will Kiril go to work tomorrow?
3. Will **Gary meet** us for dinner tomorrow?
4. We went to a movie **last night/yesterday evening**.
5. What time **are you** going to come tomorrow?
6. My sister is going to meet me at the airport. My brother **won't be** there.
7. Mr. Pang will **sell** his business and **retire** next year.
8. **Will you be** in Venezuela next year?
9. I saw Jim three **days** ago.
10. I'm **going to** graduate with a degree in chemistry.

Chapter 11: Expressing Future Time, Part 2

Exercise 1, p. 334.

Same meaning: Sentences 1, 3

Exercise 6, p. 337.

3. verb
4. adverb
5. verb
6. verb
7. adverb

Exercise 7, p. 338.

3. may be
4. may be
5. Maybe
6. may be . . . Maybe

Exercise 9, p. 339.

2. a. Maybe the teacher will give a test.
   b. The teacher may give a test.

3. a. Natalie may be home early.
   b. Natalie might be home early.

4. a. Maybe she will be late.
   b. She may be late.

5. a. Maybe it will rain tomorrow.
   b. It might rain tomorrow.

Exercise 10, p. 339.

1. may + verb
2. may + verb
3. Maybe
4. may + verb
5. Maybe
6. Maybe
7. may + verb
8. Maybe

Exercise 11, p. 340.

3. Maybe
4. may
5. Maybe
6. Maybe . . . maybe . . . may . . . may

Exercise 13, p. 341.

1. b
2. a
3. a
4. a
5. b

Exercise 15, p. 342.

1. TIME WORD: Before
   TENSE: present
   MEANING: future

2. TIME WORD: When
   TENSE: present
   MEANING: future

Exercise 16, p. 342.

2. Mr. Kim will finish his report <u>before he leaves the office today</u>.
3. I'll get some fresh fruit <u>when I go to the grocery store tomorrow</u>.
4. <u>Before I go to bed tonight</u>, I'm going to read a story to my little brother.
5. I'm going to look for a job at a computer company <u>after I graduate next year</u>.

Exercise 17, p. 342.

2. am going to buy . . . go
3. finish . . . am going to text
4. see . . . am going to ask
5. buy . . . am going to check

Exercise 18, p. 343.

2. *Order of actions: 2, 1*
   After I turn off my cell phone, I'm going to go to sleep.
   I'm going to sleep after I turn off my cell phone.
   Before I go to sleep, I'm going to turn off my cell phone.
   I'm going to turn off my cell phone before I go to sleep.

3. *Order of actions: 1, 2*
   After I spell-check the words, I'm going to turn in my essay.
   I'm going to turn in my essay after I spell-check the words.
   Before I turn in my essay, I'm going to spell-check the words.
   I'm going to spell check the words before I turn in my essay.

4. *Order of actions: 2, 1*
   Before the passengers get on the airplane, they are going to go through security.
   The passengers are going to go through security before they get on the airplane.
   After the passengers go through security, they are going to get on the airplane.
   The passengers are going to get on the airplane after they go through security.

Exercise 22, p. 345.

Correct verbs: have . . . will help

Exercise 23, p. 346.

1. gets
2. moves
3. rents
4. needs
5. loan

Exercise 25, p. 347.

2. is . . . am going to go / will go
3. am not going to stay / won't stay . . . is
4. don't feel . . . am not going to go / won't go
5. is going to stay / will stay . . . doesn't feel
6. are going to stay / will stay . . . go
7. are . . . am going to go / will go

Exercise 28, p. 348.

1. every day
2. tomorrow

Exercise 29, p. 349.

2. future activity
3. present habit
4. present habit
5. future activity
6. present habit

Exercise 30, p. 349.

1. go . . . usually stay
2. go . . . are going to stay
3. am going to have . . . go
4. usually have . . . go
5. am . . . usually stay . . . go
6. am . . . am going to stay and go
7. get . . . usually sit . . . look at
8. get . . . am going to sit . . . look at
9. walks . . . is
10. often yawn . . . stretch . . . wake
11. closes . . . turns
12. go . . . am going to stay . . . leave . . . am going to go
13. goes . . . is . . . likes . . . takes . . . is

Exercise 31, p. 351.

2. d
3. a
4. f
5. b
6. e

2. If he is hungry, he eats a piece of fruit.
3. If he is tired, he takes a nap.
4. If he gets a mosquito bite, he tries not to scratch it.
5. If he oversleeps, he skips breakfast.
6. If he gets a sore throat, he drinks tea with honey.

Exercise 32, p. 351.

1. b
2. a
3. b
4. a
5. b
6. b
7. b

Exercise 34, p. 352.

Conversation 3

Exercise 36, p. 353.

2. What do you do? (*also possible:* What do we do?)
3. What do you do? (*also possible:* What do I do?)
4. What do they do?
5. What does he do?
6. What does she do?
7. What do I do?
8. What do you do? OR What do William and you do?
   (*also possible:* What do William and I do?)

Exercise 38, p. 354.

2. did you do . . . came
3. are you going to do . . . am going to come
4. did you do . . . chatted
5. do you do . . . chat
6. are you going to do . . . am going to chat
7. are you doing right now . . . am doing
8. does Marina do . . . goes
9. are the students doing . . . are working

10. are they going to do . . . are going to take
11. did Bakari do . . . went
12. does the teacher do . . . puts . . . looks . . . says

Exercise 39, p. 355.

1. A: Are we going to be?
   B: starts

2. are we going to have
   I'll . . . make

3. A: Are you going to be
   B: won't get . . . begins
   A: I'll see

4. A: are we going to do
   B: I'll take

Exercise 40, p. 356.

2. b	5. a	8. c
3. c	6. b	9. a
4. b	7. c	10. d

Exercise 41, p. 357.

1. am going to skip (*Use* be going to *because it's a plan.*)
2. took . . . flew
3. usually walk . . . take

4. A: isn't . . . left
   B: is

5. B: lost
   B: forgot
   B: gave . . . lost
   B: stole
   B: didn't have

6. A: Are you going to stay / Will you stay
   B: am going to take . . . am going to visit
      (*Use* be going to *because it's a plan.*)
   A: are you going to be . . . will

7. B: isn't . . . left
   A: Is she going to be / Will she be
   A: did she go
   B: went

Exercise 42, p. 358.

2. We **may be** late for the concert tonight.
3. What time **are you** going to come tomorrow?
4. Amira will call us tonight when her plane **lands**.
5. Ellen **may be** at the party. OR Ellen **will be** at the party.
6. When **I** see you tomorrow, I'll return your book to you.
7. I may **not** be in class tomorrow.
8. Amin **put** his books on his desk when he walked into his apartment. OR Amin **puts** his books on his desk when he **walks** into his apartment.

9. I'll see my parents when **I return** home for a visit next July.
10. What do you **do** all day at work?

Exercise 6, p. 364.

1. can't		6. can't
2. can		7. can
3. can't		8. can't
4. can		9. can't
5. can't		10. can

Exercise 7, p. 364.

Matt is not a good person for this job. He can't speak English well, and he can't carry suitcases.

Exercise 9, p. 365.

3. A: Can Gabrielle fix her printer?
   B: No, she can't.

4. A: Can you whistle?
   B: Yes, I can.

5. A: Can Carmen ride a bike?
   B: No, she can't.

6. A: Can elephants swim?
   B: Yes, they can.

7. A: Can the doctor see me tomorrow?
   B: Yes, he/she can.

8. A: Can we have pets in the dorm?
   B: No, we can't.

Exercise 11, p. 366.

1. B: Can I
   A: He can't come . . . Can I . . . He can

2. A: Can you help
   B: I can try
   A: we can do

3. A: I can't hear . . . Can you
   B: I can't
   A: Can you do

Exercise 12, p. 367.

1. can't
2. can
3. are

Exercise 19, p. 370.

Possible answers:
2. couldn't call you
3. couldn't watch TV

4. couldn't light the candles
5. couldn't come to class
6. couldn't hear us
7. couldn't wash his clothes
8. couldn't go swimming
9. couldn't get into my car
10. couldn't go to the movie

Exercise 22, p. 372.

2. If your brother goes to the graduation party, he can **meet** my sister.
3. I couldn't **open** the door because I didn't have a key.
4. Tyler **knows** how to use sign language. He learned it when he was a child.
5. Please turn up the radio. I **can't hear** it.
6. Where **can we** meet for our study group?
7. You **cannot change** your class schedule. The deadline was last week.
8. **Do you know** how to fix a leaky faucet?
9. When Ernesto arrived at the airport last Tuesday, he **couldn't** find a parking space.
10. Excuse me. **Can you** help me? I'm looking for a pair of work boots.
11. Mr. Lo was born in Hong Kong, but now he lives in Canada. He **could not** understand spoken English before he moved to Canada, but now he **speaks** and **understands** English very well.

Exercise 23, p. 373.

1. c   4. e
2. a   5. d
3. b

Exercise 24, p. 373.

3. Kalil is bilingual. He is able to speak two languages.
4. Nola will be able to get her own apartment next year.
5. Are you able to touch your toes without bending your knees?
6. Alec wasn't able to describe the thief.
7. I wasn't able to sleep last night because my apartment was too hot.
8. My roommate is able to speak four languages. He's multilingual.
9. I'm sorry that I wasn't able to call you last night.
10. I'm sorry, but I won't be able to come to your party next week.
11. We're going to drive to San Francisco for our vacation. Will we be able to do it in one day?

Exercise 25, p. 374.

Maya's English Experience

Five years ago, Maya moved to Canada with her young children. They <u>couldn't speak</u> English. Her children started school and learned English very quickly. Maya didn't study English and <u>could</u> just <u>say</u> basic, common sentences. She only understood people who spoke very slowly and used simple language.

Maya felt very frustrated. She heard about an evening English program at a local community center. She enrolled and began to study. At first, she <u>couldn't understand</u> or <u>say</u> very much. But slowly she got better. She was excited when she went shopping and <u>could have</u> short conversations with the cashier. Her kids were also excited. They <u>could talk</u> to her in English.

Today Maya's English is pretty good. She <u>can talk</u> to friends and neighbors. She watches TV and <u>can understand</u> a lot of it. Maya and her kids speak to each other in both English and their native language. She <u>can switch</u> back and forth very easily. Maya encourages friends to take classes. She says, "Don't worry. Try it for a few months. You <u>can</u> do it!"

1. They weren't able to speak English.
2. . . . was able to (just) say basic common sentences.
3. At first, she wasn't able to understand or say very much.
4. She was excited when she went shopping and was able to have . . .
5. They were able to talk to her in English.
6. She is able to talk to friends and neighbors.
7. She watches TV and is able to understand a lot of it.
8. She is able to switch back and forth very easily.
9. You will be able to do it!

Exercise 26, p. 375.

1. A: Were you able
   B: I couldn't . . . can try

2. A: Do you know how to make
   B: can make
   A: can you teach

3. A: Are you able to understand
   B: couldn't understand . . . can understand
   A: can't understand

4. A: will you be able to
   B: wasn't able to finish . . . 'll try . . . I will be able to

5. B: I can
   A: can see . . . Can you come
   B: I can . . . don't know

Exercise 27, p. 375.

Correct response: b

Exercise 28, p. 376.

1. The shoes are too tight. Marika can't wear them. The shoes are very tight, but Mai can wear them.

2. The coat is very small, but Bruno can wear it. The coat is too small. Emily can't wear it.

3. The soup is too hot. Salman can't eat it. The soup is very hot, but Ricardo can eat it.

4. The problem is too hard. Alan can't do it. The problem is very hard, but Talal can do it.

Exercise 29, p. 378.
1. eat it.
2. buy it.
3. go camping.
4. take a break.
5. do his homework.
6. reach the cookie jar.
7. sleep.
8. lift it.

Exercise 30, p. 378.
1. too heavy.
2. too young.
3. too uncomfortable.
4. too windy.
5. too tired.
6. too expensive.
7. too small.
8. too tall.

Exercise 31, p. 379.
3. too
4. very . . . very
5. too
6. very
7. very
8. too
9. too
10. very
11. very
12. too
13. very
14. too
15. too

Exercise 32, p. 380.
Part II.
Answers will vary.
1. can remember a lot of information.
2. 248 numbers in five minutes. OR a complete deck of cards in 63 seconds.
3. memorize the first and last names with the correct spelling in 15 minutes.
4. remember all this information naturally.
5. can develop a great memory.

Part III.
1. can
2. is able to
3. was able to
4. can't
5. are able to
6. can

Exercise 33, p. 381.
2. Can **you memorize** a deck of cards?
3. I saw a beautiful diamond necklace at a store yesterday, but I couldn't **buy** it.
4. The shirt is too small. I **can't** wear it.
5. Sam Garder **knows** how to count to 1,000 in English.

6. When I was on vacation, I **could** swim every day.
7. Honeybees **are** not able to live in very cold climates.
8. Where **can we** go in the city for a good meal?
9. Hiroshi can **read** in five languages.
10. I'm late. I'm **very** sorry. I **wasn't** able to find a parking spot.

Chapter 13: Modals, Part 2: Advice, Necessity, Requests, Suggestions

Exercise 2, p. 384.
Possible answers:
2. You should take a nap.
3. You should find an ATM.
4. You should see a dentist
5. You should study harder
6. You should call the manager
7. You should call the credit card company.
8. You should sew it.
9. put on a bandaid.
10. drink tea with honey.

Exercise 4, p. 386.
3. shouldn't
4. should
5. shouldn't
6. shouldn't
7. should
8. shouldn't
9. shouldn't
10. should
11. shouldn't
12. should . . . shouldn't

Exercise 6, p. 387.
1. should
2. should
3. shouldn't
4. should
5. should
6. shouldn't
7. should
8. shouldn't

Exercise 7, p. 387.
Same meaning: Sentences 2, 3

Exercise 8, p. 388.
2. Ellen has to get a haircut.
3. The kids have to eat lunch.
4. The kids had to eat lunch.
5. Jason has to leave now.
6. Does Petra have to leave right now?
7. Why did you have to sell your car?
8. Malia doesn't have to work late.
9. The employees didn't have to work late.
10. The restaurant had to close early.

Exercise 11, p. 389.
2. A: do you have to go
   B: I have to find

3. A: does she have to leave
   B: She has to be
4. A: I had to buy
   B: did you have to buy
5. A: I have to go
   B: I have to get
6. she had to study
7. do you have to be
8. Does Ted have to find
9. A: Miki doesn't have to take
   B: Do you have to take
10. He had to stay . . . He had to finish

Exercise 12, p. 391.
1. have to
2. have to
3. have to
4. has to
5. have to
6. have to
7. has to
8. has to
9. have to
10. has to

Exercise 13, p. 391.
1. b
2. a
3. b

Exercise 15, p. 393.
2. must apply in person
3. must have a passport
4. must have a medical license
5. put on a jacket
6. must take one tablet every six hours
7. must pay the first and last month's rent
8. must pay income tax

Exercise 16, p. 394.
1. a
2. b
3. b
4. a
5. c
6. a
7. b
8. c
9. a
10. c

Exercise 18. p. 395.
(*Answers will vary.*)

Exercise 19, p. 395.
More polite: Questions 1, 3

Exercise 22, p. 397.
The sentences have the same meaning.

Exercise 27, p. 400.
1. Hurry up!
2. March!
3. Relax.
4. Wait for me!
5. Don't let go!

Exercise 28, p. 401.
1. Hold . . . Drink . . . Breathe . . . Eat
2. Wait . . . Don't forget
3. Wait . . . Do . . . Hang . . . Make . . . Put . . . Empty

Exercise 29, p. 401.
Sample answers:
1. Watch out!
2. Open, please.
3. Don't eat that!
4. Come (here).

Exercise 32, p. 403.
1. has, is able, is going
2. can, may

Exercise 33, p. 403.
3. Ø
4. to
5. Ø
6. Ø
7. to
8. Ø
9. Ø
10. Ø
11. Ø
12. Ø
13. to
14. Ø

Exercise 35, p. 405.
1. a
2. b
3. b
4. c
5. a
6. c
7. a
8. b
9. b

Exercise 36, p. 406.
1. b
2. a
3. b
4. c
5. b
6. b
7. c

Exercise 37, p. 407.
Part II.
1. b
2. a
3. b
4. a
5. b
6. a
7. b
8. a

Exercise 39, p. 409.
(*Answers may vary.*)
2. Let's go to Florida.
3. Let's go to a seafood restaurant.
4. Let's go swimming.
5. Let's go to a movie.
6. Let's walk.
7. Let's eat.
8. Let's go dancing.
9. Let's get a cup of coffee.

Exercise 41, p. 410.
2. I **will** go to the meeting tomorrow. OR
   I **can** go . . . .
3. My brother wasn't able **to call** me last night.
4. Tariq should **call** us.
5. I **had** to **go** to the store yesterday.
6. Susie! You must **not hit** your brother!

7. **Could/Would** you please hand me that book?
8. Alessandra couldn't **answer** my question.
9. Shelley can't **go** to the concert tomorrow.
10. Let's **go** to a movie tonight.
11. **Don't interrupt.** It's not polite.
12. Can **you stand** on your head?
13. I saw a beautiful dress at a store yesterday, but I couldn't **buy** it.
14. **Close** the door, please. Thank you.
15. May I **please borrow** your dictionary? Thank you.

Chapter 14: Nouns and Modifiers

Exercise 1, p. 413.
1. Picture C, noun
2. Picture A, adjective
3. Picture B, noun

Exercise 2, p. 414.
2. My grandmother is a <u>smart</u> woman.
3. English is not my <u>native</u> language.
4. The <u>busy</u> waitress poured coffee into an <u>empty</u> cup.
5. A <u>young</u> man carried the <u>heavy</u> suitcase for his <u>pregnant</u> wife.
6. I slept in an <u>uncomfortable</u> bed at an <u>old</u> hotel.

Exercise 3, p. 414.
2. Have you paid the <u>phone</u> bill yet?
3. We met Steve at the <u>train</u> station.
4. <u>Vegetable</u> soup is nutritious.
5. The <u>movie</u> theater is next to the <u>furniture</u> store.
6. The waiter handed us a <u>lunch</u> menu.
7. The <u>traffic</u> light was red, so we stopped.
8. Ms. Bell gave me her <u>business</u> card.

Exercise 4, p. 414.
1. ADJ
2. NOUN
3. NOUN
4. ADJ
5. ADJ
6. NOUN
7. ADJ
8. ADJ
9. NOUN
10. NOUN

Exercise 5, p. 415.
2. store
3. class
4. race
5. official
6. soup
7. program
8. trip
9. room
10. tickets
11. keys
12. number

Exercise 6, p. 416.
3. newspaper article
4. hotel rooms
5. office worker
6. price tag
7. airplane seats
8. park bench
9. bean soup
10. brick house

Exercise 7, p. 417.
2. a good TV show
3. dangerous mountain road
4. bad car accident
5. interesting magazine article
6. delicious vegetable soup
7. funny birthday card
8. narrow airplane seats

Exercise 8, p. 418.
1. Yes.
2. Yes.
3. a diamond . . . a large expensive diamond

Exercise 10, p. 421.
2. Asian
3. designer
4. unhappy
5. soft
6. brick
7. important
8. glass
9. Canadian

Exercise 11, p. 421.
2. delicious Thai
3. small red
4. big old brown
5. narrow dirt
6. serious young
7. beautiful long black
8. a famous old Chinese
9. thin brown leather
10. wonderful old Native American

Exercise 13, p. 423.
1. b
2. a
3. a
4. b
5. b
6. b
7. a
8. a

Exercise 15, p. 424.
1. b
2. c
3. a, b
4. a
5. b
6. b, c

Exercise 20, p. 426.

Sample answers:

2. easy
3. good
4. interesting
5. easy
6. good
7. terrible
8. sleepy
9. delicious
10. terrible
11. great
12. awful

Exercise 22, p. 427.

1. fluently
2. quickly

Exercise 23, p. 428.

1. quiet
2. quietly
3. carefully
4. careful
5. clear
6. clearly
7. careless
8. carelessly
9. easy
10. easily
11. good
12. well

Exercise 24, p. 429.

Part I.

1. fast
2. late
3. well
4. easily
5. beautifully
6. fluently
7. hard
8. early

Part II.

1. well
2. fast
3. hard
4. late
5. fluent
6. easily
7. fluently
8. beautiful

Exercise 25, p. 429.

2. correct
3. correctly
4. fast
5. quickly
6. fast
7. neat
8. neatly
9. hard
10. hard
11. honestly
12. slowly
13. quickly
14. careless
15. early
16. early
17. loudly
18. slowly . . . clearly

Exercise 26, p. 430.

Adjectives: special, popular, country, bad, huge
Adverbs: excitedly, wildly, loudly

Exercise 27, p. 431.

Sentence 3

Exercise 28, p. 432.

2. All of
3. Most of
4. Some of
5. Almost all of
6. Almost all of
7. Most of
8. All of
9. Some of
10.–13. (*free response*)

Exercise 29, p. 433.

1. NOUN: money
   QUANTITY WORD: All
   VERB AGREES WITH: money

2. NOUN: coins
   QUANTITY WORD: All
   VERB AGREES WITH: coins

Exercise 30, p. 433.

2. are
3. was
4. were
5. are
6. is
7. are . . . are
8. is
9. is
10. are
11. come
12. comes

Exercise 31, p. 434.

1. 100%
2. 30%
3. 90%
4. 70%
5. 85%

Exercise 33, p. 435.

1. c
2. a
3. c
4. a
5. b
6. c
7. b

Exercise 34, p. 435.

The verbs are all singular.

Exercise 35, p. 436.

2. book . . . is
3. students . . . are
4. student . . . is
5. teacher . . . gives
6. teachers . . . give
7. child . . . likes
8. children . . . know
9. people . . . are
10. wants
11. Do . . . students
12. Does . . . person
13. Do . . . people
14. city . . . has
15. Does

Exercise 36, p. 437.

Because it was night, Victor saw the person's reflection in the kitchen window.

7. A and F are the same.
8. F and G are similar.
9. F is similar to G.
10. G is similar to A and F but different from C.

Exercise 31, p. 471.

1. yes	4. yes	6. yes
2. yes	5. yes	7. no
3. no		

Exercise 32, p. 471.

1. Figures 1, 4, 8, and 10 are the same.
   Figures 2, 7, and 9 are the same.
2. Figure 6 is different from all the rest.
3. (Seven.)
4. Nine.
5. Eleven.

Exercise 36, p. 474.

2. like . . . alike	6. alike
3. alike	7. alike
4. like	8. like
5. like	

Exercise 37, p. 474.

1. c, e	3. d
2. a, e	4. b, e

Exercise 39, p. 475.

2. cold	9. smart
3. dirty	10. wrong
4. light	11. wet
5. dark	12. empty
6. comfortable	13. clean
7. wide	14. hard
8. hard/difficult	

Exercise 40, p. 476.

(*Answers may vary.*)
1. short
2. big/large
3. quiet
4. pretty/beautiful
5. slow
6. strong
7. inexpensive/cheap
8. lazy

Exercise 42, p. 477.

2. is	14. does
3. aren't	15. wasn't
4. was	16. didn't
5. weren't	17. can
6. do	18. will
7. can't	19. won't
8. won't	20. will
9. isn't	21. were
10. are	22. isn't
11. does	23. do
12. didn't	24. don't
13. doesn't	

Exercise 43, p. 478.

1. doesn't	6. is
2. can't	7. wasn't
3. did	8. didn't
4. were	9. won't
5. do	10. will

Exercise 47, p. 480.

1. d	4. b	7. b
2. b	5. a	8. a
3. c	6. d	9. d

Exercise 48, p. 481.

2. A monkey is **more intelligent** than a cow.
3. My grade on the test was **worse than** yours. You got **a better** grade.
4. Soccer is one of **the** most popular spor**ts** in the world.
5. Felix speaks English more **fluently** than Ernesto.
6. Girls and boys are **different**. Girls are different **from** boys.
7. A rectangle and a square **are** similar.
8. Nola's coat is similar **to** mine.
9. Victor's coat is **the** same **as** mine.
10. Nicolas and Malena aren't **the** same height. Nicolas is **taller** than Malena.
11. Professor Wilson teaches full-time, but her husband **doesn't**.
12. Your pen **and my pen are alike**. OR Your pen **is like my pen**.
13. My cousin is the same age **as** my brother.
14. What is **the prettiest** place in the world?
15. For me, chemistry **is more** difficult than biology.

Exercise 37, p. 438.

2. b	5. b	7. a
3. a, b	6. a	8. a, b
4. a		

Exercise 38, p. 439.

2. anything/something
3. anything
4. something
5. anything
6. anything/something
7. someone/somebody
8. anyone/anybody
9. anyone/anybody
10. someone/somebody
11. anyone/anybody/someone/somebody
12. something
13. anything
14. anything/something
15. someone/somebody
16. anyone/anybody/anything
17. anything/anyone/anybody
18. anyone/anybody
19. Someone/Somebody
20. anything
21. anyone/anybody/someone/somebody . . . something

Exercise 40, p. 441.

1. yes	4. yes
2. no	5. yes
3. yes	6. yes

Exercise 41, p. 441.

1. a	4. c	6. c
2. b	5. a	7. b
3. d		

Exercise 42, p. 442.

Engaged	Jack	Jim	Jake	John	Jill	Julie	Joan	Jan
yes			x					x
no	x	x		x	x	(x)	x	

2. It can't be Joan. She's already married.
3. Clues 3 and 4 work together. It can't be Jill or Jack because they met at Jill's sister's wedding one year ago. The facts (above) say that the engaged couple met just five months ago.
4. See Clue 3. So far, the answers are "no" for Julie, Joan, Jill, and Jack. Since there is only one woman left, Jan is the engaged woman.
5. Clues 5 and 7 work together. Jan's boyfriend is a medical student, so that rules out Jim (who is a computer-science student).

6. (*unnecessary clue*)
7. See Clue 5.
8. (*unnecessary clue*)
9. It can't be John, since Jan doesn't love him. The only man left is Jake. Jan and Jake are the engaged couple.

Exercise 43, p. 442.

2. I didn't see **anyone/anybody** at the mall.
3. At the library, you need to do your work **quietly**.
4. I walk in the park every **day**.
5. Mr. Spencer teaches English very **well**.
6. The answer looks **clear**. Thank you for explaining it.
7. Every grammar test **has** a lot of difficult questions.
8. I work hard every **day**.
9. We saw a pretty **flower** garden in the park.
10. Galina drives a **small blue** car.
11. **Every student** in the class **has** a grammar book.
12. The work will take a long time. We can't finish **everything** today.
13. Everybody in the world **wants** peace.

Chapter 15: Making Comparisons

Exercise 1, p. 445.

Checked sentences: 2, 3

Exercise 2, p. 446.

2. smaller than
3. bigger than
4. more important that
5. easier than
6. more difficult than
7. longer than
8. heavier than
9. more expensive than
10. sweeter than
11. hotter than
12. better than
13. worse than
14. farther/further than

Exercise 3, p. 446.

2. deeper than
3. more important than
4. lazier than
5. taller than
6. heavier than
7. more difficult than
8. hotter . . . than
9. thinner than
10. warmer . . . than

11. better than
12. longer than
13. more intelligent than
14. shorter than
15. worse than
16. farther/further . . . than
17. stronger than
18. curlier than
19. more nervous . . . than
20. happier than
21. more uncomfortable than

Exercise 6, p. 448.

1. cold	7. safer
2. colder	8. safe
3. colder	9. safer
4. happier	10. fresh
5. happy	11. funny
6. happy	12. funnier

Exercise 7, p. 449.

Possible answers:
2. sweeter than
3. warmer/colder/hotter than
4. more comfortable than
5. cheaper
6. faster than
7. more intelligent than
8. higher than
9. brighter than
10. more expensive than
11. easier than
12. more important than

Exercise 12, p. 452.

COMPARATIVE	SUPERLATIVE
2. smaller than	the smallest
3. heavier than	the heaviest
4. more comfortable than	the most comfortable
5. harder than	the hardest
6. more difficult than	the most difficult
7. easier than	the easiest
8. better than	the best
9. hotter than	the hottest
10. cheaper than	the cheapest
11. more interesting than	the most interesting
12. prettier than	the prettiest
13. farther than/further than	the farthest/the furthest
14. stronger than	the strongest
15. worse than	the worst

Exercise 13, p. 453.

2. the longest
3. the most interesting
4. the highest
5. the tallest

6. the biggest
7. the shortest
8. fastest
9. the farthest/furthest
10. the most beautiful
11. the most famous
12. the best
13. the largest
14. the most comfortable
15. the best
16. the smallest
17. the most expensive
18. the easiest
19. the most important
20. the worst

Exercise 14, p. 454.

1. no	6. no
2. yes	7. yes
3. yes	8. yes
4. yes	9. yes
5. yes	10. yes

Exercise 15, p. 455.

4. older than
5. older than
6. younger than
7. the oldest
8. Alice
9. Sachi
10. Karen . . . Sachi . . . Alice

Sample completions:
11. Brad is the weakest.
12. Lars is stronger than Keith.
13. Keith is stronger than Brad.
14. Lars is the strongest.
15. A car is more expensive than a bike.
16. A bike is less expensive than a motorcycle.
17. A motorcycle is less expensive than a car.
18. A car is the most expensive.
19. Carol's test/grade is the best/the highest.
20. Mary's test/grade is the worst/the lowest.
21. Steve's test/grade is higher than Mary's.
22. Carol's test/grade is higher than Steve's.
23. *Love in the Spring* is more interesting than *Introduction to Psychology* (to me).
24. *Murder at Night* is more boring than *Love in the Spring* (to me).
25. *Introduction to Psychology* is the least interesting (to me).
26. *Love in the Spring* is the most interesting (to me).

Exercise 16, p. 458.

1. longer than
2. the longest
3. larger than

4. the largest
5. the highest
6. higher than
7. bigger than
8. smaller than
9. the largest
10. bigger than
11. larger than
12. better . . . than
13. the best
14. more comfortable . . . the most comfortable
15. easier than
16. A: worse
   B: worse than

Exercise 17, p. 459.

2. prettier	7. the biggest
3. short	8. shorter than
4. the nicest	9. long
5. small	10. the cheapest
6. bigger	

Exercise 22, p. 462.

Part I.
1. c	3. a
2. a	4. b

Part II.
5. c
6. a

Part III.
7. c
8. b

Part IV.
9. (1) Asia
   (2) Africa
   (3) North America
   (4) Antarctica
   (5) South America
   (6) Europe
   (7) Australia

Part V.
10. c
11. b
12. b

Part VI.
14. a	17. a
15. a	18. a
16. d	19. a

Exercise 23, p. 466.

Comparisons: easier than, cheaper than, cheaper, more convenient (and) modern, one of the best

Exercise 25, p. 467.

2. more quickly than
3. more beautifully than
4. the most beautifully
5. harder
6. the hardest
7. more carefully
8. earlier
9. the earliest
10. better than
11. the best
12. more clearly
13. more fluently
14. the most fluently

Exercise 26, p. 468.

2. more beautiful than
3. neater than
4. the neatest
5. more neatly
6. the most neatly
7. more clearly than
8. better than
9. better than
10. the best
11. later than
12. the most clearly
13. sharper than
14. more artistic than
15. more slowly than
16. the longest

Exercise 27, p. 468.

2. the fastest
3. harder than
4. the hardest
5. more dangerous than
6. more loudly than
7. more slowly than
8. heavier than
9. clearer than
10. more clearly

Exercise 29, p. 470.

1. yes	4. yes
2. no	5. no
3. yes	6. yes

Exercise 30, p. 470.

3. C is different from D.
4. B is the same as D.
5. B and D are the same.
6. C and D are different.

NOTES

NOTES